ACCOUNTING

INFORMATION SOURCES

ER

MANAGEMENT
INFORMATION
GUIDE : : 18

ACCOUNTING

INFORMATION SOURCES

Rosemary R. Demarest

[Chief Librarian
Price Waterhouse & Co.
New York, New York]

An Annotated Guide to the Literature, Associations and Federal Agencies Concerned with Accounting

GALE RESEARCH COMPANY • BOOK TOWER • DETROIT, MICHIGAN

OTHER BOOKS IN THE
MANAGEMENT INFORMATION GUIDE SERIES

Write for Complete List

TRANSPORTATION—Edited by Kenneth Metcalf, Henry Ford Museum.

BUSINESS TRENDS AND FORECASTING—Edited by James Woy, Mercantile Library, Free Library of Philadelphia.

PACKAGING—Edited by Gwendolyn Jones, Librarian, St. Regis Paper Co.

GOVERNMENT REGULATION OF BUSINESS INCLUDING ANTITRUST—Edited by Beatrice S. McDermott and Freada A. Coleman, Librarians, Dewey, Ballantine, Bushby, Palmer & Wood, and Winthrop, Stimson, Putnam & Roberts.

SYSTEMS & PROCEDURES INCLUDING OFFICE MANAGEMENT—Edited by Chester Morrill, Jr., Program Officer, Chief, Program and Management Branch, Army Comptroller Division, National Guard Bureau, Departments of the Army and Air Force.

ELECTRONIC INDUSTRIES—Edited by Gretchen R. Randle, Librarian, The Thomas Newcomen Memorial Library, The Newcomen Society in North America.

INTERNATIONAL BUSINESS AND FOREIGN TRADE—Edited by Lora Jeanne Wheeler, Librarian, The American Institute for Foreign Trade.

FOOD AND BEVERAGE INDUSTRIES—Edited by Albert Vara, Senior Professional Assistant, Business Section, Paley Library, Temple University.

COMPUTERS AND DATA PROCESSING—Edited by Chester Morrill, Jr., Program Officer, Chief Program and Management Branch, Army Comptroller Division, National Guard Bureau, Departments of the Army and Air Force.

COMMERCIAL LAW INFORMATION SOURCES—Edited by Julius J. Marke, Professor of Law and Law Librarian, and Edward J. Bander, Assistant Professor of Law and Associate Law Librarian, New York University School of Law.

ACCOUNTING INFORMATION SOURCES—Edited by Rosemary R. Demarest, Chief Librarian, Price Waterhouse & Company, New York.

INVESTMENT INFORMATION—Edited by James B. Woy, Mercantile Library, Free Library of Philadelphia.

RESEARCH IN TRANSPORTATION: LEGAL/LEGISLATIVE AND ECONOMIC SOURCES AND PROCEDURE—Edited by Kenneth U. Flood, Fred V. Henkel Professor of Food Industry Logistics, University of Missouri at Columbia.

ETHICS IN BUSINESS CONDUCT: SELECTED REFERENCES FROM THE RECORD--PROBLEMS, ATTEMPTED SOLUTIONS, ETHICS IN BUSINESS EDUCATION—Edited by Portia Christian, formerly Reference Librarian School of Business Administration, Indiana University, Bloomington, Indiana with Richard Hicks, Undergraduate Librarian, Indiana University, Bloomington, Indiana.

PUBLIC RELATIONS INFORMATION SOURCES—Edited by Alice Norton, Library Public Relations, New York, New York.

AMERICAN ECONOMIC AND BUSINESS HISTORY INFORMATION SOURCES—Edited by Robert W. Lovett, Curator of Manuscripts and Archives, Baker Library, Harvard Business School.

INSURANCE INFORMATION SOURCES—Edited by Roy Edwin Thomas.

Library of Congress Catalog Card Number 70-120908

$14.50

CONTENTS

CONTENTS

CONTENTS

FOREWORD

Management processes continue to grow more complex and the range of factors relevant to contemporary decision-making mounts apace. Inevitably, the volume of published information and the number of institutions and agencies which aid in the identification of factual material increase correspondingly. The variety of materials, publications, and institutions useful in providing the factual basis for informed management judgments varies considerably from one field to another. Often, the businessman, government official, student, and librarian will lack a comprehensive and organized inventory of the resources available for fact finding in a particular field. One inevitable consequence is that the opportunity to apply appropriate factual information to the problem-solving process may be lost.

The MANAGEMENT INFORMATION GUIDE SERIES is being developed expressly in order to overcome this deficiency in basic business research tools. Each volume is edited by one or more individuals known to be expert in the subject matter of the field as well as in the information resources applicable to the problems of that field. Each is devoted to a topic of broad interest to business and professional personnel. Each work in the series is designed to direct the user to key sources by arranging, describing, and indexing published sources as well as the programs and services of organizations, agencies, and facilities, which in combination make up the total information scene of each of the fields covered.

PAUL WASSERMAN
Series Editor

PREFACE

Accounting often is called the language of business since it is a primary tool in supplying the dependable and significant information required for management and operation of an entity and for the reports that have to be sumitted to meet fiduciary responsibilities to investors and to comply with regulatory requirements of stock exchanges and governmental agencies. In an investor-owned enterprise system, as typified in the United States, the responsibilities and authorities for accounting and financial reporting of business enterprises constitute a mosaic pattern in which the primary responsibility and authority of the board of directors and management is supplemented by secondary responsibilities and authorities of governmental regulatory agencies, stock exchanges and independent certified public accountants.

In this highly developed industrial economy the body of knowledge, or literature, of accountancy necessarily flows from numerous sources. It is diversified, complex and never static. A basic guidebook for the identification of authoritative sources and for specific subject and industry references is essential for anyone wishing to perform competently in the fields of corporate accounting, government regulation, education and professional public accounting.

This volume of the Management Information Guide series has been designed to fulfill the foregoing need. In my opinion Rosemary Demarest has performed an outstanding service and one of maximum usefulness to all who have responsibilities in the field of accountancy.

Paul Grady, C.P.A.
Partner (retired), Price Waterhouse & Co.

INTRODUCTION

The literature of accounting is so voluminous that not only would it be an impossible task to list all the written material on the subject, but such a list would be virtually useless. In making a selective compilation of the better-known works, further simplification has been attempted by dividing this guide into two main parts - Modern Accounting and Accounting Literature.

In reviewing the background of modern accounting, we list the books which show how accounting has evolved through the years into the vital profession it is today. Modern accounting practice is influenced both by the accepted accounting principles set by professional accounting associations and by the rules and regulations of government agencies. The associations and their accounting publications and the federal agencies and their accounting regulations are listed in separate sections.

Publications used in tax practice and publications describing management advisory services by CPAs, both important aspects of modern accounting, are also covered in the first portion of the book.

The major part of this work deals with the literature of accounting. Bibliographies always suffer from the time lag between their preparation and their publication. Inevitably, some excellent accounting books will be published while this guide to the literature is being processed. We have tried to cover material published in 1969 with some early 1970 entries. For later publications, the bibliographies and indexes in Section 6 should enable the reader to keep up to date.

Out-of-print books are included only when they are authoritative works in their fields. They can, after all, be consulted at the libraries of the American Institute of Certified Public Accountants and the larger accounting firms.

In the final section are listed the publications which would make up a basic accounting library.

The author wishes to express her thanks to all those at Price Waterhouse & Co. who were so helpful during the preparation of this guide, especially to John Bettenhausen for his constructive criticisms and suggestions. Thanks are also due to Catherine De Lorenzo for typing the manuscript and to the author's brother, Daniel Demarest, for his endless proofreading.

It is hoped that this guide will be useful not only to librarians, students and researchers, but also to the individual accounting practitioner who does not have access to a large accounting library. In its pages we hope that he will find publications which will help him in all aspects of his practice.

Rosemary R. Demarest
May 20, 1970

Section 1

MODERN ACCOUNTING

BACKGROUND

Section 1

BACKGROUND

Accounting has a long history. It was practiced in the most basic form during the Babylonian and Assyrian civilizations. Records of Greek and Roman accounting are both numerous and fascinating. There are in existence today inscriptions and fragments of a marble stele detailing the costs of constructing the temple of Athena in the Parthenon, built in 434-433 B. C.

However, modern accounting dates from the thirteenth century with the adoption of double-entry bookkeeping by the great medieval merchant houses in the Italian cities of Venice, Florence and Milan. Luca Pacioli's SUMMA DE ARITHMETICA, GEOMETRIA, PROPORTIONI ET PROPORTIONALITA (All that is Known of Arithmetic, Geometry and Proportion), published in Venice in 1494, was the first known accounting textbook and contains his classic treatise on double-entry bookkeeping. Pacioli, a celebrated scholar and mathematician who included Leonardo da Vinci among his closest friends, was not the originator of this accounting technique. He simply recorded "the method of Venice" which was in common practice at that time.

For several centuries there was no noticeable advance in the development of accounting. Then, abruptly, during the nineteenth century, the increasing complexity of industry and commerce led to a need for more effective control. Bookkeeping was of necessity expanded into sophisticated accounting systems and simple record-keeping developed into a method whereby men could supervise and control vast enterprises. Public accounting with its "attest" function evolved from responsibility to third parties and from the tremendous increase in public ownership of business. In modern times the advent of the computer has added a a significant major tool to accounting, the full implications of which are only recently being assessed.

The works below relate to the history of accounting up to as late as 1954.

Anyon, James T. RECOLLECTIONS OF THE EARLY DAYS OF AMERICAN ACCOUNTANCY, 1883-1893. New York: priv. ptd., 1925. 68p. frontis. (o.p.)

Reviews the formation of the American Association of Public Accountants, the predecessor of the American Institute of Certified Public Accountants, and the beginnings of public accounting in America.

Bentley, Harry C. A BRIEF TREATISE ON THE ORIGIN AND DEVELOPMENT

OF ACCOUNTING. Boston: Bentley School of Accounting and Finance, 1929. 31p. pap. (o.p.)
Chiefly composed of quotations from various sources of information concerning accounting history.

Bentley, Harry C. and Leonard, Ruth S. BIBLIOGRAPHY OF WORKS ON ACCOUNTING BY AMERICAN AUTHORS. Vol. 1, 1796-1900; Vol. II, 1901-1934. Boston: Harry C. Bentley, 1934-1935. 205p. (o.p.)
Historical bibliography of books and pamphlets on various aspects of accounting.

Brown, Richard. A HISTORY OF ACCOUNTING AND ACCOUNTANTS. London: Frank Cass & Co., Ltd., first ed. 1905; new impression, 1968. 475p. Bibliography of bookkeeping. illus.
Comprehensive study of the history of accounting in Europe and Great Britain until 1900. One chapter on American accounting history.

Brown, R. Gene and Johnson, Kenneth S. PACIOLI ON ACCOUNTING. New York: McGraw-Hill Book Co., 1963. 162p. biblio., portrait.
Interesting discussion of Luca Pacioli, the man, prefaces a translation of his bookkeeping treatise and reproduction of his entire SUMMA.

Carey, John L. THE RISE OF THE ACCOUNTING PROFESSION. Vol. 1: FROM TECHNICIAN TO PROFESSIONAL, 1896-1936. New York: American Institute of Certified Public Accountants, 1969. 387p.
The first of two volumes in which the author will cover the history of the accounting profession in the United States from 1896 through 1967.

DePaula, F. R. M. DEVELOPMENTS IN ACCOUNTING. London: Sir Isaac Pitman & Sons, Ltd., 1948. 287p. facs. (o.p.)
A compilation of papers covering primarily the development of accounting principles, financial planning and control in industry, and education of accountants.

Edwards, James Don. HISTORY OF PUBLIC ACCOUNTING IN THE UNITED STATES. East Lansing, Michigan: Michigan State University, 1960. 382p. biblio.
Reviews in some detail events in the history of American public accounting.

Edwards, James Don and Salmonson, Roland F. CONTRIBUTIONS OF FOUR ACCOUNTING PIONEERS: KOHLER, LITTLETON, MAY, PATON. East Lansing, Michigan: Michigan State University, 1961. 238p.
Digests of articles by Eric L. Kohler, A. C. Littleton, George O. May and William A. Paton arranged chronologically. Brief biographies and a photograph of each of the four men are included.

Garner, S. Paul. EVOLUTION OF COST ACCOUNTING TO 1925. University, Alabama: University of Alabama Press, 1954. 430p. Selected biblio.
Emphasis is placed upon origin and development of cost practices and basic theories. The author uses the conclusion date of 1925, since "the development of accounting procedures for deriving so-

called actual factory costs had attained at least a temporary climactic stage by that time."

Green, Wilmer L. HISTORY AND SURVEY OF ACCOUNTANCY. Brooklyn, New York: Standard Text Press, 1930. 288p. biblio. illus. (o.p.)

A review of European and American accounting history. Has been described as "useful but superficial."

Hatfield, Henry Rand. "An Historical Defense of Bookkeeping." In Baxter, W. T. and Davidson, Sidney, STUDIES IN ACCOUNTING THEORY. Homewood, Illinois: Richard D. Irwin, 1962. pp. 1-13.

Originally delivered as a paper before the American Association of University Instructors in Accounting on December 29, 1923, this article was first published in the April 1924 issue of THE JOURNAL OF ACCOUNTANCY. A notably well-written, condensed review of early accounting literature and the historical development of accountancy from its inception through the early years of this century.

Kafer, Karl. THEORY OF ACCOUNTS IN DOUBLE-ENTRY BOOKKEEPING (Monograph 2). Urbana, Illinois: Center for International Education and Research in Accounting, University of Illinois, 1966. 76p. charts. pap.

First section presents an interesting critical analysis of theories of accounts of both past and contemporary writers.

Littleton, A. C. ACCOUNTING EVOLUTION TO 1900. New York: American Institute Publishing Company, 1933. 392p. (Available from Russell & Russell Publishers, subsidiary of Atheneum Publishers.)

Scholarly study of the evolution of double-entry bookkeeping and its eventual expansion into accounting.

Littleton, A. C. DIRECTORY OF EARLY AMERICAN PUBLIC ACCOUNTANTS (Bulletin No. 62). Urbana, Illinois: University of Illinois, 1942. 39p. charts, forms, tables. pap. (o.p.)

Summarizes historical development of accounting and lists public accountants in New York, Philadelphia and Chicago for the years 1850 through 1899.

Littleton, A. C. "On Accounting History." In his ESSAYS ON ACCOUNTANCY, Part One. Urbana, Illinois: University of Illinois Press, 1961. pp. 3-188.

An essay devoted to the history of accounting which is part of a superb collection of extracts from articles written by Professor Littleton.

Littleton, A. C. and Yamey, B. S. STUDIES IN THE HISTORY OF ACCOUNTING. London: Sweet & Maxwell, Ltd., 1956. 392p. facs.

An excellent selection of essays on various aspects of accounting history from 600 B. C. to 1900 A. D.

Littleton, A. C. and Zimmerman, V. K. ACCOUNTING THEORY: CONTINUITY AND CHANGE. Englewood Cliffs, New Jersey: Prentice-Hall, 1962. 262p.

Excellent presentation of the history of accounting theory.

May, George O. FINANCIAL ACCOUNTING, A DISTILLATION OF EXPERIENCE. New York: MacMillan, 1943. 283p. (o.p.)

A classic in accounting literature. The early chapters cover the historical development of the art of accounting.

May, George O. TWENTY-FIVE YEARS OF ACCOUNTING RESPONSIBILITY, 1911-1936, ESSAYS AND DISCUSSIONS. New York: American Institute Publishing Co., Inc., 1936. 798p. (o.p.)
A collection of papers interpreting aspects of accounting history and thought in the first half of the twentieth century, by the dean of American accountancy.

Montgomery, Robert H. FIFTY YEARS OF ACCOUNTANCY. New York: Ronald Press, 1939. 680p. (o.p.)
Reminiscences by a leader of the early days of American public accounting.

Pacioli, Frater Luca. AN ORIGINAL TRANSLATION OF THE TREATISE ON DOUBLE-ENTRY BOOKKEEPING, trans. by Pietro Crivell. London: The Institute of Bookkeepers, Ltd., 1924. 144p. port., facs. (o.p.)
An exact translation of Pacioli's account of double-entry bookkeeping. Bibliography of principal works referring to Pacioli's treatise is included.

Pacioli, Frater Luca. ANCIENT DOUBLE-ENTRY BOOKKEEPING, translated by John B. Geijsbeck. Denver, Colorado: John B. Geijsbeck, 1914. 180p. abridged. (o.p.)
Lively translation of the first printed account of double-entry bookkeeping.

Parker, R. H. "Accounting History: a Select Bibliography." ABACUS (Sydney University Press), Vol. 1, No. 1. September, 1965. pp.62-84.
Good annotated bibliography of articles and books, classified by subject.

Peloubet, Maurice E. "The Historical Development of Accounting." In Backer, Morton, ed., MODERN ACCOUNTING THEORY, 2nd ed. New York: Prentice-Hall, 1966. pp.5-27.
Treats briefly the historical development of accounting as influenced by changing social and economic conditions.

Peragallo, Edward. ORIGIN AND EVOLUTION OF DOUBLE-ENTRY BOOKKEEPING: A STUDY OF ITALIAN PRACTICE FROM THE FOURTEENTH CENTURY. New York: American Institute Publishing Co., 1938. 156p. biblio. facs., forms. (o.p.)
An excellent detailed review of the development of double-entry from its beginnings into a well-defined system of bookkeeping, with numerous facsimiles from actual journals and ledgers.

Stacy, Nicholas A. H. ENGLISH ACCOUNTANCY, A STUDY IN SOCIAL AND ECONOMIC HISTORY, 1800-1954. London: Gee & Co., 1954. 295p. biblio.
Accountancy reviewed in context of world events.

Woolf, Arthur H. A SHORT HISTORY OF ACCOUNTANTS AND ACCOUNTANCY. London: Gee & Co., 1912. 285p. biblio. (o.p.)
Reviews systems of accounting from Egyptian times. Section on evolution of bookkeeping. Section on the origin and development of professional accountants. Excellent bibliography of works

published 1494-1800.

Yamey, B. S., et al. ACCOUNTING IN ENGLAND AND SCOTLAND: 1543-1800, DOUBLE-ENTRY IN EXPOSITION AND PRACTICE. London: Sweet & Maxwell, 1963. 228p. biblio.

Extracts from English books on double-entry bookkeeping, including sets of early account-books which serve to illustrate ditterences between early practice of accounting and that of today. Interesting bibliography of English-language books on accounting from 1543 through 1800.

Section 2

MODERN ACCOUNTING

RISE AS A PROFESSION

Section 2

RISE AS A PROFESSION

With the introduction of cost accounting and auditing accompanied by the gradual development of accounting theory, accounting became a sophisticated and complicated art. It was only natural that the experts in this field should get together to form professional associations whose standards of admission differentiated between the numerous uncertified "accountants" and the comparatively few certified practitioners of the early days. These associations have become of primary importance to the modern accounting world as leaders in the development of generally accepted accounting principles for the entire profession.

Illustrating the accounting associations' concern with accounting principles and standards, an interesting bibliography appeared in Carmen Blough's "Accounting & Auditing Problems" column of the February 1963 issue of THE JOURNAL OF ACCOUNTANCY (Vol. 115, no. 2, pp.73-8), entitled "Selected Accounting Research Bibliography, Publications of the Principal Accounting Organizations in the United States." Under subject classifications such as accounting theory, auditing, budgeting, leases, etc. the various associations' publications on each subject are listed. Associations covered are the American Accounting Association, American Institute of Certified Public Accountants, Financial Executives Institute, Institute of Internal Auditors and National Association of Accountants.

Professional accounting associations are to be found in all major countries, but, since those of Great Britain and Canada are of vital importance to the U.S. accountant, theirs are the only foreign publications listed here. Of course, any accountant working on accounts of a company located in a foreign country would obtain information concerning the accepted accounting requirements and practices of that country. An excellent digest of the differences in accounting principles and auditing procedures in the United States and abroad is found in chapter 26 and Appendices C and D of SEC ACCOUNTING PRACTICE AND PROCEDURE, by Louis H. Rappaport (2nd ed., rev., New York: Ronald Press, 1966).

Names of the professional societies of foreign countries can be obtained from various sources. The library of the American Institute of Certified Public Accountants or the business section of any large public library would provide such information. In 1964 the Institute published PROFESSIONAL ACCOUNTING IN 25 COUNTRIES, summarizing current accounting regulations and practices in those countries. In addition, certain material on accounting in foreign countries can be found in "International Accounting," Section 8 of this book.

We also refer to the state accounting societies which play an increasingly important role in modern accounting. An alphabetical listing of these societies with their addresses is given in Appendix A and titles of their journals are listed in Section 9, "Periodicals."

A number of trade associations have developed uniform systems of accounts adapted to their particular industries. A representative number of such associations are listed in this book, but others can be found classified by industry in the three-volume ENCYCLOPEDIA OF ASSOCIATIONS, the sixth edition of which was published in 1970 by Gale Research Company, Book Tower, Detroit, Michigan 48226. This encyclopedia includes a volume containing bimonthly supplements which keep the basic volumes up to date.

We have included only those publications of particular interest to the accounting profession, but complete lists of their publications are available from all the associations listed here.

UNITED STATES ACCOUNTING ASSOCIATIONS

American Accounting Association, 1507 Chicago Avenue, Evanston, Illinois 60201. Established in 1916 as the Association of University Instructors in Accounting. The present name was adopted in 1936 when the association extended its membership to include all those interested in accounting and undertook to formulate accounting principles and standards applicable to financial statements.

An excellent history of the association was written to commemorate its 50th anniversary in 1966 by Stephen A. Zeff entitled THE AMERICAN ACCOUNTING ASSOCIATION: ITS FIRST FIFTY YEARS. Not only does the author review the association's influence and activities but also traces the evolution of accounting principles and standards during that period.

The Association issues a number of special research studies in addition to the following.

THE ACCOUNTING REVIEW, quarterly.

ACCOUNTING AND REPORTING STANDARDS FOR CORPORATE FINANCIAL STATEMENTS, 1957 rev. 64p. pap. (Superseded by 1966 statement of Basis Accounting Theory).
First issued in 1936 as, "Tentative Statement of Accounting Principles Underlying Corporate Financial Statements." Revised in 1941 and 1948 with a series of eight supplementary statements added through 1954, the 1957 revision was the work of the association's Committee on Concepts and Standards Underlying Corporate Financial Statements.

EFFECTS OF PRICE LEVEL CHANGES ON BUSINESS INCOME, CAPITAL AND TAXES, by Ralph C. Jones. 1956. 199p. charts, tables. pap.

MONOGRAPH SERIES, Nos. 1-. 1937-. This series contains some of the classics of accounting literature.

No. 1: PRINCIPLES OF PUBLIC UTILITY DEPRECIATION, by Perry Mason.
No. 2: FINANCIAL STATEMENTS, by M. B. Daniels. (o.p.)
No. 3: AN INTRODUCTION TO CORPORATE ACCOUNTING, by W. A. Paton and A. C. Littleton.

No. 4: THE ENTITY THEORY OF CONSOLIDATED STATEMENTS, by Maurice Moonitz.
No. 5: STRUCTURE OF ACCOUNTING THEORY, by A. C. Littleton.
No. 6: THE PHILOSOPHY OF AUDITING, by R. K. Mautz and H. A. Sharaf.
No. 7: AN INQUIRY INTO THE NATURE OF ACCOUNTING, by Louis Goldberg.

PRICE LEVEL CHANGES AND FINANCIAL STATEMENTS, BASIC CONCEPTS AND METHODS, by Perry Mason. 1956. 32p. charts, tables. pap.

PRICE LEVEL CHANGES AND FINANCIAL STATEMENTS, CASE STUDIES OF FOUR COMPANIES, by Ralph C. Jones. 1956. 189p. charts, tables. pap.

A STATEMENT OF BASIC ACCOUNTING THEORY. 1966. 106p. Prepared as a guide to educators, practioners, etc., this statement seeks "to identify the field of accounting...to establish standards by which accounting information may be judged; to point out possible improvements in accounting practice... ."

American Institute of Certified Public Accountants, 666 Fifth Avenue, New York, New York 10019. Incorporated in 1887 as the American Association of Public Accountants, the first organized group of professional accountants in the United States. The name was changed in 1916 to the Institute of Accountants in the United States of America and shortened in 1917 to the American Institute of Accountants. In 1936 the association merged with the American Society of Certified Public Accountants, retaining the name American Institute of Accountants. The present name was adopted in June 1957.

This is the national professional society of certified public accountants in the United States. Its stated objectives are to "unite the certified public accountants of the several states, territories, possessions and the District of Columbia; to promote and maintain high professional and moral standards within the profession...and for the certified public accountant certificate...to advance accounting research...to encourage all CPAs to perform the entire range of management services consistent with their professional competence, ethical standards and responsibilities... ."

The Institute is governed by a Council consisting of members in practice, proportional representation being given to all "states, territories, or possessions of the United States or the District of Columbia." The Council also includes all past presidents of the Institute and individuals designated as Council members by each of the state societies of certified public accountants.

A large number of committees and boards assist the Council in the administration of the Institute's activities. Of particular interest to anyone interested in accounting reference sources are the Accounting Principles Board, the Committee on Auditing Procedure, the Committee on the Management of an Accounting Practice and the Committee on Management Services. The Director of Research and his staff carry out the Institute's important accounting research programs, including the publication of "Accounting Research Studies." In 1968 the Institute's Accounting Research Association was incorporated as a non-tax-able business league in order to provide an opportunity for members "to contribute to the financial support of an intensified program of professional research." Members of the Association receive the ARA NEWSLETTER which discusses the progress of Institute research projects and the activities of the Accounting Principles Board.

The library of the American Institute of CPAs was established in 1918 and has a vast collection of reference material, including over 14,000 books. The library is primarily intended for service to members and is open to the public for reference only. It has a very interesting collection of old and rare accounting books.

In addition to the following publications, numerous other special studies are issued by various committees or the Institute's research department. An annotated listing of publications with their prices is available from the Institute.

JOURNAL OF ACCOUNTANCY, monthly.

MANAGEMENT SERVICES, bimonthly.

ACCOUNTANTS INDEX, biennially. Bibliographies and indexes. The authoritative accounting bibliographic index, described more fully in Section 6.

ACCOUNTING PRACTICE MANAGEMENT HANDBOOK. 1962. 952p. Seeks to provide "guidance on all major activities involved in the successful management of an accounting practice." These areas include fees, development of a practice, staff personnel and office management, as well as accounting reports, records and procedures.

ACCOUNTING RESEARCH STUDIES. Nos. 1-. 1961-. Prepared under the Institute's accounting research program, "the purpose of these studies is to discuss and thoroughly document specific problems, expose matters for consideration and experimentation, and recommend solutions prior to the issuance of official pronouncements by the Accounting Principles Board." (see Opinions of the Accounting Principles Board.)

No. 1: THE BASIC POSTULATES OF ACCOUNTING, by Maurice Moonitz. (1961)

No. 2: "CASH FLOW" ANALYSIS AND THE FUNDS STATEMENT, by Perry Mason. (1961)

No. 3: A TENTATIVE SET OF BROAD ACCOUNTING PRINCIPLES FOR BUSINESS ENTERPRISES, by Robert T. Sprouse and Maurice Moonitz. (1961)

No. 4: REPORTING OF LEASES IN FINANCIAL STATEMENTS, by John H. Myers. (1962)

No. 5: A CRITICAL STUDY OF ACCOUNTING FOR BUSINESS COMBINATIONS, by Arthur R. Wyatt. (1963)

No. 6: REPORTING THE FINANCIAL EFFECTS OF PRICE-LEVEL CHANGES (staff-written). (1963)

No. 7: INVENTORY OF GENERALLY ACCEPTED ACCOUNTING PRINCIPLES FOR BUSINESS ENTERPRISES, by Paul Grady. (1965)

No. 8: ACCOUNTING FOR THE COST OF PENSION PLANS, by Ernest L. Hicks. (1965)

No. 9: INTERPERIOD ALLOCATION OF CORPORATE INCOME TAXES, by Homer Black. (1968)

No. 10: ACCOUNTING FOR GOODWILL, by George R. Catlett and Norman O. Olson. (1968)

No. 11: FINANCIAL REPORTING IN THE EXTRACTIVE INDUSTRIES, by Robert E. Field. (1969)

ACCOUNTING TRENDS AND TECHNIQUES, Nos. 1-. 1948-. pap.
Detailed annual survey of financial statement practices in a selected group of approximately 600 corporate annual reports. 500 additional reports reviewed in less detail.

APB ACCOUNTING PRINCIPLES, 2 vols. Chicago: Commerce Clearing House, 1968-.
A looseleaf service which keeps up to date all current Accounting search Bulletins and Accounting Principles Board Pronouncements on accounting principles.
Vol. 1 contains the APB pronouncements arranged under major subject headings, covered by a detailed index. Several appendices cross-reference sections of the text to specific pronouncements and provide a chronological schedule of changes in the pronouncements. Vol. 2 contains Accounting Research Bulletins 43-51, Accounting Terminology Bulletins 1-4 and all APB Opinions and Statements. A paper back edition of the current volumes is published annually by Commerce Clearing House for the AICPA.

AUDITING & EDP, by Gordon B. Davis. 1968. 353p. charts, forms, tables.
The result of a special AICPA Auditing EDP Task Force, this volume discusses all aspects of the examination of corporations using computers for record-keeping. Chapters 2 through 7 discuss typical procedures in the management and control of data processing systems. Chapters 8 through 12 cover specific audit procedures. Chapters 13 through 15 treat the problems inherent in integrated systems, service centers and time sharing. Includes a detailed glossary, pp.299-323.

AN AUDITOR'S APPROACH TO STATISTICAL SAMPLING, Nos. 1-. 1967-. supplements.
A series of programmed learning texts on statistical sampling techniques in auditing, prepared by Teaching Systems Corporation.

No. 1: AN INTRODUCTION TO STATISTICAL CONCEPTS AND ESTIMATION OF DOLLAR VALUES.
No. 2: SAMPLING FOR ATTRIBUTES.
No. 3: STRATIFIED RANDOM SAMPLING.
No. 4: DISCOVERY SAMPLING.

CASE STUDIES IN AUDITING PROCEDURE: Nos. 1-. 1947-. pap.

A series sponsored by the Committee on Auditing Procedure to illustrate actual application of auditing procedures.

No. 1: A LOADING AND HAULING EQUIPMENT MANUFACTURER.
No. 2: A NEWSPAPER PUBLISHER. (o.p.)
No. 3: A DEPARTMENT STORE. (o.p.)
No. 4: A PUBLIC UTILITY. (o.p.)
No. 5: A CORN PROCESSING COMPANY (o.p.)
No. 6: A MANAGEMENT INVESTMENT COMPANY OF THE OPEN-END TYPE.
No. 7: A GRAIN COMPANY. (o.p.)
No. 8: A STEEL FABRICATING COMPANY; A SMALL RESTAURANT. (o.p.)
No. 9: A WHOLESALE DISTRIBUTOR OF NEWSPAPERS AND MAGAZINES. (o.p.)

No. 10: A SMALLER COMMERCIAL FINANCE COMPANY (o.p.)
No. 11: A HOSPITAL.
No. 12: A MEDIUM-SIZED "SMALL LOAN" COMPANY; AN ELECTRONIC EQUIPMENT MANUFACTURER.
No. 13: AN INDUSTRIAL MACHINE COMPANY; A SMALL LOAN (CONSUMER FINANCE) COMPANY.
No. 14: A MEDIUM-SIZED DAIRY.

CASE STUDIES IN INTERNAL CONTROL. Nos. 1-2. 1950. pap.
A series sponsored by the Committee on Auditing Procedure to illustrate the manner in which an accountant evaluated internal control and applied his findings in an actual audit.

No. 1: THE TEXTILE COMPANY.
No. 2: THE MACHINE MANUFACTURING COMPANY.

CPA EXAMINATIONS, OFFICIAL QUESTIONS AND UNOFFICIAL ANSWERS. 1945-. (Only three most recent volumes currently available at any time.)
Bound volumes published every three years, containing the questions and answers for the six CPA examinations given during those years.

CPA EXAMINATION QUESTION AND ANSWER SUPPLEMENTS. 1961-. pap.
Published twice a year, these contain the complete text of the most recent CPA examination questions and unofficial answers in pamphlet form.

COMPUTER RESEARCH STUDIES, prepared by System Development Corporation, 1966-.
Studies on the impact which computers are having on the public accounting profession.

INDUSTRY AUDIT GUIDES. 1956-. pap.
These guides are designed to familiarize the independent accountant with the problems encountered in the audits of various industries. The titles are: AUDITS OF BROKERS OR DEALERS IN SECURITIES, 1956; AUDITS OF SAVINGS AND LOAN ASSOCIATIONS, 1962; AUDITS OF CONSTRUCTION CONTRACTORS, 1965; AUDITS OF FIRE AND CASUALTY INSURANCE COMPANIES, 1966; AUDITS OF VOLUNTARY HEALTH AND WELFARE ORGANIZATIONS, 1967; AUDITS OF BANKS, 1968; AUDITS OF PERSONAL FINANCIAL STATEMENTS, 1968; MEDICARE AUDIT GUIDE, 1969; AUDITS OF BANKS, SUPPLEMENT, 1969.

MANAGEMENT OF AN ACCOUNTING PRACTICE. Nos. 14-. 1961-. pap. (Bulletins 1-13 originally published as "Economics of Accounting Practice" are included in 1962 AICPA publication entitled ACCOUNTING PRACTICE MANAGEMENT HANDBOOK.)

These bulletins give actual case histories in modern accounting practice management.

MANAGEMENT SERVICES HANDBOOK, edited by Henry de Vos. 1964. 408p. charts, graphs. (o.p.)
A guide to the solutions of specific problems as well as a source of general information in the area of management services.

MANAGEMENT SERVICES TECHNICAL STUDIES. No. 1-. 1965-. pap.

Each study is intended to cover in depth a specific problem area in the field of management services. The text material is followed by a number of case studies.

No. 1: COST ANALYSIS FOR PRODUCT LINE DECISIONS.
No. 2: COST ANALYSIS FOR PRICING AND DISTRIBUTION POLICIES.
No. 3: COST ANALYSIS FOR EXPANSION OR CONTRACTION OF A BUSINESS.
No. 4: ANALYSIS FOR PURCHASING AND FINANCING PRODUCTIVE EQUIPMENT.
No. 5: ANALYSIS FOR PURCHASE OR SALE OF A BUSINESS.
No. 6: PRACTICAL TECHNIQUES AND POLICIES FOR INVENTORY CONTROL.
No. 7: TECHNIQUES FOR FORECASTING PRODUCT DEMAND.
No. 8: MANAGEMENT INFORMATION SYSTEMS FOR THE SMALLER BUSINESS.

OPINIONS OF THE ACCOUNTING PRINCIPLES BOARD. Nos. 1-. 1962-. pap.

In 1961 the Accounting Principles Board was established, superseding the Committee on Accounting Procedure and the Committee on Terminology. (Bulletins issued by these committees have been published in Volume Two of the APB ACCOUNTING PRINCIPLES service.) The APB OPINIONS are issued from time to time on accounting problems of current importance and interest. These opinions are based on careful study of the problem by the Board, which is composed of a select group of accountants. Before issuing an opinion, the Board gives careful consideration to statements by its predecessor, the Committee on Accounting Procedures, the Accounting Research Studies and views of accountants in public and private practice.

No. 1: NEW DEPRECIATION GUIDELINES AND RULES. November 1962.
No. 2: ACCOUNTING FOR THE "INVESTMENT CREDIT." December 1962.
No. 3: THE STATEMENT OF SOURCE AND APPLICATION OF FUNDS. October 1963.
No. 4: ACCOUNTING FOR THE "INVESTMENT CREDIT" (amending No. 2). March 1964.
No. 5: REPORTING OF LEASES IN FINANCIAL STATEMENTS OF LESSEE. September 1964.
No. 6: STATUS OF ACCOUNTING RESEARCH BULLETINS. October 1965.
No. 7: ACCOUNTING FOR LEASES IN FINANCIAL STATEMENTS OF LESSORS. May 1966.
No. 8: ACCOUNTING FOR THE COST OF PENSION PLANS. November 1966.
No. 9: REPORTING THE RESULTS OF OPERATIONS. December 1966.
No. 10: OMNIBUS OPINION - 1966. December 1966.

No. 11: ACCOUNTING FOR INCOME TAXES. December 1967.
No. 12: OMNIBUS OPINION - 1967. December 1967.
No. 13: AMENDING PARAGRAPH 6 of APB OPINION No. 9, APPLICATION TO COMMERCIAL BANKS. March 1969.
No. 14: ACCOUNTING FOR CONVERTIBLE DEBT AND DEBT ISSUED WITH STOCK PURCHASE WARRANTS. March 1969.
No. 15: EARNINGS PER SHARE. May 1969.

PRACTICE REVIEW BULLETINS, Nos. 1-. 1966-. pap.
The Committee on Practice Review was established in 1962 to encourage compliance with generally accepted auditing standards through education and persuasion. The committee reviews specific audit reports that seem to raise questions concerning the application of accepted standards. Only reports of members of the AICPA are so reviewed. Nos. 1 and 2: DEPARTURES FROM GENERALLY ACCEPTED AUDITING STANDARDS AND ACCOUNTING PRINCIPLES. These bulletins report certain principal types of departures from the generally accepted auditing standards as given in Chapter 2 of STATEMENTS ON AUDITING PROCEDURE, No. 33.

SPECIAL BULLETINS, Nos. 1-33. 1920-29. pap. (o.p.)
Interesting early bulletins consisting of questions received and answered by the American Institute of Accountants through their library and Bureau of Information.

STATEMENTS ON AUDITING PROCEDURE. Nos. 1-. 1939-. pap.

Issued by the Committee on Auditing Procedure, these statements are highly esteemed expressions of accounting principles and procedures.

Statement Nos. 1-32 were replaced by STATEMENTS ON AUDITING PROCEDURE No. 33, AUDITING STANDARDS AND PROCEDURES in December 1963. Essentially a codification of the substance of earlier pronouncements by the Committee on Auditing Procedure, this statement deals with responsibility and function of the independent auditor and sets forth generally accepted auditing standards of a general nature for field work and reports.

No. 34: LONG-TERM INVESTMENTS. September 1965.
No. 35: LETTERS FOR UNDERWRITERS. November 1965.
No. 36: REVISION OF "EXTENSIONS OF AUDITING PROCEDURE" RELATING TO INVENTORIES. August 1966.
No. 37: PUBLIC WAREHOUSES - CONTROLS AND AUDITING PROCEDURES FOR GOODS HELD. September 1966.
No. 38: UNAUDITED FINANCIAL STATEMENTS. September 1967.
No. 39: WORKING PAPERS. September 1967.
No. 40: REPORTS FOLLOWING A POOLING OF INTERESTS. October 1968.
No. 41: SUBSEQUENT DISCOVERY OF FACTS EXISTING AT THE DATE OF THE AUDITOR'S REPORT. October 1969.

STATEMENTS ON RESPONSIBILITIES IN TAX PRACTICE. Nos. 1-.

1964-. pap.
A series of statements "intended to constitute a body of opinion on what are good standards of tax practice, delineating the extent of a CPA's responsibility to his client, the public, the Government and his profession."

No. 1. SIGNATURE OF PREPARER. September 1964.
No. 2: SIGNATURE OF REVIEWER: ASSUMPTION OF PREPARER'S RESPONSIBILITY. August 1965.
No. 3: ANSWERS TO QUESTIONS ON RETURNS. August 1966.
No. 4: RECOGNITION OF ADMINISTRATIVE PROCEEDINGS OF A PRIOR YEAR. October 1966.
No. 5: USE OF ESTIMATES. February 1969.

WORKING WITH THE REVENUE CODE. 1955-. pap.
Annual publication describing how leading tax accountants are interpreting the more difficult provisions of the Internal Revenue Code as they apply to actual tax situations.

American Society of Women Accountants, 327 South LaSalle Street, Chicago, Illinois 60604. Founded in 1938. Professional society of women accountants, educators and others engaged in accounting work. Publication: THE WOMAN C.P.A., bimonthly, published jointly with American Woman's Society of Certified Public Accountants.

American Woman's Society of Certified Public Accountants, 327 LaSalle Street, Chicago, Illinois 60604. The national society of women accountants. Publication: THE WOMAN C.P.A., bimonthly, published jointly with American Society of Women Accountants. Other bulletins on special aspects of accounting.

Association of Water Transportation Accounting Officers, P.O. Box 53, Bowling Green Station, New York, New York 10004. Founded in 1912. Membership is composed of certified public accountants as well as accountants and financial officers of companies engaged in water transportation. Its aim is to promote greater uniformity in water transportation accounting systems and government reports. Publication: BULLETIN, bimonthly.

Bank Administration Institute, 303 South Northwest Highway, P.O. Box 500, Park Ridge, Illinois 60068. Founded in 1924 as the Associated Conference of Bank Auditors and Comptrollers. In 1959, the name was changed to NABAC, The Association for Bank Audit, Control and Operation. The present name was adopted in 1968. The association was formed "to conduct research and foster education in bank accounting, control, operations and personnel administration."

It sponsors a three-year summer course at the University of Wisconsin. A number of special committees, e.g. Accounting, Auditing and Personnel Administration, issue reports in their fields. The Research Institute also publishes equipment evaluation and systems studies. In addition to the following publications, the Bank Administration Institute issues numerous other pamphlets on specific aspects of bank auditing and operation.

ACCOUNTING BULLETINS, 1-. 1964-.
Issued by the Accounting Commission, these bulletins are intended to discuss current bank accounting problems.

BULLETINS.
No. 1: SECURITIES ACCOUNTING, revised 1967.
No. 2: CAPITAL AND EARNINGS ACCOUNTING, 1965.
No. 3: LOAN LOSS AND RELATED RESERVE ACCOUNTING, 1966.

THE MAGAZINE OF BANK ADMINISTRATION, monthly.

NABAC MANUAL OF BANK ACCOUNTING, AUDITING AND OPERATION, 3rd. ed. Chicago: 1963. 290p. forms. loose-leaf. Chart of accounts, pp.7-13.
One of the most authoritative manuals on bank accounting.

Data Processing Management Association, 505 Busse Highway, Park Ridge, Illinois 60068. Founded in 1951 as the National Machine Accountants Association, the present name was adopted in 1962. Composed chiefly of managers and supervisors of data processing installations handling accounting, management controls and automatic processing. Includes certified public accountants, systems and procedures men, programmers, etc. Offers a Certificate in Data Processing for which annual examinations are conducted in about 50 cities in United States and Canada. Publication: JOURNAL OF DATA MANAGEMENT, monthly.

Federal Government Accountants Association, 1523 L Street, N.W., Washington, D.C. 20005. Founded in 1950, this professional association of accountants, auditors, comptrollers and budget officers in the federal government service is pledged to the improvement and furtherance of professional accounting principles and standards in that service.

FEDERAL ACCOUNTANT, quarterly.

FGAA NEWS NOTES, irregular.

FGAA YEAR BOOK, annual.

RESEARCH BULLETINS, Nos. 1-. 1961-.
Issued by the association's National Research Committee, these bulletins are the result of a recent emphasis on the research mission of the FGAA. Bulletin No. 1, AUDIT SAMPLING IN ACTION, 1962; Bulletin No. 2, INTERNAL AUDITING REVIEW AND APPRAISAL IN THE FEDERAL GOVERNMENT, 1962.

Financial Executives Institute, 50 West 44th Street, New York, New York 10036. Established in 1931 as Controllers Institute of America. Present name adopted in 1962. The objectives of the Institute are "to develop a progressive concept of financial management," to educate the public about this concept and "to provide financial executives with a medium through which they may receive and exchange ideas in the field of business management."

The research arm of the Institute, the Financial Executives Research Foundation is a nonprofit organization which was founded in November 1944 under the name of Controllership Foundation "to conduct fundamental research and publish authoritative material in the field of business management."

BUSINESS BUDGETING, prepared by B.H. Sord and G.A. Welsch, 1958.

BUSINESS ELECTRONICS REFERENCE GUIDE SERIES, Vols. 1-4, 1954-1958.

FINANCIAL EXECUTIVE, monthly.

FINANCIAL REPORTING BY DIVERSIFIED COMPANIES, by R.K. Mautz, 1968.

MERGERS AND ACQUISITIONS: PLANNING AND ACTION, by C.I. Drayton, et al, under the direction of G.R. Young, 1963.

WHOLE-DOLLAR ACCOUNTING, 1957.

Hospital Financial Management Association, 840 North Lake Shore Drive, Chicago, Illinois 60611. Founded in 1946 as the American Association of Hospital Accountants "to bring about closer cooperation among hospital accountants in order to promote uniformity and efficiency in hospital accounting." Present name adopted in 1968. Membership composed of persons associated directly or indirectly with hospitals and health care facilities. Publication: HOSPITAL FINANCIAL MANAGEMENT, ten times a year.

The Institute of Internal Auditors, 60 Wall Street, New York, New York 10005. Established in 1941, this is the recognized professional organization in the field of internal auditing. Its objectives are "to establish and maintain high standards of professional conduct, honor and character among internal auditors" and to publish material on "practices and methods pertinent to the subject of internal auditing."

INTERNAL AUDITOR, quarterly.

OPERATIONAL AUDITING HANDBOOK, by Bradford Cadmus. 1964. Describes the operating and control problems of seven specific business functions (purchasing, traffic, scrap, receiving operations, facilities control, advertising and insurance), with suggested techniques for dealing with each problem.

RESEARCH COMMITTEE REPORTS, Nos. 1-. 1953-.
Excellent reports dealing with internal audit and control of various business operations and departments. The following are examples: No. 2, INTERNAL AUDIT AND CONTROL OF A PURCHASING DEPARTMENT, 1955; No. 11, A GUIDE TO ORGANIZATION AND ADMINISTRATION OF AN INTERNAL AUDITING DEPARTMENT, 1962; No. 14, SURVEY OF INTERNAL AUDITING IN THE LIFE INSURANCE INDUSTRY, 1964. A full listing of these reports is available from the Institute.

Insurance Accounting and Statistical Association, P.O. Box 139, Kansas City, Missouri 64141. Founded in 1928, this association admits as associate members independent public accountants, actuarial and management consultants, statisticians and statistical organizations. Publication: THE INTERPRETER, monthly.

Municipal Finance Officers Association of the United States and Canada, 1313 East 60th Street, Chicago, Illinois 60637. Founded in 1906. Membership is composed of auditors, controllers, treasurers and other accounting officials of municipal units. The association's National Committee on Governmental Accounting was formed in 1934 as the National Committee on Municipal Accounting. This Committee is composed of representatives on municipal accounting from fifteen major professional accounting and municipal associations, the Canadian Dominion Bureau of Statistics and the U.S. Bureau of the Census. Publishes numerous books and bulletins covering such subjects as standard account classifications, uniform terminology, forms for municipal financial statements, etc.

GOVERNMENTAL ACCOUNTING, AUDITING AND FINANCIAL REPORTING, by the National Committee on Governmental Accounting. Chicago: 1968. 248p. forms, tables.
The authoritative work on governmental accounting. Describes principles and procedures of accounting, budgeting, auditing and financial reporting for all governmental units other than national governments and their agencies.

MUNICIPAL FINANCE, quarterly.

MUNICIPAL FINANCE NEWS LETTER, semimonthly.

National Association of Accountants, 505 Park Avenue, New York, New York 10022. Founded in 1919 as the National Association of Cost Accountants. First meeting on October 13 and 14 in Buffalo, New York was composed of 40 men from leading accounting firms and manufacturing concerns and representatives of several accounting schools. The present name was adopted in 1967 to denote the wider range of interest covered by the association today. Membership, which has increased to over 58,000 members with 210 active local chapters, is composed of accountants in industry, public accounting, governmental agencies, teaching, etc. Primarily interested in management accounting, the NAA issues a number of authoritative research studies, both as separate pamphlets and as sections of its monthly magazine.

ACCOUNTING PRACTICE REPORTS, 1-16. 1955-1963.
Interesting series of reports "designed to organize and accelerate the exchange of information on industrial accounting practice." Typical titles include: CONTROLLING AND ACCOUNTING FOR SUPPLIES, No. 1, 1955; MODIFYING THE CALENDAR TO MEET BUSINESS NEEDS, No. 3, 1956; DEVELOPMENT AND REPORTING OF VARIANCES, No. 15, 1962.

MANAGEMENT ACCOUNTING, monthly.

RESEARCH MONOGRAPHS, Nos. 1-. 1965-. Based on doctoral dissertations in the field of management accounting.

Monograph 1: FINANCIAL ANALYSIS TECHNIQUES FOR EQUIPMENT REPLACEMENT DECISIONS, by Elly Vassilatou-Thanopoulos. May 1965.

Monograph 2: ACCOUNTING INFORMATION IN MANAGERIAL DECISION-MAKING FOR SMALL AND MEDIUM MANUFACTURERS, by Gary A. Luoma. December 1967.

Monograph 3: SENSITIVITY ANALYSIS IN MAKING CAPITAL INVESTMENT DECISIONS, by William C. House, Jr. February 1968.

Monograph 4: MAJOR CHANGES CAUSED BY THE IMPLEMENTATION OF A MANAGEMENT INFORMATION SYSTEM, by Harold M. Sollenberger. June 1968.

Monograph 5: EFFECTS OF FEDERAL INCOME TAXES ON CAPITAL BUDGETING, by James W. Edwards. 1969.

RESEARCH REPORTS, 34-43. 1959-67. (Nos. 1-33 were issued as RESEARCH SERIES, 1943-58.)
These research studies carry out NAA's objectives to "disseminate

knowledge of managerial accounting techniques and to encourage wider adoption of the best practices." Recent reports include CURRENT APPLICATION OF DIRECT COSTING, No. 37, 1961; TECHNIQUES IN INVENTORY MANAGEMENT, No. 40, 1964; LONG-RANGE PROFIT PLANNING, No. 42, 1964; FINANCIAL ANALYSIS TO GUIDE CAPITAL EXPENDITURE DECISIONS, No. 43, 1967.

RESEARCH STUDIES IN MANAGEMENT PLANNING AND CONTROL, No. 1-. 1968-.

No. 1: COMPUTER-BASED INFORMATION SYSTEMS FOR MANAGEMENT, by Neil C. Churchill, et al. Offers results of a survey of current state of the art in industrial applications of computers. Present applications and future plans are contrasted.

RESEARCH STUDIES IN MANAGEMENT REPORTING, No. 1-. 1968-.

No. 1: EXTERNAL REPORTING FOR SEGMENTS OF A BUSINESS, by Morton Backer and Walter B. McFarland. Presents findings and conclusions of an NAA study on this subject.

No. 2: A FRAMEWORK FOR FINANCIAL REPORTING BY DIVERSIFIED COMPANIES, by Alfred Rappaport and Eugene M. Lerner.

National Association of Hotel and Motel Accountants, 28 Duncan Avenue, Jersey City, New Jersey 07306. The professional society for hotel and motel accountants, founded with the purpose of developing uniform systems of accounts for hotels and motels. Conducts education and training programs. Publication: BULLETIN, monthly.

National Association of Tax Accountants, P.O. Box 38, Colorado Springs, Colorado. Founded in 1943 to promote the standards of practice in all federal and state tax matters. Publication: TAX TOPICS, monthly.

National Society of Accountants for Cooperatives, Box 4765, Duke Station, Durham, North Carolina 27706. Founded in 1935 with the intention of uniting persons engaged in accounting and auditing services for cooperative and non-profit associations. Publication: COOPERATIVE ACCOUNTANT, quarterly.

National Society of Public Accountants, 1717 Pennsylvania Avenue, N.W., Washington, D.C. 20006. Founded in 1945 as the professional society of public accountants. Publication: NATIONAL PUBLIC ACCOUNTANT, monthly.

Society of Insurance Accountants, 111 Hamilton Street, Rockville Centre, New York. Founded in 1960 by merger of Insurance Accountants Association and the Association of Casualty Accountants and Statisticians. Special committees on accounting and auditing.

FOREIGN ACCOUNTING ASSOCIATIONS

The Canadian Institute of Chartered Accountants, 250 Bloor Street East, Toronto 5, Ontario, Canada. Each of the ten Canadian provinces has its own Institute of Chartered Accountants, but the Canadian Institute of Chartered Accountants is the main body. All members of the provincial Institutes are automatically members of the Canadian Institute. Incorporated in 1902 as The Dominion Association of Chartered Accountants, the present name was adopted in 1951. The founders of The Dominion Association were men who were dissatisfied with the way in which the affairs of the provincial Institutes were handled. However, it proved impossible to compete with these Institutes. In 1910 a major policy change led to the Association providing a means of cooperation between the Institutes and to the establishment of uniform standards of accounting examinations in Canada. Issues numerous books and reports on various aspects of accounting and business management in addition to the following publications.

AUDIT TECHNIQUES STUDIES, 1965-.
A series of bulletins issued by the Study Group on Audit Techniques, intended to assist auditors in specific problems and suggest methods for the continuing improvement of audit techniques. MATERIALITY IN AUDITING, 1965; INTERNAL CONTROL IN THE SMALL BUSINESS, 1967; INTERNAL CONTROL AND PROCEDURAL AUDIT TESTS, 1968; CONFIRMATION OF ACCOUNTS RECEIVABLE, 1969.

THE CANADIAN CHARTERED ACCOUNTANT, monthly.

CICA HANDBOOK. 1968-. loose-leaf.
The official handbook of the Canadian Institute, this includes a description of the background and organization of the Institute, its charter, bylaws, officers and committees and certain relevant statistics. Revisions are issued from time to time.

The main portion of the CICA HANDBOOK, "Research Recommendations," contains the currently effective recommendations on accounting and auditing practices made by the Accounting and Auditing Research Committee which were previously issued as separate bulletins. This portion is divided into four sections: general accounting, general auditing, specific items and specialized areas. These subjects are covered by an excellent topical index.

FINANCIAL REPORTING IN CANADA, 1953-.
Biennial study prepared by the Research Department giving information from annual reports of 325 Canadian companies.

RESEARCH STUDIES, Nos. 1-. 1963-.
Issued by the Committee on Accounting and Auditing Research, this series presents specific accounting and auditing problems prepared by individuals or groups chosen by the committee for that particular study.

No. 1: USE AND MEANING OF "MARKET" IN INVENTORY VALUATION, by Gertrude Mulcahy.
No. 2: ACCOUNTING PROBLEMS IN THE OIL AND GAS INDUSTRY, by W.B. Coutts.
No. 3: ACCOUNTING FOR THE COSTS OF PENSION PLANS, by W.B. Coutts and R.B. Dale-Harris.
No. 4: RELIANCE ON OTHER AUDITORS, by T.A.M. Hutchinson.
No. 5: ACCOUNTING FOR COSTS OF FINANCING, by H.S. Moffett.
No. 6: OVERHEAD AS AN ELEMENT OF INVENTORY COSTS, by J.K. Walker and G. Mulcahy.
No. 7: THE HOSPITAL AUDIT (staff written).
No. 8: FINANCIAL REPORTING FOR NON-PRODUCING MINING COMPANIES (staff written).
No. 9: FINANCE COMPANIES - THEIR ACCOUNTING, FINANCIAL STATEMENT PRESENTATION, AND AUDITING, by St. Elmo V. Smith.
No. 10: CANADIAN UNIVERSITY ACCOUNTING, by R.M. Skinner.

Institute of Chartered Accountants in England and Wales, Moorgate Place, London, E.C. 2, England, U.K. Incorporated by Royal Charter granted by Queen Victoria in 1880. A supplemental charter granted in 1948 states that the Institute "has pursued the objects of the original charter and has aimed at the elevation of the accountancy profession as a whole and the promotion of its efficiency and usefulness by compelling the observance of strict rules of conduct as a condition of membership and by setting up a high standard of professional and general education and knowledge... ." This continues to be the aim of the Institute today. In addition to the following, numerous statements and reports are issued by the Council and the Taxation and Research Committee.

ACCOUNTANCY, monthly.

THE ACCOUNTANCY PROFESSION IN THE UNITED KINGDOM, September 1966. 28p. pap.
A brief pamphlet describing the history, present structure, nature and scope of the profession. Includes section on professional ethics.

THE HISTORY OF THE INSTITUTE OF CHARTERED ACCOUNTANTS IN ENGLAND AND WALES, 1880-1965, AND OF ITS FOUNDER ACCOUNTANCY BODIES, 1870-1880. London: Wm. Heinemann, Ltd., 1966.
Records "the emergence and development" of British accounting from the formation of the Institute of Accountants in London in 1870 to the present day. Includes brief bibliographical notes on each of the founder firms and of several of the leading members of the Institute.

RECOMMENDATIONS ON ACCOUNTING PRINCIPLES, Governing Council. No. 1-. 1942-.
These recommendations are issued in the hope that they "will be helpful to members in advising, in appropriate cases, as to what is regarded as the best practice." Although not binding on the members, the recommendations are acknowledged to set the generally accepted accounting principles of British accountancy. We list here the Recommendations currently in effect.

N 9: DEPRECIATION OF FIXED ASSETS.
N 12: RISING PRICE LEVELS IN RELATION TO ACCOUNTS.
N 13: ACCOUNTANTS' REPORTS FOR PROSPECTUSES: FIXED ASSETS AND DEPRECIATION.
N 15: ACCOUNTING IN RELATION TO CHANGES IN THE PURCHASING POWER OF MONEY.
N 16: ACCOUNTANTS' REPORTS FOR PROSPECTUSES: ADJUSTMENTS AND OTHER MATTERS.
N 17: EVENTS OCCURRING AFTER THE BALANCE SHEET DATE.
N 18: PRESENTATION OF BALANCE SHEET AND PROFIT AND LOSS ACCOUNT.
N 20: TREATMENT OF INVESTMENTS IN THE BALANCE SHEETS OF TRADING COMPANIES.
N 21: RETIREMENT BENEFITS.
N 22: TREATMENT OF STOCK-IN-TRADE AND WORK IN PROGRESS IN FINANCIAL ACCOUNTS.
N 23: HIRE PURCHASE, CREDIT SALE AND RENTAL TRANSAC-

TIONS.

N 24: ACCOUNTING TREATMENT OF INVESTMENT GRANTS.
N 25: THE ACCOUNTING TREATMENT OF MAJOR CHANGES IN THE STERLING PARITY OF OVERSEAS CURRENCIES.
N 26: LAND COMMISSION ACT 1967: ACCOUNTING IMPLICATIONS.
N 27: TREATMENT OF TAXATION IN ACCOUNTS OF COMPANIES.
N 28: THE ACCOUNTS OF INVESTMENT TRUST COMPANIES.
N 29: TRUST ACCOUNTS

STATEMENTS ON AUDITING, Governing Council. U 1-. 1961-. These statements are issued "for the guidance of members in determining their audit procedure."

U 1: GENERAL PRINCIPLES OF AUDITING.
U 3: AUDITS OF BUILDING SOCIETIES.
U 4: INTERNAL CONTROL.
U 5: AUDITORS' REPORTS ON GROUP ACCOUNTS.
U 7: VERIFICATION OF DEBTOR BALANCES: CONFIRMATION BY DIRECT COMMUNICATION.
U 9: ATTENDANCE AT STOCKTAKING.
U10: AUDITORS' REPORTS: FORMS AND QUALIFICATIONS.
U11: STOCK-IN-TRADE AND WORK IN PROGRESS.
U12: AUDITORS' WORKING PAPERS.
U13: AUDITORS' REPORTS UNDER THE FRIENDLY AND INDUSTRIAL AND PROVIDENT SOCIETIES ACT 1968.
U14: INTERNAL CONTROL IN A COMPUTER-BASED ACCOUNTING SYSTEM.
U15: THE AUDIT OF COMPUTER-BASED ACCOUNTING SYSTEMS.

OTHER ASSOCIATIONS

American Management Association, 135 West 50th Street, New York, New York 10020. Founded in 1923 by the merger of several management societies, the AMA "has as its basic concern the improvement of management skills and techniques." Conducts over 1,000 meetings annually throughout the United States, including management courses for executives and courses in specialized fields such as marketing, systems and procedures, personnel, etc. Maintains extensive library for use of members. Publishes an excellent management salary survey, EXECUTIVE COMPENSATION SERVICE. Issued in 1967, a cumulative TEN-YEAR INDEX OF AMA PUBLICATIONS (1957-1966) which is supplemented annually. This index of articles, reports and books is classified by subject and is an extremely useful reference tool in its field.

COMPENSATION REVIEW, quarterly.

HOSPITAL SUPERVISION, semimonthly.

MANAGEMENT NEWS, monthly.

MANAGEMENT REPORTS, irregular.

MANAGEMENT REVIEW, monthly.

MANAGER'S LETTER, monthly.

PERSONNEL, bimonthly.

RESEARCH STUDIES, irregular.

SUPERVISORY MANAGEMENT, monthly.

Financial Analysts Federation, 80 Federal Street, Boston, Massachusetts 02110. A federation of 41 societies in the United States and Canada with a membership of over 11,600 practicing investment analysts. Aim is "the constant upgrading of its members' analytical abilities and professional status." In 1963 the Federation established as a separate entity the Institute of Chartered Financial Analysts which awards to Federation members the designation C.F.A. after a three-year course of study and examination.

CORPORATE REPORTING FOR THE PROFESSIONAL INVESTOR, by Corliss D. Anderson. Boston: 1962. 114p. facs., photos. pap.
A monograph dealing with the areas of financial reporting which the investment analysts feel could be treated in more detail in the corporate annual report.

FINANCIAL ANALYSTS JOURNAL, bimonthly.

National Association of Regulatory Utility Commissioners (NARUC), 3327 Interstate Commerce Building, Washington, D.C. 20044. Founded in 1899, this is the professional association of state and federal regulatory commissioners with jurisdiction over transportation agencies and public utilities.

BULLETIN, irregular.
The official organ of NARUC. Published one or more times a week, the BULLETIN lists events affecting regulation of all utilities and includes digests of important regulatory commission and court decisions.

INTERPRETATIONS OF UNIFORM SYSTEM OF ACCOUNTS FOR ELECTRIC, GAS AND WATER UTILITIES. Washington, D.C.: 1967, supplements to date. v.p. loose-leaf.
A summary of interpretations to the uniform systems of accounts adopted by NARUC in 1957 and 1958. Additional interpretations are added as a need for clarification on certain points becomes apparent.

PROCEEDINGS, annual.

PUBLIC UTILITY DEPRECIATION PRACTICES. Washington, D.C.: 1968. 447p. charts, tables.
Gives practical operating practices and methods for determining the depreciation of public utility property for regulatory purposes. Numerous supporting charts and graphs.

REPORTS. Washington, D.C.: 1939-.
Prepared by the Committee on Depreciation. The most important of these annual reports is the single volume containing the 1943 and 1944 reports. The 1943 report was the result of a four-year study of depreciation methods and included the committee's recommendations. The 1944 report contains objections to these recommendations raised within the utility industry and modifications of certain sections of the earlier report. Together, these reports give a clear picture of depreciation methods used by most utilities.

UNIFORM SYSTEM OF ACCOUNTS FOR ELECTRIC UTILITIES, 1958.
Class A & B - Accounts for utilities having annual electric operating revenues of $1,000,000 or more; 169p. Class C - Account for utilities having annual electric operating revenues of $150,000; 125p. Class D - Accounts for utilities having annual electric operating revenues

of less than $150,000; 59p.

UNIFORM SYSTEM OF ACCOUNTS FOR GAS UTILITIES, 1958.
Class A & B - Accounts for utilities having annual gas operating revenues of $1,000,000 or more; 212p. Class C - Accounts for utilities having annual gas operating revenues of $150,000 or more but less than $1,000,000; 137p. Class D - Accounts for utilities having annual gas operating revenues of less than $150,000; 66p.

UNIFORM SYSTEM OF ACCOUNTS FOR WATER UTILITIES, 1957.
Class A & B - Accounts for utilities having annual water operating revenues of $250,000 or more; 128p. Class C - Accounts for utilities having annual water operating revenues of $50,000 or more but less than $250,000; 100p. Class D - Accounts for utilities having annual water operating revenues of less than $50,000; 64p.

National Industrial Conference Board, 845 Third Avenue, New York, New York 10022. Founded in 1916. Membership composed of business organizations, trade associations, government bureaus, colleges, labor unions, libraries and individuals.

CANADIAN STUDIES, 1959-.

CONFERENCE BOARD RECORD, monthly.

CUMULATIVE INDEX OF NICB PUBLICATIONS.
Annually-revised, classified, annotated index to the NICB published research material. Not to be considered a comprehensive index of all past material since the introduction specifies "only material believed to have current application is included." Available without charge to Associates of NICB upon request to the Board's Information Service Division.

ECONOMIC ALMANAC, annual. (Published by Crowell-Collier & Macmillan Company, New York and Collier-Macmillan, Ltd., London.)
A handbook of economic information to be used in connection with current economic and management questions. Includes a glossary of business terms.

EXPERIENCES IN MARKETING MANAGEMENT, 1962-.

MANAGING THE MODERATE-SIZED COMPANY, 1966-.

STUDIES IN BUSINESS ECONOMICS, 1945-.

STUDIES IN BUSINESS POLICY, 1944-.

STUDIES IN PERSONNEL POLICY, 1937-.

STUDIES IN PUBLIC AFFAIRS, 1965-.

National Retail Merchants Association, 100 West 31st Street, New York, New York 10001. Founded in 1911 as the National Retail Dry Goods Association. Name changed in 1958. Membership composed of people active in department, chain and specialty stores. Publications: STORES, monthly.

THE NRMA Controllers Congress is the accounting section of the Association and has issued numerous publications of value on accounting in the retail field. The more important publications and the serials include: RETAIL CONTROL, monthly; DEPARTMENTAL MERCHANDISING AND OPERATING RESULTS, annual; OPERATING RESULTS OF DEPARTMENT AND SPECIALTY STORES, annual; RETAIL ACCOUNTING MANUAL, 1962; and RETAILERS' FEDERAL TAX MANUAL, a series of chapters written by tax practitioners, edited by J. J. Bliss, 1965.

New York Stock Exchange, 11 Wall Street, New York, New York 10005. Organized formally in 1792 by a group of 24 men who signed the original brokers' agreement and held daily meetings under a buttonwood tree standing on the site now occupied by No. 68 Wall Street.

We include the New York Stock Exchange in this section because it has a long history of cooperation with the accounting profession in raising the standards of financial reporting. The 1930 correspondence between the Exchange and The American Institute of Accountants resulted in the historical document, AUDITS OF CORPORATE ACCOUNTS, which was the earliest of the cooperative efforts. Currently, the listing requirements of the New York Stock Exchange are an important influence on the reporting standards of today.

We list below the major publications of the Exchange, but a number of other pamphlets on various aspects of the securities business are available from the Publications Division.

COMPANY MANUAL. loose-leaf. Amendments are sent indefinitely to all holders of the MANUAL.
Gives up-to-date, comprehensive coverage of New York Stock Exchange policies, procedures and regulations for listed companies and their securities. Financial statement requirements are given in Section A4. Appendices include procedure to be followed in original and subsequent listing on the Exchange and other relevant information such as fees, listing forms, etc.

THE EXCHANGE, monthly.
Presents articles of current interest to shareholders.

NEW YORK STOCK EXCHANGE FACT BOOK, annual.
A handbook containing statistical series and certain historical data issued by the Exchange and some relevant information by other organizations.

NEW YORK STOCK EXCHANGE GUIDE, 3 vols. Chicago: Commerce Clearing House. Loose-leaf.
Vol. 1: DIRECTORY.
Vol. 2: CONSTITUTION AND RULES.
Vol. 3: RELATED LAWS AND REGULATIONS.
The official publication of the directory, constitution, rules and policies of the Exchange relating to member firms. Separate paperback editions of Vols. 1 and 2 are published each year by Commerce Clearing House. Rules and policies administered by the Department of Member Firms concerning financial statements and reports are covered in New York Stock Exchange Rules 415–425 which comprise sections 2415-2425 of Vol. 2 of the GUIDE.

NEW YORK STOCK EXCHANGE MONTHLY REVIEW, monthly.
Compilation of current securities markets financial statistics.

Practising Law Institute, 1133 Avenue of the Americas, New York, New York 10036. Founded in 1938 to provide training for lawyers in new developments in the law and new legal techniques. Publishes approximately 75 monographs which are revised and updated regularly on subjects of interest primarily to lawyers but also to accountants in the tax field.

Robert Morris Associations (National Association of Bank Loan Officers and Credit Men), Philadelphia National Bank Building, Philadelphia, Pennsylvania 19107. Founded in 1914 in honor of Robert Morris (1734-1806) who played a large part in financing the American Revolution. Statement of purpose, dated April 1965, declares the purpose of the association, "to foster and promote a sound economy through continuous improvement in principles and practices of commercial bank lending." The Association conducts research in credit and related subjects; improves methods of gathering, compiling, analyzing and disseminating credit data; promotes a closer relationship between mercantile and financial credit men.

JOURNAL OF COMMERCIAL BANK LENDING, monthly.

STATEMENT STUDIES, annual.
A compilation of average balance sheets for 185 different lines of business in manufacturing, wholesaling and retailing.

Section 3

GOVERNMENTAL REGULATION

Section 3

GOVERNMENTAL REGULATION

Increased public interest in and concern with financial and accounting matters have led inevitably to regulation of accounting practices by governmental agencies entrusted with law administration and enforcement. This trend has developed largely during the last half century, starting with the classification of accounts for steam railroads issued by the Interstate Commerce Commission in the early 1900's. The influence of governmental regulations upon both the recordkeeping of regulated industries and the general accounting thought and concepts of the profession has been very strong. The issuing of government-prescribed uniform systems of accounts for regulated industries and the fact that certain administrative agencies, such as the Securities and Exchange Commission, have substantial authority in the case of financial statements required to be filed with them have made federal regulation a force to be reckoned with in the accounting world today.

Governmental regulation of accounting practice is prevalent throughout the world. However, with the following two exceptions we shall deal here only with the regulations issued by United States administrative agencies. The 1967 COMPANIES ACT of Great Britain (London: Her Majesty's Stationery Office, 1967. 136p. pap.) and the 1965 CANADA CORPORATIONS ACT (Ottawa: Queens Printer, 1965. pap.), together with the various Companies Acts of the Canadian Provinces are of considerable interest to an American accountant. Gee & Co. (Publishers) Ltd. has issued a GUIDE TO THE ACCOUNTING REQUIREMENTS OF THE COMPANIES ACTS 1948-1967 (London: 1967. 36p. pap.), a summary of the statutory requirements relating to the production of annual accounts of companies. An OFFICE CONSOLIDATION OF THE CANADA CORPORATIONS ACT, R.S.C. 1952, c.53 AS AMENDED BY 1964-65, c.52 (138p. pap.) with an excellent index is available from the Queen's Printer in Ottawa.

An accountant with a foreign client should, of course, familiarize himself with the governmental accounting regulations of that country. The library of the American Institute of Certified Public Accountants would be a good source of such information. In 1964 the Institute published PROFESSIONAL ACCOUNTING IN 25 COUNTRIES which summarizes current accounting regulations and practices in the countries covered.

We list here only the United States federal regulatory agencies. However, our state commissions have some powers of particular interest to accountants. For example, public utilities are regulated by state commissions both as to rates and accounting. Decisions of federal and state commissions are listed in PUBLIC UTILITIES REPORTS, CONTAINING DECISIONS OF THE REGULATORY COMMISSIONS AND OF STATE AND FEDERAL COURTS. (1st-3rd series. Annual digest; biweekly advance sheets. Washington, D.C.: Public Utilities Reports, Inc., 1915- .) This publisher has also issued two cumulative digests: P.U.R. DIGEST, 1915-1932, and P.U.R. DIGEST, 2d SERIES, 1933-1962 with supplements to date. Another aspect of state regulation, that of the sale of securities, is comprehensively covered in the Commerce Clearing House service BLUE SKY LAW REPORTER.

We include in this section the federal agencies' publications directly applicable to accounting regulations, although these agencies issue many other publications of interest. For example, all federal agencies issue annual reports which contain much valuable material. Lists of their publications are available directly from the various agencies.

An annotated bibliography of material on governmental regulation was published by Gale Research Company in 1967, entitled GOVERNMENT REGULATION OF BUSINESS INCLUDING ANTITRUST (Management Information Guide 11), by Beatrice S. McDermott and Freada A. Coleman.

The best source of general information on federal agencies is the U.S. GOVERNMENT ORGANIZATION MANUAL, published annually by the Office of the Federal Register and sold by the U.S. Government Printing Office. Much of the historical information on the agencies included here was taken from the MANUAL. A brief listing of publications of federal departments and agencies can be found in the MANUAL's Appendix B. An even more comprehensive listing of federal agency publications is found in the GUIDE TO U.S. GOVERNMENT SERIALS AND PERIODICALS, by John L. Andriot, published in 1967 by Documents Index, Box 195, McLean, Virginia 22101.

Atomic Energy Commission, 1717 H Street N.W., Washington, D.C. 20545. Established by the Atomic Energy Act of 1946 to provide and administer programs for research, development and production of atomic energy and special nuclear materials. Of particular interest to accountants is the fact that this agency conducts procurement relating to the Atomic Energy Development Program. Commerce Clearing House publishes a looseleaf ATOMIC ENERGY LAW REPORTS service with weekly supplements which contains a section on the AEC procurement regulations.

Of increasing importance are the regulations of the AEC concerning private ownership of special nuclear materials, which became effective in 1969. These regulations are discussed in the CCH ATOMIC ENERGY LAW REPORTS service. The regulations are also available from the Washington, D.C. office of the Atomic Energy Commission.

ATOMIC ENERGY COMMISSION PROCUREMENT REGULATIONS. Washington, D.C.
Although these regulations are patterned after the Armed Services Procurement Regulations, there are important differences. Of special importance are Parts 9-15 concerning contract cost principles.

Bureau of the Budget, Executive Office Building, Washington, D.C. 20503. Created by the Budget and Accounting Act of 1921, which located the Bureau in the Treasury Department but placed it under the immediate direction of the

President. The Bureau's chief responsibility is to assist in the preparation of and to control the administration of the federal budget. However, another important function of the Bureau is to "advise the executive departments and agencies of the government with respect to improved administrative organization and practice." In this capacity, the Bureau of the Budget under the 1965 Poverty Program issued in August 1965 a circular entitled "Audit of Federal Grants-in-Aid to State and Local Governments" (Circular No. A-73) which set forth policies to be followed in these audits. Each federal agency conducting grant programs was instructed to "establish audit policies for guidance of its internal or independent auditors."

Civil Aeronautics Board, 1825 Connecticut Avenue, Washington, D.C. 20428. Established by the Civil Aeronautics Act of 1938 under title of Civil Aeronautics Authority, "with broad responsibilities for 'encouragement and development' of U.S. civil aviation and vested with safety and economic rule-making and ajudicatory powers." Present name was adopted June 30, 1940. The Board regulates the accounting practices of air carriers and requires them to file monthly financial and operating reports.

The following CAB Publications are available on subscription basis from the U.S. Government Printing Office.

AIR CARRIER FINANCIAL STATISTICS, quarterly.

ECONOMIC REGULATIONS, revised to date, which contain the CAB uniform system of accounts, procedural regulations and policy statements.

UNIFORM SYSTEM OF ACCOUNTS AND REPORTS FOR CERTIFICATED ROUTE AIR CARRIERS, 1961, revised to January 1, 1969.

An excellent service covering the CAB regulations is published by Rules Service Company, 1001 15th Street, N.W., Washington, D.C. 20005. The various sections which may be subscribed to separately cover the Economic Regulations, Procedural Regulations, Safety Investigation Regulations, Special Regulations (included with subscription to the Economic Regulations) and Policy Statements.

Comptroller of the Currency (Treasury Department), 15th Street & Pennsylvania Avenue N.W., Washington, D.C. 20220. The Office of the Comptroller of the Currency was created in 1863 as an integral part of the National Banking System. It issues regulations on organization, operation and examination of national banks.

Under the disclosure requirements of the Securities Acts amendments of 1965 (for details see the Securities and Exchange Commission in this section) the Comptroller was assigned the responsibility of enforcing the requirements in the case of all national banks. Regulations effective September 1, 1964 were issued in August 1964 regarding financial information required to be given to stockholders, and more extensive regulations were issued on May 1, 1967 covering all reports to be distributed on or after June 30, 1967. The following manuals, all available from the Comptroller of the Currency, are of interest to accountants.

COMPTROLLER'S MANUAL FOR NATIONAL BANKS: LAWS, REGULATIONS, RULINGS. Washington, D.C. 1963-. loose-leaf. "Combines the laws relating to national banks, the regulations of the Comptroller and the rulings of the Comptroller interpreting and applying the laws and regulations and general principles of prudent banking."

COMPTROLLER'S MANUAL FOR REPRESENTATIVES IN TRUST: REGULATIONS, INSTRUCTIONS, OPINIONS. Washington, D.C.: 1963-. forms. loose-leaf.

COMPTROLLER'S POLICY GUIDELINES FOR NATIONAL BANK DIRECTORS. Washington, D.C.: September 1964. forms. loose-leaf.

INSTRUCTIONS, PROCEDURES, FORMS FOR NATIONAL BANK EXAMINERS. Washington, D.C.: September 1964. forms. loose-leaf.

Department of Defense, The Pentagon, Washington, D.C. 20301. Successor to the National Military Establishment created by the National Security Act of 1947. Establishes government policies and procedures relating to national security. In this capacity, the Defense Department has issued uniform policies and procedures relating to procurement of property, supplies and services related to our national defense, both within and without the United States. The direct procurement is administered by either the Air Force, Army, Navy or Defense Supply Agency.

ARMED SERVICES PROCUREMENT REGULATIONS. Washington, D.C.: U.S. Government Printing Office, 1969-. loose-leaf. Available on subscription basis.

The most important of the government procurement regulations. Some implementation of these regulations, peculiar only to the purchasing activities, have been set forth in the AIR FORCE PROCUREMENT INSTRUCTIONS, NAVY PROCUREMENT DIRECTIVES and ARMY PROCUREMENT PROCEDURES.

DEFENSE SUPPLY PROCUREMENT REGULATIONS, also an implementation, are issued by the Defense Supply Agency, an agency of the Department of Defense, subject to DOD policies, directives and instructions. This agency conducts coordinated procurement of assigned items and services utilized by all branches of the Department of Defense.

The most vitally important section in the ARMED SERVICES PROCUREMENT REGULATIONS as far as audit activity is concerned is Section XV, Contract Cost Principles. This contains general cost principles and procedures for the determination and allowance of costs in connection with the negotiation and administration of cost-reimbursement type contracts and contains guidelines for use, where appropriate, in the evaluation of costs in connection with certain negotiated fixed-price type of contracts and contracts terminated for the convenience of the Government.

Other important sections are: Section 3, paragraph 807.4: Certificate of Current Cost or Pricing Data; Section 3, paragraph 808. 2 - 808.7: Weighted Guidelines Method; Section 7, paragraph 104.29: Clause for Price Reduction for Defective Cost or Pricing Data.

Department of Health, Education and Welfare, 330 Independence Avenue S.W., Washington, D.C. 20201. Created by the Reorganization Act of 1953, this department was established to improve the administration of government agencies which promote the general welfare in the fields of health, education and social security. Issues accounting regulations concerning payments under the health insurance for the aged program (Medicare).

HOSPITAL MANUAL, rev. ed. Washington, D.C.: U.S. Government Printing Office, April 1967. 122p. illus. pap.
A procedural manual designed for use by all hospitals which will be billing for services furnished under Medicare.

PRINCIPLES OF REIMBURSEMENT FOR PROVIDER COSTS. Washington, D.C.: U.S. Government Printing Office, May 1966. 30p. pap.
Presents the Medicare accounting regulations for allowable and unallowable costs and discusses the methods by which costs of services to Medicare beneficiaries are determined.

PROVIDER REIMBURSEMENT MANUAL. Washington, D.C.: U.S. Government Printing Office, 1967. 19p. pap.
For use by intermediaries in computing reasonable costs of services furnished under Medicare.

Department of Housing and Urban Development, 1626 K Street N.W., Washington, D.C. 20410. Established in September 1965 to "assist the President in achieving maximum coordination of various Federal activities which have a major effect upon urban community, suburban or metropolitan development... ."

The Federal Housing Authority carries out programs of loan and mortgage insurance authorized by the National Housing Act for the Department of Housing and Urban Development. In this capacity the FHA has issued the following:

HANDBOOK OF FHA REQUIREMENTS GOVERNING FISCAL OPERATIONS, ACCOUNTING, AND FINANCIAL REPORTS FOR MULTIFAMILY HOUSING PROJECTS (OTHER THAN COOPERATIVE HOUSING) INSURED UNDER THE NATIONAL HOUSING ACT (FHA No. 2230), revised October 1966. Washington, D.C.: U.S. Government Printing Office, 1966. 17p. pap.
Intended as a guide to project management and professional accountants in the interest of obtaining uniform financial information. Includes requirements for maintenance of account books and the submission of financial reports as well as facsimiles of forms and schedules to be used.

Federal Communications Commission, Post Office Building, Washington, D.C. 20554. Created by the Communications Act of 1934 which it administers, the Commission is composed of seven members. Copies of the Act, revised to date, are available from the U.S. Government Printing Office. All volumes of FCC RULES AND REGULATIONS are available separately on a subscription basis.

STATISTICS OF COMMUNICATIONS COMMON CARRIERS, annual. Washington, D.C.: U.S. Government Printing Office, 1939-.

UNIFORM SYSTEM OF ACCOUNTS FOR CLASS A AND CLASS B TELEPHONE COMPANIES, September 1965...CLASS C, January 1961 (FCC Rules and Regulations, Vol. 8, parts 31 and 33). Washington D.C.: U.S. Government Printing Office. 105p. pap.

UNIFORM SYSTEM OF ACCOUNTS FOR RADIOTELEGRAPH CARRIERS (FCC Rules and Regulations, Vol. 9, part 34). Washington, D.C.: U.S. Government Printing Office. pap.

UNIFORM SYSTEM OF ACCOUNTS FOR WIRE-TELEGRAPH AND OCEAN-CABLE CARRIERS. (FCC Rules and Regulations, Vol. 9, part 35). Washington, D.C.: U.S. Government Printing Office. pap.

Federal Credit Unions Bureau (Department of Health, Education and Welfare, Social Security Administration), 330 Independence Avenue S.W., Washington, D.C. 20201. Established in 1948 to assume functions of the Federal Credit Union System, this bureau functions as a program bureau of the Social Security Administration, subject to the direction of the Commissioner of Social Security. The HANDBOOK FOR FEDERAL CREDIT UNIONS, available from the U.S. Government Printing Office, contains background information on and general operation policies of federal credit unions.

ACCOUNTING MANUAL FOR FEDERAL CREDIT UNIONS. Washington, D.C.: U.S. Government Printing Office, 1965. 186p. pap. Contains accounting procedures to be used by federal credit unions. Revisions to the manual are sent automatically to all federal credit unions.

Federal Deposit Insurance Corporation, 550 17th Street N.W., Washington, D.C. 20429. First organized in 1933 under authority of the Federal Reserve Act, this agency became a separate entity in 1950 under the Federal Deposit Insurance Act. Its chief purpose is to insure the deposits of all banks which are entitled to the benefits of insurance under the Federal Deposit Insurance Act.

Under the disclosure requirements of the Securities Acts Amendments of 1964 (for details see the Securities and Exchange Commission in this section) the Corporation was assigned the responsibility of enforcing the amendments in cases of insured banks not subject to the Comptroller of the Currency or the Federal Reserve System. The FDIC bank securities disclosure regulations and forms are available from the Washington office of the Corporation. They were also published in Part III of the Tuesday, January 12, 1965 issue of the FEDERAL REGISTER, Vol. 30, No. 7.

Federal Home Loan Bank Board, 101 Indiana Avenue N.W., Washington, D.C. 20552. The Federal Home Loan Bank System was created by the authority of the Federal Home Loan Bank Act of July 22, 1932. Previously a constituent agency of the Housing and Home Finance Agency, the Federal Home Loan Bank Board was made an independent agency in 1955. Its purpose is to provide a credit reserve for savings and home-financing institutions.

Each insured institution, commencing January 1, 1968, is required to be audited regularly by a qualified public accountant or a qualified internal auditor. With reference to this regulation, the Board issued in April 1966 a "Statement of Policy Concerning Acceptability of Auditors and Audits" directed to the banks under its jurisdiction.

CHART OF ACCOUNTS FOR FEDERAL SAVINGS AND LOAN ASSOCIATIONS. Washington, D.C.: April 1955. 20p. pap.

INDEPENDENT AUDITS. Washington, D.C.: November 14, 1966. 8p. A statement directed toward and containing specific instructions for the independent auditors who would be examining the institutions insured by the Board after the date of January 1, 1968.

Federal Power Commission, General Accounting Office Building, 441 G Street N.W., Washington, D.C. 20426. First created in 1920 as a commission consisting of the Secretaries of War, Agriculture and the Interior, the present five-man agency was established in 1930. The Commission prescribes and enforces uniform systems of accounts for both privately-owned public utilities engaged in the transmission of electric energy in interstate commerce and for natural gas pipeline companies engaged in the transportation or sale of natural gas in interstate commerce. Utilities operating in only one state are primarily subject to the state commission as to rates but under certain circumstances may be subject also to FPC jurisdiction and accounting. Current reporting of the FPC's activities is available in a bimonthly service, FURA-CURRENT SERVICE-FPC, published by Public Utilities Reports, Inc., 332 Pennsylvania Building, Washington, D.C. 20004.

The statutes administered by the FPC include the Federal Power Act and the Natural Gas Act. Texts of these acts as amended to date are available from the U.S. Government Printing Office, Washington, D.C.

FPC publications available from FPC directly:

ACCOUNTING RELEASES, AR 1-. 1964-.
Contain informal interpretations of the Uniform Systems of Accounts to be followed in the absence of specific references on the prescribed accounting regulations and other authoritative decisions of the Commission.

FPC Form No. 1 - Annual report of Electric Utilities and Licensees (Classes A and B), 1965.

FPC Form No. 1M - Annual Report of Municipal Electric Utilities (Having Annual Electric Revenues of $250,000 or more), revised December 1964.

FPC Form No. 2 - Annual report of Natural Gas Companies (Classes A and B), 1962.

FPC NEWS, weekly.
Compilation of press releases, rate changes and formal documents. Available without charge from the FPC.

NEWS DIGEST, weekly.
Compilation of news items intended primarily for the information of members and staff of the FPC but also available to the public on subscription basis.

FPC publications available only from Government Printing Office:

RU, issued irregularly.
All orders in rule-making dockets, available without charge from the FPC.

RO, issued irregularly.
All numbered opinions, available without charge from the FPC.

FPC REPORTS, OPINIONS AND DECISIONS, semi-annual. 1931-.

REGULATIONS UNDER THE FEDERAL POWER ACT, March 31, 1964, revised to date. looseleaf. Available on subscription basis.

REGULATIONS UNDER THE NATURAL GAS ACT, August 1, 1967, revised to date. looseleaf. Available on subscription basis.

RULES OF PRACTICE AND PROCEDURE, in effect January 1, 1966,

revised to date. looseleaf. Available on subscription basis.

STATISTICS OF ELECTRIC UTILITIES IN THE UNITED STATES, CLASSES A AND B PRIVATELY OWNED COMPANIES, annual. 1937-. (Available vols. prior to 1957 sold by FPC.) loose-leaf. Available on sub-subscription basis.

STATISTICS OF ELECTRIC UTILITIES IN THE UNITED STATES, CLASSES A AND B PUBLICLY OWNED, annual. 1946-. (Available vols. prior to 1957 sold by FPC) loose-leaf. Available on subscription basis.

STATISTICS FOR INTERSTATE NATURAL GAS PIPELINE COMPANIES, annual. 1944-. (Available vols. prior to 1958 sold by FPC.) loose-leaf. Available on subscription basis.

UNIFORM SYSTEM OF ACCOUNTS PRESCRIBED FOR NATURAL GAS COMPANIES (CLASS A AND B, C, AND D), subject to the provisions of the Natural Gas Act, in effect on September 1, 1968.

UNIFORM SYSTEM OF ACCOUNTS PRESCRIBED FOR PUBLIC UTILITIES AND LICENSEES. (Class A, B, C and D Companies). Available on subscription basis.

Federal Reserve System, Board of Governors of the Federal Reserve System, 20th Street & Constitution Avenue N.W., Washington, D.C. 20551. Established under the Federal Reserve Act of December 23, 1913 "to provide for the establishment of Federal Reserve Banks, to furnish an elastic currency, to afford means of rediscounting commercial paper, to establish a more effective supervision of banking in the United States... ."

The Board of Governors determines monetary, credit and operating policies for the entire system of member banks and issues rules and regulations under the Federal Reserve Act.

FEDERAL RESERVE BULLETIN, monthly.

REGULATIONS A - Y, RULES OF ORGANIZATION AND RULES OF PROCEDURE. Washington, D.C.: 1930-.
Entire series available without charge on request to the Board of Governors, Federal Reserve System which also maintains a mailing list for this series.

Of particular interest to accountants are Regulations D (Reserves of Member Banks), G (Credit by Persons other than Banks, Brokers or Dealers for Purpose of Purchasing or Carrying Registered Equity Securities), Q (Payment of Interest on Deposits), T (Credit by Brokers, Dealers, and Members of National Securities Exchanges), U (Loans by Banks for the Purposes of Purchasing or Carrying Registered Stocks) and Y (Bank Holding Companies). Regulation F (Securities of Member State Banks), effective January 1, 1965, was issued pursuant to the Reserve Board's new responsibilities of enforcing the Securities Acts Amendments of 1964 (for details see the Securities and Exchange Commission in this section) in the case of all state-chartered banks that are members of the Federal Reserve System. Regulation F and Forms F-1, F-5 and F-7 are available from the Board of Governors, Federal Reserve System, Washington, D.C.

General Accounting Office, 441 G Street N.W., Washington, D.C.

20548. Created in 1921 to assist the Congress in providing legislative control over the receipt, disbursement and application of public funds.

ACCOUNTING PRINCIPLES AND STANDARDS FOR FEDERAL AGENCIES. Washington, D.C.: 1965. 93p. pap.
A reprint of three chapters and related explanatory transmittal sheet of Title 2, as of June 30, 1965, of the GAO POLICY AND PROCEDURES MANUAL FOR GUIDANCE OF FEDERAL AGENCIES. Consists of revised instructions for obtaining Comptroller General approval of federal agency accounting systems as well as a restatement of principles and standards of accounting to be observed by federal agencies. Available without charge from the GAO.

ACCOUNTING PROCEDURES FOR FEDERAL AGENCIES. Washington, D.C.: 1962. 32p. charts. pap.
Shows how the accrual basis of accounting and simple fund control procedures can be applied to federal agencies having predominantly personal service costs.

AUDITS OF GOVERNMENT CONTRACTS. Washington, D.C.: U.S. Government Printing Office, 1966. 31p. pap.
Outlines the authority, purposes, objectives and related reporting practices of the GAO in carrying out its responsibilities to contractors subject to GAO audit.

THE GAO REVIEW, quarterly.

GENERAL ACCOUNTING OFFICE POLICY AND PROCEDURES MANUAL FOR GUIDANCE OF FEDERAL AGENCIES. Washington, D.C.: U.S. Government Printing Office. loose-leaf. Available on subscription basis.
Official medium through which the Comptroller General issues the principles, standards and requirements for accounting to be observed by federal departments and agencies as well as the uniform procedures for use by federal agencies. Includes regulations governing the relationships of the GAO with other federal agencies and with individuals and private concerns doing business with the government.

REVIEW GUIDE FOR FEDERAL AGENCY ACCOUNTING SYSTEMS. Washington, D.C.: 1966. 45p. pap.
A checklist designed to help federal agencies review their accounting systems in relation to the standards and requirements prescribed by the Comptroller General.

General Services Administration, 18th and F Streets N.W., Washington, D.C. 20405. Established by the Federal Property and Administrative Services Act of 1949 to provide for the Government an economical and efficient system for the maintenance of its property and records. Of particular interest to accountants is the fact that this agency conducts a major portion of procurement for all federal agencies other than the Department of Defense, the National Aeronautics and Space Administration and the Atomic Energy Commission. In some instances it procures certain in-house supplies for these agencies.

FEDERAL PROCUREMENT REGULATIONS. Washington, D.C.: U.S. Government Printing Office, 1964-. loose-leaf. Available on subscription basis.

Prescribes the policies and procedures for procurement by all agencies of the Government other then DOD - NASA - AEC. GSA uses these regulations without implementation, whereas other buying agencies such as Federal Aviation Agency, Department of Health, Education and Welfare, Department of Interior, etc., because of procurement peculiar to their needs, have issued some implementation to these regulations which should be referred to when dealing with these agencies.

Internal Revenue Service (Treasury Department), 1111 Constitution Avenue N.W., Washington, D.V. 20224. The office of Commissioner of Internal Revenue was created by the Internal Revenue Act of July 1, 1862 to administer the internal revenue laws of the United States.

CUMULATIVE BULLETIN, weekly. Washington, D.C.: U.S. Government Printing Office, 1922-. Available on subscription basis.
Announcement of official rulings and procedures of the IRS, decisions of the Tax Court, Treasury decisions, Executive Orders, etc. relating to internal revenue matters.

CUMULATIVE LIST OF ORGANIZATIONS DESCRIBED IN SECTION 170 (c) OF THE INTERNAL REVENUE CODE OF 1954, rev. ed., 1968 (IRS Publication 78). Washington, D.C.: U.S. Government Printing Office. Biennial vols. and cumulative supplements available on subscription basis.
List of non-profit organizations, contributions to which are deductible by donors for federal income tax purposes.

DEPRECIATION GUIDELINES AND RULES (IRS publication 456). Washington, D.C.: U.S. Government Printing Office, rev. August 1964. 92p. tables.
Provides guideline lives for approximately 75 classes of assets.

INTERNAL REVENUE BULLETIN, monthly.

LOOSE LEAF REGULATIONS SERVICE. Washington, D.C.: U.S. Government Printing Office, 1961-. Available on subscription basis.
Includes all tax regulations issued by IRS except those on alcohol, tobacco, certain firearm taxes and those issued under tax conventions.

STATISTICS OF INCOME, annual. Part 1, INDIVIDUAL TAX RETURNS. Part 2, CORPORATION INCOME TAX RETURNS. Washington, D.C.: U.S. Government Printing Office, 1918-.
Issued in preliminary form after approximately 14 months, in final form after approximately 18 months. Various supplementary parts issued separately, e.g., U.S. BUSINESS TAX RETURNS, annual, FIDUCIARY, GIFT AND ESTATE TAX RETURNS, biennial. Available on subscription basis.

TAX GUIDE FOR SMALL BUSINESS, annual. Washington, D.C.: U.S. Government Printing Office.
For the business or professional man who needs information about federal taxes in establishing, operating or disposing of his business.

TAX GUIDE FOR U.S. CITIZENS ABROAD, annual. Washington, D.C.: U.S. Government Printing Office.
Designed to help United States citizens residing or working abroad to understand the exemption from Federal Income Tax for income earned

aboard.

YOUR FEDERAL INCOME TAX, annual. Washington, D.C.: U.S. Government Printing Office.
A simplified explanation of federal tax laws as they apply to individuals.

Interstate Commerce Commission, 12th Street & Constitution Avenue N.W., Washington, D.C. 20423. Created by the Interstate Commerce Act of 1887. Regulates all common carriers engaged in interstate commerce and in foreign commerce which takes place within the United States. The Commission consists of eleven members appointed by the President for overlapping terms. An interesting four-volume work on the ICC which is now out of print but available in the larger public and accounting libraries is THE INTERSTATE COMMERCE COMMISSION, A STUDY IN ADMINISTRATIVE LAW AND PROCEDURE by I. L. Sharfman. New York: Commonwealth Fund, 1931-1937.

In addition to the publications listed below, the commission publishes forms to be used in the annual reports of the carriers under its jurisdiction. These may be obtained from the ICC Washington office.

INTERSTATE COMMERCE COMMISSION DECISIONS. Washington, D.C.: U.S. Government Printing Office, 1887-.
Volumes are issued under the classifications: Finance Docket, Motor Carriers, Traffic, Valuation Docket. Available on subscription basis.

TRANSPORT STATISTICS IN THE UNITED STATES. Washington, D.C.: U.S. Government Printing Office, 1887-.
Formerly published in annual volumes, this report is now issued in sections. Available on subscription basis.

UNIFORM SYSTEM OF ACCOUNTS FOR CARRIERS BY INLAND AND COASTAL WATERWAYS..., as amended to July 1, 1959. Washington, D.C.: U.S. Government Printing Office.

UNIFORM SYSTEM OF ACCOUNTS FOR CLASS 1 AND CLASS 11 COMMON AND CONTRACT MOTOR CARRIERS OF PASSENGERS, rev. to January 1, 1969. Washington, D.C.: U.S. Government Printing Office.

UNIFORM SYSTEM OF ACCOUNTS FOR CLASS 1 COMMON AND CONTRACT MOTOR CARRIERS OF PROPERTY, rev. to date. Washington, D.C.: U.S. Government Printing Office.

UNIFORM SYSTEM OF ACCOUNTS FOR ELECTRIC RAILWAYS, rev. to date. Washington, D.C.: U.S. Government Printing Office.

UNIFORM SYSTEM OF ACCOUNTS FOR FREIGHT FORWARDERS, rev. to date. Washington, D.C.: U.S. Government Printing Office.

UNIFORM SYSTEM OF ACCOUNTS FOR MARITIME CARRIERS PRESCRIBED BY THE INTERSTATE COMMERCE COMMISSION, effective January 1, 1951, with subsequent orders. Washington, D.C.: U.S. Government Printing Office.

UNIFORM SYSTEM OF ACCOUNTS FOR PIPE LINE COMPANIES, rev. to date. Washington, D.C.: U.S. Government Printing Office.

UNIFORM SYSTEM OF ACCOUNTS FOR RAILROAD COMPANIES, as amended to January 1, 1968 with subsequent orders. Washington, D.C.: U.S. Government Printing Office.
The ICC also issues INTERPRETATIONS OF THE UNIFORM SYSTEM

OF ACCOUNTS FOR RAILROAD COMPANIES, effective 1962 (Accounting Circular no. 130), with subsequent circulars. Washington, D.C.: U.S. Government Printing Office, 1962.

UNIFORM SYSTEM OF ACCOUNTS FOR REFRIGERATOR CAR LINES, effective January 1, 1960. Washington, D.C.: U.S. Government Printing Office.

Maritime Administration (Department of Commerce), General Accounting Office Building, 441 G Street N.W., Washington, D.C. 20235. Originally created in 1936 as an independent agency, the United States Maritime Commission. This agency was abolished and its functions transferred to Department of Commerce in the Reorganization Plan of 1950. In 1961 the Federal Maritime Commission was established as an independent agency in charge of regulatory matters under the various shipping and merchant marine acts. The Maritime Administration administers programs authorized by the Merchant Marine Act, 1936, as amended, and related shipping statutes to assist the development, promotion and operation of the United States merchant marine.

Regulations and rules of practice and procedure under the Maritime Administration and the Federal Maritime Commission are published in the CODE OF FEDERAL REGULATIONS - TITLE 46, PARTS 150 to 199 and PARTS 200 TO END, rev. to January 1, 1970, with annual cumulative supplements. Washington, D.C.: U.S. Government Printing Office. Available on subscription basis.

GENERAL ORDERS, Nos. 1-. Washington, D.C.: 1936-.
A number of these orders are of importance to accountants. General Order 22 is the chart of accounts for shipping companies.

MANUAL OF PROCEDURES, ACCOUNTING INSTRUCTIONS, Nos. 1-. Washington, D.C.: 1955-.
Distributed to all subsidized operators directly from the Commission's Office of Finance.

UNIFORM SYSTEM OF ACCOUNTS FOR MARITIME CARRIERS, PRESCRIBED BY THE INTERSTATE COMMERCE COMMISSION FOR MARITIME CARRIERS, AND BY THE MARITIME ADMINISTRATION FOR OPERATING-DIFFERENTIAL SUBSIDY CONTRACTORS, effective January 1, 1951. Washington, D.C.: 1950. 81p. pap.

National Aeronautics and Space Administration, Washington, D.C. 20546. Established by the National Aeronautics and Space Act of 1958. Responsibility is to "plan, direct and conduct aeronautical and space activities" for peaceful scientific purposes and to coordinate with the Department of Defense all space activities having military implications. This agency conducts procurement relating to the National Space Act.

NATIONAL AERONAUTICS AND SPACE ADMINISTRATION PROCUREMENT REGULATIONS. Washington, D.C.: U.S. Government Print Office, 1964-. loose-leaf. Available on subscription basis.
These regulations are modeled after the ARMED SERVICES PROCUREMENT REGULATIONS even as to section numbering. The major difference is in the section concerning patent rights. Section XV, "Contract Cost Principles", is similar to the ASPR, but different in certain areas such as research and development allowances.

Office of Economic Opportunity, 1200 19th Street N.W., Washington, D.C.

20506. Established within the Executive Office of the President by the Economic Opportunity Act of 1964. Purpose is to "eliminate the paradox of poverty in the midst of plenty in this Nation by opening to everyone the opportunity for education and training, the opportunity to work and the opportunity to live in decency and dignity."

ACCOUNTING SYSTEM SURVEY AND AUDIT GUIDE FOR COMMUNITY ACTION PROGRAM GRANTS. Washington, D.C.: 1967. v.p. pap.
Designed to assist independent accountants and auditors of public agencies to understand the special requirements for audit coverage of OEO grant programs referred to as Community Action Programs. These concern programs of both urban and rural communities to fight poverty as well as programs to raise living standards for migrant and seasonally employed workers.

COMMUNITY ACTION PROGRAM GUIDE, 2 vols. Washington, D.C.: 1965. pap.
Vol. 1- INSTRUCTIONS FOR APPLICANTS, October 1965. Instructions for developing, conducting and administering a community action program. Vol. 2 - FINANCIAL INSTRUCTIONS, June 1965. Instructions for financial management of community action program funds.

GUIDE FOR GRANTEE ACCOUNTING. Washington, D.C.: March 1966.
Contains guides to satisfactory accounting procedures and certain mandatory requirements which apply to all OEC grantees.

Office of Labor-Management and Welfare-Pension Reports (Department of Labor), 14th Street & Constitution Avenue N.W., Washington, D.C. 20210. Formed in 1963 as a consolidation of the Bureau of Labor-Management Reports and the Office of Welfare and Pension Plans. The Bureau of Labor-Management Reports was created in 1959 for the purpose of administering and enforcing those provisions of the Labor-Management Reporting and Disclosure Act of 1959 for which the Secretary of Labor is responsible.

FORM LM-2. LABOR ORGANIZATION ANNUAL REPORT (REVISED). Washington, D.C.: May 1964.
Annual report form to be filed by labor organizations.

FORM LM-3. LABOR ORGANIZATION ANNUAL REPORT (REVISED). Washington, D.C.: 1964.
Simplified annual report form for smaller labor organizations.

The Office of Welfare and Pension Plans was created in 1962 for the purpose of administering and enforcing the provisions of the Welfare and Pension Plan Disclosure Act of 1959. Prior to 1962 financial reporting of welfare and pension plans was optional. A regulation of May 26, 1962 made mandatory the filing of the following forms:

FORM D-1. PLAN DESCRIPTION REPORTING FORM D-1, PLANS DISCLOSURE ACT, effective June 18, 1962. Washington, D.C.: U.S. Government Printing Office, 1966.
This form is used for filing descriptions of welfare and pension plans.

FORM D-2. ANNUAL REPORT FORM D-2, AND PENSION PLANS DISCLOSURE ACT, rev. 1965. Washington, D.C.: U.S. Government Printing Office, 1966.

The annual report form to be filed by welfare and pension plans.

Renegotiation Board, 1910 K Street N.W., Washington, D.C. 20446. Created by Renegotiation Act of 1951 as an independent agency with powers previously conferred upon War Contracts Price Adjustment Board in 1944. The main purpose of the Renegotiation Board is to eliminate excessive profits from contracts having a direct connection with the national defense effort. Commerce Clearing House, 4025 W. Peterson Avenue, Chicago, Illinois 60646, publishes a service on government contracts which covers the Renegotiation Board regulations.

INSTRUCTIONS FOR FILING RENEGOTIATION REPORTS. Washington, D.C.: U.S. Government Printing Office, January 1965.
Designed to assist in the preparation of a report to the Board. Includes copies of RB Form 1 (Standard Form of Contractor's Report) and RB Form 90 (Statement of Non-Applicability).

RENEGOTIATION BOARD REGULATIONS UNDER THE RENEGOTIATION ACT OF 1951. March 1, 1964, rev. to date. Washington, D.C.: U.S. Government Printing Office. Available on subscription basis.
Gives requirement for filing by contractors and details of renegotiation procedure by the Board. Subscription includes the RENEGOTIATION BULLETINS and RENEGOTIATION RULINGS.

Rural Electrification Administration (Department of Agriculture), 14th Street & Independence Avenue S.W., Washington, D.C. 20250. Operating under the Rural Electrification Act of May 20, 1936, this agency administers loan programs for rural electrification and rural telephone service. The REA requires its borrowers to have their accounts audited each year by certified public accountants.

ABC's OF ACCOUNTING AND INTERPRETATION OF FINANCIAL STATEMENTS FOR REA-FINANCED RURAL ELECTRIC SYSTEMS (REA Bulletin, No. 180-3), Washington, D.C.: U.S. Government Printing Office, August 1962. 37p. forms. pap.
Written for the directors of rural electric systems, this gives a simplified explanation of basic accounting principles and reviews electric cooperative accounting and its financial statements.

AUDIT OF REA BORROWERS' ACCOUNTING RECORDS (REA Bulletin, no. 185-1 [Electric] and REA Bulletin, no. 465-1 [Telephone]). Washington, D.C.: U.S. Government Printing Office, November 1963. 85p. tables. pap.
Gives the auditing and reporting requirements of both the REA electric and telephone programs. Sample audit reports of both an electric distribution cooperative and a Class A or B commercial telephone company are included.

MONTHLY FINANCIAL AND STATISTICAL REPORT (REA Form 7). Washington, D.C.: U.S. Government Printing Office, October 1965. v.p.
Form to be filed in accordance with instructions in UNIFORM SYSTEM OF ACCOUNTS PRESCRIBED FOR ELECTRIC BORROWERS.

UNIFORM SYSTEM OF ACCOUNTS PRESCRIBED FOR ELECTRIC BORROWERS OF THE RURAL ELECTRIFICATION ADMINISTRATION (REA Bulletin 181-1), effective January 1, 1961. Washington, D.C.: U.S. Government Printing Office, 1961. 182p. pap.

Based on uniform system of accounts prescribed by the Federal Power Commission but "modified to the extent considered appropriate to the accounting needs of the electric borrowers financed by REA."

Securities and Exchange Commission, 500 N. Capitol Street N.W., Washington, D.C. 20549. Created under authority of the Securities Exchange Act of 1934, the SEC was organized on July 2, 1934 as an independent, bipartisan, quasi judicial agency of the U.S. Government. The general objective of the statues administered by the commission is to regulate the U.S. securities markets and protect the interests of the public and investors against malpractices in the offering and sale of securities. The Commission also has advisory responsibilities to Federal Districts Courts under Chapter X of the National Bankuptcy Act.

The statutes administered by the SEC include the Securities Act of 1933, the Securities Exchange Act of 1934, the Public Utility Holding Company Act of 1935, the Trust Indenture Act of 1939, the Investment Company Act of 1940 and the Investment Advisers Act of 1940. Texts of the acts as amended to date are available from the U.S. Government Printing Office, Washington, D.C. Regulation S-X, described below, is of primary importance to accountants working with these Acts.

The SEC is composed of five members of which no more than three can be of the same political party, appointed by the President, with the advice and consent of the Senate, for 5-year terms, one term ending each year. Major operating units are the Division of Corporation Finance, Division of Corporate Regulation and the Division of Trading and Exchanges. The Chief Accountant is the Commission's principal adviser on all matters of financial accounting and reporting.

It is generally recognized that the SEC has probably contributed more toward improving financial reporting in the United States than any other federal agency. Under the Securities Laws the SEC has the authority to prescribe for a registration statement whatever accounting principle, method or statement it deems appropriate for the protection of the investor. However, instead of imposing a rigid and uniform set of accounting practices upon the business community, the SEC generally has permitted the accounting profession itself to develop generally accepted accounting principles. The commission has, in fact, contributed to this evolution of principles through its relations with the American Institute of Certified Public Accountants, the stock exchanges and public accounting firms. Today the SEC will accept for financial statements filed, application of accounting principles which have substantial authoritative support even if the commission believes other principles may be more appropriate, provided it has not already announced its position on the point involved.

A number of articles have appeared in accounting journals on the accounting requirements of the SEC. The following are books which would be of particular interest to accountants dealing with the Commission:

Loss, Louis. SECURITIES REGULATION, 2nd ed., 3 vols. Boston: Little, Brown, 1961.

McCormick, Edward T. UNDERSTANDING THE SECURITIES ACT AND THE S.E.C. New York: American Book Company, 1948. 327p. (o.p.)

Rappaport, Louis H. SEC ACCOUNTING PRACTICE AND PROCEDURE, 2nd ed., rev. printing. New York: Ronald Press, 1966. v.p.

Commerce Clearing House and Prentice-Hall each publish a service relating to the Acts administered by the SEC and its rules and regulations which are listed in Section 10, Services. Three New York City printers also issue SEC services: Appeal Printing Company, 130 Cedar Street; Pandick Press, Inc., 345 Hudson Street; and Sorg Printing Company, Inc., 80 South Street. Current reporting of the work of the SEC under the Public Utility Holding Company Act is available in the service FURA-CURRENT SERIES-SEC, published by Public Utilities Reports, Inc., 332 Pennsylvania Building, Washington, D.C. 20004.

In April 1968 the SEC published a 35-page pamphlet entitled "The Work of the Securities and Exchange Commission," which describes both the nature and scope of the commission's work and the limits of its authority.

The Commission maintains a mailing list for all new or amended rules under the various acts it administers. Forms and regulations to be used in financial statements, registration statements, reports, etc. (such as Form 10-K, the annual report form for registered commercial and industrial companies) are available from the SEC. A number of printing firms also publish the more important forms and regulations and distribute them free of charge. Three New York City printers who perform this service are: Appeal Printing Company, 130 Cedar Street; Bowne & Company, Inc., 345 Hudson Street; and Sorg Printing Company, Inc., 80 South Street.

The SEC issues a number of other regular releases as well as special studies. A complete listing of Commission releases is available from the SEC Division of Administrative Services, 500 N. Capitol Street, N.W., Washington, D.C. 20549.

On August 20, 1964 the president signed into law The Securities Acts Amendments of 1964 which increased substantially the number of companies required to register their securities with the SEC. Under these amendments all companies with assets of over $1,000,000 and 750 or more stockholders at the close of their first fiscal year after July 1, 1964 became subject to the reporting, proxy and insider trading requirements of the Securities Exchange Act of 1934. As of July 1, 1966, companies with 500 or more stockholders were similarly affected.

The requirements of this law relating to banks were removed from the SEC and transferred to the appropriate agency: Comptroller of the Currency, Federal Deposit Insurance Corporation or the Federal Reserve Board (for details of their publications, look under the names of these agencies in this section).

The importance of The Securities Acts Amendments of 1964 to all practicing accountants is obvious. PUBLIC LAW 88-467 itself is available from the U.S. Government Printing Office. Commerce Clearing House has included a law as a separate section of its service FEDERAL SECURITIES LAW REPORTS, no. 3, August 7, 1964, and has also published an indexed 94-page pamphlet entitled SECURITIES ACTS AMENDMENTS OF 1964 WITH EXPLANATION.

The Practising Law Institute, 1133 Avenue of the Americas, New York, New York 10038, has issued a three-volume publication dealing with the 1964 Securities Acts Amendments entitled HOW TO COMPLY WITH THE NEW SEC RULES. This consists of a workbook volume containing SEC forms, etc., a transcript volume containing a transcript of a forum on the SEC admendments conducted by the Institute, and a broker-dealer volume containing regulations of the SEC, National Association of Securities Dealers, Inc. and the New York

Stock Exchange.

ACCOUNTING SERIES RELEASES, Nos. 1-, 1937-.
Releases containing the SEC interpretations of its new and amended rules and regulations which are indispensable to the practicing accountant. A compilation of releases Nos. 1-112 is available from the U.S. Government Printing Office, Washington 25, D.C. Later releases may be obtained directly from the SEC which also maintains a free mailing list for this series.

COMPILATION OF RELEASES, COMMISSION OPINIONS, AND OTHER MATERIAL DEALING WITH MATTERS FREQUENTLY ARISING UNDER THE INVESTMENT COMPANY ACT OF 1940, OCTOBER 1967. Washington, D.C.: U.S. Government Printing Office, 1967. 94p. pap.

COMPILATION OF RELEASES DEALING WITH MATTERS FREQUENTLY ARISING UNDER THE SECURITIES ACT OF 1933, APRIL 30, 1965 Washington, D.C.: U.S. Government Printing Office, 1965. 77p. pap.
Interesting compilations which do not claim to be exhaustive, but which include the releases referred to most frequently under these Acts.

DIRECTORY OF COMPANIES FILING ANNUAL REPORTS WITH THE SEC UNDER THE SECURITIES EXCHANGE ACT OF 1934. Washington, D.C.: 1958-. pap.
Annual publication listing all companies except investment companies, government and foreign, filing annual reports with the SEC, presented both alphabetically and by industry classification.

GENERAL RULES AND REGULATIONS UNDER THE INVESTMENT COMPANY ACT OF 1940, as in effect November 1, 1968. Washington, D.C.: U.S. Government Printing Office, 1962. 57p. pap.

GENERAL RULES AND REGULATIONS UNDER PUBLIC UTILITY HOLDING COMPANY ACT OF 1935, as in effect August 1, 1963. Washington, D.C.: U.S. Government Printing Office, 1963. 61p. pap.

GENERAL RULES AND REGULATIONS UNDER SECURITIES ACT OF 1933, as in effect November 1, 1968. Washington, D.C.: U.S. Government Printing Office, 1968. 92p. pap.

GENERAL RULES AND REGULATIONS UNDER SECURITIES EXCHANGE ACT OF 1934, as in effect October 16, 1968. Washington, D.C.: U.S. Government Printing Office, 1968. 141p. pap.

INVESTMENT ADVISERS ACT OF 1940 AND GENERAL RULES AND REGULATIONS THEREUNDER, as in effect January 1, 1969. Washington, D.C.: U.S. Government Printing Office, 1969. 21p. pap.

REGULATION S-X, as in effect September 1, 1968. Washington, D.C.: U.S. Government Printing Office, 1968. 88p. pap.
Constantly updated regulation giving the form and content of financial statements under the 1933, 1934, 1935 Acts and the Investment Company Act of 1940.

RULES OF PRACTICE AND RULES RELATING TO INVESTIGATIONS AND CODE OF BEHAVIOR GOVERNING EX PARTE COMMUNICA-

CATION BETWEEN PERSONS OUTSIDE THE COMMISSION AND DECISIONAL EMPLOYEES, rev. as of August 1968. Washington, D.C.: U.S. Government Printing Office, 1968. 39p. pap.

SEC DECISIONS AND REPORTS, Vols. 1–. Washington, D.C.: U.S. Government Printing Office, 1934–. Available on subscription basis. Bound texts of the SEC decisions.

SEC NEWS DIGEST, daily. Available on subscription basis from the U.S. Government Printing Office.
A daily resumé of orders, decisions, rules and rule proposals issued by the Commission. Includes summary of financing proposals contained in Securities Act registration statements.

TRUST INDENTURE ACT OF 1939 AND GENERAL RULES AND REGULATIONS THEREUNDER as in effect August 1, 1963. Washington, D.C.: U.S. Government Printing Office, 1936. 43p. pap.

Small Business Administration, 1441 L Street N.W., Washington, D.C. 20416. Established in 1953 as the federal agency to serve small business. Provides financial counseling and loans to small businessmen. Several of the bulletins in the various series listed below give suggested accounting and bookkeeping systems for small businesses. Two complete lists of currently available titles can be obtained from any of the field offices of the SBA: one lists free publications available from the SBA, the other lists "for sale" items available from the U.S. Government Printing Office. These lists are issued twice a year.

MANAGEMENT AIDS FOR SMALL MANAUFACTURERS, Nos. 1–. Washington, D.C.: 1952–. Irregular. Free on SBA mailing list. Annual compilation volumes available from U.S. Government Printing Office.

MANAGEMENT RESEARCH SUMMARIES. Nos. 1–. Washington, D.C.: 1960–. Irregular. Free on SBA mailing list.

SMALL BUSINESS BULLETINS/BIBLIOGRAPHIES. Nos. 1–. Washington, D.C.: 1958–. Irregular but frequent. Free from SBA, no mailing list.
Excellent bibliographies on a great variety of subjects of interest to the small businessman.

SMALL BUSINESS MANAGEMENT SERIES. Nos. 1–. Washington, D.C.: 1952–. Irregular. Available from U.S. Government Printing Office.

SMALL BUSINESS RESEARCH SERIES. Nos. 1–. Washington, D.C.: 1960–. Irregular. Available from U.S. Government Printing Office.

SMALL MARKETERS AIDS, Nos 1–. Washington, D.C.: 1954–. Free on SBA mailing list. Annual compilation volumes available from U.S. Government Printing Office.

STARTING AND MANAGING SERIES, Nos. 1–. Washington, D.C.: 1958–. Irregular. Available from U.S. Government Printing Office.

A SURVEY OF FEDERAL GOVERNMENT PUBLICATIONS OF INTEREST TO SMALL BUSINESS, 3rd ed. Washington, D.C.: U.S. Government Printing Office, 1969. 85p. pap.

A listing of publications issued by government agencies which are useful to small businessmen. Arranged by industry or subject.

TECHNICAL AIDS FOR SMALL MANUFACTURERS. Nos. 1-. Washington, D.C.: 1952-. Irregular. Free on SBA mailing list. Annual compilation volumes available from U.S. Government Printing Office.

Under the Small Business Investment Company Act of 1958, the Small Business Administration is empowered to license, regulate and help finance privately organized and privately operated small business investment companies. Copies of the Act, amended to date, are available from the U.S. Government Printing Office, Washington, D.C. 20402. These small business investment companies provide venture capital, chiefly in the form of long-term loans or equity-type financing to qualified small business concerns.

In addition to reports issued to stockholders, SBICs licensed under the Small Business Investment Act of 1958 are required to submit annually to the SBA a detailed financial report prepared on prescribed forms (SBA Form 468) and accompanied by the opinion of an independent public accountant. By regulation, such opinion is to contain certain required scope comments and supplementary account analysis. Semiannual unaudited reports are also required by the Small Business Administration. In addition, field audits of each SBIC are conducted by the Small Business Administration each year.

SBA Publications Relating to SBICs:

AUDIT AND EXAMINATION GUIDE FOR SMALL BUSINESS IN VESTMENT COMPANIES (SBA RULES AND REGULATIONS, Part 107, appendix 1). Washington, D.C.: 1968-.
Revised annually, this guide is intended to inform licensees under the Small Business Investment Act of the minimum requirements of their audits and examination. Not a complete manual of procedure.

SYSTEM OF ACCOUNTS CLASSIFICATIONS FOR SMALL BUSINESS INVESTMENT COMPANIES, 2nd rev. Washington, D.C.: 1966.
This is Part III of the volume, SBA RULES AND REGULATIONS and is constantly revised and updated.

Tax Court of the United States, Internal Revenue Building, 12th Street Constitution Avenue N.W., Washington, D.C. 20224. Created as the U.S. Board of Tax Appeals by the Revenue Act of 1924. The change to present name was made by The Revenue Act of 1942. The Tax Court has jurisdiction over proceedings involving Internal Revenue claims and similar matters.

REPORTS OF THE COURT. Monthly consolidated issue and bound semiannual volumes. Washington, D.C.: U.S. Government Printing Office, 1942-. Available on subscription basis.

Section 4

TAX PRACTICE

Section 4

TAX PRACTICE

The increasing complexity of the U.S. tax laws and the expanding number of taxpayers has led in recent years to a growing need for tax accounting services. A tax return is, after all, basically a financial statement and as such is often reviewed by an expert tax accountant. Many a small businessman who has never before required accounting assistance is obliged to seek it now in the preparation of his returns. On the other hand, large corporations with tax departments of their own often want a review of their returns by independent accountants and this is quite commonly undertaken in conjunction with audit engagements.

One of the important services rendered by the tax accountant is that of keeping abreast of the numerous changes in tax laws and regulations as well as current court decisions and rulings which affect his clients. This involves covering a voluminous field of tax literature, magazines and services.

Tax matters are covered in a number of the indexes listed in Section 6, "Bibliographies and Indexes." A Commerce Clearing House service entitled FEDERAL TAX ARTICLES, which summarizes articles and notes published in legal, accounting and tax journals, is devoted entirely to the tax field. Another index covering all public finance material, including tax services, periodicals, etc. is the TAX INSTITUTE BOOKSHELF, published by the Tax Institute of America, 457 Nassau Street, Princeton, New Jersey 08540. However, since it is published only twice a year, this index is not always current.

The tax service known as the STANDARD FEDERAL TAX REPORTS, published by Commerce Clearing House, 4025 West Peterson Avenue, Chicago, Illinois 60646, or FEDERAL TAXES published by Prentice-Hall, Inc., Englewood Cliffs, New Jersey is an essential part of a basic tax library. In fact, larger libraries include both services. Although the major emphasis in these services is on income taxes, special volumes on excise taxes and estate and gift taxes are available as part of the complete service.

In addition to these standard services, excellent supplemental services include MERTENS LAW OF FEDERAL INCOME TAXATION, published by Callaghan & Co., 6141 North Cicero Avenue, Chicago, Illinois 60646; the Rabkin and Johnson FEDERAL INCOME, GIFT AND ESTATE TAXATION, published by Mathew Bender & Co., 1275 Broadway, Albany, New York 12201; TAX COORDINATOR, published by Tax Research Institute of America, 589 Fifth Avenue, New York, New York 10017; and Prentice-Hall's TAX IDEAS. The Institute for Business Planning,

2 West 13th Street, New York, New York 10011, also publishes a very useful tax service, TAX PLANNING AND TAX PLANNING IDEAS, which may be purchased completely or in part. The choice of these supplemental services necessarily depends upon individual tastes, the needs of the particular business and the amount budgeted for this purpose.

The weekly INTERNAL REVENUE BULLETINS which are accumulated in bound form semiannually by the Internal Revenue Service are required reading for an accountant striving to keep up to date in tax practices. Current decisions and bound volumes of the TAX COURT REPORTS (formerly issued as BOARD OF TAX APPEALS REPORTS) are also valuable reference material. Both the current decisions and bound volumes of the reports containing previous years' decisions may be obtained from the U.S. Government Printing Office. In addition, both Commerce Clearing House and Prentice-Hall have special looseleaf services containing the current Tax Court decisions and publish the "memorandum" opinions of the Court not published by the U.S. Government Printing Office.

Either U.S. TAX CASES (Commerce Clearing House) or AMERICAN FEDERAL TAX REPORTER (Prentice-Hall) is a good source for other than Tax Court cases (e.g., Federal District Courts, Courts of Appeal and the U.S. Supreme Court).

The Division of General Education of New York University, New York City, conducts an annual two-week Institute on Federal Taxation during which authoritative members of the accounting and legal professions deliver lectures on current aspects of federal taxation. These lectures are published annually by Mathew Bender & Co., Inc., 1275 Broadway, Albany, New York 12201 and often contain material of value to the tax accountant. Other excellent tax institutes are held by the University of Chicago (published annually in the December issue of TAXES Magazine), Tulane University, University of Southern California and other universities.

The Practising Law Institute, 1133 Avenue of the Americas, New York, New York 10036 issues a number of publications which are of interest to the accountant in tax practice. The Fundamentals of Federal Taxation series which includes such items as TAX ACCOUNTING METHODS AND PERIODS, by Langdon Day (1963) and DEDUCTIONS AND CREDITS, by Allen J. Parker (1962) is very useful. The Library for Estate Practice series includes the fifth edition of ESTATE PLANNING, by Joseph Trachtman (1964) among other pamphlets. A catalog of the Institute's publications is available upon request.

The Bureau of National Affairs, Inc., 1231 24th Street, N.W., Washington, D.C. 20037 has published since 1959 an excellent series of TAX MANAGEMENT PORTFOLIOS FOR EXECUTIVES. Each portfolio covers a specific subject such as foreign tax credit (Portfolio No. 5-2nd) or stock dividends and stock rights (Portfolio No. 94). Each portfolio contains a comprehensive bibliography of rulings, regulations, cases and articles as well as references in the conventional tax services to the subject under analysis.

There are a number of magazines in the tax field which are of particular interest to tax accountants. The following, all of which are listed in Section 9, "Periodicals," are among the best known: JOURNAL OF TAXATION, THE TAX EXECUTIVE, TAX LAW REVIEW, TAXATION FOR ACCOUNTANTS and TAXES-THE TAX MAGAZINE. Several of the law journals such as the HARVARD LAW REVIEW, the COLUMBIA LAW REVIEW and the YALE LAW JOURNAL often carry articles relating to tax problems.

The following newsletters, all described in Sections 9 and 10, are also helpful to the tax accountant: ACCOUNTANTS' WEEKLY REPORT, DAILY REPORT FOR EXECUTIVES, J.K. LASSER TAX REPORT, KIPLINGER TAX LETTER, TAX BAROMETER, TAX POLICY, TAXES ON PARADE, U.S. TAX WEEK.

A number of the accounting handbooks such as THE ACCOUNTANT'S HANDBOOK and THE ACCOUNTING PRACTICE MANAGEMENT HANDBOOK (AICPA) contain sections on the tax practice of the CPA. We list below a few of the standard tax references which would be useful in an accountant's library. This is not to be considered by any means a comprehensive tax library. As mentioned earlier, tax services are covered in Section 10, Services.

American Institute of Certified Public Accountants. STATEMENTS ON RESPONSIBILITIES IN TAX PRACTICE. New York: 1964- . pap.

A series of statements issued by the AICPA Committee on Federal Taxation intended to keep the CPA informed concerning his responsibilities in his tax practice toward clients, the public, the Government and his profession.

No. 1: Signature of Preparer, 1964.
No. 2: Signature of Reviewer, 1965.
No. 3: Answers to Questions on Returns, 1966.
No. 4: Recognition of Administrative Proceedings of a Prior Year, 1966.
No. 5: Use of Estimates, 1969.

American Institute of Certified Public Accountants. WORKING WITH THE REVENUE CODE. New York: 1956- . Compilation of articles drawn from the JOURNAL OF ACCOUNTANCY's "Tax Clinic." Revised and updated each year.

Arranged by code section number and subject. Detailed index.

Bardes, Philip, et al. MONTGOMERY'S FEDERAL TAXES, 39th ed. New York: Ronald Press, 1964. v.p.

Published regularly since 1918, this book is now edited by various partners of Lybrand, Ross Bros. & Montgomery. Instead of offering direct quotations of law and regulations, the editors and contributors extract the essence of the rules of federal income taxation and present them in simplified form. Each chapter concludes with a summary of tax-planning suggestions.

Bickford, Hugh C. SUCCESSFUL TAX PRACTICE, 4th ed. Englewood Cliffs, New Jersey: Prentice-Hall, 1967. 464p. forms.

A working manual which covers all aspects of conducting a tax practice. Intended as a guide to tax problems, not a theoretical discussion of tax law.

Bittker, Boris I. and Eustice, James S. FEDERAL INCOME TAXATION OF CORPORATIONS AND SHAREHOLDERS, 2nd ed. Hamden, Connecticut: Federal Tax Press, 1966, annual supplement. 774p.

This volume began as a set of materials for an advanced income tax course at Yale Law School. Revised and expanded, it presents a comprehensive introduction to federal income tax problems. The annual supplement keeps it up to date.

Lowndes, Charles L.B. and Kramer, Robert. FEDERAL ESTATE AND GIFT TAXES (Holbrook Series), 2nd ed. St. Paul, Minnesota: West Publishing Co., 1962. 951p.

Deals primarily with the substance of federal estate and gift taxes rather than with the procedural aspects, although there are single chapters on the procedural phases of each of these taxes. Final section is on tax planning for estates.

Raby, William L. THE INCOME TAX AND BUSINESS DECISIONS. Englewood Cliffs, New Jersey: Prentice Hall, 1964. 448p. forms, tables.

A textbook which contrasts tax accounting and financial accounting, showing their influence upon each other. Part 1 describes the nature of income and how tax regulations influence decisions. Part 2 outlines basic framework of the federal income tax. Part 3 (comprising two-thirds of the book) describes specific transactions.

Sellin, Henry, ed. TAXATION OF DEFERRED EMPLOYEE AND EXECUTIVE COMPENSATION. Englewood Cliffs, New Jersey: Prentice-Hall, 1960. 733p.

Covers not only the tax aspects, but also the economic and administrative aspects of non-qualified deferred compensation plans, qualified pension and profit sharing plans and stock options. Composed of 27 chapters each written by a different authority.

Stanley, Joyce and Kilcullen, Richard. THE FEDERAL INCOME TAX, A GUIDE TO THE LAW, 4th ed. Tucson, Arizona: Tax Club Press, 1961; Supplement, June 1964. 416p.

Cumulative supplements published at intervals. Directed toward professional men who are not tax specialists, this book provides discussions of sections of the Internal Revenue Code in the order in which they appear. Important court cases are also covered.

Section 5

MANAGEMENT ADVISORY SERVICES

Section 5

MANAGEMENT ADVISORY SERVICES

A major development in modern accounting has been the increasing participation of certified public accountants in providing management advisory services. Accountants have long been aware of their responsibility to use their professional expertise to guide their clients into improved methods of control, financial reporting, budgeting, etc. But the need of business for outside consultants to cope with its complex problems began to develop urgently only in the middle years of this century. Providing these advisory services has by now become an almost universal practice and the firm's CPA, an accredited professional already familiar with the company's financial situation, is often in an excellent position to render competent consulting assistance to his clients.

Since World War II there has been a tremendous increase in these consulting services by the accounting profession. All the larger accounting firms have established management advisory services departments. Even the small practitioner, encouraged to assist his clients in aspects of their business other than the traditional auditing and tax work, has developed skills for effective business consulting in certain functional specialities.

In 1959 the Long-range Objectives Committee of the American Institute of Certified Public Accountants started to study the nature and direction of the management service function in the public accounting profession. The results of the study were presented to the Institute's Council in 1961 and the Council issued the following resolution: "It is an objective of the Institute, recognizing that management services activities are a proper function of CPAs, to encourage all CPAs to perform the entire range of management services consisrent with their professional competence, ethical standards and responsibility."

In 1959 the Institute began to publish the series of bulletins on MANAGEMENT SERVICES BY CPAs which was discontinued in 1963. In 1964 the increased interest in management consulting by accountants led to the introduction of the bimonthly magazine, MANAGEMENT SERVICES and the publication of the MANAGEMENT SERVICES HANDBOOK, now out of print. These were followed in 1965 by MANAGEMENT ADVISORY SERVICES GUIDELINE SERIES and in February 1969 by the series entitled STATEMENTS ON MANAGEMENT ADVISORY SERVICES.
by the series entitled STATEMENTS ON MANAGEMENT ADVISORY SERVICES.
These AICPA publications, together with those of other management associations such as the American Management Association, the Association of Consulting Management Engineers and the Administrative Management Society are of great assistance to the accountant involved in management consulting.

As further evidence of world-wide interest in management services by CPAs, in 1964 the five major accounting organizations in England, Scotland and Wales established a joint program to give a special examination and a diploma in "subjects which may be broadly described as management accounting services." This Joint Diploma Scheme went into effect on January 1, 1966 and the first written examination was held in June of that year.

There have been a number of excellent magazine articles on management advisory services by certified public accountants and in recent years an increasing number of books have been published on this important aspect of modern accounting. The following references include chapters in various accounting reference works.

Adamson, Lee J., et al. ACCOUNTANTS' DATA PROCESSING SERVICES, MODERN METHODS IN SERVING SMALL CLIENTS. New York: Ronald Press, 1964. 202p. charts, forms. chart of accounts. biblio.
Designed as a practical handbook for accountants considering the adoption of machine accounting for client write-up work.

American Institute of Certified Public Accountants. MANAGEMENT ADVISORY SERVICES GUIDELINE SERIES, No. 1- . New York: 1968- . pap.
A series of bulletins offering guidance in the administrative and technical areas of management advisory services by CPAs. No. 1: GUIDELINES FOR ADMINISTRATION OF THE MANAGEMENT ADVISORY SERVICES PRACTICE, 1968.

American Institute of Certified Public Accountants. MANAGEMENT SERVICES HANDBOOK, THE ACCOUNTANT'S CONTRIBUTION TO PLANNING, SYSTEMS AND CONTROLS, ed. by Henry De Vos. (o.p.) New York: 418p. forms.
A guide to the solutions of specific problems as well as a source of general information in the area of management services.

American Institute of Certified Public Accountants. MANAGEMENT SERVICES TECHNICAL STUDIES, No. 1- . New York: 1965- . pap.
Each study covers a particular problem area in the field of management services. Case studies are included. Titles of these STUDIES are listed in Section 2 under publications of the AICPA.

American Institute of Certified Public Accountants. STATEMENTS ON MANAGEMENT ADVISORY SERVICES, No. 1- . New York: 1969- . pap.
A series of statements recommending standards for rendering management advisory services. No. 1: TENTATIVE DESCRIPTION OF THE NATURE OF MANAGEMENT ADVISORY SERVICES BY INDEPENDENT ACCOUNTING FIRMS, February 1969. No. 2: COMPETENCE IN MANAGEMENT ADVISORY SERVICES, February 1969. No. 3: Role in Management Advisory Services, September 1969.

Arizona Society of Certified Public Accountants. Management Services Committee. A BASIC BIBLIOGRAPHY FOR A MANAGEMENT SERVICES LIBRARY. Phoenix, Arizona: December 1967. 12p. pap.
Classified listing of the better-known books and periodicals on management services. Publishers and their addresses are included.

Arnstein, William E. and Burstein, Herman. MANAGEMENT SERVICES BY ACCOUNTING FIRMS. New York: Ronald Press, 1967. 454p. charts,

graphs, tables.
Covers a wide range of management techniques employed by CPA firms in helping their clients. Major sections on administration, sales and marketing, manufacturing, data processing and office services.

Association of Consulting Management Engineers, Inc. COMMON BODY OF KNOWLEDGE REQUIRED BY PROFESSIONAL MANAGEMENT CONSULTANTS. New York: September 1957. 59p. charts.
Defines the various areas of knowledge in which the management consultant should be proficient in order to offer professional counsel to business and industry.

Association of Consulting Management Engineers, Inc. PERSONAL QUALIFICATIONS OF MANAGEMENT CONSULTANTS, rev. ed. New York: 1966. 39p. pap.
Defines the capacities and attributes which are required of an individual in order to be a successful management consultant.

Association of Consulting Management Engineers, Inc. PROFESSIONAL PRACTICES IN MANAGEMENT CONSULTING, rev. ed. New York: 1966. 109p.
Although this excellent little handbook was written for professional business consultants, it is equally applicable to the CPA in his client relationships and especially relevant to the accountant in management advisory services.

Beyer, Robert. "The Growth of CPA Management Services." In American Institute of Certified Public Accountants, ACCOUNTING & THE COMPUTER. New York: 1966. pp.183-94.
Includes the historical background of the CPA's growing involvement with the management problems of his clients.

Brown, Harry G. "How to Organize and Operate a Management Advisory Service." In Prentice-Hall, Inc., COMPLETE GUIDE TO A PROFITABLE ACCOUNTING PRACTICE, 1965. pp.365-96. biblio.
Lists the types of management services most likely to be offered by accountants.

Holmes, Arthur W. "Management Advisory Services." In AUDITING: PRINCIPLES AND PROCEDURE, 6th ed., vol. 1. Homewood, Illinois: Richard D. Irwin Co., 1964. chap. 27.
Brief summary of the development of management advisory services in the CPA field. Includes a list of different services together with the type of specialists who may be requested by the client or by the CPA to deal with them.

Montgomery, Robert H. "Management Services." In MONTGOMERY'S AUDITING, 8th ed., by Norman J. Lenhart and Philip L. Defliese. New York: Ronald Press, 1957. chap. 24.
Lists the types of management services the accountant can be expected to handle.

Redfield, James E. A STUDY OF MANAGEMENT SERVICES BY CERTIFIED PUBLIC ACCOUNTANTS (Research Monograph No. 23). Austin, Texas: Bureau of Business Research, University of Texas, 1961. 153p. tables. biblio.
An interesting monograph based on a survey of Texas accounting

firms, supplemented by interviews with accounting practitioners.

Storich, Albert J. HOW ACCOUNTANTS CAN BUILD A PROFITABLE MANAGEMENT SERVICES PRACTICE. Englewood Cliffs, New Jersey: Executive Reports Corporation, 1968. v.p. charts, forms, tables.

Offers techniques and guidelines to assist accountants in providing management services. Sections on pricing, internal control, cash management, credit and collection, buy versus lease, personnel administration, relocation, assisting non-profit organizations.

Wellington, Roger. "Enlarging a Practice Through Management Services." In ACCOUNTANT'S ENCYCLOPEDIA, vol. 4. New York: Prentice-Hall, 1962. chap. 36.

Gives specific suggestions as to how the accountant can function as a business consultant.

Whiteside, Conon D. ACCOUNTANT'S GUIDE TO PROFITABLE MANAGEMENT ADVISORY SERVICES. Englewood Cliffs, New Jersey: Prentice-Hall, 1969. 442p. charts, facs., photos.

Offers advice on how the individual practitioner can use his expert technical skill and experience to solve his client's management and operational problems.

Section 6

BIBLIOGRAPHIES AND INDEXES

Section 6

BIBLIOGRAPHIES AND INDEXES

We have included in this section not only those bibliographies and indexes specifically directed to accounting subjects, but also the more general indexing and abstracting services in which subjects of interest to accountants can be found.

The two most important business newspapers, THE NEW YORK TIMES and THE WALL STREET JOURNAL, each publish indexes, the former semimonthly, cumulated annually, and the latter monthly, cumulated annually.

In addition to their indexes described below, both the American Institute of Certified Public Accountants and the National Association of Accountants publish annual lists of suggested material for an accounting library. These lists are available from the associations on request.

"Accounting and Budgeting." In Dartmouth College, Amos Tuck School of Business Administration, A READING LIST ON BUSINESS ADMINISTRATION, 7th rev. Hanover, New Hampshire: 1958. pap. Sec. 7.

Sound bibliography of basic accounting publications of interest to businessmen. Classified by subject.

American Bar Association. Section of Corporation, Banking and Business Law. Committee on Business Law Libraries. RECOMMENDED LAW BOOKS, edited by Richard Sloan. Chicago: 1969. 319p.

Excellent annotated listing of law books, arranged by subject. Symbols indicate entries suggested for purchase by all law offices, medium-sized and large offices, and large offices only.

American Institute of Certified Public Accountants. ACCOUNTANTS' INDEX. New York: 1921. Supplements, 1923- .

Detailed bibliography of accounting literature arranged by author, subject and title. Includes sections on accounting from nonaccounting publications. First volume covers years from 1912 to 1920. Biennial supplements to date. Indispensable to an accounting library.

Bentley, Harry C. and Leonard, Ruth S. BIBLIOGRAPHY OF WORKS ON ACCOUNTING BY AMERICAN AUTHORS, 2 vols. Vol. I, 1796-1900; Vol. II, 1901-1934. Boston: Harry C. Bentley, 1934-1935. 205p. (o.p.)

Historical bibliography of books and pamphlets on various aspects of accountancy.

Blough, Carman G. "Selected Accounting Research Bibliography." JOURNAL OF ACCOUNTANCY, vol. 115, no. 2. February 1963, pp.73-8.
Annotated bibliography of research publications of the principal United States accounting organizations: American Accounting Association, American Institute of Certified Public Accountants, Financial Executives Institute, Institute of Internal Auditors and National Association of Accountants.

"Books on Accounting." LIBRARY JOURNAL, vol. 85, no. 5. March 1, 1960, pp.919-21.
A bibliography of 23 accounting books which were chosen by nine highly qualified members of the American Institute of Certified Public Accountants as a basic selection of accounting literature for use by the lay public in public libraries. Not to be considered as a recommended accounting library due to its limited scope.

Brooklyn Public Library, Science and Industry Division and Business Library. SERVICE TO BUSINESS AND INDUSTRY. Brooklyn, New York: 1951- .
Bibliographies of publications in subject fields of interest to businessmen. Accounting publications included in annual "Business Books" list, in addition to an occasional issue devoted to accounting publications. Issued monthly from September to June. Free on request.

Cleveland Public Library, Business and Technology Department. BUSINESS AND TECHNOLOGY SOURCES. Cleveland, Ohio: 1929- .
Bibliographies on subjects of interest to businessmen. July - September 1966 issue entitled "Public Accounting Practice." Issued irregularly. Available on minimal subscription.

Commerce Clearing House, Inc. ACCOUNTING ARTICLES. Chicago: 1965- . loose-leaf.
Annotated listing of articles appearing in the major accounting magazines and a number of periodicals in allied fields. Institutes, workshops and books relating to accounting and management services are also included. Indexed by topic and by author. Monthly supplements.

Commerce Clearing House, Inc. FEDERAL TAX ARTICLES. Chicago: 1962- . loose-leaf.
Summarizes articles and notes on federal taxes published in legal, accounting and tax journals. The initial 1962 Reporter backtracks to cover descriptions of articles appearing since the adoption of the 1954 Internal Revenue Code. Monthly supplements.

Funk & Scott Publishing Company. FUNK & SCOTT INDEX OF CORPORATIONS AND INDUSTRIES. Cleveland, Ohio: 1959- . loose-leaf.
Index to articles published in business magazines and newspapers and in brokerage house reports. Classified both by subject matter

and by corporate name. Published weekly with monthly, semiannual and annual cumulative issues.

Harvard University. Graduate School of Business Administration. Baker Library. BUSINESS LITERATURE: AN ANNOTATED LIST FOR STUDENTS AND BUSINESSMEN, ed. by Lorna Daniells. Boston. 1968. 139p. pap.

Excellent annotated listing of books and magazines covering the principal areas of business. The sections on finance and control are of particular interest to accountants.

Harvard University. Graduate School of Business Administration. Baker Library. SELECTED BUSINESS REFERENCES (Reference List No. 24). Boston: 1965. 72p. pap.

Although its primary purpose is to introduce Harvard Business School students to the reference resources of Baker Library, this excellent bibliography contains many entries of interest to accountants. Arrangement is by type of source, i.e. indexes and abstracts, dictionaries, directories, etc.

Institute of Internal Auditors. BIBLIOGRAPHY OF INTERNAL AUDITING. New York: 1967. 112p. pap.

Annotated bibliography of literature of internal auditing which covers all relevant material on internal auditing that has been published in English from 1950 through 1965.

Keith Business Library. MANAGEMENT INDEX. Ottawa, Canada: 1963- .

A monthly guide to new American, Canadian and British publications of interest to management. Classified by subjects. Indexes on individual subject categories as well as the complete index available on subscription basis.

"Literature of Accounting." In SOURCES OF BUSINESS INFORMATION by Edwin T. Coman, Jr. Berkeley: University of California Press, 1964. Chap. 8.

Includes not only annotated listings of the more important accounting indexes, handbooks, textbooks, magazines and services but also a checklist of accounting sources.

Morris, Robert, Associates. SOURCES OF COMPOSITE FINANCIAL DATA, A BIBLIOGRAPHY, 2nd ed. Philadelphia: 1967. 24p. pap.

A listing of current publications which gives composite balance sheet and/or profit and loss ratios on a number of business lines. Separate sections on manufacturing, wholesaling, retailing and service fields. Includes addresses of publishers and prices of publications listed.

National Association of Accountants. TOPICAL INDEX. New York: 1946. Cumulative supplements, 1952 and 1960.

A classified bibliography which covers NAA research reports, accounting practice reports and annual conferences as well as all articles appearing in the monthly MANAGEMENT ACCOUNTING. First volume covers April 1920 to April 1946. Annual supplements appear as a section of the August issue of MANAGEMENT ACCOUNTING.

Public Affairs Information Service. PUBLIC AFFAIRS INFORMATION SERVICE. New York: 1914- .

Excellent subject listing of publications printed in English throughout the world, relating to economics and public affairs. Weekly, with periodic cumulations including annual bound volume.

Public Library of Newark, New Jersey. Business Library. BUSINESS LITERATURE. Newark, New Jersey: 1927- .

Excellent bibliographies of current publications on various subjects of interest to businessmen. Slanted more toward the accounting field than the other public library bibliographies. For example, the April - May 1963 issue was, A SUGGESTED BOOKSHELF FOR THE MANAGERIAL ACCOUNTANT. Issued irregularly. Available on minimal subscription.

Tax Institute of America. TAX INSTITUTE BOOKSHELF. Princeton, New Jersey: 1944- . pap.

Classified listing of current published material on the various aspects of public finance. Issued semiannually.

Thomson, A.W. and Yamey, B.S. "Bibliography of Bookkeeping and Accounts - 1494 to 1650." ACCOUNTING RESEARCH, vol. 9, no. 4. October, 1958, pp.239-57.

Chronological listing of early books on accounting. Includes a bibliography of books on history of accounting and a detailed listing of references in those books to the authors of early accounting works.

H.W. Wilson Company. BUSINESS PERIODICALS INDEX. New York: 1958- . Previously included in THE INDUSTRIAL ARTS INDEX which was discontinued in 1957.

Subject index to material in business periodicals. Monthly, except July, with periodic cumulations including annual bound volume.

H.W. Wilson Company. READERS GUIDE TO PERIODICAL LITERATURE. New York: 1904- .

An index to selected U.S. general and nontechnical periodicals. Semimonthly with periodic cumulations including annual bound volume.

Section 7

HANDBOOKS

Section 7

HANDBOOKS

American Institute of Certified Public Accountants. ACCOUNTING PRACTICE MANAGEMENT HANDBOOK. New York: 1962. 952p.

Seeks to cover all aspects of administering a public accounting practice. Replaces the CPA HANDBOOK.

American Institute of Certified Public Accountants. MANAGEMENT SERVICES HANDBOOK, Henry de Vos, ed. New York: 1964. 418p. (o.p.)

Provides answers to specific management problems in addition to covering the general field of management services.

Black, Henry C. BLACK'S LAW DICTIONARY WITH GUIDE TO PRONUNCIATION, 4th rev. ed. St. Paul, Minnesota: West Publishing Co., 1968. 1882p.

A handy one-volume reference containing an unusually complete collection of legal terms.

Bogen, Jules I. FINANCIAL HANDBOOK, 4th ed., rev. printing. New York: Ronald Press, 1968. v.p.

Standard reference work on all aspects of financial practice.

Cadmus, Bradford. OPERATIONAL AUDITING HANDBOOK. New York: Institute of Internal Auditors, 1964. 474p. tables.

Gives the operating and control problems of seven aspects of a business: purchasing, scrap, traffic, receiving operations, facilities control, advertising and insurance and describes specific methods of handling each function.

Carson, Gordon B., ed. PRODUCTION HANDBOOK, 2nd ed. New York: Ronald Press, 1958. v.p. charts, diagrs., forms, illus., tables.

Covers all aspects of production management and control from policy formation to operating procedures.

Dickey, Robert I., ed. ACCOUNTANTS' COST HANDBOOK, 2nd ed. New York: Ronald Press, 1960. v.p.

Comprehensive volume giving practical information on the whole range of accounting for costs.

Fiske, Wyman P. and Beckett, John A., eds. INDUSTRIAL ACCOUNTANT'S HANDBOOK. Englewood Cliffs, New Jersey: Prentice-Hall, 1954. 1072p.

Covers both fundamental and specialized aspects of industrial cost accounting.

Greisman, Bernard, ed. J. K. LASSER'S BUSINESS MANAGEMENT HANDBOOK, 3rd ed., rev. and expanded. New York: McGraw-Hill Book Co., 1968. 784p. charts.

A collection of writings by various authorities on aspects of business management requiring a particular expertise. Accounting and cost accounting systems are covered in chapters 8 and 10 respectively.

Kohler, Eric. DICTIONARY FOR ACCOUNTANTS, 4th ed. Englewood Cliffs, New Jersey: Prentice-Hall, 1970. 464p. tables.

Although this excellent dictionary is not strictly a handbook, we list it in this section because its treatment of accounting terms is far more comprehensive than its title indicates. Has been described as "a dictionary in the Johnsonian tradition." Essential for an accountant's library.

Lasser, J.K., ed. HANDBOOK OF AUDITING METHODS. New York: Van Nostrand, 1953. 769p.

First section treats general auditing methods. Second section covers auditing methods for 71 specific industries, each chapter written by an auditor experienced in that field.

Lasser, J.K., ed. STANDARD HANDBOOK FOR ACCOUNTANTS. New York: McGraw-Hill Book Co., 1956. v.p. (o.p.)

Covers the various aspects of the practice of accountancy, ranging from office procedures to relationships with clients.

Lasser Institute, J.K., ed. HANDBOOK OF ACCOUNTING METHODS, 3rd ed. New York: Van Nostrand, 1964. 976p. forms.

Short first section covers basic accounting system practice. Second section is composed of 66 chapters on specific accounting problems of various industries, businesses, etc., each written by a different contributor.

Lazzaro, Victor, ed. SYSTEMS AND PROCEDURES, A HANDBOOK FOR BUSINESS AND INDUSTRY, 2nd ed. Englewood Cliffs, New Jersey: Prentice-Hall, 1968. 544p. charts, forms, tables.

The more important of the systems and procedures techniques are covered by various authorities in this handbook: work measurement, EDP, PERT, forms control, budgeting, management information systems, etc. Chapter 5, pp.90-121, concerns the management audit.

Lipkin, Lawrence, et al. ACCOUNTANTS HANDBOOK OF FORMULAS AND TABLES. Englewood Cliffs, New Jersey: Prentice-Hall, 1963. 340p. tables.

Contains formulas such as simple interest, depreciation, ratio analysis, etc. constantly used by accountants. Appendix includes the standard mathematical tables, e.g. compound interest, annuity, random digit, etc.

Maynard, Harold B., ed. HANDBOOK OF BUSINESS ADMINISTRATION. New York: McGraw-Hill Book Co., 1967. v.p. biblio. charts, tables.

Contributed by top management men in business and the professions, the chapters in this book cover all aspects of management methods. Accounting and control is covered in Section 10.

Maynard, Harold B., ed. INDUSTRIAL ENGINEERING HANDBOOK, 2nd ed.

New York: McGraw-Hill Book Co., 1963. v.p. charts, diagrs., forms, tables.

Comprehensive reference work on all phases of industrial engineering.

McNierney, Mary A., ed. DIRECTORY OF BUSINESS AND FINANCIAL SERVICES, 6th ed. New York: Special Libraries Association, 1963. 192p.

A selected list of business, economic and financial publications that are issued periodically with regular supplements.

Munn, Glenn G. ENCYCLOPEDIA OF BANKING AND FINANCE, 6th ed., rev. by F.L. Garcia. Boston: Bankers Publishing Co., 1962. 789p. facs., tables.

Excellent detailed definitions of financial terms and concepts.

Prentice-Hall, Inc. ACCOUNTANTS' ENCYCLOPEDIA. Englewood Cliffs, New Jersey: 1962. 4 vols. forms.

Prepared by the publisher's Professional Accounting Publications Editorial Board and 45 contributing authorities, this encyclopedia seeks to cover all the various phases of accountancy.

Prentice-Hall, Inc. CORPORATE TREASURER'S AND CONTROLLER'S ENCYCLOPEDIA, 4 vols. Englewood Cliffs, New Jersey: 1958.

A guide to the efficient performance of the duties of corporate financial officers.

Prentice-Hall, Inc. ENCYCLOPEDIA OF ACCOUNTING FORMS AND REPORTS, 3 vols. Englewood Cliffs, New Jersey: 1964. forms.

Vol. 1 - Forms and reports used in an accounting practice.
Vol. 2 - Forms and reports used in accounting systems.
Vol. 3 - Forms and reports used in specific industries.

Prentice-Hall, Inc. ENCYCLOPEDIA OF AUDITING TECHNIQUES, ed. by Jennie M. Palen, 2 vols. Englewood Cliffs, New Jersey: 1966. charts, forms.

Describes auditing procedures to be applied to 38 types of business organizations and activities. First chapter, by Miss Palen, outlines typical auditing procedures in some detail; second chapter deals exclusively with audits of electronically produced records. In the remaining chapters the various authors describe specific audits within specific industries or services.

Prentice-Hall, Inc. ENCYCLOPEDIA OF COST ACCOUNTING SYSTEMS, 3 vols. Englewood Cliffs, New Jersey: 1965. charts, illus., tables.

Outlines cost accounting systems for 32 industries.

Williams, Robert I. and Doris, Lillian. ENCYCLOPEDIA OF ACCOUNTING SYSTEMS, 5 vols. Englewood Cliffs, New Jersey: Prentice-Hall, 1956. forms.

Describes and illustrates accounting systems for a variety of industries, businesses and professions.

Wixon, Rufus. ACCOUNTANTS' HANDBOOK, 4th ed. New York: Ronald Press, 1956. v.p. (5th ed. to be published in 1970).

Standard reference work which treats in compact form all aspects of commercial and financial accounting. Numerous references to other accounting works increase its value to the reader wishing to study a particular aspect more thoroughly. Essential for an accountant's library.

Section 8

BOOKS

Section O

BOOKS

The literature of accounting is more extensive than that of any other aspect of business. It would be impractical to include in this section all the available books on accounting and the various aspects of accountancy, so a selective approach has been used.

Out-of-print books have been included only when these are still considered among the definitive works in their respective fields. Their status has been indicated by the symbol (o.p.). These books can be found in the larger public libraries or in the libraries of the American Institute of Certified Public Accountants and of the larger private accounting firms.

Where books have been reissued by a different publishing company, we have identified the original publisher in the citation but have added in brackets the name of the company from which the book is currently available.

We have included only English-language works and have concentrated on material published in the United States. A few British accounting classics are listed and several translations of foreign works are included in the "International Accounting" section, but very few other foreign books have been included.

Magazine articles have not been included since they are far too numerous to list effectively. The ACCOUNTANTS INDEX, published biennially by the American Institute of Certified Public Accountants does an excellent job of indexing accounting articles as well as books, proceedings of institutes, etc. The monthly Commerce Clearing House service ACCOUNTING ARTICLES attempts to keep up with the current literature and includes a brief description of the subject matter of each article. In addition, an extremely interesting collection of accounting articles of historical interest was published in the 1965 book, SIGNIFICANT ACCOUNTING ESSAYS, edited by Maurice Moonitz and A.C. Littleton.

Some theses on accounting matters have been listed in this section, but undoubtedly a larger number have been omitted. There is no regularly published comprehensive list of titles of accounting theses. Since 1967, the January issue of THE ACCOUNTING REVIEW has included a section entitled "Research in Accounting," covering the previous year. This is a classified listing which gives the author's name, title of thesis, where it was submitted and the completion date. The January issue each year of THE JOURNAL OF BUSINESS (Graduate School of Business, University of Chicago) contains a classified list of accepted doctoral dissertations which includes a section on accounting. The

Committee on Research Review of the American Accounting Association compiled information on research projects in accounting, covering both masters' essays and doctoral dissertations for the years 1950 through 1959. These are listed in the following issues of THE ACCOUNTING REVIEW: July 1951, January 1952, April 1953, April 1954, April 1955, April 1956, July 1957, October 1958, October 1959 and October 1960. A more recent detailed listing entitled "(Research Projects in Accounting 1964 (and expected completion date)", by John H. Myers on page 1079 of the October 1964 issue of THE ACCOUNTING REVIEW, includes both doctoral and faculty research. Copies of theses are usually available on loan from the library of the university to which they were submitted. If they are not permitted to be withdrawn, microfilm or xerographic copies can be purchased from University Microfilms, 300 North Zeeb Road, Ann Arbor, Michigan 48106.

Only a few of the numerous manuals of accounting systems published by industry associations are listed in the following pages. Others can often be obtained directly from the trade associations in the various fields. A classified listing of associations by subject fields is available in ENCYCLOPEDIA OF ASSOCIATIONS, 6th ed., Vol. 1, published in 1970 by Gale Research Company. An excellent collection of industry accounting manuals is maintained by the National Association of Accountants and is available (for reference purposes only) in the association's library. In 1967, the NAA issued a list of trade association accounting manuals currently available which includes the names of the issuing associations and the prices. This list is available without charge from the NAA.

Several reference works contain accounting systems for a number of different industries. Among them are the HANDBOOK OF AUDITING METHODS, 1953, and the HANDBOOK OF ACCOUNTING METHODS, 1964, both edited by the J. K. Lasser Institute (Van Nostrand). The ENCYCLOPEDIA OF ACCOUNTING SYSTEMS, five volumes, 1956, by Robert I. Williams and Lillian Doris (Prentice-Hall) and the ENCYCLOPEDIA OF AUDITING TECHNIQUES, two volumes, 1966, edited by Jennie M. Palen (Prentice-Hall) each cover a variety of industries and services.

A 1951 book, now out of print, SPECIALIZED ACCOUNTING SYSTEMS by Henry Heaton Baily (New York: John H. Wiley & Sons, 1951) contains several still useful chapters on such fields as grain and stock brokerage, railroads, motor carriers, air transportation, building and loan associations and public utilities on which not much printed information is available.

Information on accounting in numerous specific fields not included in the following pages can be located in the ACCOUNTANTS' INDEX. This index covers articles, pamphlets, doctoral theses, etc. and is by far the most comprehensive accounting index available.

For fields regulated by governmental agencies and not included in this section, such as federal credit unions, see also Section 3, "Governmental Regulation."

What follows is a classified, selective list of the better-known English-language books and pamphlets on accounting, almost all of which were published in the United States.

ACCOUNTANCY PROFESSION

See also Section 1, Background and Section 2, Rise as a Profession

Andersen, Arthur & Co. THE FIRST FIFTY YEARS, 1913-1963. Chicago: 1963. 213p. portraits.

Traces the development and expansion of the firm from its founding by Arthur Andersen in 1913 to its present position with Leonard Spacek, who succeeded Mr. Andersen in 1947 as managing partner.

Ashworth, John. CAREERS IN ACCOUNTING. New York: Henry Z. Walck, Inc., 1963. 109p. photos.

Describes opportunities in public, governmental and corporate accounting fields. Chapter on qualifications of a good accountant.

Carey, John L. THE CPA PLANS FOR THE FUTURE. New York: American Institute of Certified Public Accountants, 1965. 541p.

Considers in some detail how accountants can adapt most successfully to changing times.

Cashin, James A. CAREERS AND OPPORTUNITIES IN ACCOUNTING. New York: Dutton, 1965. 224p. illus., photos.

Gives information on all aspects of the accounting profession: its history, the various branches in which an accountant may specialize, and "the educational background and general aptitudes necessary for success in the field." Includes a chapter on opportunities for woman accountants.

Commerce Clearing House, Inc. ACCOUNTANCY LAW REPORTER, 2 vols. Chicago: 1953- . loose-leaf.

Published in cooperation with the American Institute of Certified Public Accountants, this service covers all laws regulating the practice of public accounting in all states, the District of Columbia and the territories and possessions of the U.S. Gives rules and regulations of each state's board of accountancy covering admission to the C.P.A. examination. Arranged alphabetically by state.

DeMond, C.W. PRICE WATERHOUSE & CO. IN AMERICA, A HISTORY OF A PUBLIC ACCOUNTING FIRM. New York: 1951. 356p. illus., portraits. (o.p.)

Covers the operations of the American firm from 1877, when the firm of Jones and Caesar was formed in New York City as an agent of the London firm, to 1944.

Ernst & Ernst. A HISTORY OF THE FIRM. Cleveland, Ohio: 1960. 94p. portraits.

Describes the first 53 years of the firm's operation.

Haskins & Sells. HASKINS & SELLS, THE FIRST FIFTY YEARS, 1895-1945. New York: 1947. 98p. portraits.

The presentation of the first 50 years of the firm of Haskins and Sells is combined with vivid descriptions of life in New York City during that era.

Lafrentz, F.W. & Co. A HALF CENTURY OF ACCOUNTING, 1899-1949. New York: 1949. 53p. facs., portraits. (o.p.)

A brief description of the history of F.W. Lafrentz & Co. under the leadership of Ferdinand William Lafrentz.

Lybrand, Ross Bros. & Montgomery. FIFTIETH ANNIVERSARY, 1898-1948. New York: 1948. 168p. portraits.

A history of the firm which includes a bibliography of books, pamphlets and articles written by members of the firm and staff.

ACCOUNTANTS' EDUCATION

American Institute of Accountants. CONTEMPORARY ACCOUNTING, A REFRESHER COURSE FOR PUBLIC ACCOUNTANTS, Thomas W. Leland, ed. New York: 1945. looseleaf. (o.p.)

Intended primarily to be of service to returning CPA veterans of World War II, this compilation of views by 38 of the leading practitioners of the day is still of historical interest.

American Institute of Certified Public Accountants. Committee on Education and Experience Requirements for CPAs. REPORT OF THE COMMITTEE ON EDUCATION AND EXPERIENCE REQUIREMENTS FOR CPAs. New York: March 1969. 65p. pap.

Contains discussion on and the text of ten recommendations on policies concerning experience and educational requirements for CPAs, which were adopted by the AICPA Council in May 1969, becoming statements of Institute policy. Chief among the recommendations are that the CPA certificate be considered evidence of basic professional competence and that five years of college study can be substituted for the present education and two or three-year experience requirement.

American Institute of Certified Public Accountants. Committee on Relations with Universities. ACCOUNTING EDUCATION. New York: 1963. 81p. tables. pap.

Summaries of five seminars on the future of accounting education held in 1961-2. Also includes a questionnaire sent to participants in the seminars and summaries of their responses.

Churchill, Neil C., et al. AUDITING MANAGEMENT GAMES AND ACCOUNTING EDUCATION. Homewood, Illinois: Richard D. Irwin, 1964. 108p. figures, tables.

Describes a course in Graduate School of Industrial Administration, Carnegie Institute of Technology in which first-year graduate students audit "firms" run by second-year students as part of Institute's Management Game, a requirement of master's degree. Examples are included.

Commerce Clearing House, Inc. ACCOUNTANCY LAW REPORTER, 2 vols. Chicago: 1953- . loose-leaf.

Published in cooperation with the American Institute of Certified Public Accountants, this service covers all laws regulating the practice of public accounting in all states, the District of Columbia and the territories and possessions of the U.S. Gives rules and regulations of each state's board of accountancy covering admission to the C.P.A. examination. Arranged alphabetically by state.

Commission on Standards of Education and Experience for Certified Public Accountants. STANDARDS OF EDUCATION AND EXPERIENCE FOR CERTIFIED PUBLIC ACCOUNTANTS. Ann Arbor, Michigan: Bureau of Business Research, University of Michigan, 1956. 151p.

Issued by a commission formed of outstanding individuals in the accounting profession, this report was one of the earliest efforts to formulate standards of education and experience for CPAs.

Gordon, Robert Aaron and Howell, James Edwin. HIGHER EDUCATION FOR BUSINESS. New York: Columbia University Press, 1959. 511p

Sponsored by the Ford Foundation. Published in the same year as EDUCATION OF AMERICAN BUSINESSMEN, sponsored by the Carnegie Corporation. These excellent studies make several definite recommendations for accounting education.

International Conference on Accounting Education. PROCEEDINGS, September 30, October 1, 2 and 3, 1962. Urbana, Illinois: Center for International Education and Research in Accounting, University of Illinois, 1962. 137p. photos. pap.

Interesting collection of papers covering the state of accounting education and research in various countries.

Pierson, Frank C., et al. THE EDUCATION OF AMERICAN BUSINESSMEN, A STUDY OF UNIVERSITY-COLLEGE PROGRAMS IN BUSINESS ADMINISTRATION. New York: McGraw-Hill Book Co., 1959. 760p.

Sponsored by Carnegie Corporation. Chapter 14 on "Accounting" was written by Professor Robert G. Cox. This volume and Gordon and Howell's HIGHER EDUCATION FOR BUSINESS are considered landmarks in the study of business education.

Roy, Robert H. and MacNeil, James H. HORIZONS FOR A PROFESSION: THE COMMON BODY OF KNOWLEDGE FOR CERTIFIED PUBLIC ACCOUNTANTS. New York: American Institute of Certified Public Accountants, 1967. 354p. charts, illus., tables.

Sponsored jointly by the Carnegie Foundation and the AICPA. This study describes the kind of financial information and analytical methods which will "serve the business world of the future" and the knowledge and characteristics which will be required of the CPA to succeed in that world.

ACCOUNTING

This section contains only those publications which cover the whole field of accounting and cannot be allocated to any of the more specialized sections.

American Institute of Certified Public Accountants. PAPERS PRESENTED AT THE...ANNUAL MEETING. New York: 1938-1954. pap. (o.p.)

Publication of papers as separate volumes discontinued with the 1954 papers. Thereafter, selected papers have been published in the JOURNAL OF ACCOUNTANCY.

American Institute of Certified Public Accountants. YEARBOOKS. New York: 1904-1947. (o.p.)

Contain the complete proceedings of annual meetings, reports of all committees, lists of members and firms. Since 1947 these sections have been published separately.

Andersen, Arthur & Co. DICCIONARIO DE TERMINOS CONTABLES Y COMERCIALES. DICTIONARY OF ACCOUNTING AND BUSINESS TERMS. [Chicago]: 1962. 228p. pap.

Designed for the firm's employees in Spanish-speaking countries, this is an excellent Spanish-English and English-Spanish listing of accounting terms. Appendices include weights and measures, numbers and fractions, and currencies of member countries of the International Monetary Fund.

Edwards, James D. and Salmonson, Roland F. CONTRIBUTIONS OF FOUR ACCOUNTING PIONEERS: KOHLER, LITTLETON, MAY, PATON. East Lansing, Michigan: Michigan State University, 1961. 238p. photos.

Digests of selected articles by Eric L. Kohler, A.C. Littleton, George O. May and William A. Paton. Arranged chronologically, these views of two leading teachers and two leading practitioners are most interesting. Includes biographies and a photograph of each man.

Florida, University of. ACCOUNTING SERIES, No. 1- . 1964- . Gainesville, Florida: Accounting Department, College of Business Administration, University of Florida. pap.

A series of booklets on all aspects of accounting.

No. 1 - FINANCIAL AND MANAGERIAL REPORTING BY CERTIFIED PUBLIC ACCOUNTANTS.

No. 2 - ANNOTATED BIBLIOGRAPHY OF ELECTRONIC DATA PROCESSING.

No. 3 - THE AMERICAN ACCOUNTING ASSOCIATION-SPONSORED STATEMENTS OF STANDARDS FOR CORPORATE FINANCIAL REPORTS, A PERSPECTIVE, By Harvey T. Deinzer.

No. 4 - ASPECTS OF CONTEMPORARY ACCOUNTING.

Grady, Paul, ed. MEMOIRS AND ACCOUNTING THOUGHT OF G.O. MAY. New York: Ronald Press, 1962. 313p. biblio. ports.

Part I: "Memoirs," written by G.O. May.

Part II: "Accounting Thought," a compilation of Mr. May's major utterances on accounting matters.

Part III: "Thoughts Across the Years," contains a number of Mr. May's epigrams on accounting and other matters.

Haskins & Sells. SELECTED PAPERS. New York: 1955- . Annual volume of representative papers presented by members of Haskins & Sells throughout the year. A cumulative index in each volume is classified by subject.

Ingalls, Edmund F. PRACTICAL ACCOUNTING AND AUDITING PROBLEMS, 3 vols. New York: American Institute of Certified Public Accountants, 1966.

Contains case studies from files of Institute's Technical Information Service for the period 1958-62.

INTERNATIONAL CONGRESS OF ACCOUNTANTS, 1st-9th. Various publishers, 1904-67.

First, St. Louis, 1904; Second, Amsterdam, 1926; Third, New York, 1929; Fourth, London, 1933; Fifth, Berlin, 1938; Sixth, London, 1952; Seventh, Amsterdam, 1957; Eighth, New York, 1962; and Ninth, Paris, 1967.

Through the 7th Congress, 1957, the complete texts of all papers were published. The technical papers of the 8th Congress were mimeographed and distributed to participants. The 9th Congress issued a publication entitled NEW HORIZONS OF ACCOUNTING, which contained summaries of the technical papers presented at the various sessions.

Kohler, Eric. A DICTIONARY FOR ACCOUNTANTS, 4th ed. New York: Prentice-Hall, 1970. 161p. tables.
Treatment of accounting terms is far more comprehensive than title indicates. Has been described as "a dictionary in the Johnsonian tradition." Essential for an accountant's library.

Littleton, A.C. ESSAYS ON ACCOUNTANCY. Urbana, Illinois: University of Illinois Press, 1961. 637p.
An excellent collection of extracts from Professor Littleton's articles, grouped under four principal areas: accounting history, accounting theory, the profession and accounting education.

McAnly, H.T. SELECTED WRITINGS ON ACCOUNTING AND RELATED SUBJECTS. [Cleveland, Ohio]: Ernst & Ernst, 1963. 303p. exhibits.
A collection of articles published since 1940 by the author, the director of management services of Ernst & Ernst.

May, George O. TWENTY-FIVE YEARS OF ACCOUNTING RESPONSIBILITY, 1911-1936, ESSAYS AND DISCUSSIONS. New York: American Institute Publishing Co., Inc., 1936. 435p. (o.p.)
A collection of papers interpreting aspects of accounting history and thought in the first part of the twentieth century.

Ohio State University. INSTITUTE ON ACCOUNTING, PROCEEDINGS. Columbus, Ohio: 1938- . pap.
Sponsored by the Department of Accounting, College of Commerce and Administration, Ohio State University.

Prentice-Hall, Inc. ACCOUNTANTS' ENCYCLOPEDIA, 4 vols. New York: 1962. forms.
Prepared by the publisher's Professional Accounting Publications Editorial Board and 45 contributing authorities, this encyclopedia seeks to cover all the various phases of accountancy.

Taggart, Herbert F., ed. PATON ON ACCOUNTING, WRITINGS OF W.A. PATON. Ann Arbor, Michigan: Graduate School of Business Administration, University of Michigan, 1964. 713p. biblio.
A selection of articles written by Professor Paton during his distinguished teaching career of over 40 years.

U.S. Securities and Exchange Commission. ACCOUNTING SERIES RELEASES, Nos. 1- . Washington, D.C.: 1937- .
Issued as necessary, these releases contain the SEC interpretations of its accounting rules and regulations. A compilation of Nos. 1-112 is available from the U.S. Government Printing Office.

Later releases may be obtained from the SEC. A free mailing list is maintained by the SEC for this series.

Wixon, Rufus. ACCOUNTANTS' HANDBOOK, 4th ed. New York: Ronald Press, 1956. v.p. (5th ed. to be published in 1970).
Standard reference work which covers all aspects of commercial and financial accounting. Numerous references to other accounting

works increase its value to the reader wishing to study a particular aspect more thoroughly. Essential for an accountant's library.

ACCOUNTING AND AUDITING TEXTBOOKS

See also CPA Examinations and Management Accounting

Only the better known textbooks are listed here. Others can be found under the subjects "Accounting" and "Auditing" in SUBJECT GUIDE TO BOOKS IN PRINT, published annually by R. R. Bowker Company.

Anderson, W.T., et al. ACCOUNTING: BASIC FINANCIAL, COST, AND CONTROL CONCEPTS. New York: John H. Wiley & Sons, 1965. 808p. forms, tables.

Anthony, Robert N. ESSENTIALS OF ACCOUNTING. Reading, Massachusetts: Addison-Wesley, 1964. 158p. forms.

Programmed instruction designed to help the student teach himself the basic concepts of accounting.

Barr, Ben B. and Grinaker, Robert L. SHORT AUDIT CASE: THE VALLEY PUBLISHING COMPANY. Homewood, Illinois: Richard D. Irwin, 1964. v.p. forms.

Illustrates the basic principles of audit field work.

Bedford, Norton M. INTRODUCTION TO MODERN ACCOUNTING. New York: Ronald Press, 1968. 754p. charts, tables.

Bedford, Norton M., et al. ADVANCED ACCOUNTING, AN ORGANIZATIONAL APPROACH, 2nd ed. New York: John H. Wiley & Sons, 1967. 842p. tables.

Bierman, Harold, Jr. FINANCIAL ACCOUNTING THEORY. New York: Macmillan; London: Collier-Macmillan, Ltd., 1965. 412p. pap.

Bierman, Harold, Jr. and Drebin, Allan R. FINANCIAL ACCOUNTING: AN INTRODUCTION. New York: Macmillan, 1968. 432p. forms.

Bierman, Harold, Jr. and Drebin, Allan R. MANAGERIAL ACCOUNTING: AN INTRODUCTION. New York: Macmillan, 1968. 413p. charts, forms.

Black, Homer A., et al. ACCOUNTING IN BUSINESS DECISIONS: THEORY, METHOD, AND USE, 2nd ed. Englewood Cliffs, New Jersey: Prentice-Hall, 1967. 990p. charts, tables.

Braden, Andrew W. and Allyn, Robert G. ACCOUNTING PRINCIPLES. Princeton, New Jersey: D. Van Nostrand, 1963. 689p. forms.

Cashin, James A. and Owens, Garland C. AUDITING, 2nd ed. New York: Ronald Press, 1963. 857p. forms.

Coughlan, John W. GUIDE TO CONTEMPORARY THEORY OF ACCOUNTS. Englewood Cliffs, New Jersey: Prentice-Hall, 1965. 563p. figures.

Although basically a text for the theory portion of the CPA examination, this book has some reference value for the practicing accountant.

Davidson, Sidney, ed. PRINCIPLES OF ACCOUNTING (Management Edition). Chicago: Educational Methods, 1966. 201p. pap.

A programmed text showing how accounting can be useful in the management of a business.

Deinzer, Harvey T. DEVELOPMENT OF ACCOUNTING THOUGHT. New York: Holt, Rinehart & Winston, 1965. 192p. biblio.

A "syllabus" prepared for graduate courses in accounting theory, designed to stimulate "inquiry into accounting treatment rules." Readings at end of each chapter.

Dixon, Robert L., et al. ESSENTIALS OF ACCOUNTING. New York: Macmillan, 1966. 757p. tables.

Edwards, James Don, et al. ACCOUNTING, A PROGRAMMED TEXT, rev. ed 2 vols. Homewood, Illinois: Richard D. Irwin, 1970. facs., tables.

A programmed elementary accounting text covering financial accounting, financial management and managerial accounting.

Esquerré, Paul Joseph. THE APPLIED THEORY OF ACCOUNTS. New York: Ronald Press, 1914. 575p. forms. (o.p.)

Still used as textbook in a number of advanced accounting theory courses, this provides a comprehensive outline of the principles of accounting.

Finney, H.A. and Miller, Herbert E. THE ACCOUNTING PROCESS. Englewood Cliffs, New Jersey: Prentice-Hall, 1963. 161p. forms.

A programmed adaptation of their PRINCIPLES OF ACCOUNTING, INTRODUCTORY, 6th ed.

Finney, H.A. and Miller, Herbert E. PRINCIPLES OF ACCOUNTING, ADVANCED, 5th ed. Englewood Cliffs, New Jersey: Prentice-Hall, 1960. 847. forms.

Constantly revised and updated. This and the two following titles generally considered to be best of the accounting textbooks.

Finney, H.A. and Miller, Herbert E. PRINCIPLES OF ACCOUNTING, INTERMEDIATE, 6th ed. Englewood Cliffs, New Jersey: Prentice-Hall, 1965. forms.

Finney, H.A. and Miller, Herbert E. PRINCIPLES OF ACCOUNTING, INTRODUCTORY, 6th ed. Englewood Cliffs, New Jersey: Prentice-Hall, 1963. 704p. forms.

Finney, H.A. and Miller, Herbert E. PRINCIPLES OF FINANCIAL ACCOUNTING, A CONCEPTUAL APPROACH. Englewood Cliffs, New Jersey: Prentice-Hall, 1968. 461p.

An introductory text covering financial accounting topics rather than those associated with managerial accounting.

Grant, Eugene L. and Bell, Lawrence F. BASIC ACCOUNTING AND COST ACCOUNTING, 2nd ed. New York: McGraw-Hill Book Co., 1964. 528p. forms. biblio.

Griffin, Charles H., et al. ADVANCED ACCOUNTING. Homewood, Illinois: Richard D. Irwin, 1966. 845p. tables.

Includes several fields not always covered in advanced accounting texts: national income accounting, measurement and quantitative accounting, and governmental accounting.

Grinaker, Robert L. and Barr, Ben B. AUDITING: THE EXAMINATION OF FINANCIAL STATEMENTS. Homewood, Illinois: Richard D. Irwin, 1965.

581p. diagrs. illus.

Harlan, Neil E. and Vancil, Richard F. CASES IN ACCOUNTING POLICY. Englewood Cliffs, New Jersey: Prentice-Hall, 1961 433p. tables.
Collection of cases designed for use with an accounting text at the intermediate or advanced level.

Holmes, Arthur W. and Overmyer, Wayne S. AUDITING: PRINCIPLES AND PROCEDURES, 7th ed., 2 vols. Homewood, Illinois: Richard D. Irwin, 1970.
Volume 2 is composed of illustrative audit papers.

Holmes, Arthur W. BASIC AUDITING PRINCIPLES, 3rd ed. Homewood, Illinois: Richard D. Irwin, 1966. 390p. tables.
Designed to fill the requirements of a short course in auditing. This book is not an abridgment of the author's AUDITING PRINCIPLES AND PROCEDURE.

Holmes, Arthur W., et al. ELEMENTARY ACCOUNTING, 3rd ed. Homewood, Illinois: Richard D. Irwin, 1962. 799p. charts.

Husband, G.R. ACCOUNTING: ADMINISTRATIVE AND FINANCIAL. Philadelphia: Chilton, 1960. 511p. graphs, tables.

Johnson, Arnold W. ADVANCED ACCOUNTING, 3rd ed. New York: Vantage Press, 1968. 595p. tables.

Johnson, Arnold W. AUDITING, PRINCIPLES AND CASE PROBLEMS. New York: Holt, Rinehart & Winston, 1959. 684p.

Johnson, Arnold W. ELEMENTARY ACCOUNTING, 4th ed. New York: Holt, Rinehart & Winston, 1962. 888p.

Johnson, Arnold W. and Kriegman, Oscar. INTERMEDIATE ACCOUNTING, 3rd ed. New York: Holt, Rinehart & Winston, 1964. 810p. tables.

Kennedy, Ralph Dale and Kurtz, Frederick Charles. INTRODUCTION TO FINANCIAL AND MANAGERIAL ACCOUNTING, 2nd ed. Scranton, Pennsylvania: International Textbook, 1966. 300p. charts, tables.

Koestler, Edward J. ADVANCED ACCOUNTING. New York: Pace & Pace, 1963. 508p. forms.

Koestler, Edward J. INTERMEDIATE ACCOUNTING. New York: Pace & Pace, 1962. 479p.

Kohler, Eric L. ADVANCED ACCOUNTING PROBLEMS, 3rd ed., 2 vols. Englewood Cliffs, New Jersey: Prentice-Hall, 1960.

Leonard, W.G. and Beard, Frank N. CANADIAN ACCOUNTING PRACTICE, 2nd ed. New York: McGraw-Hill Book Co., 1963. 512p. forms.
A textbook for Canadian students which is also of interest to U.S. accountants with Canadian clients.

Mason, Perry, et al. FUNDAMENTALS OF ACCOUNTING, 4th ed. New York: Holt, Rinehart & Winston, 1959. 910p. charts.

Mautz, R.K. FUNDAMENTALS OF AUDITING, 2nd ed. New York: John H.

Wiley & Sons, 1964. 581p.

Meigs, Walter B. and Johnson, Charles E. ACCOUNTING: THE BASIS FOR BUSINESS DECISIONS, 2nd ed. New York: McGraw-Hill Book Co., 1967. 932p. tables.

Meigs, Walter B., et al. ADVANCED ACCOUNTING. New York: McGraw-Hill Book Co., 1966. 958p. tables.

Meigs, Walter B.; et al. INTERMEDIATE ACCOUNTING, 2nd ed. New York: McGraw Hill Book Co., 1968. 917p. tables.
Second in a coordinated series of accounting texts, this volume emphasizes the importance of the income concept in accounting.

Meigs, Walter B. and Larsen, E. John. PRINCIPLES OF AUDITING, 4th ed. Homewood, Illinois: Richard D. Irwin, 1969. 857p. charts.

Milroy, Robert R., et al. ACCOUNTING THEORY AND PRACTICE: ADVANCED. Boston: Houghton Mifflin, 1961. 685p. graphs.

Milroy, Robert R. and Walden, Robert E. ACCOUNTING THEORY AND PRACTICE: INTERMEDIATE. Boston: Houghton Mifflin, 1960. 695p. tables.

Milroy, Robert R. and Walden, Robert E. ACCOUNTING THEORY AND PRACTICE: INTRODUCTORY. Boston: Houghton Mifflin, 1960. 893p. charts, tables.

Montgomery, Robert H. MONTGOMERY'S AUDITING, by Norman J. Lenhart and Philip L. Defliese, 8th ed. New York: Ronald Press, 1957. 766p.
Originally authored by Robert H. Montgomery, this unsurpassed auditing text was first published in 1912. Now prepared by partners in his accounting firm of Lybrand, Ross Bros. & Montgomery. This work also discusses accounting principles in much greater detail than one would normally expect in an auditing text.

Moonitz, Maurice and Jordan, Louis H. ACCOUNTING: AN ANALYSIS OF ITS PROBLEMS, rev. ed., 2 vols. New York: Holt, Rinehart & Winston, 1963-1964. tables.
Vol. 1: Valuation of assets and liabilities and the determination of periodic profit.
Vol. 2: Multiple proprietorship.

Morrissey, Leonard E. CONTEMPORARY ACCOUNTING PROBLEMS, TEXT AND CASES. Englewood Cliffs, New Jersey: Prentice-Hall, 1963. 653p.

Moyer, Cecil A. and Mautz, Robert K. INTERMEDIATE ACCOUNTING, A FUNCTIONAL APPROACH. New York: John H. Wiley & Sons, 1962. 602p. charts, tables.

Newlove, George H. and Garner, S. Paul. ADVANCED ACCOUNTING, 2 vols. Boston: Heath, 1951. tables. (o.p.)
Although out of print, this text is still highly valued. Vol. 1: Corporate capital and income. Vol. 2: Reorganizations, bankruptcies, fiduciaries, partnerships.

Niswonger, C. Rollin and Fess, Philip E. ACCOUNTING PRINCIPLES, 10th ed. Cincinnati: South-Western Publishing Co., 1969. 853p. tables.

Pace, Homer St. Clair and Koestler, Edward J. BASIC ACCOUNTING, 2 vols. New York: Pace & Pace, 1959-60. charts, tables.

Paton, William A. and Paton, William A., Jr. ASSET ACCOUNTING, AN INTERMEDIATE COURSE. New York: Macmillan, 1952. 567p. tables. (o.p.)

Paton, William A. and Paton, William A., Jr. CORPORATION ACCOUNTS AND STATEMENTS, AN ADVANCED COURSE. New York: Macmillan, 1955. 740p. (o.p.)

Pyle, William W. and White, John Arch. FUNDAMENTAL ACCOUNTING PRINCIPLES, 5th ed. Homewood, Illinois: Richard D. Irwin, 1969. 831p. forms.

Seiler, Robert E. PRINCIPLES OF ACCOUNTING: A MANAGERIAL APPROACH. Columbus, Ohio: Chas. E. Merrill, 1967. 903p. charts, forms.

Silvoso, Joseph A. and Bauer, Royal D.M. AUDITING, 2nd ed. Cincinnati: South-Western Publishing Co., 1965. 582p. illus., tables.

A paperback illustrative audit to accompany the text is also available.

Simons, Harry and Karrenbrock, Wilbert E. ADVANCED ACCOUNTING, COMPREHENSIVE VOLUME, 4th ed. Cincinnati: South-Western Publishing Co., 1968. 1056p. tables.

Simons, Harry and Karrenbrock, Wilbert E. INTERMEDIATE ACCOUNTING, COMPREHENSIVE VOLUME, 4th ed. Cincinnati: South-Western Publishing Co., 1964. 980p. forms.

Slavin, Albert, et al. BASIC ACCOUNTING FOR MANAGERIAL AND FINANCIAL CONTROL. New York: Holt, Rinehart & Winston, 1968. 862p. forms.

Smith, C. Aubrey and Ashburne, Jim G. FINANCIAL AND ADMINISTRATIVE ACCOUNTING, 2nd ed. New York: McGraw-Hill Book Co., 1960. 650p. charts, tables.

Specthrie, Samuel Waldo. INDUSTRIAL ACCOUNTING, 2nd ed. Englewood Cliffs, New Jersey: Prentice-Hall, 1959. 607p. forms.

Spicer, Ernest E. and Pegler, Ernest. BOOKKEEPING AND ACCOUNTS, 16th ed. Edited by W.W. Bigg, et al. London: HFL (Publishers) Ltd. 1963. 642p. charts, supplement, 1968.

One of the authoritative textbooks on accounting in England.

Spiller, Earl A., Jr. FINANCIAL ACCOUNTING, BASIC CONCEPTS. Homewood, Illinois: Richard D. Irwin, 1966. 666p.

Stettler, Howard F. AUDITING PRINCIPLES, 3rd ed. Englewood Cliffs, New Jersey: Prentice-Hall, 1970. 733p. forms.

Stettler, Howard F. SYSTEMS BASED INDEPENDENT AUDITS. Englewood Cliffs, New Jersey: Prentice-Hall, 1967. 762p. charts.

Based on the new trend toward a more comprehensive "transaction" approach to auditing as opposed to the simple balance sheet-income statement verification.

This is a successor to the author's AUDITING PRINCIPLES, which, however, continues to be available.

Tunick, Stanley B. and Saxe, Emmanuel. FUNDAMENTAL ACCOUNTING:

THEORY AND PRACTICE, 3rd ed. Englewood Cliffs, New Jersey: Prentice-Hall, 1963. 880p. charts, tables.

Vance, Lawrence L. and Taussig, Russell. ACCOUNTING PRINCIPLES AND CONTROL, rev. ed. New York: Holt, Rinehart & Winston, 1966. 796p. tables.

Welsch, Glenn A., et al. INTERMEDIATE ACCOUNTING, rev. ed. Homewood, Illinois: Richard D. Irwin, 1968. 1084p. charts, tables.

Wentworth, Gerald O., et al. THE ACCOUNTING PROCESS, A PROGRAM FOR SELF-INSTRUCTION. New York: McGraw-Hill Book Co., 1963. 272p. glossary.

A programmed text which, using the corporate form of ownership throughout, presents a generalized accounting system.

Wixon, Rufus and Cox, Robert G. PRINCIPLES OF ACCOUNTING, 2nd ed. New York: Ronald Press, 1969. 839p. charts, tables.

ACCOUNTING PRINCIPLES AND PROCEDURES

American Institute of Accountants. Special Committee on Co-operation with Stock Exchanges. AUDITS OF CORPORATE ACCOUNTS, 1932-1934. New York: 1934. 49p. pap. (o.p.)

A keystone document in accounting literature. Contains the correspondence between this AIA committee and the Committee on Stock List of the New York Stock Exchange which led to several milestone decisions in accounting history. Among them are the Exchange's decision that after July 1, 1933 all annual reports of listed companies should be audited by independent public accountants and the development of a standard form of audit certificate approved by both committees.

American Institute of Certified Public Accountants. ACCOUNTING RESEARCH STUDIES, No. 1- . New York: 1961- .

Comprehensive research studies on various specific problems issued by The Institute's Accounting Principles Board in order to stimulate discussion prior to the issuance of APB pronouncements.

American Institute of Certified Public Accountants. APB ACCOUNTING PRINCIPLES, 2 vols. Chicago: Commerce Clearing House, 1968- .

A loose-leaf service which keeps current all Accounting Research Bulletins and Accounting Principles Board pronouncements. Volume 1 contains the APB pronouncements arranged under major subject headings, covered by a detailed index. Several appendices cross-reference sections of the text to specific pronouncements and provide a chronological schedule of changes in the pronouncements. Volume 2 contains Accounting Research Bulletins 43-51, Accounting Terminology Bulletins 1-4 and all APB opinions and statements to date. A paperback edition of the current volumes is published annually by Commerce Clearing House for the AICPA.

American Institute of Certified Public Accountants. OPINIONS OF THE ACCOUNTING PRINCIPLES BOARD, No. 1- . New York: 1962- .

APB pronouncements on current accounting matters. Departures from these opinions should be disclosed in footnotes to financial statements or in audit reports of AICPA members.

Andersen, Arthur & Co. ACCOUNTING AND REPORTING PROBLEMS OF THE ACCOUNTING PROFESSION, 3rd ed. [Chicago]: 1969. 210p. pap.
Discusses 26 of "the more important accounting and reporting problems facing the accounting profession."

Andersen, Arthur & Co. ESTABLISHING ACCOUNTING PRINCIPLES - A CRISIS IN DECISION MAKING. [Chicago]: December 1965. 42p. pap.
Concerned with the establishment of uniform accounting principles and standards. Contains the draft of a bill which would create a United States Court of Accounting Appeals, although the pamphlet does not propose such a court be established.

Andersen, Arthur & Co. THE POSTULATE OF ACCOUNTING - WHAT IT IS, HOW IT IS DETERMINED, HOW IT SHOULD BE USED. [Chicago]: 1960. 43p. pap.
Presents the firm's position that "the one basic accounting postulate underlying accounting principles may be stated as that of fairness - fairness to all segments of the business community... ."

Briloff, Abraham J. THE EFFECTIVENESS OF ACCOUNTING COMMUNICATION (Praeger Special Studies in U.S. Economic and Social Development). New York: Praeger, 1967. 348p. biblio., charts, forms, tables.
A study of the communications gap between the accounting profession and both the financial community and the general public. This is accentuated by differences within the profession concerning various interpretations of generally accepted accounting principles. The author expresses a number of criticisms and several recommendations, chief among them being that accounting research be taken out of the hands of the American Institute of CPAs and "be centered in the universities."

Duke University. School of Law. "Uniformity in Financial Accounting." LAW AND CONTEMPORARY PROBLEMS, Vol. 30, No. 4, Autumn 1965. pap.
The entire issue of this magazine is devoted to a symposium of 14 articles written by men in the various fields concerned with uniform accounting practices: accountants, lawyers, investment analysts, the SEC, etc.

Grady, Paul. INVENTORY OF GENERALLY ACCEPTED ACCOUNTING PRINCIPLES FOR BUSINESS ENTERPRISES (Accounting Research Study, No. 7). New York: American Institute of Certified Public Accountants, 1965. 469p. selected biblio.
An excellent presentation of the current status of accounting principles. These principles are arranged under five headings: (A) Income and Expense, (B) Equity, (C) Assets, (D) Liabilities and (E) Financial Statements.

Hylton, Delmer P. PRINCIPLES AND PROCEDURES OF MODERN ACCOUNTING PRACTICE. Englewood Cliffs, New Jersey: Prentice-Hall, 1965. 281p.
An interesting non-objective review of current areas of controversy among accountants, e.g. price-level adjustments, evaluation of replacement costs, lease capitalization, etc. Under each major heading the author presents the current practice, a criticism of same,

and suggested changes.

Illinois. University. Center for International Education and Research in Accounting. A STATEMENT OF BASIC ACCOUNTING POSTULATES AND PRINCIPLES. Urbana, Illinois: 1964. 36p. pap.

Seeks to develop a general theory of accounting applicable to any type of enterprise.

Moonitz, Maurice. THE BASIC POSTULATES OF ACCOUNTING (Accounting Research Study, No. 1). New York: American Institute of Certified Public Accountants, 1961. 61p. pap. biblio.

An attempt to establish certain postulates to be used as framework for accounting principles.

Paton, William A. and Littleton, A.C. AN INTRODUCTION TO CORPORATE ACCOUNTING STANDARDS (American Accounting Association Monograph, No. 3). Madison, Wisconsin: American Accounting Association, reprinted 1962. 178p. pap. biblio.

Originally published in 1940, this lucid monograph by two eminent accounting teachers establishes standards by which corporation accounting can be judged.

Sanders, Thomas Henry, et al. A STATEMENT OF ACCOUNTING PRINCIPLES. New York: American Institute of Accountants, 1938; Columbus, Ohio: American Accounting Association, 1959 reprinting. 154p. pap.

A well written classic of accounting literature. Chapters on general considerations, the income statement, the balance-sheet, consolidated statements and footnotes.

Sprouse, Robert T. and Moonitz, Maurice. A TENTATIVE SET OF BROAD ACCOUNTING PRINCIPLES FOR BUSINESS ENTERPRISES (Accounting Research Study, No. 3). New York: American Institute of Certified Public Accountants, 1962. 87p. pap. biblio.

A companion publication to ARS No. 1. THE BASIC POSTULATES OF ACCOUNTING, by Professor Moonitz. This study recommends some extensions and changes of generally accepted accounting principles.

Storey, Reed K. THE SEARCH FOR ACCOUNTING PRINCIPLES. New York: American Institute of Certified Public Accountants, 1964. 65p.

Indicates that the unfinished search for a statement or code of accounting principles has been caused by the profession's failure to adopt the conceptual, logical approach rather than the practical piecemeal one. Yet the author states that the exclusive use of the conceptual approach by the American Accounting Association has proved "equally ineffective" and proposes a combination of the two approaches as the only possible solution.

U.S. Federal Reserve System. Board of Governors. APPROVED METHODS FOR THE PREPARATION OF BALANCE SHEET STATEMENTS, A TENTATIVE PROPOSAL. Washington, D.C.: U.S. Government Printing Office, 1918. 25p. (o.p.)

An important historical accounting document, this is a reprint of its UNIFORM ACCOUNTING, A TENTATIVE PROPOSAL, prepared by the American Institute of Accountants (AIA) at the request of the Federal Trade Commission, transmitted to the Federal Reserve

Board and originally published in the Federal Reserve Bulletin, April 1917.

This was twice revised by the AIA, and published as its VERIFICATION OF FINANCIAL STATEMENTS, 1929, and its EXAMINATION OF FINANCIAL STATEMENTS BY INDEPENDENT PUBLIC ACCOUNTANTS, 1936.

An interesting description of the history of these early accounting "bulletins" is given in the 1963 AICPA publication, AUDITING STANDARDS AND PROCEDURES, pp.92-4.

ACCOUNTING THEORY

American Accounting Association. A STATEMENT OF BASIC ACCOUNTING THEORY. Evanston, Illinois: 1966. 106p. pap.

Seeks "to identify the field of accounting...to establish standards by which accounting information may be judged; to point out possible improvements in accounting practice; to present a framework for accounting researchers seeking to extend the uses...and the scope of accounting subject matter... ."

This supersedes the 1957 AAA statement, ACCOUNTING AND REPORTING STANDARDS FOR CORPORATE FINANCIAL STATEMENTS AND PRECEDING STATEMENTS AND SUPPLEMENTS.

Backer, Morton, ed. MODERN ACCOUNTING THEORY, rev. Englewood Cliffs, New Jersey: Prentice-Hall, 1966. 576p.

Emphasis is placed on the major areas of controversy within the accounting profession. The contributing authorities, while expressing their own viewpoints, also explain the contrary views in these controversies. Bibliographies at the end of each chapter.

Baxter, W.T. and Davidson, Sidney, eds. STUDIES IN ACCOUNTING THEORY. London: Sweet & Maxwell; Homewood, Illinois: Richard D. Irwin, 1962. 657p.

An updating of W.T. Baxter's 1950 work, STUDIES IN ACCOUNTING, this is an excellent collection of essays on the nature of accounting by the foremost teachers and practitioners in the field. Henry Hatfield's classic 1923 paper "An Historical Defense of Bookkeeping" is the lead-off article.

Financial Executives Institute. WHOLE-DOLLAR ACCOUNTING, prepared by Florence A. May and Herbert F. Klingman. New York: 1957. 335p. biblio. charts, forms, tables.

Analyzes the concept of whole-dollar accounting, reporting in detail the experiences of 13 companies.

Garner S., Paul and Berg, Kenneth, eds. READINGS IN ACCOUNTING THEORY. Boston: Houghton Mifflin, 1966. 520p. pap.

A compilation of articles intended to be used as collateral and supplementary reading in intermediate and advanced courses in financial accounting and management.

Goldberg, Louis. AN INQUIRY INTO THE NATURE OF ACCOUNTING (American Accounting Association Monograph No. 7). Chicago: American Accounting Association, 1965. 383p. forms. pap.

The first section presents accounting in relation to economics, law, management and government. The second section covers accounting theory. The third part deals with operational problems of profit control, valuation and communication.

Hendriksen, Eldon S. ACCOUNTING THEORY. rev. ed. Homewood, Illinois: Richard D. Irwin, 1970. 663p.

Surveys the entire field of financial accounting theory, including its historical development. Selected readings at the end of each chapter.

Ijiri, Yuji. THE FOUNDATIONS OF ACCOUNTING MEASUREMENT: A MATHEMATICAL, ECONOMIC AND BEHAVIOURAL INQUIRY. Englewood Cliffs, New Jersey: Prentice-Hall, 1967. 251p. biblio. charts, graphs, tables.

Studies three types of inquiry into the foundations of accounting measurement: mathematical, in order to grasp the logical structure of accounting measurement; economic, to understand what is being measured in accounting; and behavioural, to discover how the measurement system is used by accountants and how the results influence decision makers.

Jaedicke, Robert K., et al., eds. RESEARCH IN ACCOUNTING MEASUREMENT. Evanston, Illinois: American Accounting Association, 1966. 279p. charts, tables. pap.

Composed of papers given at a seminar of accounting teachers and public practitioners held in March 1965 at the Stanford University Graduate School of Business. Broad subject coverage on the scope and setting of measurement in accounting, reliability in accounting measurements, the behavioral implications of accounting measurements and the impact of accounting measurements on the firm's external environment. Brief bibliographies included with majority of papers.

Kafer, Karl. THEORY OF ACCOUNTS IN DOUBLE-ENTRY BOOKKEEPING (Monograph 2). Urbana, Illinois: Center for International Education and Research in Accounting, University of Illinois, 1966. 76p. biblio. charts. pap.

First section describes and criticizes the best known theories of accounts of past and present-day writers. Second section attempts to develop a reliable theory of accounts to be applied in all situations.

Littleton, A.C. THE STRUCTURE OF ACCOUNTING THEORY (American Accounting Association Monograph, No. 5). Chicago: American Accounting Association, 1953. 242p. pap.

Part 1, "Nature of Accounting," is designed to show that accounting is not a loose collection of traditional methods but a "tightly knit discipline in which all parts support each other." In Part 2, "Nature of Theory," the author outlines the general concepts of accounting theory, the formulation of accounting principles and rules and the uses of theory in providing a "better understanding of accounting thought and action."

Littleton, A.C. and Zimmerman, V.K. ACCOUNTING THEORY: CONTINUITY AND CHANGE. Englewood Cliffs, New Jersey: Prentice-Hall, 1962.

282p.
Excellent presentation of the history of accounting theory.

Marple, Raymond P. TOWARD A BASIC ACCOUNTING PHILOSOPHY. New York: National Association of Accountants, 1964. 117p. exhibits, port.
With the exception of the selection from which the book title has been taken, these are reprints of articles published by the author between 1934 and 1963.

May, George Oliver. FINANCIAL ACCOUNTING, A DISTILLATION OF EXPERIENCE. New York: Macmillan, 1943. 274p. (o.p.)
A classic in accounting literature by one of the profession's outstanding members which is aptly described by its subtitle. The author's intention was "to discuss and illustrate the nature of the process of financial accounting...in the light of fifty years of accounting experience in the United States, England and elsewhere."

Moonitz, Maurice and Littleton, A.C., eds. SIGNIFICANT ACCOUNTING ESSAYS. Englewood Cliffs, New Jersey: Prentice-Hall, 1965. 529p.
Interesting compilation of famous articles by outstanding men in the accounting field which have been published since 1900. Gives a clear perspective on the development of U.S. accounting thought.

Paton, William A. ACCOUNTING THEORY WITH SPECIAL REFERENCE TO THE CORPORATE ENTERPRISE. Chicago: Accounting Studies Press, 1962. 508p.
Reprint of his doctoral dissertation which was first published in 1922. Foreword by Herbert F. Taggart.

Prince, Thomas R. EXTENSIONS OF THE BOUNDARIES OF ACCOUNTING THEORY. Cincinnati: South-Western Publishing Co., 1963. 221p. biblio. charts.
The author contends that current accounting theory and practice is primarily concerned with the short-term profit objective of the corporation. This, he feels, should be replaced by a "long-term motivational model" such as that sought in other social sciences.

Stanley, Curtis H. OBJECTIVITY IN ACCOUNTING (Michigan Business Studies, No. 5). Ann Arbor: Bureau of Business Research, Graduate School of Business Administration, University of Michigan, 1965. 131p. biblio.
Examines the nature of accounting theory and its relation to accounting practice.

Vatter, William J. THE FUND THEORY OF ACCOUNTING AND ITS IMPLICATIONS FOR FINANCIAL REPORTS. Chicago: University of Chicago Press, 1947. 145p. pap.
Treats the origins, development and principles of the fund theory and its application to commercial and industrial financial reports.

ASSET ACCOUNTING

Commerce Clearing House, Inc. 1965 DEPRECIATION GUIDE INCLUDING NEW LIBERALIZED RULES. Chicago: 1965. 176p. tables. pap.
Contains official text of basic Treasury procedures with explanations by CCH.

Coughlan, Joseph D. and Strand, William K. DEPRECIATION: ACCOUNTING,

TAXES, AND BUSINESS DECISIONS. New York: Ronald Press, 1969. v.p. charts, tables.

Covers all aspects of depreciation, including current guideline procedures, computation of depreciation and investment credit recapture.

Grant, Eugene L. and Norton, Paul T., Jr. DEPRECIATION, rev. printing. New York: Ronald Press, 1955. 504p. biblio. tables. (o.p.)

Although now out of print, still useful as a manual for the accounting and tax aspects of depreciation

Harvard University. Graduate School of Business Administration. Accounting Round Table. THE MEASUREMENT OF PROPERTY, PLANT AND EQUIPMENT. Harvard Business School Accounting Round Table, April 29-30, 1963. Boston: 1964. 86p. ports. pap.

Interesting report of a discussion by some outstanding accounting practitioners and scholars of the significant issues in current reporting of the measurement of property, plant and equipment in financial statements.

Hermanson, Roger H. ACCOUNTING FOR HUMAN ASSETS (Occasional Paper, No. 14). East Lansing, Michigan: Bureau of Business and Economic Research, Graduate School of Business Administration, Michigan State University, 1964. 69p. biblio. illus. pap.

Reviews the possibility of assigning asset status to human resources in accounting statements.

Meij, J.L., ed. DEPRECIATION AND REPLACEMENT POLICY. Chicago: Quadrangle, 1961. 235p. charts, tables.

Three chapters, "Depreciation and Obsolescence as Factors in Costing," "Depreciation and the Maintenance of Real Capital" and "Depreciation Problems and Taxation" are by individual authors. The final chapter by Professor Meij and three Dutch colleagues reviews the five current methods of handling depreciation: technical lifetime, economic lifetime, maximal goodwill, replacement value and the Terborgh theories.

National Association of Accountants. CURRENT PRACTICE IN ACCOUNTING FOR DEPRECIATION (NAA Research Series No. 33). New York: April 1, 1958. 36p. facs. pap.

The results of a research project participated in by 55 companies. Describes "purposes served by accounting for depreciation and how well these objectives are met by various depreciation practices."

Paton, William A. and William A., Jr. ASSET ACCOUNTING, AN INTERMEDIATE COURSE. New York: Macmillan, 1952. 567p. tables. (o.p.)

Designed as a textbook, this reference covers, in depth, all aspects of the accounting problems and procedures concerned with business assets.

Terborgh, George. REALISTIC DEPRECIATION POLICY. Chicago: Machinery and Allied Products Institute, 1954. 221p. charts, tables.

Offers a depreciation policy in which recoveries are adjusted for changes in the purchasing power of the dollar since the original investment.

Thomas, David A. ACCELERATED AMORTIZATION (Michigan Business Studies, Vol. 13, No. 4). Ann Arbor: Bureau of Business Research, University of Michigan, 1958. 112p. charts, tables.

An analysis which defends the use of accelerated amortization. Emphasis is placed on the administrative application of legislation permitting use of rapid amortization.

Woods, L. Milton. ACCOUNTING FOR CAPITAL, CONSTRUCTION, AND MAINTENANCE EXPENDITURES. Englewood Cliffs, New Jersey: Prentice-Hall, 1967. 190p.

Seeks to "bring together in one place" all phases of the acquisition of capital assets. Covers initiation of project, financial justification, construction and, finally, accounting for fixed assets and depreciation.

Part I: Decision, Action, Control and Follow-up; Part II: Accounting.

AUDITING

See also Accounting and Auditing Textbooks, Internal Auditing and Control

American Institute of Accountants. AUDITS OF CORPORATE ACCOUNTS, 1932-1934. New York: 1934. 49p. pap. (o.p.)

Correspondence between the AIA Special Committee on Co-operation With Stock Exchanges and the Committee on Stock List of the New York Stock Exchange.

A historical document, recording the earliest cooperative effort of the AIA and the New York Stock Exchange to develop a form of accountants' report of value to investors.

American Institute of Certified Public Accountants. AN INITIAL AUDIT (Case Studies in Auditing Procedure, No. 13). New York: 1962. pp.11-31. pap.

Describes an actual initial audit of a medium-sized light industrial manufacturer.

American Institute of Certified Public Accountants. CASE STUDIES IN AUDITING PROCEDURE, No. 1- . New York: 1947- . pap.

These case studies describe the auditing procedures which were actually followed by practitioners in particular instances. Titles are listed in Section 2, under the publications of the AICPA.

American Institute of Certified Public Accountants. CASE STUDIES IN THE OBSERVATION OF INVENTORY. New York: 1959. 62p. pap.

Shows how a group of experienced auditors satisfied themselves as to the reasonableness of physical inventory counts in seven different business enterprises.

American Institute of Certified Public Accountants. INDUSTRY AUDIT GUIDES. New York: 1956- . pap.

A series of studies, each describing features of a particular industry or business and recommending appropriate auditing and reporting practices. Titles of these Guides are listed in Section 2, under the publications of the AICPA.

American Institute of Certified Public Accountants. SPECIAL REPORTS: APPLICATION OF STATEMENT ON AUDITING PROCEDURE NO. 28. New York:

1960. 96p. pap.

Describes various types of special situations and offers numerous suggestions as to the handling of the more difficult problems.

American Institute of Certified Public Accountants. STATEMENTS ON AUDITING PROCEDURE, Nos. 1- . New York: 1939- . pap.

Auditing Statement No. 33 issued in 1963, entitled "Auditing Standards and Procedures," is a codification of earlier committee pronouncements. Includes historical background of early AICPA bulletins.

Bell, William H. and Johns, Ralph S. AUDITING, 3rd ed. New York: Prentice-Hall, 1952. 564p. (o.p.)

Although now out of print, still considered one of the most practical works on auditing.

Bigg, Walter W. PRACTICAL AUDITING, by Ernest Evan Spicer and Ernest C. Pegler, 14th ed. London: H.F.L. (Publishers) Ltd., 1965. Table of cases. 583p.

First published in 1911, this British publication covers both auditing principles and practices. Chapter XII contains specific points in different classes of audits, e.g. banks, clubs, newspapers, etc.

Brown, R. Gene. A SCIENTIFIC APPROACH TO AUDITING. Unpublished Ph. D. thesis, Ohio State University, 1961. Ann Arbor, Michigan: University Microfilms, 1965. 279p. biblio. processed.

Proposes that a more scientific, and therefore more efficient, approach to auditing would be provided by the use of quantified internal control questionnaires, internal control effectiveness indices and statistical sampling techniques.

Canadian Institute of Chartered Accountants. Study Group on Audit Techniques. MATERIALITY IN AUDITING. Toronto: 1965. 27p. tables. pap.

The first of a series of bulletins on audit techniques. Discusses the concept of materiality in relation to its effect on auditing procedures and offers guidelines to assist the auditor in deciding as to the materiality of an item. The second study in this series, INTERNAL CONTROL IN THE SMALL BUSINESS (1967), is included under Internal Audit and Control in this section.

Cooper, Vivian R.V. MANUAL OF AUDITING, 2nd ed. London: Gee & Co. (Publishers) Ltd., 1969. 704p.

A comprehensive treatise on auditing. Includes internal control questionnaires and specimen audit programs.

Johnson, James T. and Brasseaux, J. Herman. READINGS IN AUDITING, 2nd ed. Cincinnati: South-Western Publishing Co., 1965. biblio. 720p.

An interesting collection of articles on current issues and controversies concerning the issuance of audit reports. A brief introduction to each section summarizes the points of view of the authors.

Lasser, J.K., ed. HANDBOOK OF AUDITING METHODS. New York: Van Nostrand, 1953. 769p.

First section treats general auditing methods. Second section covers auditing methods for 71 specific industries, each chapter written by an auditor experienced in that field.

Mautz, R.K. and Sharaf, Hussein A. THE PHILOSOPHY OF AUDITING (American Accounting Association Monograph, No. 6). Madison, Wisconsin: American Accounting Association, 1961. 248p. pap.
Covers many aspects of auditing: concepts, independence, ethical conduct, fair presentation, etc.

Montgomery, Robert H. MONTGOMERY'S AUDITING, by Norman J. Lenhart and Philip L. Defliese, 8th ed. New York: Ronald Press, 1957. 766p.
The authoritative work on auditing. Includes a long questionnaire on internal control.

National Conference of Bankers and Certified Public Accountants. THE AUDITOR'S REPORT, ITS MEANING AND SIGNIFICANCE. New York: American Institute of Certified Public Accountants, 1967. 30p. illus. pap.
The conference is composed of an equal number of representatives from The American Bankers Association and the American Institute of CPA's and three members of Robert Morris Associates. This publication, the first to develop from their dialogues, explains clearly the auditor's function in rendering an opinion on a company's financial condition.

Nielsen, Oswald. CASES IN AUDITING. Homewood, Illinois: Richard D. Irwin, 1965. 349p. exhibits.
Lists cases covering the attest function in modern business, with emphasis placed on managerial responsibility rather than on auditing mechanics.

Palmer, Leslie E. and Bell, W.H. ACCOUNTANTS' WORKING PAPERS, rev. by Ralph S. Johns, 3rd ed. New York: Ronald Press, 1950. 488p. forms.
Part I consists of illustrative working papers and discussions of general and specific auditing techniques. Part II contains a complete set of correlated working papers on a specific audit, including a draft of the audit report.

Prentice-Hall, Inc. ENCYCLOPEDIA OF AUDITING TECHNIQUES, ed. by Jennie M. Palen, 2 vols. Englewood Cliffs, New Jersey: 1966. charts, forms.
Describes auditing procedures to be applied to 38 types of business organizations and activities. First chapter by Miss Palen, outlines typical audit procedures in some detail; second chapter deals exclusively with audits of electronically produced records. In the remaining chapters various authors describe specific audits within specific industries or services.

Ray, J.C., ed. INDEPENDENT AUDITING STANDARDS, A BOOK OF READINGS. New York: Holt, Rinehart & Winston, 1964. biblio. 510p.
A collection of 42 readings arranged under the ten "Generally Accepted Auditing Standards" of the AICPA.

Skinner, R.M. and Anderson, R.J. ANALYTICAL AUDITING, AN OUTLINE OF THE FLOW CHART APPROACH TO AUDITS. New York: Pitman, 1966. 171p. charts.
Describes an auditing technique based on a flow chart analysis.

Covers the theory and objectives of analytical auditing, explaining the two stages of the systems audit and the follow-up audit. Includes a chapter showing its application to punched card and computer systems.

AUDITING AND THE COMPUTER

Boutell, Wayne S. AUDITING WITH THE COMPUTER. Berkeley and Los Angeles: University of California Press, 1965. 181p. biblio., figures.
Explains how auditing controls can be incorporated in computer systems.

Brown, Harry L. EDP FOR AUDITORS. New York: John H. Wiley & Sons, 1968. 205p. glossary, charts, forms, tables.
Describes techniques to be used in auditing electronically processed information systems. Contains questionnaire for evaluation of internal control in the dataprocessing function.

Corcoran, A. Wayne and Istvan, Donald F. THE AUDIT AND THE PUNCHED CARD, AN INTRODUCTION. (Bureau of Business Research Monograph, No. 101.) Columbus, Ohio: Bureau of Business Research, Ohio State University, 1961. 90p. facs. pap.
Gives excellent, detailed descriptions of the auditing uses of punched-card equipment.

Davis, Gordon B. AUDITING AND EDP. New York: American Institute of Certified Public Accountants, 1968. 353p. glossary, charts, forms, tables.
Based on results of a special AICPA Auditing EDP Task Force. Covers all aspects of examination of companies using computers for recordkeeping. First chapters discuss typical procedures in the management and control of data processing systems. Chapters 8 through 12 cover specific audit procedures. Remaining chapters treat problems found in integrated systems and service centers and the training required for the auditing of EDP.

Haskins & Sells. INTERNAL CONTROL IN ELECTRONIC ACCOUNTING SYSTEMS. [New York]: 1965. 134p. forms. pap.
Describes in detail the various internal accounting control methods found only in electronic data processing systems.

Institute of Internal Auditors. INTERNAL AUDITING OF ELECTRONIC DATA PROCESSING SYSTEMS. New York: 1967. loose-leaf.
Intended to provide current information as it becomes available, this manual is based on the experience of internal auditors who have actually audited EDP systems in their companies.

Kaufman, Felix. ELECTRONIC DATA PROCESSING AND AUDITING. New York: Ronald Press, 1961. 180p. charts, graphs.
Describes control aspects of computer systems and gives generally accepted audit techniques to be used in a computer environment.

Lybrand, Ross Bros. & Montgomery. THE CONTROL AND AUDIT OF ELECTRONIC DATA PROCESSING SYSTEMS. [New York]: 1965. 56p. glossary. pap.
Chapters on auditing "around" versus auditing "through" the computer; using the computer as an audit tool; preparing for the future.

Nolan, Robert E., et al. WORK MEASUREMENT IN MACHINE ACCOUNTING, CONTROLS, INCENTIVES, SCHEDULING AND COSTING PROCEDURES. New York: Ronald Press, 1963. 286p. forms, illus., tables.

Shows how to measure and accurately control tabulating operations.

Pinkney, A. AN AUDIT APPROACH TO COMPUTERS. London: General Educational Trust of the Institute of Chartered Accountants in England and Wales, December 1966. 159p. biblio.

A concise presentation of computer auditing. Chapter 1 is a generalized presentation of audit approaches, audit trails; chapters 2 through 4 continue to review control techniques; chapters 5 and 6 are on audit tests and techniques. Appendix A, pp.123-42, is entitled "The Elements of a Computer System" and has a number of informative diagrams.

Porter, W. Thomas, Jr. AUDITING ELECTRONIC SYSTEMS. Belmont, California: Wadsworth, 1966. 125p. biblio., figures.

A clear explanation of electronic data processing and the types of control to be used in electronic systems. Also explains the use of computers in auditing.

BUDGETING

Bunge, Walter R. MANAGERIAL BUDGETING FOR PROFIT IMPROVEMENT. New York: McGraw-Hill Book Co., 1968. 239p. glossary, charts, tables.

A non-technical presentation directed toward business management which explains how a corporate budget system can be established, operated and controlled.

Dearden, John. COST AND BUDGET ANALYSIS. Englewood Cliffs, New Jersey: Prentice-Hall, 1962. 219p. charts, illus.

Covers cost accounting and analysis and budgetary control. Stresses that the true worth of these techniques is indicated by the value of the information they provide for management decisions.

Financial Executives Institute. BUSINESS BUDGETING, A SURVEY OF MANAGEMENT PLANNING AND CONTROL PRACTICES, prepared by Bernard H. Sord and Glenn A. Welsch under direction of Herbert F. Klingman. New York: 1958. 367p. charts, tables.

An analysis of budgeting practices of several hundred selected U.S. companies, based on interviews and questionnaires. A useful summary analysis of the study serves as an introduction.

Heckert, J. Brooks and Willson, James D. BUSINESS BUDGETING AND CONTROL, 3rd ed. New York: Ronald Press, 1967. 596p. charts, forms, tables.

Slanted toward the management viewpoint of budgeting as an aid in business planning.

Heiser, Herman C. BUDGETING - PRINCIPLES AND PRACTICE. New York: Ronald Press, 1959. 415p. figures, graphs.

Directed toward experienced financial managers, this is a detailed treatment of budgeting as an important management tool.

Jones, Reginald L. and Trentin, H. George. BUDGETING: KEY TO PLANNING AND CONTROL, PRACTICAL GUIDELINES FOR MANAGERS. New York: American Management Association, 1966. 253p. charts, exhibits, forms.

Written in non-technical language for businessmen.

Knight, W.D. and Weinwurm, E.H. MANAGERIAL BUDGETING. New York: Macmillan, 1964. 468p. charts, forms, tables. (o.p.)
A textbook sponsored by and published under the auspices of Budget Executives Institute which presents budgeting from the management point of view.

Lewis, Ronello B. PROFIT PLANNING FOR MANAGEMENT. Englewood Cliffs, New Jersey: Prentice-Hall, 1960. 196p. tables.
Emphasizes the "control follow-up and profitable corrective action" occuring after the budget has been completed. Numerous tables illustrate author's therories. Last two chapters cover savings and budgeting for the individual.

Mattessich, Richard. SIMULATION OF THE FIRM THROUGH A BUDGET COMPUTER PROGRAM. Homewood, Illinois: Richard D. Irwin, 1964. 102p. biblio., illus. pap.
Discusses the objectives, evolution and implementation of budget simulation before presenting the detailed budget computer program.

Rautenstrauch, Walter and Villers, Raymond. BUDGETARY CONTROL, rev. ed. New York: Funk & Wagnalls, 1968. 368p. biblio., charts, forms, tables.
A general textbook on all aspects of budgeting. Emphasis on fact that a budget, to be effective, must cover all divisions of a business. Numerous illustrations of budgetary procedures in specific industries. Includes list of data sources in addition to bibliography.

Stedry, Andrew C. BUDGET CONTROL AND COST BEHAVIOUR. Englewood Cliffs, New Jersey: Markhamn, Publishing Co., 1968. 161p. biblio.
Contrasts planning and control functions of a budget, describing mathematical models of each. A treatment of budget theory rather than a practical guide to budgeting.

Wellington, C. Oliver. A PRIMER ON BUDGETING. New York: Van Nostrand, 1949. 94p. charts, illus., tables. (o.p.)
A clearly stated, non-technical explanation of budgeting principles and procedures.

Welsch, Glenn A. BUDGETING: PROFIT-PLANNING AND CONTROL, 2nd ed. Englewood Cliffs, New Jersey: Prentice-Hall, 1964. 600p.
Stresses the practical application of profit planning. Includes numerous case studies and problems.

CPA EXAMINATIONS

See also Accountants' Education

American Institute of Certified Public Accountants. CPA EXAMINATIONS. New York: 1921- .
Past CPA examination questions and answers are published in three-year volumes. The only ones now available are the 1960-62 through the 1966-68 volumes. Twice a year, the complete texts of the most recent CPA examinations are published in paperback form as a supplement to the JOURNAL OF ACCOUNTANCY. These supplements are available on subscription basis.

American Institute of Certified Public Accountants. INFORMATION FOR CPA CANDIDATES. New York: 1970. 50p. pap.

Gives very useful information concerning such matters as requirements for sitting, emphasis and scope of examinations, suggestions for preparation, etc.

Behling, Robert P. CPA REQUIREMENTS, 2nd ed. Whitewater, Wisconsin: Wisconsin State University (Whitewater), 1968. 230p.

Covers entrance requirements for CPA examinations, the examination requirements, any additional requirements before CPA certificate is awarded and how to obtain the CPA certificate by reciprocity. Arranged alphabetically by state. Revised periodically.

Chamberlain, Henry T. and Meier, Robert A. CPA COACHING COURSE, 2nd ed., 2 vols. Englewood Cliffs, New Jersey: Prentice-Hall, 1963.

Vol. 1: Problems; Vol. 2: Solutions. Consists of 20 assignments, each containing three problems in accounting practice, ten questions on theory and eight on auditing. Twenty problems on federal taxation also provided.

Commerce Clearing House, Inc. ACCOUNTANCY LAW REPORTER, 2 vols. Chicago: - . loose-leaf.

Published in cooperation with the American Institute of Certified Public Accountants, this service covers all laws regulating the practice of public accounting in all states, the District of Columbia and the territories and possessions of the U.S. Gives rules and regulations of each state's board of accountancy covering admission to the C.P.A. examination. Arranged alphabetically by state.

Coppola, Andrew J. and Katz, Harry. BUSINESS LAW: A CPA REVIEW. New York: John H. Wiley & Sons, 1963. 765p.

Edwards, James Don and Ruswinckel, John W. THE PROFESSIONAL C.P.A. EXAMINATION, TEXT AND PROBLEMS, 2 vols. New York: McGraw-Hill Book Co., 1963.

Excellent review volumes covering the Auditing, Accounting Theory and Accounting Practice sections of the CPA examination. Volume 2 contains the solutions to all questions and problems in Volume 1. Reading references are given in each chapter of Volume 1.

Frascona, Joseph L. C.P.A. LAW REVIEW UNDER THE UNIFORM COMMERCIAL CODE, 3rd ed. Homewood, Illinois: Richard D. Irwin, 1966. 1302p.

Interesting presentation of material. Each field of law is shown separately in detail, consisting of a check list, the text for that field and the UCC or other statutory material. Use of the checklist as the text is read has proved a very effective method of learning the material.

Horngren, Charles T. and Leer, J. Arthur. CPA PROBLEMS AND APPROACHES TO SOLUTIONS, 3rd ed., 2 vols. Englewood Cliffs, New Jersey: Prentice-Hall, 1969.

A review text covering all four sections of the CPA examination. Emphasizes underlying reasons and procedures used in preparation of the solutions rather than just the solutions themselves.

Houghton, Mifflin Company. C.P.A. COACHING. Boston: 1962.
An 11 - volume coaching set for CPA candidates. Vol. 1 - BASIC HANDBOOK. Vols. 2A-2B - ACCOUNTING PRACTICE. Vol. 2C - ACCOUNTING THEORY. Vol. 2D - AUDITING. Vol. 2E - COMMERCIAL LAW. Vols. 3A-3E - SOLUTIONS.

Lavine, A. Lincoln. MANUAL ON COMMERCIAL LAW, UNIFORM COMMERCIAL CODE EDITION, 3rd ed. Englewood Cliffs, New Jersey: Prentice-Hall, 1968. 382p.
Generally considered the best of the texts to be used in preparation for the CPA commercial law examinations.

Lipscomb, P.D. LIPSCOMB'S CPA REVIEW. Englewood Cliffs, New Jersey: Prentice-Hall, 1968. 617p.
A CPA coaching text which is programmed in such a way that it can be used in homestudy.

Miller, Herbert E., ed. C.P.A. REVIEW MANUAL, 3rd ed. Englewood Cliffs, New Jersey: Prentice-Hall, 1966. 640p. charts, tables.
The best of the review manuals. Chapter 9, on taxation, published separately in revised form every few years.

Newman, Benjamin. AUDITING: A CPA REVIEW TEXT, 2nd ed. New York: John H. Wiley & Sons, 1964. 795p.
Discusses both the overall subject field of auditing and the areas which the CPA examination may be expected to cover.

Newman, Benjamin and Mellman, Martin. ACCOUNTING THEORY, A CPA REVIEW. New York: John H. Wiley & Sons, 1967. 213p.
Covers major accounting concepts and their place in the framework of generally accepted accounting theory.

Thompson, George C. and Brady, Gerald P. SHORTENED CPA LAW REVIEW, 2nd ed. Belmont, California: Wadsworth, 1965. 528p.
Offers brief but comprehensive coverage of commercial law in outline form. Interesting table on pages 8-9 shows the frequency with which various areas have been included in CPA commercial law examinations during 1952-64.

U.S. Army Audit Agency, in cooperation with the American Institute of Certified Public Accountants. PROVISIONS IN CPA LAWS AND REGULATIONS, rev. July 1, 1968. Washington, D.C.: U.S. Government Printing Office. 81p. tables. pap.
Summarizes the principal legal requirements for the issuance of CPA certificates in the various states, District of Columbia, Puerto Rico and Virgin Islands. Revisions are automatically mailed to holders of basic publication.

U.S. General Accounting Office. Office of Staff Management. OUTLINE OF AICPA ACCOUNTING RESEARCH AND TERMINOLOGY BULLETINS, FINAL EDITION. Washington, D.C.: 1962. 38p. pap.

U.S. General Accounting Office. Office of Staff Management. OUTLINE OF AICPA AUDITING STANDARDS AND PROCEDURES, STATEMENTS ON AUDITING PROCEDURE NO. 33. Washington, D.C.: 1965. 23p. pap. (o.p.)

U.S. General Accounting Office. Office of Staff Management. QUIZZER ON

AICPA ACCOUNTING RESEARCH AND TERMINOLOGY BULLETINS, FINAL EDITION. Washington, D.C.: 1962. 79p. pap.

U.S. General Accounting Office. Office of Staff Management. QUIZZER ON AICPA AUDITING STANDARDS AND PROCEDURES, STATEMENTS ON AUDITING PROCEDURE NO. 33. Washington, D.C.: 1965. 46p. pap. (o.p.)

These booklets, prepared for the GAO's Advanced Accounting and Auditing Study Program, CPA Review Course, provide excellent brief reviews of the AICPA bulletins in question. Useful for accountants preparing to sit for the CPA examination.

University of the State of New York. State Education Department. HANDBOOK 14, PROFESSIONAL EDUCATION PUBLIC ACCOUNTANCY, LAWS, RULES, INFORMATION. Albany, New York: 1966. 122p. pap.

Gives New York State rules and regulations concerning the practice of public accounting as well as requirements and regulations for CPA examinations. Includes a listing of accredited college accounting courses accepted by the State Education Department. Available without charge from the University.

CAPITAL BUDGETING

Alfred, A.M. and Evans, J.B. APPRAISAL OF INVESTMENT PROJECTS BY DISCOUNTED CASH FLOW PRINCIPLES AND SOME SHORT CUT TECHNIQUES. London: Chapman & Hall, Ltd. 1965. 71p. tables. pap.

Prepared by the Economics Department of Courtaulds, Ltd., this is an excellent guide to the short cuts in the DCF techniques which "one firm has found helpful."

Bierman, Harold Jr., and Smidt, Seymour. THE CAPITAL BUDGETING DECISION, 2nd ed. New York: Macmillan; London: Collier-Macmillan, Ltd., 1966. 432p. biblio., tables.

Covers the various methods of making investment decisions. The authors consider the present-value method superior to other methods.

Dean Joel. CAPITAL BUDGETING, TOP-MANAGEMENT POLICY ON PLANT, EQUIPMENT, AND PRODUCT DEVELOPMENT. New York and London: Columbia University Press, 1951. 186p. charts, tables.

Offers a capital budgeting system based on economic analysis of the theory of investment.

Edge, C.G. A PRACTICAL MANUAL ON THE APPRAISAL OF CAPITAL EXPENDITURE, rev. ed. (Special Study, No. 1.) Hamilton, Ontario, Society of Industrial and Cost Accountants of Canada, 1964. 214p. tables.

Covers principles and methods of evaluating capital expenditures. Discounted-cash-flow methods are applied to various types of investment problems. Also reviewed are the capital budgeting areas of estimating, evaluation of risk using sensitivity analysis, and the use of computers.

Grant, Eugene L. and Ireson, W. Grant. PRINCIPLES OF ENGINEERING ECONOMY, 4th ed. New York: Ronald Press, 1960. 574p. formulas, tables.

Explains principles and techniques of decision making in the acquisition and selling of capital goods.

BOOKS

Hackney, John W. CONTROL AND MANAGEMENT OF CAPITAL PROJECTS. New York: John H. Wiley & Sons, 1965. 320p. biblio., charts, illus., tables.

Describes in detail a control system for estimating and managing complex engineering-construction capital projects. Sections on capital-cost estimating and control, progress planning and control, value prediction and control, procedures and reports, manning the organization.

Hunt, Pearson. FINANCIAL ANALYSIS IN CAPITAL BUDGETING (The George H. Leatherbee Lectures, 1964). Boston: Graduate School of Business Administration, Harvard University, 1964. 88p. charts, tables. pap.

Offers a scheme of analysis providing a logical choice of projects to be accepted within the limit of funds provided for capital expenditures.

Istvan, Donald F. CAPITAL-EXPENDITURE DECISIONS: HOW THEY ARE MADE IN LARGE CORPORATIONS (Indiana Business Report, No. 33). Bloomington, Indiana: Bureau of Business Research, Graduate School of Business, Indiana University, 1961. 139p. forms. pap.

An interesting study based on the result of interviews with top financial officers in 48 of the largest United States corporations.

Merrett, A.J. and Sykes, Allen. THE FINANCE AND ANALYSIS OF CAPITAL PROJECTS. London: Longmans, 1963. 564p. charts, tables. (Distributed in the United States by John Wiley & Sons, Inc.).

Directed toward both the financial specialist and the non-financial executive, this book is divided into two parts. The first section covers the general aspects of capital budgeting, the second section concentrates on the more complex problems.

National Association of Accountants. FINANCIAL ANALYSIS TO GUIDE CAPITAL EXPENDITURE DECISIONS (Research Report 43). New York: 1967. 198p. biblio., charts, tables. pap.

Detailed report on current practice in the field of capital budgeting and expenditure as determined by field interviews with 28 companies. Stresses financial analysis methods. Supplements NAA Research Report 35, 1959, "Return on Capital as a Guide to Managerial Decisions."

National Association of Accountants. RETURN ON CAPITAL AS A GUIDE TO MANAGERIAL DECISIONS (Research Report 35). New York: December 1, 1959. 107p. biblio., charts, tables. pap.

Part I: Rate of return for measuring periodic profit performance;
Part II: Using rate of return in capital planning.

National Industrial Conference Board. MANAGING CAPITAL EXPENDITURES (Studies in Business Policy, No. 107), by Norman E. Pflomm. New York: 1963. 148p. charts, illus. pap.

Based on a study of capital expenditures control by 346 manufacturing companies with chapters on the capital budget, authorizing capital expenditures, financial evaluation of capital progress, controlling projects in progress, the post-completion audit. Appendix C is the Westinghouse Electric Corporation's instruction manual on "Planning and Control of Facilities Expenditures."

Solomon, Ezra, ed. THE MANAGEMENT OF CORPORATE CAPITAL. Chicago: Graduate School of Business, University of Chicago, 1959. 327p. classified biblio. charts, tables.

A compilation of 22 essays on the various problems of managing corporate capital. Sections on measuring investment worth, the cost of debt and equity funds, optimal investment decisions, and special aspects of capital measurement.

Terborgh, George. BUSINESS INVESTMENT MANAGEMENT. Washington, D.C.: Machinery and Allied Products Institute, 1967. 383p. charts, tables.

Outlines a system of planning and executing capital expenditures. Supersedes the 1958 study, BUSINESS INVESTMENT POLICY, A MAPI STUDY AND MANUAL.

Usry, Milton F. CAPITAL-EXPENDITURE: PLANNING AND CONTROL (Studies in Accounting, No. 1). Austin, Texas: Bureau of Business Research, University of Texas, 1966. 277p. biblio. charts, forms, tables. pap.

A study which defines the basic requirements of a capital-expenditure planning and control program. Supplemented by intensive field research of the Continental Oil Company and its subsidiaries. Includes four detailed case studies of the different types of capital expenditures in a producing well, a company-owned service station, the development of a new petrochemical product and a pipeline and refinery expansion project.

Vandell, Robert F. and Vancil, Richard F. CASES IN CAPITAL BUDGETING. Homewood, Illinois: Richard D. Irwin, 1962. 476p. charts, forms, tables.

Presents a series of case studies of actual problems in capital budgeting which were faced by businessmen. Chapters on measuring return on investment, evaluating risk, measuring the cost of capital, capital structure planning, choosing among financing alternatives, capital rationing, the strategy of capital budgeting. Tables for analysis of capital expenditures are included.

CONSOLIDATED STATEMENTS

A number of advanced accounting texts included in Accounting and Auditing Textbooks section include chapters on consolidated statements.

American Institute of Certified Public Accountants. "Part of the Examination Made by Other Independent Auditors." In AUDITING STANDARDS AND PROCEDURES (Statements on Auditing Procedure No. 33). New York: 1963. pp.66-9.

Discusses the responsibility of the independent auditor for reports made by other auditors on statements of a company's subsidiaries which he himself has not examined. Gives methods of disclosing the divided responsibility in either the scope or opinion paragraph of the certificate.

American Institute of Certified Public Accountants. SURVEY OF CONSOLIDATED FINANCIAL STATEMENT PRACTICES. New York: 1956. 31p. pap. (o.p.)

Survey conducted to determine how corporations handle the special problems which arise in the preparation of consolidated financial statements.

Childs, William H. CONSOLIDATED FINANCIAL STATEMENTS, PRINCIPLES AND PROCEDURE. Ithaca, New York: Cornell University Press, 1949. 368p. selected biblio.

Covers legal and institutional background of consolidated statements, including theoretical and practical aspects of the basic concept. Chapters on the consolidated balance sheet at date of acquisition and after period of acquisition, consolidated profit and loss and surplus statements, stock transactions after original acquisition, indirect and reciprocal relationships.

Hutchison, T.A.M. RELIANCE ON OTHER AUDITORS (Research Study, No. 4). Toronto: Canadian Institute of Chartered Accountants, 1964. 37p. pap.

Reviews practices in Canada, the United Kingdom and the United States of principal auditors in reviewing the accounts of sub-auditors. Details the responsibilities of the parent company auditor as well as those of the subsidiary company's auditor. Suggests that note be made of reliance on other auditors in the scope paragraph of the opinion.

Institute of Chartered Accountants in England and Wales. AUDITORS' REPORTS ON GROUP ACCOUNTS (Statements on Auditing, U5). London: 15 April 1965. 3p. pap.

States that parent company auditors who report on a consolidated group have a duty to satisfy themselves that their opinion on the group accounts is based on adequate information about each material company in the group. This would include reviewing the reports of other auditors as well as making such additional inquiries as they deem necessary.

Moonitz, Maurice. THE ENTITY THEORY OF CONSOLIDATED STATEMENTS (American Accounting Association Monograph, No. 4). Brooklyn, New York: Foundation Press, 1951. 104p. pap.

Originally published by the American Accounting Association in 1944. Offers a theory of consolidation based on the treatment of closely allied companies as a single accounting unit in spite of their divergent activities. Covers the functions of consolidated reports, the circumstances under which they should be presented and the accounting standards and principles behind their presentation.

Newlove, George Hillis. CONSOLIDATED STATEMENTS INCLUDING MERGERS AND CONSOLIDATIONS (Heath Accounting Series). Boston: Heath, 1948. 412p. coded biblio., exhibits. (o.p.)

Although now out-of-print, this extremely detailed text is still useful. Numerous illustrations and examples are included.

Rappaport, Alfred, et al, eds. PUBLIC REPORTING BY CONGLOMERATES: THE ISSUES, THE PROBLEMS, AND SOME POSSIBLE SOLUTIONS. Englewood Cliffs, New Jersey: Prentice-Hall, 1968. 172p. charts, graphs, tables.

Contains proceedings and also formal comments on the papers of a symposium held at Tulane University in October 1967.

Robson, Sir Thomas B. and Duncan, S.M. HOLDING COMPANIES AND THEIR SUBSIDIARIES. CONSOLIDATED AND OTHER GROUP ACCOUNTS, PRINCIPLES AND PROCEDURE, 4th ed. London: Gee & Co., 1969. 148p.

Intended as a practical guide for the businessman approaching consolidation for the first time.

CONTROLLERSHIP

See also Corporations - Financial Management

American Management Association. COMPANY ORGANIZATION OF THE FINANCE FUNCTION, By Edward T. Curtis. (Research Study, No. 55.) New York: 1962. 127p. charts. pap. (o.p.)

This report, based on a survey of 278 companies and accounting literature on the subject, gives an account of current industrial practice concerning the division of responsibilities among corporate financial officers.

American Management Association. THE FINANCIAL MANAGER'S JOB, ed. by Elizabeth Marting and Robert E. Finley. New York: 1964. 464p.

A collection of articles originally published by AMA in the MANAGEMENT REVIEW or in divisional publications such as the Research Studies. Covers such topics as corporate financing, capital investment, profit planning, overseas expansion, etc.

Anderson, David R. and Schnidt, Leo A. PRACTICAL CONTROLLERSHIP, rev. ed. Homewood, Illinois: Richard D. Irwin, 1961. 777p.

Examines the controllership function and the position of the controller in the modern business organization.

Bennett, Jerome V. ADMINISTERING THE COMPANY ACCOUNTING FUNCTION. Englewood Cliffs, New Jersey: Prentice-Hall, 1968. 223p. charts, forms, photo.

Emphasis on control reporting techniques. Chapters on cost accounting and control, treasury duties, planning, financial analysis, controller's role in systems planning, etc.

Cohen, Jerome B. and Robbins, Sidney M. THE FINANCIAL MANAGER, BASIC ASPECTS OF FINANCIAL ADMINISTRATION. New York: Harper & Row, 1966. 1006p. charts, tables.

A comprehensive review of the financial manager's responsibilities in the areas of planning and control. Financial theory and practical applications are both included. Suggested readings at end of each chapter.

Hassler, Russell H. and Harlan, Neil E. CASES IN CONTROLLERSHIP. Englewood Cliffs, New Jersey: Prentice-Hall, 1958. 364p. charts, forms, tables.

A series of cases developed for use at the Harvard Business School, grouped under the following subjects: nature of the controller function; internal control and internal audit; accounting policy; the role of financial analysis in the management process.

Heckert, J. Brooks and Willson, James D. CONTROLLERSHIP, 2nd ed. New York: Ronald Press, 1963. 816p. charts, forms, tables.

A general text covering the responsibilities of the controller in great detail.

Hutton, Clifford E. CONTROLLERSHIP, FUNCTION AND TRAINING (Research Monograph No. 24.) Austin, Texas: Bureau of Business Research, University of

Texas, 1962. 156p. biblio. tables. pap.
Based on questionnaires and interviews with top executives and a review of current literature, this study seeks to show how the controllership function should operate. Chapters cover the controller's position in company organization; managerial, recordkeeping and internal auditing functions; qualifications and education for controllership; experience and training requisites.

Jackson, J. Hugh. COMPTROLLER: HIS FUNCTIONS AND ORGANIZATION. Boston: Harvard University Press, 1949. 109p. charts.
The 1949 Dickinson Lecture in Accounting delivered at the Harvard University Graduate School of Business, this little book still offers a good description of the comptroller's responsibilities and his position in the corporate structure.

Lewis, Ronello B. FINANCIAL CONTROLS FOR MANAGEMENT. Englewood Cliffs, New Jersey: Prentice-Hall, 1961. 180p. charts.
A reference book for the corporate control officer. Covers in detail ten areas in which management can benefit by effectively presented financial information. Chapter 10 includes an organization chart of the financial officer's department and job description for the financial control officer.

National Industrial Conference Board. DIVISION FINANCIAL EXECUTIVES, by Carl C. Baumes. (Studies in Business Policy, No. 101.) New York: 1961. 59p. pap.
Based upon experiences of 123 manufacturing companies in allocating financial responsibilities to division and headquarters finance groups. Tabular analysis of division financial executives' authority is included.

National Industrial Conference Board. MANAGING THE FINANCIAL FUNCTION, Report No. 1- . New York: 1968- . pap. No. 1: DUTIES AND PROBLEMS OF CHIEF FINANCIAL EXECUTIVES. 34p.
Discusses the duties, problems, influence of the top financial officer in a survey of 160 corporations.

Prentice-Hall Editorial Staff. CORPORATE TREASURER'S AND CONTROLLER'S ENCYCLOPEDIA, 4 vols. Englewood Cliffs, New Jersey: Prentice-Hall, 1958.
A guide to the efficient performance of the duties of corporate treasurers and controllers.

CORPORATIONS - FINANCIAL MANAGEMENT

See also Asset Accounting, Budgeting, Capital Budgeting, Controllership, Distribution Costs, Internal Auditing and Control, Leasing, Management Accounting, Mergers and Acquisitions, and Public Offerings

Anderson, W.H. Locke. CORPORATE FINANCE AND FIXED INVESTMENT, AN ECONOMETRIC STUDY. Boston: Division of Research, Graduate School of Business Administration, Harvard University, 1964. 144p. charts, tables.
A study of investment policies of manufacturing concerns which indicates that they are strongly influenced by the firms' debt, liquidity and interest rate positions.

Anthony, Robert N., et al. MANAGEMENT CONTROL SYSTEMS, CASES AND READINGS. Homewood, Illinois: Richard D. Irwin, 1965. 698p. charts, illus., tables.

Based on a Harvard Business School course, the management of costs, profit centers and capital acquisitions are the main subjects covered in these readings and their illustrative cases. Chapters on organizational relationships and objectives; expense, financial performance, investment and information centers; long-range planning; capital budgeting.

Anthony, Robert N. PLANNING AND CONTROL SYSTEMS, A FRAMEWORK FOR ANALYSIS. Boston: Division of Research, Graduate School of Business Administration, Harvard University, 1965. 192p. chart.

Attempts to set up a framework upon which discussions of management planning and control systems can logically be based. Differentiates sharply between managerial and operational control. Concludes that among other characteristics, the central management control system should be a financial system.

Ball, Richard E. and Melnyk, Z. Lew. THEORY OF MANAGERIAL FINANCE: SELECTED READINGS. Boston: Allyn and Bacon, 1967. 632p. charts, tables. pap. biblio.

A selection of articles by a number of practicing financial managers and theoretical finance professors. Sections on capital investment, capital budgeting, cost of capital, capital structure factors in financial decisions, corporate earnings and dividend policy, financial strategy and corporate valuation.

Beranek, William. ANALYSIS FOR FINANCIAL DECISIONS. Homewood, Illinois: Richard D. Irwin, 1963. 495p. charts, tables.

A textbook on various methods of analyzing financial problems. Brief list of supplementary readings at end of each chapter.

Blecke, Curtis J. FINANCIAL ANALYSIS FOR DECISION MAKING. Englewood Cliffs, New Jersey: Prentice-Hall, 1966. 220p. charts, photo., tables.

Offers effective reporting systems, both graphic and tabular, for financial reports to management. Definitions of selected technical terms are included on pp.179-90.

Bogen, Jules I. FINANCIAL HANDBOOK, 4th ed., rev. printing. New York: Ronald Press, 1968. v.p.

Standard reference work on all aspects of financial practice.

Bradley, Joseph F. ADMINISTRATIVE FINANCIAL MANAGEMENT, 2nd ed. New York: Holt, Rinehart & Winston, 1969. 555p. biblio. charts, tables.

Applies the administrative process and financial management in providing tools for executive decisions.

Braun, Carl F. OBJECTIVE ACCOUNTING, A PROBLEM OF COMMUNICATION. Alhambra, California: C.F. Braun & Co., 1958. 81p.

Attacks the lack of communication in industrial accounting between the accounting department and management. Offers suggestions for ways in which accountants can simplify techniques, language, etc.

Casey, William J. HOW TO RAISE MONEY TO MAKE MONEY. New York: Institute for Business Planning, 1966. 275p.

Covers all aspects of the various financing alternatives available to business corporations and/or businessmen. Sections on planning, financing sources, the equity market and special financing techniques are written in clear, effective language.

Childs, John F. LONG-TERM FINANCING. Englewood Cliffs, New Jersey: Prentice-Hall, 1961. 381p. charts, illus., tables.

Designed for practical use by businessmen. Discusses not only the steps necessary to raise money for corporate expansion, but also other aspects of financial management such as capital structure, finance programs, dividend policy, etc.

Corrigan, Francis J. and Ward, Howard A., eds. FINANCIAL MANAGEMENT POLICIES AND PRACTICES. Boston: Houghton Mifflin, 1963. 621p. charts, forms, tables. pap.

A study of the acquisition and administration of funds needed in a corporate enterprise.

Davis, Hiram S. PRODUCTIVITY ACCOUNTING. Philadelphia: University of Pennsylvania Press, 1955. 194p. biblio.

Presents a method for measuring the productivity of a firm in inflationary as well as stable times by using "the ratio of total goods and services produced by an enterprise to the total economic costs incurred, both products and costs having been revalued to some selected scale of constant prices."

Dewing, Arthur S. THE FINANCIAL POLICY OF CORPORATIONS, 5th ed. 2 vols. New York: Ronald Press, 1953.

The authoritative work in the field of corporation finance. Written from the point of view of the corporate policy-maker, it gives practical guidance on all aspects of corporate financial matters.

Donaldson, Elvin F. and Pfahl, John K. CORPORATE FINANCE: POLICY AND MANAGEMENT, 3rd ed. New York: Ronald Press, 1969. 808p. charts, tables.

A college text on all aspects of corporate finance. Selected reading lists at end of each chapter.

Donaldson, Gordon. CORPORATE DEBT CAPACITY. Boston: Division of Research, Graduate School of Business Administration, Harvard University, 1961. 308p. charts, tables.

Discusses to what lengths a management should go in using long-term debt in capital financing. Selected readings listed.

Easton, Edison E. and Newton, Byron L. ACCOUNTING AND THE ANALYSIS OF FINANCIAL DATA. New York: McGraw-Hill Book Co., 1958. 449p. charts, tables.

Designed for non-accountants who need an elementary knowledge of accounting.

Eisenberg, Joseph. COST CONTROLS FOR THE OFFICE. Englewood Cliffs, New Jersey: Prentice-Hall, 1968. 255p. charts, forms, photo., tables.

Practical handbook covering office cost systems and procedures with numerous illustrations.

Foster, Le Baron R. TELLING THE COMPANY'S FINANCIAL STORY, prepared for the Financial Executives Research Foundation. New York: Financial

Executives Institute, 1964. 111p. biblio., tables.
Describes the planning and programming of financial public relations activities.

Gerstenberg, Charles W. FINANCIAL ORGANIZATION AND MANAGEMENT OF BUSINESS, 4th rev. ed. Englewood Cliffs, New Jersey: Prentice-Hall, 1959. 640p. charts, tables.
Covers the organizing of a business, its financing and management of its corporate funds, expansion, and recapitalization.

Gilbert, Lewis D. and John J. ANNUAL REPORT OF STOCKHOLDER ACTIVITIES AT CORPORATION MEETINGS. New York: 1939- . pap.
Annual report by the Gilbert brothers giving their opinion of management's handling of corporate annual meetings which they attend as stockholders. Includes their views of certain annual reports and various aspects of corporation policy of interest to stockholders such as cumulative voting, pensions, options, etc. Always contains a chapter on auditing in which the authors discuss specific accounting and auditing matters which have been raised at annual meetings during the year.

Gordon, Myron J. THE INVESTMENT, FINANCING AND VALUATION OF THE CORPORATION. Homewood, Illinois: Richard D. Irwin, 1962. 271p.
Establishes a model for explaining the valuation of a corporation which may be used to decide the most profitable investment and financing by the corporation.

Guthman, Harry G. and Dougall, Herbert E. CORPORATE FINANCIAL POLICY, 4th ed. Englewood Cliffs, New Jersey: Prentice-Hall, 1962. 795p.
Standard text on corporation finance. Covers profit planning, capital budgeting, and financial analysis in more detail than earlier editions. Selected references are given.

Humble, Thomas N. STANDARDS IN STRATEGIC PLANNING AND CONTROL, A CONCEPTUAL STUDY (Studies in Accounting, No. 2). Austin, Texas: Bureau of Business Research, University of Texas, 1966. 186p. biblio.
Offers a conceptual model of standards of performance in the area of planning and control which is tested through field research and in two case studies. Chapter II contains a survey of literature in the field.

Hunt, Pearson and Andrews, Victor. FINANCIAL MANAGEMENT: CASES AND READINGS. Homewood, Illinois: Richard F. Irwin, 1968. 946p. charts, map, tables.
The two main sections, "Funds Allocation" and "Managing the Capital Structure," are divided into several parts. In each category three to six cases are presented as well as several readings on the particular subject. Some of the articles include bibliographies.

Hunt, Pearson, et al. BASIC BUSINESS FINANCE, TEXT AND CASES, 3rd ed. Homewood, Illinois: Richard D. Irwin, 1966. 1038p. charts, illus., tables.
Written from the viewpoint of the corporate finance officer who not only provides the funds for the operation of the business but also participates in all financial planning. Covers business financing and sources of funds, types of securities, capital budgeting

and variations of capital contracts such as leasing. References for additional reading are included.

Johnson, Robert W. FINANCIAL MANAGEMENT, 3rd ed. Boston: Allyn & Bacon, 1966. 709p. charts, forms, tables.

Sections on planning and managing assets; planning the financial structure; managing short, long and intermediate-term funds; valuing business enterprises. Selected references at the end of each chapter.

Kelly, Richard J. THE ADVERTISING BUDGET, PREPARATION, ADMINISTRATION AND CONTROL. New York: Association of National Advertisers, Inc., 1967. 300p. charts, forms, tables.

Prepared under the direction of the A.N.A. Advertising Administration Control Committee, this manual covers the financial management of the corporate advertising function. Chapters on preparing the advertising budget, purchasing the advertising, advertising budgetary control and advertiser-agency financial procedures. Appendices to each chapter describe in detail actual procedures followed by different companies.

Kent, Raymond P. CORPORATE FINANCIAL MANAGEMENT, 3rd ed. Homewood, Illinois: Richard D. Irwin, 1969. 936p. forms, tables.

A textbook which combines descriptions of the principles and procedures of corporate financial policy with treatment of the techniques of decision making.

Ladd, Dwight R. CONTEMPORARY CORPORATE ACCOUNTING AND THE PUBLIC. Homewood, Illinois: Richard D. Irwin, 1963. 185p. tables.

Estimates the extent to which modern accounting has fulfilled its role of accurately informing the public as to the power and practices of the modern corporation.

Lewis, Ronello B. FINANCIAL ANALYSIS FOR MANAGEMENT. Englewood Cliffs, New Jersey: Prentice-Hall, 1959. 190p. illus. (o.p.)

Shows how management should use accounting and financial reports in making decisions.

Lewis, Ronello B. MANAGEMENT CONTROL TECHNIQUES FOR IMPROVING PROFITS. Englewood Cliffs, New Jersey: Prentice-Hall, 1962. 267p. forms, tables.

"A checklist for the profit-minded executive." Thirty chapters, with illustrations, cover the techniques to be applied to checking a company's profits.

Lindsay, Robert and Sametz, Arnold W. FINANCIAL MANAGEMENT, AN ANALYTICAL APPROACH, rev. ed. Homewood, Illinois: Richard D. Irwin, 1967. 529p. charts, tables.

Textbook which covers the general field of corporate finance, relating business practice to economic policy and theory. Suggested readings at end of each chapter.

Mayer, Raymond R. FINANCIAL ANALYSIS OF INVESTMENT ALTERNATIVES. Boston: Allyn & Bacon, 1966. 103p. selected biblio. tables. pap.

Describes three basic methods of investment analysis: present worth, uniform annual cost and rate of return techniques.

Miller, Ernest C. OBJECTIVES AND STANDARDS OF PERFORMANCE IN FINANCIAL MANAGEMENT (AMA Research Study 87). New York: American Management Association, 1968. 109p. chart, photo.

Describes how to establish objectives and standards for corporate financial management. Numerous case studies. Suggested readings, are included.

Mock, Edward J., ed. FINANCIAL DECISION MAKING. Scranton, Pennsylvania: International Textbook, 1967. 967p. charts, formulae, graphs, tables.

Collection of 60 articles on financial decision making by well-known authorities covering the phases of most interest to the financial manager. Reference lists at end of each chapter.

Mock, Edward J., ed. READINGS IN FINANCIAL MANAGEMENT. Scranton, Pennsylvania: International Textbook, 1964. 504p. charts, graphs, tables.

Contains 26 articles covering subject areas of the finance function: financial planning and control, management of assets, capital budgeting, capital structure and cost of capital, and management of corporate capital.

National Association of Accountants. CASH FLOW ANALYSIS FOR MANAGERIAL CONTROL (NAA Research Report 38). New York: October 15, 1961. 63p. illus. pap.

Summarizes experience of 42 companies in presenting financial data relevant to the management of cash assets of a business. Techniques included are: short-period cash forecasts and cash budgets; long-range cash forecasts; reports for communicating cash flow data and cash position figures to management.

National Industrial Conference Board. ALLOCATING CORPORATE EXPENSES (Studies in Business Policy, No. 108). New York: 1963. 90p. facs., tables. pap.

A comprehensive review of the pros and cons of allocation of corporate headquarter's expenses to divisions. Based on the practices of 158 companies.

National Industrial Conference Board. MANAGING COMPANY CASH (Studies in Business Policy, No. 99). New York: 1961. 123p. charts, illus., tables. pap.

A study based on the practices of over 200 companies which describes various methods of using company cash most effectively.

Norgaard, Richard L. and Vaughn, Donald E. CASES IN FINANCIAL DECISION MAKING. Englewood Cliffs, New Jersey: Prentice-Hall, 1967. 383p.

charts, tables.

Consists of 47 cases presented as a basis for group discussion. Grouped under the following headings: financial planning, working capital management, capital budgeting and cost of capital, short and intermediate term financing, long-term financing, valuation of expansion, special problems, comprehensive cases.

O'Donnell, John L. and Goldberg, Milton S. ELEMENTS OF FINANCIAL ADMINISTRATION. Columbus, Ohio: Merrill, 1962. 687p. charts, tables.

A collection of 34 essays used in the teaching of financial administration at Michigan State University. Covers fundamentals of the finance function, working capital, analytic tools, capital and long-term fund management, regulation and taxation.

Park, Colin and Gladson, John W. WORKING CAPITAL. New York: Macmillan, 1963. 222p. charts, tables.

Advocates the use of accounting techniques for more effective control of corporate funds. Working capital is defined as the relatively liquid portion of all assets and liabilities instead of the traditional difference between current assets and liabilities. The authors suggest "an operating-cycle approach to developing figures for management planning and control of the finances of a business." Financial statements would be based on this cycle rather than on a one-year fiscal or calendar period.

Rumpf, Howard A. CORPORATE LIQUIDATIONS FOR THE LAWYER AND THE ACCOUNTANT, 2nd ed. Englewood Cliffs, New Jersey: Prentice-Hall, 1965. 206p. facs., tables.

In addition to detailed explanations of the 1954 Code and Regulations, this covers the technical requirements for filing of schedules and information, the tax forms necessary and the accounting procedure for liquidation and/or dissolution of corporations.

Schindler, James S. QUASI-REORGANIZATION (Michigan Business Studies, Vo. 13, No. 5). Ann Arbor: Bureau of Business Research, School of Business Administration, University of Michigan, 1958. 186p.

A study of the quasi-reorganization procedure in which there is a complete restatement of assets, the revaluation amounts being substituted for the previous carrying amounts.

Solomon, Ezra. THE THEORY OF FINANCIAL MANAGEMENT. New York: Columbia University Press, 1963. 184p. classified biblio.

Provides a theoretical structure upon which to base financial decisions and their implementation.

Thompson, F. Corine and Norgaard, Richard L. SINKING FUNDS, THEIR USE AND VALUE. New York: Financial Executives Research Foundation, 1967. 80p. charts.

Discusses the history of sinking funds and other arrangements for payment of long term debt prior to maturity; presents a mathematical model for determining the value of a mandatory installment payment provision to the borrower and to the lender.

Walker, Ernest W. and Baughn, William H. FINANCIAL PLANNING AND POLICY. New York: Harper, 1961. 520p. charts, tables.

Focuses on the various planning stages of the financial decision.

The six parts of the book are divided into organization for financial management, necessary analysis procedures, determination of financial requirements, policies covering internal sources of funds, securing necessary funds, and other such aspects of financial management as communication, influence of taxes, etc.

Weston, J. Fred and Brigham, Eugene F. MANAGERIAL FINANCE, 3rd ed. New York: Holt, Rinehart & Winston, 1969. 848p. graphs, tables.
Emphasizes the contributions which should be made by financial managers to the planning and control aspects of business enterprises.

White, K.K. FINANCING COMPANY EXPANSION (AMA Research Study 64). New York: American Management Association, 1964. 144p. charts, illus., tables.
Describes in detail the various sources of outside funds available for corporate expansion. Selected readings are listed.

Wright, M.G. DISCOUNTED CASH FLOW. London: McGraw-Hill Publishing Company Ltd., 1968. 188p. diagrs., tables.
A clear exposition of the discounted cash flow technique and its application to capital investment appraisal.

CORPORATION-INDUSTRIAL MANAGEMENT

Only a few of the best-known titles on industrial management are listed here since the accountant's primary interest is in corporate financial management.

Alford, L.P. and Beatty, H. Russell. PRINCIPLES OF INDUSTRIAL MANAGEMENT, rev. ed. New York: Ronald Press, 1951. 801p. charts, diagrs., forms, tables.
A textbook in which emphasis is placed on the principles of management, but which includes description of detailed methods. References at end of each chapter.

Brown, Stanley M., ed. BUSINESS EXECUTIVE'S HANDBOOK, 4th ed., rev. by Lillian Doris. Englewood Cliffs, New Jersey: Prentice-Hall, 1953. 1504p.
Provides direct information on all aspects of business management from profitable advertising to accounting for the business executive.

Carson, Gordon B., ed. PRODUCTION HANDBOOK, 2nd ed. New York: Ronald Press, 1958. v.p. charts, diagrs., forms, illus., tables.
Covers all aspects of production management and control.

Dale, Ernest. ORGANIZATION. New York: American Management Association, 1967. 368p. biblio., charts, forms.
Based on a questionnaire survey covering 166 large and medium-size companies. Covers theory and objectives of organizations; how to divide and coordinate the work; the planning and carrying out of a reorganization; the effect of increasing corporate internationalization and of computers upon the organization structure.

Dean, Joel. MANAGERIAL ECONOMICS. Englewood Cliffs, New Jersey: Prentice-Hall, 1951. 637p. charts, tables.
A management classic which illustrates how economic analysis can be used in the formulation of management policy.

Greisman, Bernard, ed. J.K. LASSER'S BUSINESS MANAGEMENT HANDBOOK, 3rd ed., rev. and expanded. New York: McGraw-Hill Book Co., 1968. 784p. charts.

A collection of writings by various authorities on aspects of business management which require a certain expertise. Chapters 8 and 10 are on accounting and cost accounting systems respectively.

Heany, Donald F. DEVELOPMENT OF INFORMATION SYSTEMS. New York: Ronald Press, 1968. 421p. glossary, selected biblio., charts, forms, photos.

Outgrowth of text prepared originally for the General Electric Company's Financial Management Program and related courses. Intended to acquaint the businessman with the design, programming and administration of an information system.

Heyel, Carl, ed. THE ENCYCLOPEDIA OF MANAGEMENT. New York: Reinhold, 1963. 1112p.

A compilation of essays arranged in alphabetical order, covering all aspects of management. Designed to give the executive quick background information on any management problem which might arise. References are cited at the end of many of the entries.

Ireson, William Grant and Grant, Eugene L., eds. HANDBOOK OF INDUSTRIAL ENGINEERING AND MANAGEMENT. Englewood Cliffs, New Jersey: Prentice-Hall, 1955. 1213p. charts, diagrs., forms, maps, photos., tables.

Sections on business organization structure, managerial economics, industrial budgeting as well as the traditional time and motion study, production control, job evaluation, etc. Bibliographies at the end of each section. New edition due in 1971.

Jerome, William T., III. EXECUTIVE CONTROL: THE CATALYST. New York: John A. Wiley & Sons, 1961. 289p. charts.

Treats control as an overall management function rather than a specific financial technique. Budgeting and internal control are discussed in chapter 7, "Planning." Chapter 11, "Review and Analysis through Audit" covers internal auditing.

Maynard, Harold B., ed. HANDBOOK OF BUSINESS ADMINISTRATION. New York: McGraw-Hill Book Co., 1967. v.p. charts, tables.

A compilation of articles on business administration contributed by top management men. Section 10 covers accounting and control. Bibliographies at the end of each chapter.

Maynard, Harold B., ed. INDUSTRIAL ENGINEERING HANDBOOK, 2nd ed. New York: McGraw-Hill Book Co., 1963. v.p. charts, forms, illus., tables.

One-Hundred and nine contributors of high caliber make this one of the best of the industrial engineering references. Material is divided into ten sections: the industrial engineering function, methods, work-measurement techniques, applied work measurement, predetermined-elemental-time standards, wage and salary plans, control procedures, plant facilities, mathematical and statistical procedures, and other aspects of industrial engineering.

Newman, William H. ADMINISTRATIVE ACTION, THE TECHNIQUES OF ORGANIZATION AND MANAGEMENT, 2nd ed. Englewood Cliffs, New Jersey: Prentice-Hall, 1963. 496p. charts.

Chapters are grouped into the areas of planning, organizing, assembling resources, supervising and controlling. Selected references at the end of each chapter.

Newman, William H. and Logan, James P. BUSINESS POLICIES AND CENTRAL MANAGEMENT, 5th ed. Cincinnati: South-Western Publishing Co., 1965. 960p. selected biblio., charts, tables.
Textbook for business policy courses which explains how to analyze corporate enterprises. Includes illustrative cases.

Rautenstrauch, Walter and Villers, Raymond. ECONOMICS OF INDUSTRIAL MANAGEMENT, 2nd ed. New York: Funk & Wagnalls, 1957. 510p. charts, tables.
Part I, "Visualizing the Business," includes chapters on financial statements and their interpretation, break-even and profit and loss charts. Part II, "Industrial Cost Characteristics," covers depreciation, costs, expenses. Part III discusses the business entity as part of the national plant. (o.p.)

Solomons, David. DIVISIONAL PERFORMANCE: MEASUREMENT AND CONTROL. New York: Financial Executives Research Foundation, 1965. 319p. biblio., charts, forms, tables.
Based on a study of divisional relations and control within 25 large decentralized corporations. This is not just a survey of current practices, but an expression of the author's viewpoints and suggestions on these practices.

Terry, George R. OFFICE MANAGEMENT AND CONTROL: THE ACTIONS OF ADMINISTRATIVE MANAGEMENT, 5th ed. Homewood, Illinois: Richard D. Irwin, 1966. 809p. charts, forms, photos.
Gives fundamental principles and practices used in the organization, activation and control of successful office management.

Toan, Arthur B., Jr. USING INFORMATION TO MANAGE. New York: Ronald Press, 1968. 161p. glossary, charts, tables.
Discusses how corporate managers should use information to prevent trouble, to analyze problems and to establish positive goals.

Wylie, Harry L., ed. OFFICE MANAGEMENT HANDBOOK, 2nd ed. New York: Ronald Press, 1958. v.p. diagrs., forms, tables.
Written under the auspices of the Administrative Management Association, this is a comprehensive work offering standard principles and practices for efficient office procedures.

COST ACCOUNTING

See also Distribution Costs, Management Accounting, Research and Development Costs

American Management Association. DIRECT COSTING, A LOOK AT ITS STRENGTHS AND WEAKNESSES (Management Bulletin 54). New York: 1964. [University Microfilms] 20p. charts. pap.
Three papers containing "representative arguments" for and against direct costing.

Anton, Hector R. and Firmin, Peter A. CONTEMPORARY ISSUES IN COST ACCOUNTING. Boston: Houghton Mifflin, 1966. 543p. charts, tables.

pap.

A selection of articles on all aspects of cost accounting. Divided into eight sections, each of which includes an excellent bibliography on the particular aspect covered.

Backer, Morton and Jacobsen, Lyle E. COST ACCOUNTING: A MANAGERIAL APPROACH. New York: McGraw-Hill Book Co., 1964. 678p. charts, tables.

Combines the traditional collection of data material with the managerial uses of this material.

Basso, Lee L. COST HANDBOOK FOR THE SMALL MANUFACTURER. St. Louis, Missouri: L.B. Associates, 1964. 319p. forms.

A non-technical handbook which describes basic accounting principles as well as costing techniques.

Bennett, Earl D. COST ADMINISTRATION: ACCOUNTING FOR COST CONTROL AND PRODUCT DECISION. Englewood Cliffs, New Jersey: Prentice-Hall, 1960. 606p. charts, illus. (o.p.)

A collection of cases on the reporting of data for use in planning and controlling the firm's internal activities.

Bierman, Harold, Jr. TOPICS IN COST ACCOUNTING AND DECISIONS. New York: McGraw-Hill Book Co., 1963. 217p. charts, tables.

Applies the techniques of decision theory to cost accounting problems.

Brock, Horace R., *et al.* COST ACCOUNTING, THEORY AND PRACTICE. New York: McGraw-Hill Book Co., 1965. 341p. charts, tables.

A basic textbook covering all aspects of cost accounting.

Brummet, R. Lee. OVERHEAD COSTING, THE COSTING OF MANUFACTURED PRODUCTS (Michigan Business Studies, Vol. 13, No. 2). Ann Arbor: Bureau of Business Research, School of Business Administration, University of Michigan, 1957. 169p. charts, tables.

A monograph which discusses overhead costing from the viewpoints of both the cost accountant and management.

Carroll, Phil. OVERHEAD COST CONTROL. New York: McGraw-Hill Book Co., 1964. 314p. charts, forms, tables.

Shows how to achieve substantial profit improvement through practical analysis, assignment and control of overhead.

Clark, John Maurice. STUDIES IN THE ECONOMICS OF OVERHEAD COSTS. Chicago: University of Chicago Press, 1923. 516p.

An important historical work in the field of cost theory, which discusses overhead costing "from the standpoint of disinterested economic science."

Crowningshield, Gerald R. COST ACCOUNTING, PRINCIPLES AND MANAGERIAL APPLICATIONS rev. ed. Boston: Houghton Mifflin, 1969. 812p. charts, tables.

Applies cost concepts and techniques to such business problems as planning, decision making, internal control of operations, etc.

Dearden, John. COST AND BUDGET ANALYSIS. Englewood Cliffs, New Jersey: Prentice-Hall, 1962. 217p. tables.

Concentrates on accounting techniques which best provide the financial information needed in making short-term operating decisions. Does not consider capital investment analysis, long-term profit planning, etc.

Dickey, Robert I., ed. ACCOUNTANTS' COST HANDBOOK, 2nd ed. New York: Ronald Press, 1960. v.p.
Comprehensive volume giving practical information on the whole range of accounting for costs.

Dudick, Thomas S. COST CONTROLS FOR INDUSTRY. Englewood Cliffs, New Jersey: Prentice-Hall, 1962. 320p. charts, graphs, tables.
Outlines a number of cost control techniques for business. Discusses standard and direct cost accounting systems, overhead problems, and reporting methods.

Fiske, Wyman P. and Beckett, John A., eds. INDUSTRIAL ACCOUNTANT'S HANDBOOK. New York: Prentice-Hall, 1954. 1072p.
Covers both fundamental and specialized aspects of industrial cost accounting.

Garner, S. Paul. EVOLUTION OF COST ACCOUNTING TO 1925. University, Alabama: University of Alabama Press, 1954. 416p. selected biblio.
Emphasis placed on origin and development of cost practices.

Gillespie, Cecil. COST ACCOUNTING AND CONTROL. Englewood Cliffs, New Jersey: Prentice-Hall, 1957. 839p. charts, exhibits, forms.
A comprehensive treatment of cost accounting, cost control and cost management as a factor in business planning. Appendix 1 - Set of cost control reports for a manufacturing business. Appendix 2 - A complete budget for a manufacturing business. Appendix 3 - Annotated bibliography of selected articles on distribution costs.

Gillespie, Cecil. STANDARD AND DIRECT COSTING, 3rd ed. Englewood Cliffs, New Jersey: Prentice-Hall, 1962. 337p. charts, forms, tables.
Applies standard cost principles to the concept of direct costing. Bibliographies on direct costing, breakeven point, responsibility accounting, profit planning and working capital.

Henrici, Stanley B. STANDARD COSTS FOR MANUFACTURING, 3rd ed. (McGraw-Hill Accounting Series.) New York: McGraw-Hill Book Co., 1960. 402p. charts.
A comprehensive treatment of standard costs.

Hickey, James J. HOW TO INSTALL AND EFFECTIVELY USE DIRECT COSTING. Stratford, Connecticut: Kevmar Publications, 1965. 166p. pap.
A strong advocate of direct costing, the author gives a number of useful illustrations of its value to companies which are successfully using direct costing systems.

Horngren, Charles T. COST ACCOUNTING, A MANAGERIAL EMPHASIS, 2nd ed. Englewood Cliffs, New Jersey: Prentice-Hall, 1967. 896p. glossary, charts.
Excellent textbook presentation of the services which the accountant

can render management in the planning and control functions.

Li, David H. COST ACCOUNTING FOR MANAGEMENT APPLICATIONS. Columbus, Ohio: Merrill, 1966. 669p. charts, tables.

A textbook which details the background, the transition period and the current techniques in cost accounting, showing how it has become more valuable as a management tool.

Lynch, Richard M. ACCOUNTING FOR MANAGEMENT: PLANNING AND CONTROL. New York: McGraw-Hill Book Co., 1967. 461p. glossary, charts, tables.

A textbook which provides background information on basic cost concepts and outlines a number of management control techniques.

McNeill, Winfield I. EFFECTIVE COST CONTROL SYSTEMS. Englewood Cliffs, New Jersey: Prentice-Hall, 1965. 232p. charts, forms, tables.

Discusses in detail how to choose a cost system, its formulation and installation, how to operate it effectively and use it as a planning tool. Numerous illustrations increase the effectiveness of the text material.

Marple, Raymond P., ed. NATIONAL ASSOCIATION OF ACCOUNTANTS ON DIRECT COSTING: SELECTED PAPERS. New York: Ronald Press, 1965. 451p. illus.

A collection of readings on direct costing which have appeared in publications of the NAA from 1936 to 1964.

Matz, Adolph, et al. COST ACCOUNTING, 4th ed. Cincinnati: South-Western Publishing Co., 1967. 973p. charts, tables.

Textbook which covers both basic cost accounting methods and procedures and the value of cost techniques in management decision making and control.

Miller, Myron M. and Viosca, Robert R. USING DIRECT COSTING FOR PROFIT AND PRODUCT IMPROVEMENT. Englewood Cliffs, New Jersey: Prentice-Hall, 1967. 255p. charts, tables.

Describes management control techniques to be used to increase profits.

National Association of Accountants. NAA RESEARCH REPORTS. New York: 1959- . pap.

This series started in 1943 as the RESEARCH SERIES. Each study reviews some aspect of cost or control accounting and presents an in-depth description including the theory behind the practice.

National Industrial Conference Board. ADMINISTRATION OF COST REDUCTION PROGRAMS (Studies in Business Policy, No. 117). New York: 1965 illus., tables. pap.

Based on experiences of 204 manufacturing companies. Illustrates how the various companies run their economy programs.

Neuner, John J.W. COST ACCOUNTING: PRINCIPLES AND PRACTICE, 7th ed. Homewood, Illinois: Richard D. Irwin, 1967. 859p. charts, forms, tables.

Useful for students, businessmen and practicing accountants. Emphasizes managerial use of cost data.

Nickerson, Clarence B. MANAGERIAL COST ACCOUNTING AND ANALYSIS: TEXT, PROBLEMS AND CASES, 2nd ed. New York: McGraw-Hill Book Co., 1962. 644p. charts, forms, tables.

Combines case studies in various industries with the text material.

Pace, Homer St. Clair and Koestler, Edward J. COST ACCOUNTING. New York: Pace & Pace, 1956. 524p. charts, illus., tables.

A standard cost accounting textbook.

Prentice-Hall Editorial Staff. ENCYCLOPEDIA OF COST ACCOUNTING SYSTEMS, 3 vols. Englewood Cliffs, New Jersey: Prentice-Hall, 1965. charts, illus., tables.

Outlines cost accounting systems for 32 industries. Each chapter includes background information on the industry, discussion of the industry's functional set-up for cost control, the cost system itself and cost reporting practices.

Schiff, Michael and Benninger, Lawrence J. COST ACCOUNTING, 2nd ed. New York: Ronald Press, 1963. 664p. charts, forms, tables.

A standard textbook describing the uses of cost accounting in managerial decisions.

Shillinglaw, Gordon. COST ACCOUNTING: ANALYSIS AND CONTROL, rev. ed. Homewood, Illinois: Richard D. Irwin, 1967. 931p. charts, tables.

Excellent analysis of cost accounting and management uses of cost accounting information.

Specthrie, Samuel W. BASIC COST ACCOUNTING, 2nd ed. Englewood Cliffs, New Jersey: Prentice-Hall, 1963. 448p. charts, tables.

A textbook especially adapted to a course which concentrates on the teaching of cost procedures.

Taggart, Herbert F. COST JUSTIFICATION (Michigan Business Studies, Vol. 14, No. 3). Ann Arbor: Bureau of Business Research, Graduate School of Business Administration, University of Michigan, 1959. 606p. tables.

A major work on the Robinson-Patman Act, this book covers in detail the cost provisions of Section 2(a) of the Act from 1936 to the Spring of 1958. Includes 18 court and Federal Power Commission cases. Separately published supplements give examples of attempts to justify price differences on the basis of cost.

Supplement No. 1: THOMASVILLE CHAIR COMPANY, 1964. 62p. tables. pap. Supplement No. 2: PHILADELPHIA CARPET COMPANY and CHEMWAY CORPORATION, 1967. 64p. tables. pap.

Terrill, William A. and Patrick, A.W. COST ACCOUNTING FOR MANAGEMENT. New York: Holt, Rinehart & Winston, 1965. 694p. illus.

A textbook designed to familiarize the reader with cost control, cost analysis, and planning for certain aspects of the firm's operations.

Thomas, William E., Jr., ed. READINGS IN COST ACCOUNTING, BUDGETING AND CONTROL, 3rd ed. Cincinnati: South-Western Publishing Co., 1968. 887p.

A collection of writings on cost accounting intended to supplement the many textbooks on the subject. Sections on background and theory of cost accounting, problem areas of accounting for product and period costs, problem areas of planning and control, reports for management.

Tipper, Harry, Jr. CONTROLLING OVERHEAD. New York: American Management Association, 1966. 125p.

Directed toward the businessman who deals with the costs of overhead.

Weber, Charles. THE EVOLUTION OF DIRECT COSTING (Monograph 3). Urbana, Illinois: Center for International Education and Research in Accounting, University of Illinois, 1966. 121p. biblio., charts, tables. pap.

Chapters on fundamentals of direct costing, the development of basic techniques used in direct costing, the development of direct costing prior to World War II and the development of direct costing since World War II. References to European theories and literature on direct costing.

Woolsey, Samuel M. DIRECT COSTING TECHNIQUES FOR INDUSTRY. Englewood Cliffs, New Jersey: Prentice-Hall, 1967. 203p. charts, tables.

Explains the direct cost system in non-technical language.

Wright, Wilmer. DIRECT STANDARD COSTS FOR DECISION MAKING AND CONTROL. New York: McGraw-Hill Book Co., 1962. 235p. charts, forms, tables.

Presentation of direct standard costs as a management tool.

CREDIT AND COLLECTION

Beckman, Theodore N. CREDITS AND COLLECTIONS, MANAGEMENT AND THEORY, 8th ed. New York: McGraw-Hill Book Co., 1969. 736p. charts, forms.

Emphasis is placed on the management functions of credit business.

Chapin, Albert F. and Hassett, George, Jr. CREDIT AND COLLECTION, PRINCIPLES AND PRACTICE, 7th ed. New York: McGraw-Hill Book Co., 1960. 603p. biblio., illus., tables.

A standard text in the credit field. Part 4 is on protection and redemption of credit.

Cole, Robert H. CONSUMER AND COMMERCIAL CREDIT MANAGEMENT, 3rd ed. Homewood, Illinois: Richard D. Irwin, 1968. 631p. forms, tables.

Includes both business and consumer credit, including enlarged coverage of revolving credit and installment loan plans. Analysis and interpretation of financial statements in credit decisions are discussed in chapters 27 and 28.

Credit Research Foundation. CREDIT MANAGEMENT HANDBOOK, 2nd ed.

Homewood, Illinois: Richard D. Irwin, 1965. 812p. figures, tables.
A comprehensive manual which seeks to provide both the principles of credit management and answers to day-to-day credit problems. Section on financial statement analysis.

Ettinger, Richard P. and Golieb, David E. CREDITS AND COLLECTIONS, 5th ed. Englewood Cliffs, New Jersey: Prentice-Hall, 1962. 408p. charts, forms, tables.
Includes several chapters on items in the financial statement and analysis of these items, such as bad debt reserves, accounts receivable, etc.

Lazere, Monroe R., ed. COMMERCIAL FINANCING. New York: Ronald Press, 1968. 318p. forms.
A collection of writings on secured and non-secured business loans by authorities in both bank and commercial lending fields. Discusses financing of installment and time sales, inventory, imports and exports, real estate, equipment leases, mergers and acquisitions, etc.

National Association of Credit Management. CREDIT MANUAL OF COMMERCIAL LAWS. New York: annual.
Analyzes the Federal and State laws and regulations concerning credit functions. Indexed by subjects and states.

National Conference of Bankers and Certified Public Accountants (Section II on Financial Reporting of Borrowers). FINANCIAL STATEMENT PROVISIONS IN TERM-LOAN AGREEMENTS. New York: American Bankers Association; American Institute of Certified Public Accountants, September 1968. 16p. pap.
The second in a series of statements issued by the Conference which is composed of representatives of The American Bankers Association, The American Institute of Certified Public Accountants and Robert Morris Associates. Part 1 consists of a "point-outline," discussing in detail the various points involved in a term-loan agreement. Part 2 gives suggested wording of financial statement provisions in term-loan agreements.

Phelps, Clyde William. RETAIL CREDIT FUNDAMENTALS, 4th ed. St. Louis, Missouri: International Consumer Credit Association, 1963. 275p. forms.
Concentrates on basic functions to be performed in credit management. Sections on acquiring new business, controlling the account and collecting the account. Chapter 19 is on bookkeeping for credit control. No index.

Seidman, Walter S. ACCOUNTS RECEIVABLE AND INVENTORY FINANCING. Ann Arbor, Michigan: Masterco Press, 1957. 147p. forms.
A collection of lectures given by the author. Explains the finance business in non-technical language, covering factoring, accounts receivable, export and import financing, and installment sales financing. No index.

Shultz, William J. and Reinhardt, Hedwig. CREDIT AND COLLECTION MANAGEMENT, 3rd ed. Englewood Cliffs, New Jersey: Prentice-Hall, 1962. 655p. forms, illus., tables.
A basic textbook in the credit field. Supplementary readings at the end of each chapter.

DEPRECIATION

See Asset Accounting

DISTRIBUTION COSTS

See also Cost Accounting

American Institute of Certified Public Accountants: COST ANALYSIS FOR PRICING AND DISTRIBUTION POLICIES (Management Services Technical Study, No. 2). New York: 1965. 138p. biblio., illus., tables. pap.
First section outlines the types of analyses CPAs might be called upon to provide in the distribution cost and pricing field. Four case studies are then discussed in some detail.

Eisner, Frederick M. "Distribution Cost Accounting and Analysis." In Prentice-Hall, Inc., ACCOUNTANT'S ENCYCLOPEDIA, Vol. 1. New York: 1962. pp.385-431.
Gives detailed instructions, including illustrations, for the installation of a distribution cost accounting system based on 24 key forms.

Heckert, J. Brooks and Miner, Robert B. DISTRIBUTION COSTS, 2nd ed. New York: Ronald Press, 1954. 396p. biblio., forms, tables.
Part I discusses analysis of distribution costs.
Part II covers methods of controlling these costs. Classification of accounts is given in both parts.

Longman, Donald R. and Schiff, Michael. PRACTICAL DISTRIBUTION COST ANALYSIS. Homewood, Illinois: Richard D. Irwin, 1955. 462p. forms, tables. (o.p.)
A comprehensive review of distribution costing. Includes background on financial and cost accounting and on manufacturing cost systems.

Mossman, Frank H. DIFFERENTIAL DISTRIBUTION COST AND REVENUE ANALYSIS: A NEW APPROACH (Marketing and Transportation Paper, No. 10). East Lansing, Michigan: Bureau of Business and Economic Research, Graduate School of Business Administration, Michigan State University, 1962. 34p. charts, tables. pap.
Shows how distribution costs can be based on factors which cause variations in the marketing of a product.

Parent, André. DISTRIBUTION COSTS, THEIR CONTROL AND ANALYSIS (Special Study, No. 3). Hamilton, Ontario: Society of Industrial and Cost Accountants of Canada, 1962. 84p. biblio., charts, tables.
Studies in detail the control and analysis of advertising and selling expenses. Avalon Company case study, pp.29-66.

Schiff, Michael and Mellman, Martin. FINANCIAL MANAGEMENT OF THE MARKETING FUNCTION. New York: Financial Executives Research Foundation, 1962. 270p. charts, illus.
A study of the marketing cost control and analysis practices of 28 selected companies.

Steel Service Center Institute and National Association of Aluminum Distributors. DISTRIBUTION COST ANALYSIS FOR METALS DISTRIBUTORS: MANUAL OF INSTRUCTION. Cleveland, Ohio: 1960. v.p. charts, tables. looseleaf.

Presents suggested distribution cost analysis techniques to be used in member distributors' "Statement of Product-Line Profitability."

ECONOMICS AND ACCOUNTING

See also Price Level Changes

American Accounting Association. National Income Committee. A SURVEY OF ECONOMIC ACCOUNTING. Columbus, Ohio: 1958. 116p. biblio., tables. pap.

Reviews rather than researches the field of national economic accounting. Emphasis placed on the national income and product accounts although the flow-of-funds system, input-output tables and balance of payments accounting are also covered.

Canning, John G. THE ECONOMICS OF ACCOUNTANCY: A CRITICAL ANALYSIS OF ACCOUNTING THEORY. New York: Ronald Press, 1929. 367p. (o.p.)

A study of accounting theory and practice from the point of view of the professional student of economics.

Chambers, Raymond J. ACCOUNTING, EVALUATION AND ECONOMIC BEHAVIOR. Englewood Cliffs, New Jersey: Prentice-Hall, 1966. 388p. charts.

Interesting presentation of accounting as a principal source of current measurement of financial relationships and economic actions.

Corbin, Donald A. ACCOUNTING AND ECONOMIC DECISIONS. New York: Dodd, Mead, 1964. 745p. forms.

Presents accounting as a branch of economics dealing primarily with economic data. Financial accounting and managerial accounting are treated separately.

Dean, Joel. "Profit Measurement." In his MANAGERIAL ECONOMICS. Englewood Cliffs, New Jersey: Prentice-Hall, 1951. pp.12-28.

Shows clearly the difference between economic and accounting costs and their effect on profits.

Edey, Harold C., et al. NATIONAL INCOME AND SOCIAL ACCOUNTING, 3rd rev. ed. London: Hutchinson & Co. (Publishers) Ltd., 1967. 207p. biblio., formulas, tables.

Emphasis is placed on the meanings and purposes of social accounting rather than on the techniques.

Goldsmith, Raymond W. and Lipsey, Robert E. STUDIES IN THE NATIONAL BALANCE SHEET OF THE UNITED STATES, 2 vols. Princeton, New Jersey: Princeton University Press, 1963. charts, tables.

A study undertaken for use in analyzing the capital market structure. Volume II contains basic data on balance sheets and fund flows, presented essentially along the lines of business accounting.

Mathews, Russell. ACCOUNTING FOR ECONOMISTS, 2nd ed. Melbourne, Australia: F.W. Cheshire; Beverly Hills, California: Tri-Ocean, 1965. 604p.

biblio., charts, tables.

Sec. 1: The Accounting Framework.
Sec. 2: Accounting in Business Management.
Sec. 3: Accounting in the National Economy.

National Bureau of Economic Research. National Accounts Review Committee. THE NATIONAL ECONOMIC ACCOUNTS OF THE UNITED STATES: REVIEW, APPRAISAL AND RECOMMENDATIONS. Washington, D.C.: U.S. Government Printing Office, 1958. 202p. tables. pap.

A report to the Joint Economic Committee of the U.S. Congress authorized by the Bureau of the Budget. Presents the National Bureau's proposal, among other recommendations, for an integrated accounting system for the five segments of the national economic accounts: national income and product accounts, international balance of payments statement, flow-of-funds statement, input-output tables and the national balance sheet.

Powelson, John P. ECONOMIC ACCOUNTING. New York: McGraw-Hill Book Co., 1955. 512p. charts, tables. (o.p.)

A textbook which covers accounting principles useful to economists and "relates them to areas of economic thought." Includes both corporation and social accounts in order to familiarize the student with accounting principles and statement structure.

Ray, Delmas D. ACCOUNTING AND BUSINESS FLUCTUATIONS. Gainsville, Florida: University of Florida Press, 1960. 196p. biblio., tables.

A study of the theory that accounting methods cause business cycles or fluctuations by their effect upon business decisions concerning inventory, wages, prices, etc.

Scott, D.R. THE CULTURAL SIGNIFICANCE OF ACCOUNTS. New York: Henry Holt & Co., 1931. [Reprinted by Lucas Brothers, Columbia, Missouri, 1965.] 316p. pap.

Describes the place of accounts and accounting techniques in a process of social and economic development.

United Nations. Statistical Office. Department of Economic and Social Affairs. A SYSTEM OF NATIONAL ACCOUNTS AND SUPPORTING TABLES (Studies in Methods, Series F, No. 2, rev. 2). New York: 1964. 55p. tables. pap.

Establishes a uniform basis for national income statistics reporting. Does not include flow of funds and input-output tables.

ELECTRONIC DATA PROCESSING AND THE ACCOUNTANT

See also Auditing and the Computer, Systems

The subject of electronic data processing is covered thoroughly in Management Information Guide No. 13, ELECTRONIC INDUSTRIES, by Gretchen R. Randle, published in 1968 by Gale Research Company.

Adamson, Lee J., <u>et al</u>. ACCOUNTANTS' DATA PROCESSING SERVICES, MODERN METHODS IN SERVING SMALL CLIENTS. New York: Ronald Press, 1964. 202p. chart of accounts, biblio., charts, forms, illus.

Detailed handbook of methods to be followed in serving small clients.

American Institute of Certified Public Accountants. ACCOUNTING & THE COMPUTER. New York: 1966. 364p. glossary. (o.p.)

A selection of articles on the impact of computers on accounting practices, drawn from the Institute's JOURNAL OF ACCOUNTANCY and MANAGEMENT SERVICES and from technical papers presented at the AICPA'S 1965 annual meeting.

American Institute of Certified Public Accountants. AN APPROACH TO THE USE OF EDP IN AN ACCOUNTING PRACTICE (Computer Research Studies, No. 6). New York: 1968. 75p. biblio., forms.

Directed toward the CPA who intends to provide computer services to his clients. Includes three case studies.

Auerbach Info. Inc. AUERBACH STANDARD EDP REPORTS, 8 vols. Philadelphia: 1963- . loose-leaf.

Encyclopedic reference service covering computer systems characteristics, performances, and related technology. Useful as a reference source to the rapidly changing field of EDP. A condensed version of this service is available in the AUERBACH COMPUTER NOTEBOOK FOR ACCOUNTANTS. Subscriptions to the NOTEBOOK are available through the American Institute of Certified Public Accountants at a greatly reduced rate for Institute members.

Edge, C.G., et al. THE IMPACT OF SYSTEMS AND COMPUTERS ON MANAGEMENT AND ON THE ACCOUNTANT (Special Study No. 6). Hamilton, Ontario: The Society of Industrial and Cost Accountants of Canada, 1966. 223p. biblio., glossary, charts, photos., tables.

Describes the nature of the management function and the techniques of management science and operations research involved in decision making. Explains data processing technical terms. The final chapter assesses the future role of the accountant in computerized decision making.

Florida University. ANNOTATED BIBLIOGRAPHY OF ELECTRONIC DATA PROCESSING (Accounting Series, No. 2). Gainesville: Accounting Department, College of Business Administration, University of Florida, 1964, rev. 1968. 52p. pap.

Offers a comprehensive listing of 60 books and 300 magazine articles.

Gregory, Robert H. and Van Horn, Richard L. AUTOMATIC DATA-PROCESSING SYSTEMS, PRINCIPLES AND PROCEDURES, 2nd ed. Belmont, California: Wadsworth, 1963. 827p. charts, tables.

An excellent text covering the entire field of automatic data-processing. Sections on automatic equipment, systems design, programming and processing procedures, principles of processing systems and equipment acquisition and utilization.

Haskins & Sells. DATA PROCESSING BY ELECTRONICS, A BASIC GUIDE FOR THE UNDERSTANDING AND USE OF A NEW TECHNIQUE. New York: 1955. 113p. pap.

A broad portrayal of the EDP field and the various electronic techniques with suggestions as to preparation for the electronic systems.

Haskins & Sells. INTRODUCTION TO DATA PROCESSING, AN OUTLINE OF BASIC DATA-PROCESSING OPERATIONS AND METHODS. New York: 1957.

107p. pap.
Seeks to give the reader an understanding of the basic concepts.

Konstans, Constantine. THE EFFECTS OF DATA-PROCESSING SERVICE BUREAUS ON THE PRACTICE OF PUBLIC ACCOUNTING (MSU Business Studies). East Lansing, Michigan: Bureau of Business and Economic Research, Graduate School of Business Administration, Michigan State University, 1968. 219p. biblio., tables.
Studies current usage by accounting firms of service bureau applications in reporting financial data, preparing and analyzing information for management decisions and in auditing.

Li, David H. ACCOUNTING, COMPUTERS, MANAGEMENT INFORMATION SYSTEMS. New York: McGraw-Hill Book Co., 1968. 384p. charts, forms, illus.
Covers the computer's role in the accounting process and in the development of management information systems. Section V discusses the auditing of computerized systems.

McRae, Thomas W. THE IMPACT OF COMPUTERS ON ACCOUNTING. New York: John H. Wiley & Sons, 1964. 304p. charts, forms, tables.
The author believes that accounting training methods should be adapted to include mathematical analysis and computer arts in order to keep the role of the accountant on a professional level in the future. Exceptionally lucid explanations of how to use computer systems. Bibliography of data processing, pp.280-90.

Price Waterhouse & Co. MANAGEMENT CONTROL OF ELECTRONIC DATA PROCESSING. White Plains, New York: International Business Machines, 1965. 39p. pap.
Written for International Business Machines Corporation, this pamphlet describes in detail current methods for controlling data processing procedures. Two case studies and a checklist for reviewing adequacy of control are included.

Systems Development Corporation. COMPUTER RESEARCH STUDIES, Nos. 1-6. New York: American Institute of Certified Public Accountants, 1968. pap.
The first five studies, issued in 1966, present the results of a six-month research program on the impact of computers on the public accounting profession, undertaken by the Systems Development Corporation at the request of the Institute. Study No. 6, AN APPROACH TO THE USE OF EDP IN AN ACCOUNTING PRACTICE (1968), is the result of another special research project on this subject.

EXECUTIVE COMPENSATION

See also Pensions and Profit Sharing

American Management Association. EXECUTIVE COMPENSATION SERVICE. New York: 1956- . loose-leaf.
Excellent series of reports covering the salaries and bonuses paid in industry and commerce, the administration and control of executive compensation and various methods of compensation other than direct salary and bonus payments. Separate series of annual reports on top management, middle management, supervisory positions, administrative and technical positions. Periodic revisions

of all other volumes. Recently established INTERNATIONAL COMPENSATION series contains volumes on executive compensation in foreign countries: United Kingdom, Federal Republic of Germany, Mexico, Belgium, Netherlands, Switzerland, France, Argentina, Venezuela, Italy, Brazil, Columbia, Peru, Chile and Puerto Rico. Available on subscription basis, separately by series or in entirety.

Andersen, Arthur & Co. DEFERRED COMPENSATION PLANS, 2nd ed. [Chicago]: 1965. 76p. pap.

A nontechnical discussion of pension plans, profit-sharing plans, deferred compensation contracts and stock options.

Burgess, Leonard Randolph. TOP EXECUTIVE PAY PACKAGE. New York: Free Press of Glencoe, 1963. [Macmillan] 251p. biblio., charts, tables.

A study of the executive pay package as consisting of "salaries, bonuses (current and deferred, stock and cash), dividends on undelivered stock, pensions, deferred cash under contract, thrift and savings plan benefits, and stock option and purchase gains."

Casey, William J. PAY PLANNING, 2 vols. New York: Institute for Business Planning, Inc., 1964. loose-leaf.

A comprehensive review of all types of compensation plans: pension, profit-sharing, stock option, guaranteed pay, sickness and accident, deferred pay, etc. Section on fringe benefits. Includes actual plans used by a number of corporations. Periodically updated.

Dartnell Corporation. EXECUTIVE COMPENSATION. Chicago: 1970. 306p. tables. loose-leaf.

A study of executive earnings, salary ranges, bonus practices, supplementary pay plans and new developments in the theory and practice of executive compensation in over 1,800 companies. Lists specific compensation for various executive positions with selected companies in large number of industries.

Ewing, David W. and Fenn, Dan H., Jr., eds. INCENTIVES FOR EXECUTIVES. New York: McGraw-Hill Book Co., 1962. 236p.

Contains the papers given at the 31st Annual National Business Conference of the Harvard Business School Association, covering a number of topics related to executive compensation.

Halsey, Crawford C. and Peloubet, Maurice E. with the editorial assistance of Robert S. Holzman. FEDERAL TAXATION AND UNREASONABLE COMPENSATION. New York: Ronald Press, 1964. 180p. biblio., tables.

Reviews the situation which arises when an employee's compensation is found unreasonable for income tax purposes.

Lasser Tax Institute, J.K. and Cunnion, John D. TAX PROTECTED COMPENSATION FOR THE EXECUTIVE. Larchmont, New York: Business Reports, Inc., 1965. 222p. tables.

Using numerous examples to illustrate the text, this book reviews all types of executive compensation from the tax angle.

Lewellen, Wilbur G. EXECUTIVE COMPENSATION IN LARGE INDUSTRIAL CORPORATIONS. New York: National Bureau of Economic Research, 1968. 397p. biblio., charts, tables.

Part of a National Bureau project concerned with the effect of federal tax policies on economic growth. This study shows the extent to which supplementary payments such as stock options, deferred compensation, pension benefits and profit sharing plans have replaced salaries and bonuses.

Moore, Russell F., ed. COMPENSATING EXECUTIVE WORTH. New York: American Management Association, 1968. 280p. charts, tables.
Contributions by 11 compensation specialists on how to attract, retain and motivate competent top executives.

National Industrial Conference Board. TOP EXECUTIVE COMPENSATION, by Harland Fox (Studies in Personnel Policy No. 213). New York: 1969. 82p. charts, tables. pap.
The 13th in a series of NICB studies of the three highest-paid executives in a large number of American corporations. Broken down by industry, these studies give salary and bonus information.

Powers, James T. EXECUTIVE COMPENSATION IN RETAILING...in cooperation with Sam Flanel. New York: National Retail Merchants Association, Controllers Congress, 1966. v.p. tables. loose-leaf.
Bulk of survey is composed of tables giving the dollar salary, bonus and total compensation figures for the 18 top executive positions in the 125 participating retail firms, grouped by size of store as indicated by sales volume. Appendices give representative bonus, retirement, profit sharing and stock option plans.

Smyth, Richard C. FINANCIAL INCENTIVES FOR MANAGEMENT. New York: McGraw-Hill Book Co., 1960. [University Microfilms] 319p. charts.
Analyzes the techniques involved in the various types of financial compensation. Several chapters on the corporate organization structure, including job descriptions for top executives.

Sweeney, Daniel L. ACCOUNTING FOR STOCK OPTIONS (Michigan Business Studies, Vol. 14, No. 5). Ann Arbor: Bureau of Business Research, School of Business Administration, University of Michigan, 1960. 236p. tables.
The author feels strongly that the present accounting treatment of stock options is inadequate in that certain elements of compensation are not being charged against income. He suggests the substitution of a cash-value-of-services concept which he presents in some detail.

Washington, George T., et al. COMPENSATING THE CORPORATE EXECUTIVE, 3rd ed., 2 vols. New York: Ronald Press, 1962.
Volume 1 covers salary, profit participation and deferred compensation plans. Volume 2 covers stock, pension and insurance plans.

FINANCIAL RATIOS

Accounting Corporation of America. BAROMETER OF SMALL BUSINESS. San Diego, California: 1948- . pap.
A semiannual publication, giving balance sheet and operation data for more than 50 lines of small retail and service businesses by geographical location and by sales volume. Information is obtained from monthly financial reports submitted by Accounting Corporation clients.

Dun & Bradstreet, Inc. KEY BUSINESS RATIOS. New York: 1931- . pap.
Composed of three parts:

1. KEY BUSINESS RATIOS IN 125 LINES. Each line of business is divided into upper and lower quartile and medium ratios showing such figures as relationship of current assets to current debt, turnover of tangible net worth, net sales to net working capital, current debt to inventory, etc.
2. COST OF DOING BUSINESS IN 185 LINES - CORPORATIONS. Operating ratios derived to provide a guide as to the average amount spent by corporations for these items.
3. COST OF DOING BUSINESS FOR PROPRIETORSHIPS AND PARTNERSHIPS. Covers 102 lines of business, using ratios representing a percentage of business receipts derived from representative samples of income tax returns filed in district offices of the Internal Revenue Service.

Morris, Robert, Associates. SOURCES OF COMPOSITE FINANCIAL DATA, A BIBLIOGRAPHY. Philadelphia: 1967. 24p. pap.

An annotated listing of current publications which give composite balance sheet and/or profit and loss ratios on a number of business lines. Separate sections on manufacturing, wholesale, retail and service fields. Addresses of publishers and prices are included.

Morris, Robert, Associates. STATEMENT STUDIES. Philadelphia: 1923- . pap.

Annual compilation of composite balance sheets and income statements for different lines of business - manufacturers, wholesalers and retailers. Obtained from financial statements supplied by member banks.

News Front. 15,000 LEADING U.S. CORPORATIONS. New York: 1966. 226p. charts, graphs, tables. pap.

Analyzes the largest U.S. manufacturing and non-manufacturing corporations by 17 indexes including sales, profits, assets, employees, plants, share of the market and diversification.

Standard & Poor's Corporation. STANDARD & POOR'S INDUSTRY SURVEYS, 2 vols. New York: loose-leaf.

Annual basic surveys on approximately 50 industries contain comparative financial ratios for the top companies in each industry.

FINANCIAL STATEMENTS AND ANALYSIS

American Institute of Certified Public Accountants. ACCOUNTING TRENDS AND TECHNIQUES. New York: 1948- .

Annual survey of financial statement practices in corporation annual reports. Covers 600 annual reports in detail, reviews an additional 500.

Anderson, Corliss D. CORPORATE REPORTING FOR THE PROFESSIONAL INVESTOR: WHAT THE FINANCIAL ANALYST WANTS TO KNOW. Boston: Financial Analysts Federation, 1962. 114p. charts, graphs, photos. pap.

Reviews financial matters which financial analysts would like to have included in the stockholders' annual report.

Bevis, Herman W. CORPORATE FINANCIAL REPORTING IN A COMPETITIVE ECONOMY (Studies of the Modern Corporation, ed. by Richard Eells, Vol. 1). New York: Macmillan, 1965. 212p. tables.

Good presentation of the value of financial statements as major link between the corporation and its stockholders. Author rejects necessity of imposed uniform accounting principles, feeling that each corporate entity has different problems which should be interpreted freely and flexibly in order to present a true view to the stockholders.

Burton, John C., ed. CORPORATE FINANCIAL REPORTING: CONFLICTS AND CHALLENGES. New York: American Institute of Certified Public Accountants, 1969. 286p.

Contains papers of a symposium jointly sponsored by the AICPA, Financial Analysts Federation, Financial Executives Institute and Robert Morris Associates. First comprehensive compilation of suggestions on how to improve corporate financial reporting by both issuers and users of financial reports.

Floyd, Elizabeth R. PREPARING THE ANNUAL REPORT (AMA Research Study 46). New York: American Management Association, 1960. 112p. charts, photos., tables. pap.

Part 1 describes the various procedures followed with regard to annual report presentation by 278 companies. Part 2, a detailed analysis of 100 reports selected from AMA files and from the participants in this project, shows the relative prominence and importance of the reports' components, e.g. financial statements, president's letter, list of products, etc.

Foster, Louis O. UNDERSTANDING FINANCIAL STATEMENTS AND CORPORATE ANNUAL REPORTS, rev. enlarged ed. Philadelphia: Chilton; Ontario: Thomas Nelson & Sons, Ltd., 1968. 175p.

Slanted toward the business executive and the investor, this book explains in non-technical language the meaning and interpretation of financial statements.

Foulke, Roy A. PRACTICAL FINANCIAL STATEMENT ANALYSIS, 6th ed. New York: McGraw-Hill Book Co., 1968. 736p. tables.

Gives background, development and techniques for analyzing financial statements. Appendix: 1964 tables giving interquartile range of ratios for 72 types of businesses.

Graham, Benjamin and McGolrick, Charles. THE INTERPRETATION OF FINANCIAL STATEMENTS, 2nd rev. ed. New York: Harper & Row, 1964. 117p.

Explains corporation balance sheets and income statements in simple language.

Graham, Benjamin, et al. SECURITY ANALYSIS, PRINCIPLES AND TECHNIQUE, 4th ed. New York: McGraw-Hill Book Co., 1962. 788p. tables.

Analysis of financial statements is covered in Part 2.

Guthmann, Harry G. ANALYSIS OF FINANCIAL STATEMENTS, 4th ed. Englewood Cliffs, New Jersey: Prentice-Hall, 1953. 717p. charts, forms.

Part 1 covers general accounting principles and techniques of statement analysis. Part 2 contains chapters on the financial statements of specific industries: railroads, public utilities, mercantile and manufacturing corporations, mining, banking, insurance and holding companies. Selected reference material is also given.

Helfert, Erich A. TECHNIQUES OF FINANCIAL ANALYSIS, rev. ed.

Homewood, Illinois: Richard D. Irwin, 1967. 233p. charts, graphs, tables. pap.

A textbook which explains in non-technical language methods by which financial managers and analysts can interpret financial statements and other financial reports.

Kennedy, Ralph Dale and McMullen, Stewart Yarwood. FINANCIAL STATEMENTS: FORM, ANALYSIS, AND INTERPRETATION, 5th ed. Homewood, Illinois: Richard D. Irwin, 1968. 744p. illus., tables.

An informative guide to the understanding of financial statements. Part IV discusses financial statements of various types of business, with special attention to air carriers, railroads, public utilities and banks.

Mauriello, Joseph A. ACCOUNTING FOR THE FINANCIAL ANALYST (C.F.A. Monograph Series, No. 1). Homewood, Illinois: Richard D. Irwin, 1967. 148p. forms, tables. pap.

A summary of accounting principles, practices and terminology for use by candidates studying for the C.F.A. examination and by practising financial analysts. Also includes three chapters on financial statement analysis. Bibliographies after each chapter refer to leading textbooks and Opinions of the AICPA Accounting Principles Board.

Mautz, R.K. FINANCIAL REPORTING BY DIVERSIFIED COMPANIES. New York: Financial Executives Research Foundation, 1968. 398p. biblio., charts, tables.

Discusses whether diversified companies should report results of operations on other than total company figures. Findings are based on responses to an Investors Questionnaire answered by 218 financial analysts and investment advisors and a Corporate Questionnaire sent to 412 companies of various sizes representing all major non-regulated industries.

Miller, Donald E. THE MEANINGFUL INTERPRETATION OF FINANCIAL STATEMENTS: THE CAUSE-AND-EFFECT RATIO APPROACH. New York: American Management Association, 1966. 250p.

Intended to give the manager of a business a basic financial understanding with which to apply such analytical techniques as cash flow projections, budgets and forecasts to his own company's needs.

Myer, John N. ACCOUNTING FOR NON-ACCOUNTANTS. Rye, New York: New York University Press, 1957. 232p. forms. (Reprinted by American Research Council, 1967.)

Written in non-technical language for those who, although not accountants, require a basic knowledge of accounting in connection with their work.

Myer, John N. FINANCIAL STATEMENT ANALYSIS, 4th ed. Englewood Cliffs, New Jersey: Prentice-Hall, 1969. 288p. charts, tables.

Gives background and historical development of accounting principles and procedures and explains techniques of financial statement analysis.

Myer, John N. WHAT THE EXECUTIVE SHOULD KNOW ABOUT THE ACCOUNTANT'S STATEMENTS. Larchmont, New York: American Research

Council, 1964. 149p. charts.

Intended to acquaint the non-accounting executive with sufficient accounting knowledge to be able to thoroughly understand the financial condition of a company through the study of its financial statements.

Myer, John N. WHAT THE INVESTOR SHOULD KNOW ABOUT CORPORATE FINANCIAL STATEMENTS, 2nd ed. Larchmont, New York: American Education Council, 1965. 126p. facs.

Explains in simple language the items in financial statements, and shows how the investor can use the information they contain to estimate the financial condition of a business.

National Association of Accountants. EXTERNAL REPORTING FOR SEGMENTS OF A BUSINESS, by Morton Backer and Walter B. McFarland. New York: 1968. 112p. charts, forms, tables. pap.

Analyzes the types of segment financial information most useful to investors and creditors in their decisions concerning diversified companies and suggests that independent auditors in their opinions should accept responsibility for such segment reporting.

National Association of Accountants. FINANCIAL REPORTING FOR SECURITY INVESTMENT AND CREDIT DECISIONS, by Morton Backer. New York: 1970. 283p. tables.

The results of an extensive five year study, this book describes the types of accounting information and the financial reporting methods required by investment analysts and bankers in evaluating corporations.

Prime, John H. INVESTMENT ANALYSIS, 4th ed. Englewood Cliffs, New Jersey: Prentice-Hall, 1967. 446p.

Discusses the general field of investments, securities, security markets, investment policies and estate planning, etc. before going into the analysis of corporate financial statements.

Rappaport, Alfred, et al. PUBLIC REPORTING BY CONGLOMERATES. Englewood Cliffs, New Jersey: Prentice-Hall, 1968. 172p. biblio., forms.

Papers on aspects of public reporting of segmented profit information by U.S. corporations which were delivered at a 1967 symposium given at the Tulane University Graduate School of Business Administration. Includes a synthesis of discussions by the participants.

Ross, Howard. THE ELUSIVE ART OF ACCOUNTING. New York: Ronald Press, 1966. 199p. tables.

An excellent book which, in the author's words, "...attempts to establish what financial statements should accomplish in contrast to what they actually do accomplish, to explore some of the reasons for the apparent shortcomings, and to point out a road towards improvement."

Taylor, Robert G. AN EXAMINATION OF THE EVOLUTION, CONTENT, UTILITY AND PROBLEMS OF PUBLISHED INTERIM REPORTS. Unpublished Ph.D. thesis, Chicago University, Graduate School of Business, August 1963. 218p. tables. typewritten. (Available from University Microfilms).

Against a well-delineated background of the historical development of the published interim report, the author examines current practice including the deficiencies most often found in interim statements, and comes to the conclusion that the accounting profession has rather neglected this aspect of financial reporting.

FRAUD AND DEFALCATION

See also Internal Auditing and Control

Cardwell, Harvey. THE PRINCIPLES OF AUDIT SURVEILLANCE. Princeton: Van Nostrand, 1960. 475p. glossary, forms.

A treatise on embezzlement which proposes the establishment of "audit surveillance" as a definite audit function designed specifically to detect fraud.

Churchill, Allen. THE INCREDIBLE IVAR KREUGER. New York. Rinehart, 1957. 301p. illus., ports. (o.p.)

Biography of Ivar Kreuger which delves into the psychological background of the Match King.

Dicksee, Lawrence R. "Reports of Cases of Professional Interest." In his AUDITING, A PRACTICAL MANUAL FOR AUDITORS, 17th ed. by Brian Magee. London: Gee & Co., 1951. pp.573-852. (o.p.)

Reports of well-known British law cases held from 1887 to 1950.

Jaspan, Norman and Black, Hillel. THE THIEF IN THE WHITE COLLAR. Philadelphis: Lippincott, 1960. 254p.

A collection of cases drawn from the files of the author's management consulting firm, concerning embezzlements by white collar workers. Final chapter offers a brief "system of preventive management."

Keats, Charles. MAGNIFICENT MASQUERADE: THE STRANGE CASE OF DR. COSTER AND MR. MUSICA. New York: Funk & Wagnalls, 1964. 290p. facs., illus., ports.

A fascinating review of the famous McKesson & Robbins case of 1938.

McNew, Bennie B. and Prather, Charles L. FRAUD CONTROL FOR COMMERCIAL BANKS. Homewood, Illinois: Richard D. Irwin, 1962. 187p. biblio., tables.

Gives concrete suggestions for the prevention and detection of bank frauds. Accrual accounting recommended as an effective complement to an internal control system. Includes survey of control practices by 30 banks.

Miller, Norman C. THE GREAT SALAD OIL SWINDLE. New York: Coward-McCann, 1965. 256p.

An expanded outgrowth of the author's reporting for the WALL STREET JOURNAL on the Allied Crude Vegetable Oil Refining Corporation cas case during 1963-64.

Pratt, Lester A. BANK FRAUDS: THEIR DETECTION AND PREVENTION, 2nd ed. New York: Ronald Press, 1965. 284p. figures.

Covers all aspects of detection and prevention of bank frauds. Chapters on "The Accountant as an Expert Witness" and "Auditing Departments Employing Electronic Data Processing." Appendix summarizes on analysis, arranged by departments, of 1,144 actual bank embezzlement cases. cases.

Rogers, Keith M., as told to W.G. Whitham. DETECTION AND PREVENTION

OF BUSINESS LOSSES: HOW TO PROTECT YOUR BUSINESS AGAINST ALL TYPES OF EXTERNAL AND INTERNAL THEFTS. New York: Arco, 1962. 173p. biblio., forms.

Discusses business thefts originating both within and outside the organization. Particular emphasis on inadequate loss control procedures. Chapter on where to turn for assistance in establishing strong controls which includes a checklist giving 54 points to be reviewed in a security audit.

Schmidt, Robert Milton. LEGAL AND ACCOUNTING HANDBOOK OF FEDERAL TAX FRAUD. Englewood Cliffs, New Jersey: Prentice-Hall, 1963. 656p.

Primarily concerned with legal aspects of tax fraud except for Chapter IX, "Role of an Accountant in a Tax Fraud Case."

Shaplen, Robert. KREUGER: GENIUS AND SWINDLER. New York: Knopf, 1960. 278p. photo. (o.p.)

Interesting study of the rise and fall of Ivar Kreuger. Sections of the book were printed in three issues of THE NEW YORKER Magazine in 1959: September 26, October 3 and October 10.

Shaplen, Robert. "The Metamorphosis of Philip Musica." THE NEW YORKER, Vol. 31, No. 36-7. October 22, 1955, pp.49-87; October 29, 1955, pp. 39-87.

Tells the story of the McKesson & Robbins fraud and the man behind it.

Vallance, Aylmer. VERY PRIVATE ENTERPRISE, AN ANATOMY OF FRAUD AND HIGH FINANCE. London: Thames and Hudson, 1955. 205p. (o.p.)

A collection of stories of famous financial market frauds perpetrated in England and America since the 18th century.

INCOME AND CASH FLOW

See also Price Level Changes

Anton, Hector R. ACCOUNTING FOR THE FLOW OF FUNDS. Boston: Houghton Mifflin, 1962. 131p. biblio. pap.

A comprehensive study of flow-of-funds techniques used in business, covering both the theoretical and practical aspects of this method of analysis.

Bedford, Norton M. INCOME DETERMINATION THEORY: AN ACCOUNTING FRAMEWORK. Reading, Massachusetts: Addison-Wesley, 1965. 241p. selected biblio., tables.

An advanced course textbook, this seeks to provide a basic framework of accounting concepts of income from which future income measurements may be evolved.

Bernstein, Leopold A. ACCOUNTING FOR EXTRAORDINARY GAINS AND LOSSES. New York: Ronald Press, 1967. 341p. biblio., tables.

A guide to the presentation in the income statement of extraordinary items of gain and loss. Part I analyzes the theory and Part II discusses the current practice concerning the problem. A detailed tabular presentation of reports analyzed by the author is given on pp.203-95.

Davidson, Sidney, ed. AN INCOME APPROACH TO ACCOUNTING THEORY: READINGS AND QUESTIONS. Englewood Cliffs, New Jersey: Prentice-Hall, 1964. 593p.

A compilation of articles from current professional journals which comprise a survey of the theory and procedures of income determination. CPA examination questions and answers on accounting theory also included.

Dickerson, Peter J. BUSINESS INCOME - A CRITICAL ANALYSIS. Berkeley, California: Institute of Business and Economic Research, 1965. 93p. tables. pap.

In attempting to apply the Edwards and Bell theories (THE THEORY AND MEASUREMENT OF BUSINESS INCOME, 1961) of business income determination to an actual company's operations, the author demonstrates their value and their limitations.

Edwards, Edgar O. and Bell, Philip W. THE THEORY AND MEASUREMENT OF BUSINESS INCOME. Berkeley and Los Angeles, California: University of California Press, 1961. 341p. Selected bibliography of books and articles.

First part develops the theory of business income determination; second part presents accounting techniques for the application of the theory.

Gilman, Stephan. ACCOUNTING CONCEPTS OF PROFIT. New York: Ronald Press, 1939. 650p.

Still interesting presentation of "the more important conventions, doctrines and rules which influence the determination of accounting profits."

Jaedicke, Robert K. and Sprouse, Robert T. ACCOUNTING FLOWS: INCOME, FUNDS, AND CASH. Englewood Cliffs, New Jersey: Prentice-Hall, 1965. 175p. charts, tables. pap.

Presented as a "critical comparative discussion of the flow concepts." Relationship of the three concepts to the balance sheet and their importance in decision making are explained.

Mason, Perry. "CASH FLOW" ANALYSIS AND FUNDS STATEMENTS. (Accounting Research Study, No. 2.) New York: American Institute of Certified Public Accountants, 1961. 98p. biblio. pap.

Part I: "Cash Flow" Analysis. Describes the cash flow concept and emphasizes fact that amount of "cash flow" should not take the place of net income as indicating results of operations or change in financial position.

Part II: The Funds Statement. Describes characteristics of the funds statement, including consolidated funds statements. The author states that "a funds statement, preferably in comparative form, should be treated as a major financial statement."

National Association of Accountants. CASH FLOW ANALYSIS FOR MANAGERIAL CONTROL (NAA Research Report 38). New York: October 15, 1961. 63p. forms. pap.

Concentrates on management of cash assets of a business rather than on preparation of funds statement.

Paton, William A. CORPORATE PROFITS: MEASUREMENT, REPORTING,

DISTRIBUTION, TAXATION, A SURVEY FOR LAYMEN AND ACCOUNTANTS. Homewood, Illinois: Richard D. Irwin, 1965. 158p. tables.

A critical essay of the corporation and corporate profits. Discusses depreciation theories, inflation and financial management, cash-flow analysis, dividend policies, measurement and distribution of earnings.

Robinson, Claude. UNDERSTANDING PROFITS. Princeton, New Jersey: Van Nostrand, 1961. 534p. charts, forms, photos., tables.

An examination of corporate profits from a sociologist's viewpoint that the profit-making corporation is of value to the community.

Study Group on Business Income. CHANGING CONCEPTS OF BUSINESS INCOME. New York: Macmillan, 1952. 160p. biblio., charts. pap. (o.p.)

An historic document on the determination of business income examined from the accounting, legal and economic standpoints.

Study Group on Business Income. FIVE MONOGRAPHS ON BUSINESS INCOME. New York: American Institute of Accountants, July 1, 1950. 279p. pap. (o.p.)

Published under the auspices of the Study Group, these monographs constitute an interesting economic discussion of business income.

Thomas, Arthur L. REVENUE RECOGNITION (Michigan Business Reports, No. 49). Ann Arbor: Bureau of Business Research, Graduate School of Business Administration, University of Michigan, 1966. 175p. tables. pap.

Provides qualified support for, and examines some of the alternatives to, the Sprouse and Moonitz position on the realization rule, which was expressed in the AICPA Accounting Research Study No. 3, "A Tentative Set of Broad Accounting Principles for Business Enterprises."

Windal, Floyd W. THE ACCOUNTING CONCEPT OF REALIZATION (Occasional Paper No. 5). East Lansing, Michigan: Bureau of Business and Economic Research, Graduate School of Business Administration, Michigan State University, 1961. 90p. pap.

Treats the economic, legal and accounting concepts of realization in an effort to clarify the term in its technical accounting usage. The final chapter is a critical analysis of the realization concept itself. Brief bibliographies at the end of each chapter.

Zeff, Stephan A. and Keller, Thomas F., eds. FINANCIAL ACCOUNTING THEORY: ISSUES AND CONTROVERSIES. New York: McGraw-Hill Book Co., 1964. 466p. ports.

A collection of readings by well-known authorities which is "geared to the core of income determination theory" covered in the typical intermediate accounting course. Bibliographies at end of each section. A second volume, published 1969, covers a wider range of topics and also includes excellent bibliographies.

INTERNAL AUDITING AND CONTROL

See also Auditing, Auditing and the Computer,
Fraud and Defalcation, and Management Audit

American Institute of Certified Public Accountants. CASE STUDIES IN INTERNAL CONTROL, Nos. 1- . New York: 1950- . pap.

No. 1: Based on actual case in which internal control procedures were reviewed. Includes a detailed internal control questionnaire checklist with comments by auditor on adequacy of system. Describes case study No. 2: a case in which an accountant evaluated the internal control situation and applies his findings in an actual audit.

American Institute of Certified Public Accountants. INTERNAL CONTROL. New York: 1949. 24p. pap.

Although not recent, this pamphlet is one of the most useful introductions to internal control. Includes ten organization and procedural flow charts.

Brink, Victor Z. INTERNAL AUDITING, rev. by James A. Cashin, 2nd ed. New York: Ronald Press, 1958. 478p. chart.

Aims to be of practical use to the public accountant and corporate financial officer as well as the internal auditor. Appendix III, entitled "Review of Internal Control," is an unusually comprehensive review of procedures to be followed in an internal audit.

Cadmus, Bradford and Child, Arthur J.E. INTERNAL CONTROL AGAINST FRAUD AND WASTE. Englewood Cliffs, New Jersey: Prentice-Hall, 1953. 330p. (Available from the Institute of Internal Auditors.)

Developed as a project of the Institute of Internal Auditors. This excellent book reviews the general safeguards of internal control in a given aspect of business, e.g. billing; then gives several case histories of frauds in that particular field, pointing out omissions in the control systems which made the frauds possible.

Institute of Internal Auditors. INTERNAL AUDIT REPORTING PRACTICES (Research Committee Report, No. 10). New York: 1961. 76p. biblio. pap.

Includes excerpts from specimen audit reports as well as several complete reports.

Institute of Internal Auditors. PROCEEDINGS...INTERNATIONAL CONFERENCE. New York: 1943- . pap.

Through 1960 this annual volume was issued under separate titles. The first two volumes, 1943-4, included papers and addresses given throughout the entire season. Both the 1943 volume, INTERNAL AUDITING, A NEW MANAGEMENT TECHNIQUE and the 1944 INTERNAL AUDITING, PHILOSOPHY AND PRACTICE contain sections on the relationship of public accounting to internal auditing.

Lamperti, Frank A. and Thurston, John B. INTERNAL AUDITING FOR MANAGEMENT. Englewood Cliffs, New Jersey: Prentice-Hall, 1953. 510p. charts. (o.p.)

Emphasizes the relationship of internal auditing to management controls.

National Industrial Conference Board. INTERNAL AUDITING, by Francis J. Walsh, Jr. (Business Policy Study, No. 111.) New York: 1963. 81p. charts, forms. pap.

Based on a study of practices in 177 companies, this report covers in some detail the activities and administration of the internal auditing function. Chapter 2 on "The Internal Auditing Department" contains a number of excellent organization charts and job descriptions drawn from the companies participating in the study.

Thurston, John B. BASIC INTERNAL AUDITING PRINCIPLES AND TECHNIQUES. Scranton, Pennsylvania: International Textbook Co., 1949. 106p. chart.

The first of the internal auditing texts and still valuable for its detailed treatment of that activity.

Walker, W.A. and Davies, W.R. INDUSTRIAL INTERNAL AUDITING. New York: McGraw-Hill Book Co., 1951. [University Microfilms]. 329p. forms.

Although not a recent publication, this is generally considered one of the most practical books on internal auditing. Emphasis is placed on the requirements of industrial corporations.

INTERNATIONAL ACCOUNTING

The papers presented at the various international accounting congresses are among the most valuable sources of international accounting information. These congresses include the International Congresses of Accountants, The Inter-American Accounting Conferences, the Asian and Pacific Accounting Conventions and the European Accounting Congresses.

For publications of the Canadian Institute of Chartered Accountants and the Institute of Chartered Accountants in England and Wales, see Section 2, Rise as a Profession, Foreign Accounting Associations.

Accountants International Study Group. ACCOUNTING AND AUDITING APPROACHES TO INVENTORIES IN THREE NATIONS. London: 1968. 36p. pap.

The Accountants International Study Group is composed of members from the American Institute of Certified Public Accountants, the Canadian Institute of Chartered Accountants, the Institute of Chartered Accountants in England and Wales, the Institute of Chartered Accountants of Scotland and the Institute of Chartered Accountants in Ireland. The purpose of the Group is "to institute comparative studies as to accounting thought and practice in participating countries..." and to make reports which will be issued to members by the sponsoring Institutes. This comparative survey on inventory accounting and auditing is the first of a series planned by the Group.

American Institute of Certified Public Accountants. Committee on Foreign Affairs. ACCOUNTING FOR INTERNATIONAL TRADE AND INVESTMENT. New York: 1954. 4p. pap. (o.p.)

Although now out-of-print, this brief pamphlet is still a valid statement of the problems created by nationalistic restrictions on the practice of accounting.

American Institute of Certified Public Accountants. PROFESSIONAL ACCOUNTING IN 25 COUNTRIES. New York: 1964. v.p. exhibits.

Gives data on accounting principles, auditing standards, reporting practices and professional requirements in various countries throughout the free world. Provides illustrative financial statements in both the local language and in English.

American Institute of Certified Public Accountants. Committee on International Relations. ACCOUNTING AND OTHER REQUIREMENTS FOR THE SALE OF FOREIGN SECURITIES IN THE U.S. CAPITAL MARKET, rev. New York:

1962. 32p. pap.
Outlines general considerations for foreign companies seeking public financing in the U.S. and the requirements for financial disclosure to investors.

American Management Association. FINANCING INTERNATIONAL OPERATIONS, A GUIDE TO SOURCES AND METHODS, ed. by William D. Falcon. (Management Report No. 82.) New York: 1965. 192p. pap.
A collection of reports by executives in the financial field on the financial problems of international operations.

Andersen & Co., Arthur. DICCIONARIO DE TERMINOS CONTABLES Y COMERCIALES. DICTIONARY OF ACCOUNTING AND BUSINESS TERMS. New York: 1962. 228p. pap.
Designed for the firm's employees in Spanish-speaking countries, this is an excellent Spanish-English and English-Spanish listing of accounting terms. Appendices include weights and measures, numbers and fractions and currencies of member countries of the International Monetary Fund.

Andersen & Co., Arthur. TAX AND TRADE GUIDES. New York: 1961- pap.
These guides offer basic data on the government, laws, business organization and other information pertinent to doing business in a number of foreign countries.

Berg, Kenneth B., et al. READINGS IN INTERNATIONAL ACCOUNTING. Boston: Houghton Mifflin, 1969. 315p.
A collection of articles on various aspects of international accounting. They are arranged in four sections: international dimensions of accounting, patterns of accounting development, bridging the gap in accounting between countries and areas, and selected practical international accounting problems. Additional selected references are listed at the end of each section.

Business International. ACCOUNTING PRACTICES IN FLUCTUATING-CURRENCY COUNTRIES. New York: 1963. 20p. pap. mimeo.
A rather interesting discussion on the subject based on information "from sources which we believe to be reliable..." Includes a description of the accounting methods used by seven companies in handling international operations.

Campbell, Robert W. ACCOUNTING IN SOVIET PLANNING AND MANAGEMENT (Harvard University Russian Research Center Studies, No. 45.) Cambridge, Massachusetts: Harvard University Press, 1963. 315p. glossary, bibliographical notes, illus.
Drawn chiefly from official Soviet laws and institutions, Soviet accounting handbooks and textbooks, the author describes accounting under a planned economy.

Cooper, Vivian R.V. MANUAL OF AUDITING, 2nd ed. London: Gee & Co. (Publishers) Ltd., 1969. 704p.
The authoritative British auditing text. Includes internal control questionnaires and specimen audit programs.

Corporation Accounting Specialists Study Team. CURRENT CONDITION OF

CORPORATION ACCOUNTING IN JAPAN. Tokyo, Japan: Japan Productivity Center, International Cooperation Administration, 1959. 24p. tables. pap.

Describes briefly the state of both financial and managerial accounting in Japan.

Cowan, T.K. FINANCIAL ACCOUNTING IN NEW ZEALAND. Wellington, New Zealand: Sweet and Maxwell (N.Z.) Ltd., 1960. 318p. illus.

Emphasizes the place of the accountant as a "member of the management team" rather than simply the "technician" of financial statements. Covers thoroughly, however, all the various aspects of corporate financial accounting. Includes chapters on planning, controlling, and operating the accounting system; presentation of annual reports; holding company and group accounts; analysis and interpretation of accounting statements; price level changes; valuation of goodwill, etc.

Ernst & Ernst. INTERNATIONAL BUSINESS SERIES. Cleveland: 1964- . pap.

Describes characteristics of business entities and digests of principal taxes in various countries. Each booklet contains a glossary of terms with the English equivalent.

Fitzgerald, Alexander. FITZGERALD'S ANALYSIS AND INTERPRETATION OF FINANCIAL STATEMENTS, 4th ed. (Butterworth Tax and Commercial Series No. 23.) Sydney: Butterworth & Co., 1966. 234p. graphs, tables.

Concerned with the technique of analysis and methods of interpretation of corporate financial statements from the Australian point of view.

Foreningen af Statsautoriserede Revisorer. ALMINDELIG INFORMATION, MEDLEMSFORTEGNELSE, LOVE OG VEDTAEGTER. Copenhagen, Denmark: 1968. 134p. pap.

Annual publication of the Danish Institute, which, in addition to the usual membership information, contains the more important pronouncements of the Institute's Council. Includes the Bookkeeping Law and regulation concerning scope and contents of bookkeeping. Extracts of various laws of interest to the practising accountant are given. Issued in Danish language.

Gonzalez, Francisco F., IV. LAWS AND ETHICS OF ACCOUNTANCY IN THE PHILIPPINES. Manila, Philippines: Conanan Educational Supply, 1958. 190p.

Covers in some detail three important aspects of the accountancy profession in the Philippines: Act 3105, the 1923 act regulating the practice of public accounting; the Code of Ethics in the Philippines; and the legal responsibilities of the Philippine CPA.

Hanner, Per V.A. ACCOUNTING TECHNIQUES IN ANNUAL REPORTS OF 100 SWEDISH CORPORATIONS: 1949-1951 (English summary of Stockholm Business Research Institute Report No. 43.) Stockholm, Sweden: Stockholm Business Research Institute, 1953. 15p.

This survey is updated periodically.

Haskins & Sells. INTERNATIONAL TAX AND BUSINESS SERVICE. New York: 1965- . pap.

Intended to serve as background information when considering doing business in a foreign country, these booklets concentrate on the tax aspects of conducting a business. Available in loose-leaf binders or as separate booklets.

Hepworth, Samuel R. REPORTING FOREIGN OPERATIONS (Michigan Business Studies, Vol. 12, No. 5.) Ann Arbor, Michigan: Bureau of Business Research, University of Michigan, 1956. 211p. tables.

Explores major problem areas in investment in foreign subsidiaries and suggests accounting and reporting techniques applicable.

Institut der Wirtschaftsprüfer. DIE FACHGUTACHTEN UND STELLUNGNAHMEN. Dusseldorf, Germany: 1968.

Official opinions and positions of the German Institute, giving recommendations and directives on accounting matters which are expected to be observed by the accountancy profession in Germany. Issued in German language.

Institut der Wirtschaftsprüfer. WIRTSCHAFTSPRÜFER-HANDBUCH, 1968. Dusseldorf, Germany: 1968. 2183p.

Familiarly known as the WP HANDBUCH. Gives the history of the accountancy profession in Germany, outlining the accountant's duties and obligations, professional ethics, etc. Covers auditing standards and practice in great detail and includes a section on cost accounting. Long sections on the revised Corporation Law of 1965 and the statutory rules of civil and commercial law which might be of interest to an auditor. Consolidated statements are discussed in detail. Issued in German language.

Institute of Chartered Accountants in Australia. PROFESSIONAL CONDUCT. Sydney: January 1967- . loose-leaf.

A codification of some of the fundamental rules of the Institute and the rulings of the General Council on ethical matters. (See also PROFESSIONAL ETHICS OF THE CHARTERED ACCOUNTANT IN AUSTRALIA.)

Institute of Chartered Accountants in Australia. PROFESSIONAL ETHICS OF THE CHARTERED ACCOUNTANT IN AUSTRALIA, 2nd ed., by H.W. Chancellor. Sydney: 1963. 48p. pap.

Originally presented as a paper at an accounting congress, this guide to ethical conduct is kept current by supplements issued by the Australian Institute to its members.

Institute of Chartered Accountants in Australia. STATEMENT ON GENERAL PRINCIPLES OF PROFESSIONAL AUDITING PRACTICE. Sydney: 1960; reprinted, 1966. 12p. pap.

Discusses the nature of accounts and the auditor's responsibilities before outlining general principles governing the audit and its approach.

Institute of Chartered Accountants in Australia. STATEMENTS ON ACCOUNTING PRINCIPLES AND RECOMMENDATIONS ON ACCOUNTING PRACTICE. Sydney: February, 1968. 55p. pap.

A compilation of the Australian Institute's Recommendations which were started in 1946. These are based on the Recommendations of the Institute of Chartered Accountants of England and Wales which are generally applicable to Australian practice.

I. Presentation of Balance Sheet and Profit and Loss Account. II. Treatment of Stock-in-Trade and Work in Progress in Financial Accounts. III. Accountants' Reports for Prospectuses. Two unnumbered statements promulgated in 1946 are included since they are still current: "The Treatment of Taxation in Accounts" and "Depreciation of Fixed Assets." Two statements were issued separately in May 1968 by the Australian Institute which are based on the similarly-titled English Institute's Recommendations: AUDITOR'S REPORTS ON GROUP ACCOUNTS and QUALIFICATIONS IN AUDITORS' REPORTS.

Institute of Chartered Accountants of India. AUDIT OF BANKING COMPANIES (Research Study No. 1.) New Delhi, India: 1967. 68p. pap.
A detailed presentation of the procedures for conducting a bank audit.

Institute of Chartered Accountants of India. A GUIDE TO COMPANY AUDIT, 2nd ed. New Delhi, India: 1962. 63p. pap.
Intended to give "general guidance for the conduct of audits and accounting matters," this pamphlet takes into consideration the 1960 amendments to the Company Act of 1956.

Institute of Chartered Accountants of India. REPORT OF THE JOINT COMMITTEE ON THE FUTURE OF THE ACCOUNTANCY PROFESSION IN INDIA (supplement to THE CHARTERED ACCOUNTANT, Vol. XVII, pt. II, August 1968.) New Delhi, India: 1968. 156p. pap.
Prepared jointly with the Institute of Cost and Works Accountants of India, this report strongly recommends the establishment of a single intergrated Institute to regulate the accountancy profession in India. Recommendations on accountants' education and training as well as definite criteria of membership, administration, etc. of the proposed Institute are included. Appendix gives summary of conclusions and recommendations.

Institute of Chartered Accountants of India. STATEMENT ON AUDITING PRACTICES, 2nd ed. New Delhi, India: 1968. 82p. pap.
Describes appropriate procedures to be followed by the auditor in India. Concentrates on audits of manufacturing and trading companies.

Institute of Chartered Accountants of India. STATEMENT ON THE TREATMENT OF RETIREMENT GRATUITY IN ACCOUNTS. New Delhi, India: 1966. 15p. pap.
A guide to be used in determining the best method in accounting for retirement gratuities.

Institute of Chartered Accountants of Pakistan. WHAT IS A CHARTERED ACCOUNTANT. Karachi, Pakistan: 1963. 18p. pap.
Includes a brief history of the accountancy profession in Pakistan and a description of the current work of a Pakistani accountant. Tells how to become a member of the Institute. Has chapters on "professional conduct and ethics" and "duties and obligations of

an auditor."

Instituto Mexicano de Contadores Publicos. BOLETINES DE LA COMISION DE ORIENTACION DE PRACTICA PROFESIONAL, No. 1- . Mexico, D.F.: 1964- . pap.

A series of bulletins issued by the Institute's Committee on Professional Practice which offer recommendations on professional matters to be followed by the Mexican accountant. Issued in Spanish language only.

Instituto Mexicano de Contadores Publicos. BOLETINES DE LA COMISION PROCEDIMIENTOS DE AUDITORIA, No. 1- . Mexico, D.F.: 1956- . pap.

These bulletins, issued by the Institute's Committee on Auditing Prgctice, are similar to the AICPA STATEMENTS ON AUDITING PROCEDURE, covering the same general subject matter. Although not binding on members, they represent the generally accepted auditing standards and procedures.

A compilation of Bulletins Nos. 1-21 was published in 1965 by the Institute, entitled NORMAS Y PROCEDIMIENTOS DE AUDITORIA. Issued in Spanish language.

International Finance Corporation. ACCOUNTING AND FINANCIAL REPORTING. Washington, D.C.: August 1964. 14p. pap.

A brief presentation of the accounting practices to be followed by business enterprises dealing with the IFC.

International Finance Corporation. ILLUSTRATIVE FORM OF AUDIT REPORT (DEVELOPMENT FINANCE COMPANIES). Washington, D.C.: October 1965. 22p. pap.

A guide for development finance companies in which the IFC has invested, to which the World Bank has made loans or the International Development Association has extended credits.

International Monetary Fund. ANNUAL REPORT ON EXCHANGE RESTRICTIONS. Washington, D.C.: 1950- . pap.

An excellent review of foreign exchange information on member countries of the Fund. Includes a chronological listing of changes during the past year for each country.

Leonard, W.G. CANADIAN ACCOUNTANT'S HANDBOOK. Toronto: McGraw-Hill Company of Canada, Ltd., 1968. 572p. tables.

Handbook of accounting principles and procedures outlined in the context of Canadian laws and practices. Includes sections on federal and provincial taxes.

Mueller, Gerhard G. A BIBLIOGRAPHY OF INTERNATIONAL ACCOUNTING, rev. ed. Seattle, Washington: University of Washington, 1968. 66p. processed. pap. (Copies available from author.)

Comprehensive English-language bibliography compiled for purposes of research and graduate study in international accounting at the University of Washington. Entries are arranged by geographic areas.

Mueller, Gerhard G. INTERNATIONAL ACCOUNTING. New York: Macmillan, 1967. 269p.

Detailed textbook presentation of problems in international accounting. Part I: Comparative patterns of accounting development.
Part II: International dimensions of accounting and financial reporting practices. Selected reference lists at end of each chapter.

Mueller, Gerhard G. STUDIES IN ACCOUNTING (International Business Series), No. 1- . Seattle, Washington: Graduate School of Business Administration, University of Washington, 1962- . pap.
These small pamphlets give excellent presentations of the essentials of accounting and auditing in the countries covered: the Netherlands (No. 1), Sweden (No. 2), Argentina (No. 3), West Germany (No. 4), and Japan (No. 5). All except No. 2 include short bibliographies. An interesting review of the early pamphlets appears in the August 1965 issue of The Journal of Accountancy. May be purchased separately from the publisher.

National Association of Accountants. MANAGEMENT ACCOUNTING PROBLEMS IN FOREIGN OPERATIONS (Research Report No. 36). New York: 1960. 71p. pap.
Deals primarily with problems inherent in the translation of foreign currencies in financial reports to management.

National Council of Chartered Accountants (S.A.) SOUTH AFRICAN CHARTERED ACCOUNTANT'S HANDBOOK. Johannesburg, South Africa: 1964. loose-leaf.
Contains authoritative statements issued by the National Council as well as Rules of Professional Conduct.
Section A: Statements on Auditing.
A1 - Auditing Principles and Standards
A2 - Stock in Trade and Work in Progress
A3 - Electronic Data Processing Systems

Section B: General Statements.
B1 - Guide to Incoming Auditors Following a Change in the Appointment
B2 - The Duties of Members of the Provincial Societies in Public Practice in Respect of Unlawful Acts or Unlawful Defaults of their Clients Including Officers and Employees of Clients Acting in the Performance of their Duties to Clients

All statements are issued in both English and Afrikaans.

New Zealand Society of Accountants. Board of Research and Publications. STATEMENTS ON ACCOUNTING AND AUDITING PRACTICE, No. 1- . Wellington, New Zealand: 1964- . pap.
Originally published in the Society's journal, THE ACCOUNTING JOURNAL, as "Tentative Statements on Accounting Practice" and "Tentative Statements on Auditing Practice." Although these pronouncements "do not represent official Society policy, nor will conformity with them be mandatory in any way," they are generally considered to indicate majority views concerning accounting and auditing standards in the various fields covered.

Statements on Accounting Practice:

B-1 Presentation of Company Balance Sheets and Profit and Loss Accounts, September 1966.

Statements on Auditing Practice:

C-1 General Principles of Auditing, September 1966.
C-2 Events after Balance Date: The Auditor's Responsibility, September 1966.

Peat, Marwick, Mitchell & Co. INTERNATIONAL TAX AND BUSINESS GUIDE TO... [New York]: 1967- .

Handbooks outlining trading conditions in foreign countries. The first of the series deals with Italy.

Philippine Institute of Certified Public Accountants. ACCOUNTING PRINCIPLES BULLETINS, No. 1- . Manila, Philippines: November 1968- . pap.

Bulletin No. 1, BASIC CONCEPTS IN ACCOUNTING FOR BUSINESS ENTERPRISE, lists ten basic concepts with explanatory comments on each.

Philippine Institute of Certified Public Accountants. AUDIT BULLETINS, No. 1- . Manila, Philippines: 1949- . pap.

Official pronouncements of the Philippine Institute on auditing matters. Bulletin No. 15, GUIDES TO IMPLEMENTATION OF THE GENERALLY ACCEPTED AUDITING STANDARDS, issued in 1968, is the most comprehensive of the series, covering all aspects of the auditor's work.

Price Waterhouse & Co. INFORMATION GUIDES FOR THOSE DOING BUSINESS OUTSIDE THE UNITED STATES OF AMERICA. [New York]: 1959- . pap.

A series of guides on business conditions in countries in which Price Waterhouse & Co. has offices. Booklets regularly revised and updated.

Rappaport, Louis H. "Differences in Accounting Principles Generally Accepted in the United States as Compared with those in Certain Foreign Countries." In his SEC ACCOUNTING PRACTICE AND PROCEDURE, 2nd ed., rev. New York: Ronald Press, 1966. v.p. Appendix C.

Rappaport, Louis H. "Differences in Auditing Standards and Procedures in the United States as Compared with those in Certain Foreign Countries." In his SEC ACCOUNTING PRACTICE AND PROCEDURE, 2nd ed., rev. New York: Ronald Press, 1966. v.p. Appendix D.

Rydell, Ferd. THE ACCOUNTING PROFESSION IN PAKISTAN, INDIA, BURMA AND THAILAND: A COMPARATIVE STUDY. Karachi, India: Institute of Business Administration, University of Karachi, 1960. 272p. pap.

Reviews the current state of the accounting profession in these countries. The author emphasizes in his introduction the fact that the profession in these countries is still in a developing stage and that their present program of industrialization is placing the accountant in a far more important position than he previously held. Lack of funds and trained personnel are the major problems to be faced in the future.

Schmalenbach, Eugen. DYNAMIC ACCOUNTING, 12th ed., translated from the German by G.W. Murphy and Kenneth S. Most. London: Gee & Co., 1959. 222p.

Originally published in 1908, this book is authored by one of the foremost proponents of the dynamic accounting theory - that the important aspect of an annual accounting is the measurement of expense and revenue and its detailed presentation in a profit and loss statement.

Seidler, Lee J. THE FUNCTION OF ACCOUNTING IN ECONOMIC DEVELOPMENT: TURKEY AS A CASE STUDY (Praeger Special Studies in International Economics and Development). New York: Praeger, 1967. 366p. glossary, biblio., tables.

Examines in detail the relationship of accounting to taxation, price regulation, establishment of capital markets and control of state enterprises in the developing industrialization of Turkey.

Spicer, Ernest E. and Pegler, Ernest. BOOK-KEEPING AND ACCOUNTS, 16th ed., ed. by W.W. Bigg, et al. London: HFL (Publishers) Ltd., 1963. 642p. charts. supplement, 1968.

The authoritative textbook on accounting in England. The 1968 supplement incorporates the changes brought about by the Companies Act, 1967.

Union Europeenne des Experts Comptables, Economiques et Financiers. UEC - TEN YEARS. Paris: 1962. 32p.

A superficial review of the first ten years of the UEC, highlighting the founding members.

INVENTORY

Accountants International Study Group. ACCOUNTING AND AUDITING APPROACHES TO INVENTORIES IN THREE NATIONS. London: 1968. 36p. pap.

A survey of comparative practices in accounting and auditing for inventories in Canada, the United Kingdom and the United States. The Accountants International Study Group is composed of representatives from the American Institute of CPAs, the Canadian Institute of chartered Accountants, the Institute of Chartered Accountants in England and Wales, the Institute of Chartered Accountants of Scotland and the Institute of Chartered Accountants in Ireland. Sources and references are listed.

Alfandary-Alexander, Mark. AN INQUIRY INTO SOME MODELS OF INVENTORY SYSTEMS. Pittsburgh, Pennsylvania: University of Pittsburgh Press, 1962. 116p. biblio., charts. pap.

Applies simulation methods to policy evaluation in an inventory problem.

American Institute of Certified Public Accountants. CASE STUDIES IN THE OBSERVATION OF INVENTORY. New York: 1959. 62p. pap.

Seven case studies of auditing procedures used in actual practice by CPAs observing the taking of physical inventories in various types of businesses.

American Institute of Certified Public Accountants. PRACTICAL TECHNIQUES AND POLICIES FOR INVENTORY CONTROL (Management Services Technical

Study, No. 6). New York: 1968. 79p. biblio., charts. pap.
Shows how the CPA can help his client by identifying costs on which to base the inventory policy and by providing a "fresh outside approach" to his client's inventory problems. Includes four case studies.

Ammer, Dean S. MATERIALS MANAGEMENT. Homewood, Illinois: Richard D. Irwin, 1962. 457p. selected classified biblio., charts, facs., forms, photos.
A textbook on "integrated materials management," which the author describes as a combination of the functions of production and material control, nonproduction stores, purchasing, traffic, receiving and shipping.

Brown, Robert Goodell. DECISION RULES FOR INVENTORY MANAGEMENT. New York: Holt, Rinehart & Winston, 1967. 410p. charts, formulas, tables.
Offers a case history of a theoretical company with inventory problems which are solved by various mathematical techniques.

Brown, Robert Goodell. STATISTICAL FORECASTING FOR INVENTORY CONTROL. New York: McGraw-Hill Book Co., 1959. 250p. biblio., glossary, charts, graphs.
Written in non-technical language, this book is directed toward the business executive as well as the systems engineer. Mathematical simulation models are included as appendices.

Buchan, Joseph and Koenigsberg, Ernest. SCIENTIFIC INVENTORY MANAGEMENT. Englewood Cliffs, New Jersey: Prentice-Hall, 1963. 537p. charts, diagrams, tables.
Elementary explanation of the derivation and use of the economic lot size formula for replenishment of stock.

Hadley, G. and Whitin, G.M. ANALYSIS OF INVENTORY SYSTEMS. Englewood Cliffs, New Jersey: Prentice-Hall, 1963. 464p. charts, diagrams.
Presents practical techniques of preparing and analyzing mathematical models of inventory systems.

Hanssmann, Fred. OPERATIONS RESEARCH IN PRODUCTION AND INVENTORY CONTROL. New York: John H. Wiley & Sons, 1962. 266p. charts, formulas.
Offers a mathematical formulation of scientific production and inventory control. Bibliographies at the end of each chapter; also a bibliography of inventory theory and its applications.

Hoffman, Raymond A. INVENTORIES, A GUIDE TO THEIR CONTROL, COSTING, AND EFFECT UPON INCOME AND TAXES. New York: Ronald Press, 1962. 382p. tables. Currently being revised.
A definitive work on the accounting principles applicable to inventories.

Lavery, Kenneth R. SELECTIVE INVENTORY MANAGEMENT (Special Study No. 4). Hamilton, Canada: The Society of Industrial and Cost Accountants of Canada, 1964. 101p. selected biblio., forms, tables.
Shows how to make the transition from a mathematical formula to a workable inventory system.

McNair, Malcolm P. and Hersum, Anita C. RETAIL INVENTORY METHOD AND LIFO. New York: McGraw-Hill Book Co., 1952. 466p. tables. (o.p.)

Describes both the "retail method" of inventory valuation based on selling rather than cost price of article and "LIFO," the last-in first-out method.

Magee, John F. and Boodman, David M. PRODUCTION PLANNING AND INVENTORY CONTROL, 2nd ed. New York: McGraw-Hill Book Co., 1967. glossary, charts, tables.

A practical work on inventory planning and control, directed toward the operating executive concerned with inventory planning and decisions. Limited mathematical formulas in the main text; a few are found in Appendices A-C. Numerous graphs and charts.

Mulcahy, Gertrude. USE AND MEANING OF "MARKET" IN INVENTORY VALUATION (Research Study, No. 1). Toronto: Canadian Institute of Chartered Accountants, 1963. 40p. biblio. pap.

Examines the term "market" in the inventory valuation phrase "the lower of cost or market." Appendix I discusses the official pronouncements of the AICPA and the Institute of Chartered Accountants in England and Wales.

Naddor, Eliezer. INVENTORY SYSTEMS. New York: John H. Wiley & Sons, 1966. 355p. references and biblio., charts, tables.

Presents various operations research solutions to the inventory control problem.

National Association of Accountants. TECHNIQUES IN INVENTORY MANAGEMENT (NAA Research Report No. 40). New York: February 1, 1964. 119p. selected biblio., charts, tables.

An in-depth study written in non-technical language describing how a company decides how much and when to order. Forty-three organizations participated in the field survey.

Prabhu, N.U. QUEUES AND INVENTORIES, A STUDY OF THEIR BASIC STOCHASTIC PROCESSES (Applied Probability and Statistics Series). New York: John H. Wiley & Sons, 1965. 287p. formulas.

Presents mathematical formulas for queueing and inventory models. References at the end of each chapter.

Prichard, James W. and Eagle, Robert H. MODERN INVENTORY MANAGEMENT. New York: John H. Wiley & Sons, 1965. 431p. glossary, tables.

A textbook which is also directed toward the administrator of an inventory control system. The author uses graphic and algebraic proofs of modern inventory management systems rather than higher mathematical techniques.

Starr Martin K. and Miller, David W. INVENTORY CONTROL: THEORY AND PRACTICE. Englewood Cliffs, New Jersey: Prentice-Hall, 1962. 368p. glossary, biblio., charts, graphs.

Emphasizes the uses of mathematical methods in solving inventory problems.

Walker, J.K. and Mulcahy, G. OVERHEAD AS AN ELEMENT OF INVENTORY COSTS (Research Studies, No. 6). Toronto: Canadian Institute of

Chartered Accountants, 1965. 27p. biblio. pap.
Explains the basic techniques of direct costing and absorption costing and gives an evaluation of their relative merits.

Welch, W. Evert. SCIENTIFIC INVENTORY CONTROL. Greenwich, Connecticut: Management Publishing Corp., 1956. [Technical Book Company] 158p. charts, tables.
Intended to bridge the gap between most industrial practices and the techniques of operations research and linear programming, this book presents a "scientific method" leading to greater precision in inventory management.

LAW

American Bar Association. Section of Corporation, Banking and Business Law. Committee on Business Law Libraries. RECOMMENDED LAW BOOKS, edited by Richard Sloan, Chicago: 1969. 319p.
Excellent annotated listing of law books, arranged by subject. Symbols indicate entries suggested for purchase by all law offices, medium-sized and large offices, and large offices only.

Andersen, Arthur & Co. CASES IN PUBLIC ACCOUNTING PRACTICE, 7 vols. New York: 1960-62.
Comprehensive presentation of a series of cases which have established important precedents in the practice of public accounting.
Vol. 1: THE AICPA INJUNCTION CASE. RE: ACCOUNTING RESEARCH BULLETIN NO. 44 (REVISED). 309p.
Vol. 2: THE ALTON WATER COMPANY DEFERRED TAX CASE. 304p.
Vols. 3 & 4: THE PHILADELPHIA TRANSPORTATION COMPANY CASE. RE: INCOME INTEREST ON BONDS. 2 vols.
Vols. 5 & 6: SEC ADMINISTRATION POLICY. RE: BALANCE-SHEET TREATMENT OF DEFERRED INCOME-TAX CREDITS. 2 vols.
Vol. 7: INTERSTATE COMMERCE COMMISSION JURISDICTION OVER FINANCIAL STATEMENTS IN REPORTS TO STOCKHOLDERS. 136p.

Andersen, Arthur & Co. RETURN ALLOWED IN PUBLIC UTILITY RATE CASES, 2 vols. [Chicago]: [1964] tables.
Volume 1 covers cases 1915-54.
Volume 2 covers cases 1955-61.

Anderson, Ronald A. and Kumpf, Walter A. BUSINESS LAW, PRINCIPLES AND CASES. Cincinnati: South-Western Publishing Co. 1967. 960p. glossary.
A textbook presentation of the fundamental principles of business law. The complete 1962 text of the Uniform Commercial Code is included as an appendix.

Anderson, Ronald A. and Kumpf, Walter A. BUSINESS LAW: UNIFORM COMMERCIAL CODE (Comprehensive volume), 8th ed. Cincinnati: South-Western, 1968. 909p. glossary.

A textbook offering a detailed account of the legal framework of business. Appendix contains the 1962 text of the Uniform Commercial.code.

Bergh, Louis O. and Conyngton, Thomas. BUSINESS LAW, 6th ed. New York: Ronald Press, 1964. 1006p. glossary, forms.
Combines a detailed presentation of legal business problems with the basic principles of the law.

Black, Henry C. BLACK'S LAW DICTIONARY WITH GUIDE TO PRONUNICATION. 4th rev. ed. St. Paul, Minnesota: West Publishing Co., 1968. 1882p.
A handy one-volume reference containing an unusually complete collection of legal terms.

Dickerson, R.W.V. ACCOUNTANTS AND THE LAW OF NEGLIGENCE. Toronto: Canadian Institute of Chartered Accountants, 1966. 663p.
An excellent discussion of the subject of negligence and of accountants' legal responsibilities relating to negligence under Anglo-American jurisdictions. Covers damages, contributory negligence, gross negligence and fraud, duty to third parties, etc. Appendix A reports a number of cases in their entirety.

Dohr, James L., et al. ACCOUNTING AND THE LAW, CASES AND MATERIALS, 3rd ed. Brooklyn: Foundation Press, 1964. 713p. biblio. (o.p.)
A law course textbook which explains the background and techniques of accounting, its relationship to the legal profession, the principles of accounting and the law applicable to financial statements, and the accounting problems found in drafting legal instruments.

Hills, George S. THE LAW OF ACCOUNTING AND FINANCIAL STATEMENTS. Boston: Little, Brown, 1957. 352p. (o.p.)
Intended as a reference work for both accountants and lawyers working with financial statements, this study "considers the legal concepts which have been derived from judicial decisions and statutory enactments concerning accounting principles and practices." Table of cases is given.

Lavine, A. Lincoln. MODERN BUSINESS LAW, 2nd ed. Englewood Cliffs, New Jersey: Prentice-Hall, 1963. 860p. glossary.
A basic text on business law. Sections on contracts, agency, employment, sales, negotiable instruments, partnership, corporations, real property, personal property, bailments and carriers, liens and secured transactions, security relationships, wills and estates, bankruptcy.

Levy, Saul. ACCOUNTANTS' LEGAL RESPONSIBILITY. New York: American Institute of Certified Public Accountants, 1954. 288p. (o.p.)
Reprints in full, various, well-known accounting court cases.

Prentice-Hall Editorial Staff. THE CORPORATE SECRETARY'S HANDBOOK. Englewood Cliffs, New Jersey: Prentice-Hall, 1964. 392p. illus., tables.
A reference book for corporate secretaries which provides a general outline of their role together with practical details of their responsibilities.

Robert, William J., et al. DILLAVOU AND HOWARD'S PRINCIPLES OF BUSINESS LAW, 8th ed. Englewood Cliffs, New Jersey: Prentice-Hall, 1967. 1088p. glossary.
General textbook on business law using the text-case method of presentation. Detailed presentation of the Uniform Commercial Code.

Rohrlich, Chester. ORGANIZING CORPORATE AND OTHER BUSINESS ENTERPRISES, 4th ed. Albany, New York: Mathew Bender Co., 1967. 632p.

A well-known handbook primarily directed toward lawyers engaged in the organization of a new business.

Simon, Sidney I. ACCOUNTING AND THE LAW. New Brunswick, New Jersey: Bureau of Economic Research, Rutgers - The State University, 1965. 158p. pap.

A collection of essays which review the impact of legal decisions on accounting principles.

United States Corporation Company. CORPORATION MANUAL, 2 vols. New York: 1910- . Published annually.

Gives complete texts of the corporate laws of each of the 50 states, Puerto Rico and District of Columbia, arranged alphabetically. This publisher also issues separate annual paperback volumes on business laws of Delware and New York with annotated texts.

LEASING

See also Asset Accounting, and Corporations - Financial Management

American Institute of Certified Public Accountants. Accounting Principles Board. ACCOUNTING FOR LEASES IN FINANCIAL STATEMENTS OF LESSORS (Opinion No. 7). New York: May 1966. 10p. pap.

Expresses the APB's opinions on accounting for the revenue and expenses related to property leased to others as well as on accounting for the investment in such property.

American Institute of Certified Public Accountants. Accounting Principles Board. REPORTING OF LEASES IN FINANCIAL STATEMENTS OF LESSEE (Opinion No. 5). New York: September 1964. 9p. pap.

Expresses the APB's opinions on the proper methods for implementing generally accepted accounting principles in accounting for assets, liabilities, income and expense with regard to leases and sale and leasebacks.

Andersen, Arthur & Co. ACCOUNTING FOR LEASES. [Chicago]: August, 1962. 45p. pap.

Discusses the "reporting of property-use rights acquired and the obligations and costs incurred in the financial statements of lessees."

Australian Hire Purchase and Finance Conference. REPORT ON METHODS OF ASSESSING DEFERRED INCOME. [Sydney, Australia]: 1963. v.p. tables. pap.

The conference recommends the "Collins" actuarial factors be used in conjunction with a ratio method in apportioning interest income on long-term contracts. Numerous explanatory tables and appendices.

Australian Society of Accountants. ACCOUNTING FOR HIRE PURCHASE TRANSACTIONS (Statements on Accounting Practice, No. 3). Melbourne, Australia: December, 1958. (Supplement to The Australian Accountant.) 47p. tables. pap.

Describes origin, development and legal background of hire purchase, before detailing current practices and committee recommendations for profit determination and presentation of financial statements of finance companies.

Cohen, Albert H. LONG TERM LEASES: PROBLEMS OF TAXATION, FINANCE AND ACCOUNTING (Michigan Business Studies, Vol. 11, No. 5). Ann Arbor, Michigan: Bureau of Business Research, School of Business Administration, University of Michigan, 1954. 149p. biblio., tables. pap.

Explains and illustrates proposed accounting treatment for assets, liabilities and expenses related to long-term leases. Covers development of long-term leases, provisions and financing aspects of leases of real property.

Culliton, James W. MAKE OR BUY. Boston: Division of Research, Graduate School of Business Administration, Harvard University, reprinted 1961. 128p. biblio. pap.

A consideration of the problems fundamental to the decision whether to manufacture or buy materials, accessory equipment, fabricating parts and supplies.

Eiteman, Wilford John and Davisson, Charles N. THE LEASE AS A FINANCING AND SELLING DEVICE (Bureau of Business Research Report No. 20). Ann Arbor, Michigan: Bureau of Business Research, School of Business Administration, University of Michigan, 1951. [University Microfilms] 108p. charts, tables.

Reviews the pros and cons of the lease as a financial device.

Gross, Harry. MAKE OR BUY. Englewood Cliffs, New Jersey: Prentice-Hall, 1966. 255p. biblio., tables.

Provides quantitative and qualitative guidelines to assist management in the analysis of make-or-buy decisions.

Harvard Business Review. LEASE FINANCING. Boston: 1955-59. v.p. charts, tables. pap.

A collection of reprints of seven articles and seven letters on lease financing which appeared in the HARVARD BUSINESS REVIEW. One of the best, "Illusion in Lease Financing," by Donald R. Gant (HBR, March-April 1959) analyzes the significance of long-term commitments involved in leasing, describes the similarity between lease financing and debt, compares the costs of loans and leases and suggests methods of improving financial statements.

Institute of Chartered Accountants in Australia. THE TREATMENT OF "INCOME YET TO MATURE" IN THE ACCOUNTS OF FINANCE AND OTHER COMPANIES AND THE PRINCIPLE AND METHODS OF APPORTIONING "INCOME YET TO MATURE." Sydney, Australia: [1960-61] 4p. pap.

Two pronouncements, issued together, endorsed by the Council of the Institute, relating to presentation and accounting for assets and income of finance and hire purchase companies.

Jackson, James F., Jr. AN EVALUATION OF FINANCE LEASING (Studies in Banking and Finance, No. 6). Austin, Texas: Bureau of Business Research, Graduate School of Business, The University of Texas at Austin, 1967. 149p. biblio., tables. pap.

Adapted from a doctoral study, this report evaluates leasing versus purchase in terms of cost, cash flow and financial-structure flexibility. Tax aspects are also covered. No index.

Law, Warren A. and Crum, M. Colyer. EQUIPMENT LEASING AND COMMERCIAL BANKS. Chicago: Association of Reserve City Bankers, June 1963

61p. biblio. pap.
This report, prepared for the trustees of the Bankers Research Fund, analyzes past and current participation of commercial banks in financial leasing of equipment and evaluates the legal, economic and tax problems that will be encountered in permissible direct leasing. Introduction gives concise information on the status of the leasing industry, the practical advantages of leasing and its future growth.

Lee, Samuel J. INTRODUCTION TO LEASING. Studio City, California: Coda Publications, 1965. 199p. biblio.
A comprehensive review of all aspects of leasing as it affects the lessee, the lessor and the investor financing a lease. Bibliography includes section on accounting aspects.

Machinery and Allied Products Institute and Council for Technological Advancement. LEASING OF INDUSTRIAL EQUIPMENT. Washington, D.C.: 1965. 160p. tables.
Contains material presented at a symposium covering accounting, tax and financing aspects of equipment leasing.

McMichael, Stanley L. and O'Keefe, Paul T. LEASES: PERCENTAGE, SHORT AND LONG TERM, 5th ed. Englewood Cliffs, New Jersey: Prentice-Hall, 1959. 525p. Definitions. forms, tables.
A comprehensive treatment of real estate leasing.

Metz, Donald H. LEASING: STANDARDS AND PROCEDURES. Kaukauna, Wisconsin: Thomas Publications, Ltd., 1968. v.p. glossary, forms, photos, tables. loose-leaf.
Written in non-technical language, this manual describes the fundamentals of equipment leasing. Sections on lease or buy, interest, depreciation and investment credit, insurance, regulations (federal, state and local), accounting, computing lease payments, lease contracts, forms and documents, automobile and truck leasing.

Myers, John H. REPORTING OF LEASES IN FINANCIAL STATEMENTS (Accounting Research Study, No. 4). New York: American Institute of Certified Public Accountants, 1962. 143p. biblio. pap.
Covers both theory and practice of presentation of leases in financial statements with suggestions for treatment of long-term leases. Analyzes various arguments for and against recognizing future rentals as liabilities.

National Industrial Conference Board. LEASING IN INDUSTRY (Business Policy Study, No. 127), by Henry G. Hamel. New York: 1968. 117p. tables. pap.
Discusses advantages and disadvantages of leasing; describes third-party professional lessors and their services; outlines methods of negotiating a lease and selecting a lessor; explains how to evaluate a lease proposal; and reviews the treatment of leases in financial statements. Seven case studies are included.

Nelson, A. Tom. THE IMPACT OF LEASES ON FINANCIAL ANALYSIS (Occasional Paper No. 10). East Lansing, Michigan: Bureau of Business and Economic Research, Graduate School of Business Administration, Michigan State University, 1963. 107p. exhibits, tables. pap.

Suggests capitalization of leases in financial statements rather than current practice of reporting leases in accounts with inadequate footnote disclosure.

Saulnier, Raymond Joseph and Jacoby, Neil H. FINANCING EQUIPMENT FOR COMMERCIAL AND INDUSTRIAL ENTERPRISE (Studies in Business Financing, 5). New York: National Bureau of Economic Research, 1944 [University Microfilms] 111p. charts, tables. pap.

Presents the findings of a study on the financing of installment purchases of income-producing equipment. Traces the development of this technique and describes its operating methods.

Terborgh, George. LEASE-PURCHASE ALTERNATIVES (Studies in the Analysis of Business Investment Projects, No. 5). Washington, D.C.: Machinery and Allied Products Institute, 1961. 32p. charts, tables. pap.

Written from the point of view of the user of the goods. Not only analyzes the problem of whether to rent or buy, but also shows how to estimate the effect of inflation in making this decision.

Vancil, Richard F. LEASING OF INDUSTRIAL EQUIPMENT, with TABLES FOR THE ANALYSIS OF FINANCIAL ALTERNATIVES AND CAPITAL EXPENDITURES, by Jerome Bracken and Charles J. Christenson. New York: McGraw-Hill Book Co., 1963. 297p. charts, tables.

Emphasis is placed on the economics of leasing and the factors to be considered by management in making a leasing decision. To explain appropriate methods of investigation and analysis of leasing transactions, the fundamentals of leases and operations of lessors are described. Technical procedures to compute the capitalized value of a lease are outlined and required financial tables are included.

MANAGEMENT ACCOUNTING

See also Accounting, Accounting and Auditing Textbooks, Controllership, Corporations - Financial Management, and Cost Accounting

American Management Association. REPORTING FINANCIAL DATA TO MANAGEMENT, ed. by William D. Falcon. New York: 1965. 159p. charts, tables. pap.

A compilation of case studies showing what certain companies are doing in various areas of financial reporting to improve the effectiveness of their reports.

Anthony, Robert N. MANAGEMENT ACCOUNTING PRINCIPLES, rev. ed. Homewood, Illinois: Richard D. Irwin, 1970. 490p. charts, tables.

Approaches accounting from the viewpoint of the user of accounting information. Book is adapted from material in author's MANAGEMENT ACCOUNTING, TEXT AND CASES.

Anthony, Robert N. MANAGEMENT ACCOUNTING, TEXT AND CASES, 4th ed. Homewood, Illinois: Richard D. Irwin, 1970. 811p. charts, forms, tables.

Emphasizes the managerial uses of accounting data.

Beyer, Robert. PROFITABILITY ACCOUNTING FOR PLANNING AND CONTROL. New York: Ronald Press, 1963. 377p. charts, forms, tables.

Presents a management information system covering performance control, managerial decisions, and the determination of annual earnings in a form which insures the consistency of the data used.

Burns, Thomas J., ed. THE USE OF ACCOUNTING DATA IN DECISION MAKING. Columbus, Ohio: College of Commerce and Administration, Ohio State University, 1966. 260p. pap.

Proceedings and papers from accounting symposiums held at Ohio State University on March 23 and April 14, 1966. Participants included five decision makers from industrial corporations and five from non-industrial concerns. The former group presented papers on the use of internal accounting data in decision making, the latter group covering the use of external accounting data. Four accounting professors, having read the papers, presented written critiques of the papers in advance of each meeting.

Childs, William H. ACCOUNTING FOR MANAGEMENT CONTROL. New York: Simmons-Boardman, 1960. 734p. charts, forms. (o.p.)

Textbook emphasizing the use of the accounting method to assist management in the control of corporate financial activities and in investment of corporate funds.

Dykeman, Francis C. FINANCIAL REPORTING SYSTEMS AND TECHNIQUES. Englewood Cliffs, New Jersey: Prentice-Hall, 1969. 220p. charts, tables.

Shows how technological advances and new measurement techniques have increased the effectiveness of management reporting systems.

Fertig, Paul E., et al. USING ACCOUNTING INFORMATION, AN INTRODUCTION. New York: Harcourt, Brace & World, Inc., 1965. 607p. glossary, charts, tables.

Covers managerial uses of accounting as well as generally accepted accounting principles and uses of financial statements.

Florida. University. FINANCIAL AND MANAGERIAL REPORTING BY CERTIFIED PUBLIC ACCOUNTANTS (Accounting Series, No. 1). Gainesville, Florida: Accounting Department, College of Business Administration, University of Florida, n.d. 62p. charts, tables. pap.

Comprised of papers presented at the University's institute on this subject held on December 13-14, 1962.

Fremgen, James M. MANAGERIAL COST ANALYSIS. Homewood, Illinois: Richard D. Irwin, 1966. 500p. graphs, tables.

Emphasizes use of costs by management rather than techniques of financial cost presentation. Gives detailed procedures to be used with cost accounting information for management planning and control.

Gardner, Fred V. PROFIT MANAGEMENT AND CONTROL. New York: McGraw-Hill Book Co., 1955. 285p. charts, tables. pap.

Section 1 gives basis for profit control, while Section 2 shows use of breakeven points in management decisions.

Goetz, Billy E. and Klein, Frederick R. ACCOUNTING IN ACTION, ITS MEANING FOR MANAGEMENT. Boston: Houghton Mifflin, 1960. 725p. charts, formulas, tables.

Textbook which directs the student's attention to the role of accounting information in management decision making. Part 1, Orientation: Accounting as a Basis for Managerial Planning and Control; Part 2, The Accounting System; Part 3, Accounting: the Calculus of Management; Part 4, Accounting and the Social Sciences. Suggested readings at end of most chapters.

Gordon, Myron J. and Shillinglaw, Gordon. ACCOUNTING: A MANAGEMENT APPROACH, 4th ed. Homewood, Illinois: Richard D. Irwin, 1969. 855p.

Explains in layman's terms how accounting functions as a management tool.

Gray, John C., et al. ACCOUNTING INFORMATION AND BUSINESS DECISIONS: A SIMULATION. New York: McGraw-Hill Book Co., 1964. 41p. forms. pap.

A noncomputerized simulation intended to show the student how the accounting information system is used in business decisions.

Greene, William C. CASE PROBLEMS IN MANAGERIAL ACCOUNTING. New York: Holt, Rinehart & Winston, 1964. 124p. figures.

Presents case problems found in various business situations. Each case revolves around a specific accounting topic.

Haseman, Wilbur C. MANAGEMENT USES OF ACCOUNTING. Boston: Allyn & Bacon, 1963. 797p. charts, forms, tables.

Intended for the non-accounting student or businessman, this book describes the use of accounting by managers in cost control and decision-making.

Horngren, Charles T. ACCOUNTING FOR MANAGEMENT CONTROL: AN INTRODUCTION, 2nd ed. Englewood Cliffs, New Jersey: Prentice-Hall, 1970. 606p. glossary, graphs, tables.

Shows uses and limitations of accounting for management control. Describes various methods in which accounting may direct attention to problems inherent in current planning.

Keller, I. Wayne and Ferrara, William L. MANAGEMENT ACCOUNTING FOR PROFIT CONTROL, 2nd ed. New York: McGraw-Hill Book Co., 1966. 744p. charts, forms, tables.

Presents an inter-related system of accounting, planning, controlling and reporting for industrial and commercial businesses.

Kohler, Eric. L. ACCOUNTING FOR MANAGEMENT. Englewood Cliffs, New Jersey: Prentice-Hall, 1965. 275p. tables.

Written for the businessman. Explains not only the general background and vocabulary of the accountant, but also the value of accounting in expanding the scope of a business.

Lewis, Ralph E. PLANNING AND CONTROL FOR PROFIT, rev. ed. New York: Harper & Row, 1970. 230p. charts.

Shows how the use of accounting, especially budgetary procedures, in the planning and control area can improve profits. Covers the uses and limitations of coventional adcounting statements, marketing, research and development, administrative costs and capital budgeting.

Li, David H. ACCOUNTING FOR MANAGEMENT ANALYSIS. Columbus, Ohio: Merrill, 1964. 579p. charts, tables. (o.p.)

Describes management's contribution toward making accounting more meaningful.

Lynch, Richard M. ACCOUNTING FOR MANAGEMENT: PLANNING AND CONTROL. New York: McGraw-Hill Book Co., 1967. 461p. glossary, charts, tables.

Discusses management's problems with planning and control programs which have been decided upon through accounting analysis.

McFarland, Walter B. CONCEPTS FOR MANAGEMENT ACCOUNTING. New York: National Association of Accountants, 1966. 176p. illus.

Emphasizes the kind of information to be presented to management by accountants rather than the method of reporting. The major uses of this financial information are defined as "profit planning and measuring financial performance by projects, by products and markets and by management responsibilities." These aspects are covered in some detail.

Malchman, Lawrence H. and Slavin, Albert. FOUNDATIONS OF ACCOUNTING FOR MANAGERIAL CONTROL. Philadelphia: Chilton, 1961. 831p. tables.

A first-year accounting textbook which stresses accounting as a tool for management control as well as a source of financial data.

Mattessich, Richard. ACCOUNTING AND ANALYTICAL METHODS: MEASUREMENT AND PROJECTION OF INCOME AND WEALTH IN THE MICRO - AND MACRO-ECONOMY. Homewood, Illinois: Richard D. Irwin, 1964. 552p. biblio., charts, tables. (o.p.)

Interesting presentation which "affords a bridge between accounting and operations research."

Moore, Carl L. and Jaedicke, Robert K. MANAGERIAL ACCOUNTING, 2nd ed. Cincinnati: South-Western Publishing Co., 1967. 722p. charts, forms, tables.

The authors review the general field of management, the role of the accountant in the industrial field and the use to be made by management of accounting data.

Moore, Francis E. and Stettler, Howard F. ACCOUNTING SYSTEMS FOR MANAGEMENT CONTROL. Homewood, Illinois: Richard D. Irwin, 1963. 708p. tables.

Shows how to prepare an accounting system which will be effective from the standpoint of management demands.

Murphy, Mary E. MANAGERIAL ACCOUNTING. Princeton, New Jersey: Van Nostrand, 1963. 278p.

A rather elementary textbook designed for management accounting courses. No problems or case materials are included in the book, but are available upon request to the publisher.

National Association of Cost Accountants. PRESENTING ACCOUNTING INFORMATION TO MANAGEMENT (Research Series No. 28, N.A.C.A. Bulletin, Vol. XXXVI, No. 4, December 1954, sec. 3). New York: 1954.

52p. charts, tables. pap.
Deals with accounting reports as a method of financial communication with management. Thirty companies participated and their practices are included as case examples.

Peloubet, Maurice E. THE FINANCIAL EXECUTIVE AND THE NEW ACCOUNTING. New York: Ronald Press, 1967. 237p.
Designed to show the corporate executive just what the certified public accountant can do for him. Tells how the capabilities of the CPA or his firm can be judged and how the client and accountant can cooperate to their best advantage. Glossary of terms used in statistics and operations research is included.

Rossell, James H. and Frasure, William W. MANAGERIAL ACCOUNTING. Columbus, Ohio: Merrill, 1964. 633p. biblio., charts, forms, tables.
Describes how accounting by providing financial information to management can assist in control of current operations and formulation of policy decisions.
Part I: Financial Accounting Concepts, Evaluations, and Planning Guides.
Part II: Cost Accounting Concepts, Controls and Decision Guides.

Smith, Richard L. MANAGEMENT THROUGH ACCOUNTING. Englewood Cliffs, New Jersey: Prentice-Hall, 1962. 457p.
Illustrates how accounting information can be used by management in the functions of appraisal, diagnosis, planning and control.

Van Voorhis, Robert H., et al. USING ACCOUNTING IN BUSINESS. Belmont, California: Wadsworth Publishing Co., 1962. 480p. charts, tables.
Explains in non-technical terms how businessmen can use accounting records and reports to increase their efficiency.

Williams, Thomas H. and Griffin, Charles H. MANAGEMENT INFORMATION: A QUANTITATIVE ACCENT. Homewood, Illinois: Richard D. Irwin, 1967. 726p. charts, tables.
A text which applies mathematical quantitative methods to the solving of business problems.

MANAGEMENT AUDIT

See also Internal Audit and Control

Cadmus, Bradford. OPERATIONAL AUDITING HANDBOOK. New York: Institute of Internal Auditors, 1964. 474p. tables.
Demonstrates the way in which the techniques of internal auditing may be applied to a number of management functions. Covers in detail seven specific functions: purchasing; traffic; scrap, salvage and surplus materials; receiving operations; facilities; advertising and sales promotion; insurance.

Leonard, William P. THE MANAGEMENT AUDIT. Englewood Cliffs, New Jersey: Prentice-Hall, 1962. 238p. (o.p.)
Step-by-step guide to the audit of management. When completed, this audit can serve for future evaluation.

Martindell, Jackson. THE APPRAISAL OF MANAGEMENT, FOR EXECUTIVES AND INVESTORS, rev. ed. New York: Harper & Row, 1965. 253p.

charts, tables.

Presents the American Institute of Management's "Management Audit" method of evaluation of a business which is composed of ten categories: economic function, corporate structure, health of earnings, service to stockowners, research and development, directorate analysis, fiscal policies, production efficiency, sales vigor and executive evaluation.

Martindell, Jackson. "Management Audit." In Heyel, Carl, ed., THE ENCYCLOPEDIA OF MANAGEMENT. New York: Reinhold, 1963. pp.461-6.

Defines briefly but clearly the management audit procedure and the categories of business activities evaluated in such an audit.

National Industrial Conference Board. PERSONNEL AUDITS AND REPORTS TO TOP MANAGEMENT, by Geneva Seybold (Personnel Policy Study, No. 191). New York: 1964. 149p. forms, tables.

Describes methods used by management in 132 companies to evaluate personnel policies, procedures and practices.

Peloubet, Sidney W. and Heaton, Herbert. INTEGRATED AUDITING. New York: Ronald Press, 1958. 282p. forms.

A presentation of auditing concepts and techniques as an integral part of management controls.

U.S. Small Business Administration. MANAGEMENT AUDIT FOR SMALL MANUFACTURERS, by Philip M. Faucett (Small Business Management Series, No. 29). Washington, D.C.: U.S. Government Printing Office, 1963. 63p. pap.

Using an approach similar to that used in financial auditing, 15 categories of questions are listed to be answered by the owner-manager on a "do-it-yourself" basis. Appendix A is a classified listing of Small Business Administration management publications.

U.S. Small Business Administration. MANAGEMENT AUDIT FOR SMALL RETAILERS, by John W. Wingate (Small Business Management Series, No. 31). Washington, D.C.: U.S. Government Printing Office, 1964. 56p. pap.

Uses the "do-it-yourself" approach similar to the above volume, slanted to the retail field.

MANAGEMENT OF AN ACCOUNTING PRACTICE

American Institute of Certified Public Accountants. ACCOUNTING PRACTICE MANAGEMENT HANDBOOK. New York: 1962. 952p.

Covers all aspects of administering a public accounting practice. Replaces the CPA HANDBOOK.

American Institute of Certified Public Accountants. MANAGEMENT OF AN ACCOUNTING PRACTICE, Bulletins 14- . (Bulletins 1-13, issued originally as "Economics of an Accounting Practice" series have been incorporated in the ACCOUNTING PRACTICE MANAGEMENT HANDBOOK.) New York: 1961-

Bulletins describing actual facts, procedures and case histories involved in managing an accounting practice.

Lasser, J.K., ed. STANDARD HANDBOOK FOR ACCOUNTANTS. New York: McGraw-Hill Book Co., 1956. v.p. (o.p.)

Covers all aspects of the practice of accountancy, ranging from office procedures to relationships with clients.

Murphy, Mary E. ADVANCED PUBLIC ACCOUNTING PRACTICE. Homewood, Illinois: Richard D. Irwin, 1966. 587p.

Seeks to cover all aspects of the practice of accountancy from a consideration of professional ethics and legal responsibilities of CPAs to a review of professional recruitment and staff compensation within the profession. Bibliographies at end of each chapter.

Prentice-Hall, Inc. "Administering the Accountant's Practice." In ACCOUNTANT'S ENCYCLOPEDIA, 4 vols. Englewood Cliffs, New Jersey: 1962. Vol. IV, part IX.

Chapters on fees, office practices, staff development, tax practice, the accountant's own accounting system and time-saving techniques in servicing the smaller client.

Prentice-Hall, Inc. COMPLETE GUIDE TO A PROFITABLE ACCOUNTING PRACTICE. Englewood Cliffs, New Jersey: 1965. 797p. charts, forms.

Written in non-technical language, this is the result of a combined effort of the Prentice-Hall editorial staff and 20 accounting professors and practitioners. Covers operations of an accounting office, accounting and various management advisory services.

Prentice-Hall, Inc. "Expanding the Accountant's Practice." In ACCOUNTANT'S ENCYCLOPEDIA, 4 vols. Englewood Cliffs, New Jersey: 1962. Vol. IV, part VIII.

Chapters on enlarging a practice through management services, expanding personal services to owners of close corporations and obtaining new business.

Rotramel, Denny D. IMPROVING YOUR ACCOUNTING PRACTICE. Englewood Cliffs, New Jersey: Prentice-Hall, 1965. 248p. forms.

An outline of acceptable practices and procedures which can be used as a guide for a local accounting firm.

MANAGEMENT SERVICES BY CPAS

See Section 5, Management Advisory Services, for publications in this field.

MERGERS AND ACQUISITIONS

Alberts, William W. and Segall, Joel E. THE CORPORATE MERGER. Chicago: University of Chicago Press, 1966. 287p.

Proceedings of a seminar sponsored by the University of Chicago Graduate School of Business. Explores some of the major problems of corporate growth by merger.

American Institute of Certified Public Accountants. ANALYSIS FOR PURCHASE OR SALE OF A BUSINESS (Management Services Technical Study, No. 5). New York: 1967. 177p. biblio., tables. pap.

This study is concerned with the practical application of business judgment in preparing an analysis of the economic consequences of a merger or sale transaction for presentation to clients entering such negotiations. Four case studies are included.

American Institute of Certified Public Accountants. BUSINESS COMBINATIONS (Accounting Research Bulletin No. 48). New York: 1967. 3p. pap.

This bulletin gives the characteristics which differentiate between a purchase and a pooling of interests.

American Institute of Certified Public Accountants. "Intangible Assets." In RESTATEMENT AND REVISION OF ACCOUNTING RESEARCH BULLETINS (Accounting Research Bulletin No. 43). New York: 1953. chap. 5. pap. (Reprinted in APB ACCOUNTING PRINCIPLES, Vol. 2, 1968.)

This chapter in Bulletin 43 deals specifically with accounting for intangible assets acquired by the issuance of securities or purchased for cash or other consideration. It does not cover accounting for intangibles developed in regular course of business activity, such as advertising, research, etc.

American Management Association. CORPORATE GROWTH THROUGH MERGER AND ACQUISITION (Management Report, No. 75). New York: 1963. [University Microfilms] 156p. charts, tables. pap.

A compilation of readings by 17 authoritative management men on various aspects of mergers and acquisitions, from the searching through the financing and purchasing to the final integration.

Catlett, George R. and Olson, Norman O. ACCOUNTING FOR GOODWILL (Accounting Research Study, No. 10). New York: American Institute of Certified Public Accountants, 1968. 198p. selected biblio. pap.

Controversial study which recommends the elimination of the "pooling of interest" accounting method in business combinations. Also recommends that amounts paid for goodwill in a merger or acquisition be treated in the financial accounts "as a reduction of stockholders' equity at the time of the combination."

Choka, Allen D. BUYING, SELLING AND MERGING BUSINESSES. Philadelphia: American Law Institute, Joint Committee on Continuing Legal Education, 1965. 204p. pap.

Primarily directed toward lawyers involved in merger transactions. Chapter 2 covers financial statements. Brief bibliographies at end of each chapter.

Dellenbarger, Lynn E., Jr. COMMON STOCK VALUATION IN INDUSTRIAL MERGERS. Gainesville, Florida: University of Florida Press, 1966. 168p. biblio., charts, tables.

Analyzes the determinant factors of relative common equity value in fifty selected corporate mergers.

Financial Executives Research Foundation. MERGERS AND ACQUISITIONS: PLANNING AND ACTION, by Clarence I. Drayton, et al, under the direction of G. Richard Young. New York: 1963. 237p. biblio., tables.

First section, "Planning," examines assessment factors to be considered before a merger. Second section, "Action," describes techniques of searching, exploring, evaluating and negotiating. Chapter X is on legal, tax and accounting aspects.

Fox, Byron E. and Eleanor M. CORPORATE ACQUISITIONS AND MERGERS. New York: Mathew Bender, 1968. 800p. tables. loose-leaf.

Covers the legal, tax and antitrust aspects of acquisitions and mergers.

Hennessy, J.H., Jr. ACQUIRING AND MERGING BUSINESSES. Englewood

Cliffs, New Jersey: Prentice-Hall, 1966. 286p.

Designed to provide the executive interested in buying or selling a business with knowledge of the operating problems he will encounter. Chapters 1 through 4 gives general background information on valuation techniques, tax and legal matters, etc. Chapters 5 through 10 cover corporate planning, organization, administration and execution of the acquisition project; bargaining and closing; post-merger integration problems and antitrust considerations. Public and employee relations are covered in the final chapter.

Hutchison, G. Scott, ed. THE BUSINESS OF MERGERS AND ACQUISITIONS. New York: Presidents Publishing House, 1968. 430p. charts, tables.

Thirty-one business executives contribute their experiences in planning, negotiating and completing a sale, merger or acquisition. No index.

Linowes, David F. MANAGING GROWTH THROUGH ACQUISITION. New York: American Management Association, 1968. 192p.

Describes techniques used by businessmen who have been successful in acquiring going concerns to supplement their companies' resources and to insure their future growth. Brief list of references.

McCarthy, George D. ACQUISITIONS AND MERGERS. New York: Ronald Press, 1963. 353p. tables.

A practical guide covering the accounting and financial aspects of mergers and acquisitions.

Mace, Myles L. and Montgomery, George G., Jr. MANAGEMENT PROBLEMS OF CORPORATE ACQUISITIONS. Cambridge, Massachusetts: Graduate School Business Administration, Harvard University, 1962. 276p.

Uses the case study method in reviewing the merger-acquisition process.

Narver, John C. CONGLOMERATE MERGERS AND MARKET COMPETITION. Berkeley, California: University of California Press, 1967. 155p. tables.

A study of the effect of conglomerate mergers upon competition which concludes that such mergers can either promote or decrease competition depending upon conditions in "the pertinent market." Covers current trends and legislative history of conglomerate mergers as well as reviewing several conglomerate merger actions under Section 7 of the Clayton Act.

National Industrial Conference Board. MERGERS AND MARKETS, 6th ed., by Betty Bock (Studies in Business Economics, No. 100). New York: 1968. 223p. pap.

Excellent study of the economic content of the court decisions, complaints and orders issued to date under the Merger Act of 1950. Appendices cover: status of merger cases brought, 1966-7; selected basic facts alleged in new merger complaints, 1966-7; principal requirements of consent orders, 1966-7; merger decisions in litigated cases, 1951 to date. For pre-1966 developments in the first three appendices, reference must be made to the fourth and fifth editions of this book.

Practising Law Institute. MERGING, BUYING AND SELLING BUSINESSES. New York: 1966. 22p. pap.

Compilation of chapters contributed by members of PLI on legal aspects of corporate mergers and sales. The three sections cover techniques of acquisition and sale, tax aspects for buyer and seller and annotated forms for the transaction.

Scharf, Charles A. TECHNIQUES FOR BUYING, SELLING AND MERGING BUSINESSES. Englewood Cliffs, New Jersey: Prentice-Hall, 1964. 258p. forms.

Emphasizes legal and tax aspects of mergers.

Short, Robert A. BUSINESS MERGERS, HOW AND WHEN TO TRANSACT THEM. Englewood Cliffs, New Jersey: Prentice-Hall, 1967. 223p. photo.

Directed toward management engaging in a merger transaction for the first time, this guidebook covers such factors as economic objections, negotiation techniques, legal requirements, going public and how to manage the merged firm.

U.S. Department of Justice. MERGER GUIDELINES. Washington, D.C.: May 30, 1968. 27p. pap. mimeo.

Guidelines outlining the Department of Justice's standards for determining whether to oppose corporate mergers or acquisitions under Section 7 of the Clayton Act.

U.S. Federal Trade Commission. REPORT ON CORPORATE MERGERS AND ACQUISITIONS. Washington, D.C.: U.S. Government Printing Office, May 1955. 218p. charts, tables. pap. (o.p.)

Historical document on mergers and acquisitions. Based on data available in the FTC files, this study gives detailed statistics on merger activity during the years from 1948 through 1954. Also discusses procedures followed in corporate acquisitions and the competitive consequences of mergers and acquisitions.

Wichita. University. BUYING AND SELLING A SMALL BUSINESS. Wichita, Kansas: 1963. 157p. biblio. pap.

Financed by a Small Business Administration grant, this study presents a step-by-step procedure to be followed in a buy-sell transaction. Part 2 includes abstracts of actual transactions. Financial statement presentation is covered in some detail on pp.112-139.

Wyatt, Arthur R. A CRITICAL STUDY OF ACCOUNTING FOR BUSINESS COMBINATIONS (Accounting Research Study, No. 5). New York: American Institute of Certified Public Accountants, 1963. 146p. biblio. pap.

Gives historical background of business combinations before discussing the "pooling of interests" concept versus purchase accounting.

OPERATIONAL AUDITING

See Management Audit

OPERATIONS RESEARCH

See also Statistical and Mathematical Methods

Ackoff, Russell L. and Sasieni, Maurice W. FUNDAMENTALS OF OPERATIONS RESEARCH. New York: John H. Wiley & Sons, 1968. 467p. charts, formulas.

Chapters 1 through 4 outline general aspects and methods used in

OR. Remaining chapters cover specific problems such as those of allocation, inventory queuing, etc., and the problems inherent in implementing and controlling the solutions. Bibliographies at end of each chapter.

Ackoff, Russell L., and Rivett, Patrick. A MANAGER'S GUIDE TO OPERATIONS RESEARCH. New York: John H. Wiley & Sons, 1963. 117p. biblio.

Excellent guide for the layman. Last chapter suggests a number of additional readings.

Baumol, William J. ECONOMIC THEORY AND OPERATIONS ANALYSIS, 2nd ed. Englewood Cliffs, New Jersey: Prentice-Hall, 1965. 620p. graphs, tables.

Exphasis is on mathematical economic theory rather than operations research. References at end of each chapter.

Beer, Stafford. DECISION AND CONTROL: THE MEANING OF OPERATIONAL RESEARCH AND MANAGEMENT CYBERNETICS. New York: John H. Wiley & Sons, 1966. 556p. charts, graphs.

Traces the historical background of operations research and examines its infinite possibilities in assisting management to solve decision and control problems.

Bursk, Edward C. and Chapman, John F., eds. NEW DECISION MAKING TOOLS FOR MANAGERS. Cambridge, Massachusetts: Harvard University Press, 1963. 413p. charts, tables.

Mathematical programming as an aid in the solving of business problems.

Charnes, Abraham and Cooper, W.W. MANAGEMENT MODELS AND INDUSTRIAL APPLICATIONS OF LINEAR PROGRAMMING, 2 vols. New York: John H. Wiley & Sons, 1961. biblio., graphs, tables.

Covers applications, computational methods and the underlying mathematics of linear programming applications.

Churchman, C. West, et al. INTRODUCTION TO OPERATIONS RESEARCH. New York: John H. Wiley & Sons, 1957. 645p. charts, diagrs., tables.

Prepared from lecture material for a course at Case Institute of Technology. Bibliographies at end of each chapter.

Dorfman, Robert, et al. LINEAR PROGRAMMING AND ECONOMIC ANALYSIS. New York: McGraw-Hill Book Co., 1958. 539p. biblio., charts, graphs.

Provides a broad outline of the theory of linear programming and its relationship to traditional economic theory and analysis.

Langhoff, Peter, ed. MODELS MEASUREMENT AND MARKETING. Englewood Cliffs, New Jersey: Prentice-Hall, 1965. 216p. biblio., charts, graphs.

Directed toward the non-technical executive, these papers presented at meetings of the Market Research Council, explain clearly the various tools of the mathematical sciences.

Miller, David W. and Starr, Martin K. EXECUTIVE DECISIONS AND OPERATIONS RESEARCH. Englewood Cliffs, New Jersey: Prentice-Hall, 1960. 456p. biblio., charts, tables.

Shows the value of operations research to the executive in solving his problems. The OR problems presented in chapter 3 are classified not by techniques used but by fields in which they fall: marketing, production, administration.

Operations Research Society of America. INTERNATIONAL ABSTRACTS IN OPERATIONS RESEARCH. Baltimore, Maryland: bimonthly.

Published for the International Federation of Operational Research Societies, this listing provides a comprehensive listing of current literature on operations research. Brief abstracts of the articles are given.

Operations Research Society of America. PROGRESS IN OPERATIONS RESEARCH, 3 vols. Volume 1 (Publications in Operations Research No. 5) edited by Russell L. Ackoff. Volume 2 (Publications in Operations Research No. 9) edited by David B. Hertz and Roger T. Eddison. Volume 3 (Publications in Operations Research No. 16) edited by Julius S. Aronofsky. New York: John H. Wiley & Sons, 1961, 1964, 1969.

Volume 1 consists of chapters contributed by various authorities on the technical progress of operations research. In Volume 2 the emphasis is placed on the progress of operations research in its application to industrial and governmental problems. Volume 3 discusses the relationship between operations research and the computer.

Saaty, Thomas L. MATHEMATICAL METHODS OF OPERATIONS RESEARCH. New York: McGraw-Hill Book Co., 1959. 433p. formulas, tables.

Describes mathematical theories and techniques utilized by operations research workers. References at end of each chapter.

Sasieni, Maurice, et al. OPERATIONS RESEARCH, METHODS AND PROBLEMS. New York: John H. Wiley & Sons, 1959. 328p. tables.

A good textbook. Material presented in the form of problems which are worked out against a background of pertinent discussion. Bibliographies at end of each chapter.

Schlaifer, Robert. PROBABILITY AND STATISTICS FOR BUSINESS DECISIONS. New York: McGraw-Hill Book Co., 1959. 744p. Index of symbols, charts, tables.

A "nonmathematical introduction to the logical analysis of practical business problems in which a decision must be reached under uncertainty."

PENSIONS AND PROFIT SHARING

See also Executive Compensation

American Institute of Certified Public Accountants. ACCOUNTING FOR THE COST OF PENSION PLANS (Accounting Principles Board Opinion, No. 8). New York: November 1966. 37p. glossary. pap.

Offers the Accounting Principles Board's opinions with regard to the recommendations in the Accounting Research Study No. 8, of the same title, written by Ernest Hicks and published in 1965.

American Institute of Certified Public Accountants. ACCOUNTING FOR THE COST OF PENSION PLANS: TEXT AND EXPLANATORY COMMENTS ON APB OPINION NO. 8. New York: 1968. 109p. glossary. charts, tables.

pap.

Contains the text of APB Opinion No. 8 as well as five articles which first appeared in the Journal of Accountancy. These articles cover in detail some of the more difficult aspects in the application of APB Opinion 8.

American Management Association. THE TOTAL APPROACH TO EMPLOYEE BENEFITS, edited by Arthur J. Deric. New York: 1967. 128p. chart, tables. pap.

Demonstrates the new total approach concept of analyzing employee benefits. Plans are discussed in five sections on survivor benefits, retiree benefits, hospital, surgical and medical coverages, income replacement and other fringe benefits.

Andersen, Arthur & Co. DEFERRED COMPENSATION PLANS, 2nd ed. [Chicago]: 1965. 76p. pap.

Discusses advantages and disadvantages of various types of pension plans, profit-sharing plans, deferred compensation contracts and stock options.

Bankers Trust Company. 1970 STUDY OF INDUSTRIAL RETIREMENT PLANS. New York: 1970. 313p. tables. pap.

The bulk of this study (Section 3, pp.81-263) is devoted to a detailed tabulation of actual plans classified by type of industry or service instead of by name. Section 1 discusses trends in retirement plans. Section 2 gives explanatory comments on 1965-70 amendments to some of the pension plans described in Section 3, indicating progressive liberalization of terms. New editions of this report are issued every four or five years.

Bankers Trust Company. 1967 STUDY OF EMPLOYEE SAVINGS PLANS. New York: 1967. 132p. tables. pap.

A survey of employees savings plans in 132 companies. The findings of the survey are summarized on pp.7-44. The remainder of the pamphlet contains details of each of the 132 plans.

Bernstein, Merton C. THE FUTURE OF PRIVATE PENSIONS. New York: Free Press of Glencoe, 1964. 394p. tables.

Reviews thoroughly the many aspects of existing private pension plans and suggests improvements such as transferable pension credits and a pension credit clearinghouse.

Biegel, Herman C., et al. PENSIONS AND PROFIT SHARING, 3rd ed. Washington, D.C.: Bureau of National Affairs, Inc., 1964. 283p. tables, forms.

In this standard reference work the eight chapters, each by a different expert in the pension field, cover all aspects of pension planning: tax problems, financing, costs, administration, etc.

Bureau of National Affairs, Inc. FEDERAL-STATE REGULATION OF WELFARE FUNDS, rev. ed. Washington, D.C.: 1962. 271p. forms.

Explains the original 1958 Welfare and Pension Plans Disclosure Act and the 1962 amendments which added strengthening reguirements concerning the filing and publishing of annual reports among other aspects of pension regulation.

Council of Profit Sharing Industries. PROFIT SHARING MANUAL, 3rd ed., edited by Joseph B. Meier. Chicago: 1957. 436p. forms, photos.

The first three chapters cover the philosophy, planning and implementation of profit sharing. The remaining portion of the book is devoted to a representative collection of currently active profit sharing plans. These are grouped under cash plans, deferred plans, combined plans and special plans.

Council of Profit Sharing Industries. SUCCESSFUL PROFIT SHARING PLANS - THEORY AND PRACTICE, edited by Donald X. Murray. Chicago: 1968. 166p. charts, photos.

A compilation of articles originally published in the council's magazine PROFIT SHARING. Includes survey reports and data gathered by the Council's technical information service.

Coutts, W.B. and Dale-Harris, R.B. ACCOUNTING FOR THE COSTS OF PENSION PLANS (Research Study, No. 3). Toronto: Canadian Institute of Chartered Accountants, 1963. 13p. pap.

Discusses the characteristics of pension plans, the accounting problems involved and proposed accounting treatment.

Cramer, Joe J., Jr. ACCOUNTING AND REPORTING REQUIREMENTS OF THE PRIVATE PENSION TRUST (Indiana Business Information Bulletin No. 55). Bloomington, Indiana: Bureau of Business Research, Graduate School of Business, Indiana University, 1965. 111p. pap.

Proposes more detailed financial reporting of the private pension trust, perhaps as a supplement to the corporation's published financial statements.

Dietz, Peter O. PENSION FUNDS: MEASURING INVESTMENT PERFORMANCE. New York: Macmillan; Toronto: Collier-Macmillan Canada, Ltd., 1966. 183p. biblio., charts, tables.

This study, dealing with noninsured private pension plans, concentrates on measurement of portfolio quality and return on investment rather than on the actuarial aspects.

Haskins & Sells. THE PENSION SYSTEM IN THE UNITED STATES. [New York]: 1964. 67p. biblio., tables. pap.

Explains the principal types of pension plans and the various methods of financing pension costs.

Hicks, Ernest L. ACCOUNTING FOR THE COST OF PENSION PLANS (Accounting Research Study, No. 8). New York: American Institute of Certified Public Accountants, 1965. 159p. biblio. pap.

A comprehensive study of all the problems of pension plan accounting from which the author draws his own conclusions and recommendations.

Lybrand, Ross Bros. & Montgomery. FUNDAMENTAL CONCEPTS UNDERLYING PENSION PLAN FINANCING AND COSTS, by Frederick P. Sloat and David V. Burgett [New York]: 1970. 54p. index of terms. pap.

Includes a description of various types of pension plans currently in use and related funding methods.

McGill, Dan M. FUNDMENTALS OF PRIVATE PENSIONS, 2nd ed. Homewood, Illinois: Richard D. Irwin, 1964. 441p. tables.

Explains the background of the pension plan movement before detailing the basic features of today's private pension plan. This second edition "draws a sharp distinction between the accruing costs of a pension plan in the accounting sense and the financial policies pursued by the employer in the face of these accruals." A chapter is devoted to each of these topics.

Marples, William F. ACTUARIAL ASPECTS OF PENSION SECURITY. Homewood, Illinois: Richard D. Irwin, 1965. 230p. tables.

Published for the Pension Research Council of the Wharton School of Finance and Commerce, University of Pennsylvania. Discusses actuarial cost methods, funding programs, multiemployer pension plans, etc., as well as the role and responsibilities of the actuary in pension planning.

Melone, Joseph J. and Allen, Everett T., Jr. PENSION PLANNING: PENSIONS, PROFIT SHARING, AND OTHER DEFERRED COMPENSATION PLANS. Homewood, Illinois: Dow Jones-Irwin, Inc., 1966. 416p. charts, tables.

Excellent basic text on all types of deferred compensation programs.

Metzger, B.L. PROFIT SHARING IN PERSPECTIVE IN AMERICAN MEDIUM-SIZED AND SMALL BUSINESS, 2nd ed. Evanston, Illinois: Profit Sharing Research Foundation, 1966. 243p. biblio., charts, forms, illus., tables.

Statistics show that one of every five companies with 50 or more employees has some type of profit sharing plan. Chapters on coverage, objectives, ratings and characteristics of various plans as well as one on "guides to sound planning."

National Industrial Conference Board. SHARING PROFITS WITH EMPLOYEES, by F. Beatrice Brower (Studies in Personnel Policy, No. 162). New York: 1957. 92p. tables. pap. (o.p.)

Covers profit sharing plans that include the rank-and-file employee, excluding plans restricted to clerical or salaried employees except in such cases as banks where such clerks constitute the majority of employees.

Peat, Marwick, Mitchell & Co. ACCOUNTING FOR PENSION COSTS, by E.H. Owen and L. Werner. New York: 1967. 47p. pap.

Discusses problems which arise in applying AICPA Opinion 8, "Accounting for the Cost of Pension Plans." Five case studies of different types of pension plans are covered in some detail.

Rothman, David C. ESTABLISHING & ADMINISTERING PENSION & PROFIT SHARING PLANS & TRUST FUNDS (Taxation Practice Handbook 20). Philadelphia: Joint Committee on Continuing Legal Education of the American Law Institute and the American Bar Association, 1967. 259p. pap.

Good handbook covering all aspects of pension and profit sharing plan organization and administration. Includes an annual checklist for the administrator of these plans.

U.S. President. Committee on Corporate Pension Funds and Other Private Retirement and Welfare Programs. PUBLIC POLICY AND PRIVATE PENSION PROGRAMS, A REPORT TO THE PRESIDENT ON PRIVATE EMPLOYEE RETIREMENT PLANS. Washington, D.C.: U.S. Government Printing Office, January 1965. v.p. chart, tables. pap.

The committee issues a number of recommendations. One is that "a vesting requirement is necessary if private pension plans are to serve the broad social purpose justifying their favored tax status." Another is the strengthening of minimum standards for adequate funding of pension plans.

American Institute of Certified Public Accountants. FINANCIAL STATEMENTS RESTATED FOR GENERAL PRICE-LEVEL CHANGES (APB Statement No. 3). New York: 1969. 72p. pap.

Offers the conclusions and recommendations of the Accounting Principles Board concerning the presentation of general price-level information. Presentation of such information is not mandatory.

American Institute of Certified Public Accountants. REPORTING THE FINANCIAL EFFECTS OF PRICE-LEVEL CHANGES (Accounting Research Study, No. 6). New York: 1963. 290p. biblios. pap.

Describes the meaning of price-level adjustments, the techniques of making these adjustments and the methods of disclosing the effects of price-level changes in financial statements. Recommends that disclosure of price-level changes should be given in fully adjusted statements as a supplement to the conventional financial statements.

Gynther, R.S. ACCOUNTING FOR PRICE-LEVEL CHANGES: THEORY AND PROCEDURES. London: Pergamon Press, 1966. 270p. pap.

The author seeks to show that the effects of changing prices can and should be incorporated into accounting systems on a day-to-day basis.

Hendricksen, Eldon S. PRICE-LEVEL ADJUSTMENTS OF FINANCIAL STATEMENTS - AN EVALUATION AND CASE STUDY OF TWO PUBLIC UTILITY FIRMS. Pullman, Washington: Bureau of Economic and Business Research, School of Economics and Business, Washington State University, 1961. 133p. tables.

Introduction gives concepts and objectives of price-level changes. Chapter 2 compares adjusted and unadjusted financial statements. Chapter 3 reviews the choice of an index. Chapters 4 and 5 evaluate the adjustment results and the counterbalancing effects of capital additions and technological improvements.

Institute of Chartered Accountants in England and Wales. Research Committee. ACCOUNTING FOR STEWARDSHIP IN A PERIOD OF INFLATION. London: Research Foundation of the Institute of Chartered Accountants in England and Wales, August 1968. 24p. tables. pap.

An expression of opinion by the Research Committee which does not claim to represent the views of the Council. Discusses the various calculations required to measure the effects of inflation on stewardship accounts prepared on the conventional historical cost basis.

Jones, Ralph Coughenour. EFFECTS OF PRICE LEVEL CHANGES ON BUSINESS INCOME, CAPITAL AND TAXES. [Columbus, Ohio]: American Accounting Association, 1956. 207p. charts, tables. pap.

Studies the effects of inflation on monetary and nonmonetary accounts and shows ways in which statements adjusted for changes in the value of the dollar can be useful to management, investors and the government.

Jones, Ralph Coughenour. PRICE LEVEL CHANGES AND FINANCIAL STATEMENTS - CASE STUDIES OF FOUR COMPANIES. [Columbus, Ohio]: American Accounting Association, 1956. 189p. charts, tables. pap.

Studies the effects of inflation on four major companies by adjusting their financial statements for price-level changes. The historical cost approach is used but the invested costs are restated in a constant-value unit which is equal to the purchasing power of the dollar at a selected "base date." Historical dollar values are converted into constant-value units by using the U.S. Bureau of Labor Statistics Consumers' Price Index.

Mason, Perry. PRICE LEVEL CHANGES AND FINANCIAL STATEMENTS, BASIC CONCEPTS AND METHODS. Columbus, Ohio: American Accounting Association, 1956. 28p. tables. pap.

This is the introductory booklet in the major AAA research project on the advisability of restating conventional accounting figures with the use of a general price-level index so that each dollar will represent the same amount of general purchasing power. Discusses the nature of price levels and index numbers and describes the techniques used in making price-level adjustments in financial statements.

May, George O. BUSINESS INCOME AND PRICE LEVELS, AN ACCOUNTING STUDY. New York: July 1, 1949. 132p. pap. (o.p.)

A comprehensive study of the relationship of price-level changes to accounting principles. Prepared at the request of the American Institute of Accountants' Study Group on Business Income, for whom Mr. May served as research consultant.

National Industrial Conference Board. INFLATION AND CORPORATE ACCOUNTING (Studies in Business Policy, No. 104). New York: 1962. 100p. biblio., charts, facs, tables. pap.

A non-technical presentation of methods used or proposed to combat the effect of inflation on financial statement presentation.

Paton, William A., Jr. A STUDY IN LIQUIDITY, THE IMPACT OF INFLATION ON MONETARY ACCOUNTS (Michigan Business Studies, Vol. 14, No. 2). Ann Arbor, Michigan: Bureau of Business Research, School of Business Administration, University of Michigan, 1958. 182p. charts, tables.

Analyzes the effects of inflation on "monetary items" in the accounts of 52 sample non-financial corporations over the December 31, 1942 to December 31, 1952 period.

Sweeney, Henry W. STABILIZED ACCOUNTING. New York: Holt, Rinehart & Winston, 1964. 274p. tables.

Originally published in 1936, this is one of the accounting classics. The new edition contains forewords by Roy B. Kester and W.A. Paton. Main theme is a method of expressing financial statements on the basis of an index of the general price level.

Wilk, Lionel A. ACCOUNTING FOR INFLATION. London: Sweet & Maxwell, 1960. 196p. biblio.

Proposes a revision of the present form of accounts based on historical cost in which the yardstick applied to the changing dollar would be an index of the purchasing power of money.

PROFESSIONAL ETHICS

American Institute of Certified Public Accountants. CODE OF PROFESSIONAL ETHICS...AND INTERPRETIVE OPINIONS, as amended December 31, 1969. New York: 1970. 31p. pap.

Pamphlet reissued whenever revisions occur. Proposed and newly adopted articles of the Code of Professional Ethics and numbered opinions appear first in THE CPA, monthly publication of the Institute.

Carey, John L. and Doherty, William O. ETHICAL STANDARDS OF THE ACCOUNTING PROFESSION. New York: American Institute of Certified Public Accountants, 1966. 330p.

An updating of the 1956 PROFESSIONAL ETHICS OF CERTIFIED PUBLIC ACCOUNTANTS, by John L. Carey, this volume is the definitive work on professional ethics for the accountancy profession in the United States. Part One covers principles of ethics, independence, professional competence and attitude; Part Two deals separately with ethical responsibilities in auditing, tax practice and management services; Part Three discusses relations with clients and fellow practitioners and lists forms of organization, descriptions of accounting firms and the manner in which the practice should be carried on.

Casler, Darwin J. THE EVOLUTION OF CPA ETHICS: A PROFILE OF PROFESSIONALIZATION (Occasional Paper No. 2). East Lansing, Michigan: Bureau of Business and Economic Research, Graduate School of Business Administration, Michigan State University, 1964. 139p. bibliographic notes. pap.

Analyzes the evolution of various rules of ethics and the social environment in which they were established.

Levy, Saul. ACCOUNTANTS' LEGAL RESPONSIBILITY. New York: American Institute of Certified Public Accountants, 1954. 288p. (o.p.)

A reprinting in full of chapter 6 of the 1952 CPA HANDBOOK, published by the AIA. Includes a collection of leading cases and articles.

PUBLIC OFFERINGS

For additional regulations issued by the Securities and Exchange Commission, see publications listed under SEC in Section 3, Governmental Regulation.

See also entries under Brokerage in Specialized Accounting section.

American Institute of Certified Public Accountants. LETTERS FOR UNDERWRITERS (Statements on Auditing Procedure 35). New York: November 1965. 32p. pap.

Offers guides for independent accountants in the preparation of "comfort letters" in connection with the distribution of securities.

American Institute of Certified Public Accountants. A MANAGEMENT

INVESTMENT COMPANY OF THE OPEN-END TYPE (Case Studies in Auditing Procedure, No. 6). New York: 1947. 48p. pap.

Case study submitted by a member of the Institute's Committee an Auditing Procedure covering an actual examination of a mutual fund.

American Stock Exchange. AMERICAN STOCK EXCHANGE GUIDE. New York: Commerce Clearing House, April 1968- . loose-leaf.

Contains policies applicable to companies with securities listed on The American Stock Exchange. Contains sections on requirements for original and additional listings. Part 6 gives specifications for annual and quarterly reports.

Bromberg, Alan R. SECURITIES LAW - FRAUD - SEC RULE 10b-5. New York: McGraw-Hill Book Co., 1967. 385p. biblio. Updated quarterly. loose-leaf.

Part 1: Relates Rule 10b-5 to other state and federal fraud rules.
Part 2: Examines the application of 10b-5 to a number of varied public and private transactions.
Part 3: Discusses 10b-5 in relation to key legal concepts and procedures.

Friend, Irwin, *et al.*, eds. INVESTMENT BANKING AND THE NEW ISSUES MARKET. Cleveland, Ohio: World Publishing, 1967. 608p. forms, tables.

A detailed report of the findings of a study by the Securities Research Unit of the University of Pennsylvania's Wharton School of Finance and Commerce under a grant from the Investment Bankers Association of America. Covers the first quarter of 1962 with some tracing of principal developments from 1935 through 1963.

Investment Dealers Digest. CORPORATE FINANCING, 1950-1966, 3 vols. New York: 1962-1967.

These volumes (1950-61, 1961-63, 1964-66) are compiled from the semiannual CORPORATE FINANCING DIRECTORY issued by the same publisher. They contain a record of all public and private offerings by U.S. and foreign corporations and foreign governments. Also include secondary offers, private placements of over $500,000, underwritten ICC offers. Arranged alphabetically by issuing corporation or government, under which are listed the date of issuance, description of the offering and the name of the underwriter.

Investment Dealers Digest. CORPORATE FINANCING DIRECTORY. New York: 1942- . pap.

Semiannual compilation of all U.S. corporate financing during that period. Part 1, Alphabetical by Issuers; Part 2, Alphabetical by Underwriters; Part 3, Rights and Exchange Offerings; Part 4, Secondary Offerings; Part 5, Corporate Syndicate Personnel; Part 6, Syndicate Heads (with total amount of underwritings and number of issues); Part 7, Corporate Issuers Placed Privately (alphabetically by name and alphabetically by agent, Canadian issues included); Part 8, Canadian Financing (corporate and provincial), alphabetically by underwriters.

Loss, Louis. SECURITIES REGULATION, 2nd ed., 3 vols. Boston: Little, Brown, 1961.

The most detailed of the works on the S.E.C. Kept up to date by supplements.

McCormick, Edward T. UNDERSTANDING THE SECURITIES ACT AND THE S.E.C. New York: American Book Co., 1948. 335p. biblio., table of cases, decisions and opinions. (o.p.)

Still valuable for its clear presentation of the historical and sociological background from which the S.E.C. evolved.

Moffet, H.S. ACCOUNTING FOR COSTS OF FINANCING (Research Study, No. 5). Toronto: Canadian Institute of Chartered Accountants, 1964. 29p. biblio. pap.

Examines "accounting for discounts, premiums and issue costs related to funded debt." Also discusses these terms in relation to equity share issues.

New York Stock Exchange. COMPANY MANUAL. New York: 1954- . loose-leaf.

Presents the policies, requirements, procedures and practices of the New York Stock Exchange. Includes a section on the procedure for listing on the Exchange. Section A4 deals with financial statements required, both annual and interim.

Rappaport, Louis H. SEC ACCOUNTING PRACTICE AND PROCEDURE, 2nd ed., rev. printing. New York: Ronald Press, 1966. v.p.

The authoritative text on accounting for the SEC. The revised printing contains a new chapter on SEC problems of foreign companies.

Robinson, Gerald J. GOING PUBLIC, SUCCESSFUL SECURITIES UNDERWRITING. New York: Clark, Boardman, 1961. 353p.

Introductory text on the subject covering the underwriting contract, federal and state securities laws and federal income tax aspects.

U.S. Securities and Exchange Commission. ACCOUNTING SERIES RELEASES. Washington, D.C.: 1937- .

Releases which contain the SEC interpretations of its new and amended rules and regulations. Paperback compilation of Nos. 1-112 is available from the U.S. Government Printing Office. The SEC maintains a free mailing list for current releases.

Winter, Elmer L. A COMPLETE GUIDE TO MAKING A PUBLIC STOCK OFFERING. Englewood Cliffs, New Jersey: Prentice-Hall, 1962. 269p.

A non-technical guide for executives who plan to "go public."

RECORDS RETENTION

Financial Executives Institute. CORPORATE RECORDS RETENTION, 3 vols. New York: 1958-60. (Volumes 1 and 2 now out of print.)

Vol. 1: A Guide to U.S. Federal Requirements.
Vol. 2: A Guide to Canadian Federal and Provincial Requirements.
Vol. 3: A Guide to Requirements of State Governments of the U.S.

Detailed analyses of record retention requirements of the above governments and governmental agencies. Volume 1 is arranged by industry, Volume 2 by province and Volume 3 alphabetically.

Mitchell, William E. RECORDS RETENTION, rev. ed. Evansville, Indiana: Ellsworth Publishing Co., 1967. 72p. tables. pap.

Starting off with a recommended retention schedule, this book covers government, federal and state tax regulations. Chapters on payroll records, government contracts, classified information.

New Jersey Society of Certified Public Accountants. A FAST GUIDE TO RECORD RETENTION, by Morris B. Kadin, ed. by Theodore Cohn. Newark, New Jersey: August 1967. 33p. pap.

A handy outline of record retention recommendations, arranged on an alphabetic schedule.

Office of the Federal Register (National Archives and Records Service, General Services Administration). GUIDE TO RECORD RETENTION REQUIREMENTS. Washington, D.C.: U.S. Government Printing Office. v.p. pap.

Annual guide to legal requirements as to "what records must be kept, who must keep them and how long they must be kept." Early each year the daily FEDERAL REGISTER prints this guide as Part II of one issue. It is then reissued in booklet form by the U.S. Government Printing Office.

Record Controls, Inc. RETENTION AND PRESERVATION OF RECORDS WITH DESTRUCTION SCHEDULES, 7th ed. Chicago: 1967. 62p. biblio., forms, tables. pap.

Shows how to organize a records retention program and gives federal and state laws affecting records retention. Regularly updated.

RESEARCH AND DEVELOPMENT COSTS

American Management Association. THE CASE FOR RESEARCH ACCOUNTABILITY, by William G. McLoughlin (Management Bulletin 98). New York: 1967. 23p. pap.

Explains why R & D, as a definite profit center, should be treated the same way as conventional capital investments for accounting purposes.

McFadden, J.A., Jr. and Tuska, C.D. ACCOUNTING AND TAX ASPECTS OF PATENTS AND RESEARCH. Princeton, New Jersey: Van Nostrand, 1960. 327p. forms.

Part 1 covers accounting for research and development costs, patent prosecution expenses, patent infringement and litigation expenses, patent account structure, patent amortization methods, and patent income. Part 2 deals with taxes on patent income or sales.

National Association of Cost Accountants. "Accounting for Research and Development Costs" (Research Series, No. 29). N.A.C.A. BULLETIN, Vol. 36, No. 10, June 1955, sec. 3. 62p. pap.

Excellent presentation of problems of accounting for company-operated research programs. Covers practices of 35 companies.

National Industrial Conference Board. MARKETING, BUSINESS AND COMMERCIAL RESEARCH IN INDUSTRY (Studies in Business Policy, No. 72). New York: 1955. 88p. charts, forms. pap.

Section 7 is on "Budgeting and Accounting" and each of the 20 case studies include a section on that company's method of accounting for research expenditures.

Quinn, James Brian. EVALUATING RESEARCH AND DEVELOPMENT (Tuck Bulletin, No. 22). Hanover, New Hampshire: The Amos Tuck School of Business Administration, Dartmouth College, September 1959. 20p. brief biblio. pap.

Presents a system of evaluating and controlling individual segments of a research program.

Villers, Raymond. RESEARCH AND DEVELOPMENT: PLANNING AND CONTROL. New York: Financial Executives Research Foundation, Inc., 1964. 199p. biblio., charts, tables.

The practices of 34 companies and two institutions form the basis for this study of R & D functions in industrial corporations.

SMALL BUSINESS

For serial publications of the U.S. Small Business Administration, as well as SBA regulations, see Section 3, Governmenral Regulation.

American Institute of Certified Public Accountants. "Sources and Means of Financing." In MANAGEMENT SERVICES HANDBOOK. New York: 1964. p. 101-25. (o.p.)

Discusses financial requirements and equity financing sources of small business.

Basso, Lee L. COST HANDBOOK FOR THE SMALL MANUFACTURER. St. Louis, Missouri: L.B. Associates, 1964. 319p. forms.

Written in non-technical language in order to be easily understood by the small businessman, this handbook explains basic accounting principles as well as costing techniques.

Broom, H.N. and Longenecker, Justin G. SMALL BUSINESS MANAGEMENT, 2nd ed. Cincinnati: South-Western Publishing Co., 1966. 842p. charts, tables.

A good comprehensive review of small business in the American economy, its problems and peculiarities. Covers the environment of small business; the problems of starting a new business; financial, marketing and production management of the small firm; legal and governmental relationships. A reading reference list is included.

Canadian Institute of Chartered Accountants. Study Group on Audit Techniques. INTERNAL CONTROL IN THE SMALL BUSINESS. Toronto: 1967. 37p. pap.

Concentrates on problems presented in auditing an organization dominated by an owner-manager or an employee-manager. Includes an internal control questionnaire for small businesses.

Gibson, James L. and Haynes, W. Warren. ACCOUNTING IN SMALL BUSINESS DECISIONS. Lexington, Kentucky: University of Kentucky Press, 1963. 133p.

A study of the influence accounting data has upon the basic decisions made by small businessmen. Based on a review of 100 case studies. Certain chapters are devoted to different types of small businesses with models showing how decisions can be well handled.

Institute of Continuing Legal Education. SMALL BUSINESS FINANCING LIBRARY, 3 vols., ed. by Jay V. Grimm, Robert L. Knauss and Bernard Goodwin. Ann Arbor, Michigan: 1966. v.p. biblio., forms, tables.

For the lawyer who is called upon to handle financial as well as legal work for a small business client. Contains numerous forms, checklists, financial plans and agreements. Includes "authoritative articles" on the subject in each section.

Krentzman, Harvey C. MANAGING FOR PROFITS. Washington, D.C.: U.S. Government Printing Office, 1968. 170p. forms. pap.

Issued by the Small Business Administration, this book is intended as a review of and a supplement to courses cosponsored in recent years by the SBA with various business and educational institutions. Contains practical advice on marketing, advertising, systems, financial management, credit and collection, accounting and statistics, budgeting and expense control, etc. Bibliographies at the end of each chapter.

New York. State. Department of Commerce. THE MANAGEMENT PROBLEMS OF A GROWING BUSINESS, by Dale Zand (Small Business Bulletin, No. 4). Albany, New York: 1958. 17p. pap.

Discusses the transition from "worker" to "manager" and describes some of the major functions required of a small business manager.

U.S. Small Business Administration. COST ACCOUNTING FOR SMALL MANUFACTURERS, by R. Lee Brummet. Washington, D.C.: 1953. 99p. biblio., charts, facs., tables. pap.

Expresses in relatively simple terms the fundamentals of job order and process cost accounting systems, use of ledgers and journals, principles of accounting for material, labor and overhead.

U.S. Small Business Administration. MANAGEMENT AUDIT FOR SMALL MANUFACTURERS, by Philip M. Faucett (Small Business Management Series, No. 29). Washington, D.C.: U.S. Government Printing Office, 1963. 63p. pap.

Using an approach similar to that used in financial auditing, 15 categories of questions are listed to be answered by the owner-manager on a "do-it-yourself" basis. Appendix A is a classified listing of Small Business Administration management publications.

U.S. Small Business Administration. MANAGEMENT AUDIT FOR SMALL RETAILERS, by John W. Wingate (Small Business Management Series, No. 31). Washington, D.C.: U.S. Government Printing Office, 1964. 56p. pap.

Uses the "do-it-yourself" approach similar to the above volume, slanted to the retail field.

U.S. Small Business Administration. PUBLIC ACCOUNTING SERVICES FOR SMALL MANUFACTURERS, by Robert E. Witschey (Small Business Management Series, No. 5). Washington, D.C.: 1954. 21p. biblio. pap.

A brief report directed to the non-financial small businessman, pointing out the areas in which the independent public accountant can be of great assistance.

Whiteside, Conon D. ACCOUNTING SYSTEMS FOR SMALL AND MEDIUM-SIZED BUSINESS. Englewood Cliffs, New Jersey: Prentice-Hall, 1961. 264p. forms.

Describes accounting systems for wholesale, retail and service trades as well as for the small or medium-sized manufacturer.

Zeff, Stephan A. USES OF ACCOUNTING FOR SMALL BUSINESS (Michigan

Business Report, No. 39). Ann Arbor, Michigan: Bureau of Business Research, University of Michigan, 1962. 79p. pap.

Directed toward the non-accountant, this includes a concise description of financial statements of a small manufacturing firm and shows how a simple bookkeeping system can be useful in evaluation and financial control.

Zwick, Jack. A HANDBOOK OF SMALL BUSINESS FINANCE, 7th ed. (Small Business Management Series, No. 15). Washington, D.C.: U.S. Small Business Administration, 1965. 86p. pap.

Describes concepts and tools of financial analysis to help the small businessman interpret financial data. Several chapters on financial statements. Sources of further information including a bibliography.

SPECIALIZED ACCOUNTING

Although a number of industry accounting manuals have been included in the following sections, there are undoubtedly many in existence which are not listed here. Anyone interested in obtaining further information on accounting for any particular industry should contact the trade associations in that field. A comprehensive listing of these associations is given in the ENCYCLOPEDIA OF ASSOCIATIONS, 6th ed., Vol. 1, published in 1970 by Gale Research Company.

An extensive file of industry accounting manuals is available for reference purposes in the library of the National Association of Accountants. A 1967 listing of manuals currently available can be obtained from the NAA library.

Also, several of the accounting handbooks listed in Section 7 of this book are comprehensive volumes covering the accounting for a large number of different industries.

ADVERTISING AGENCIES

Andersen, Arthur & Co. MANUAL OF ADVERTISING AGENCY ACCOUNTING. New York: Committee on Agency Administration, American Association of Advertising Agencies, 1955. 123p. charts, tables. pap. (o.p.)

Intended as a guide to be adapted to individual agencies' needs and requirements. Chart of accounts.

Barton, Roger. "Financial Operations." In his ADVERTISING AGENCY OPERATIONS AND MANAGEMENT. New York: McGraw-Hill Book Co., 1955. chap. 17.

Describes briefly cost accounting, budgeting, financial reporting practices of agencies.

Farrand, George N. "The Financial Management of Advertising Agencies." ADVERTISING AGENCY, Vol. 47, April, June, August, November 1954; Vol. 48, February, May 27, June 24, September 16, 1955. (o.p.)

This excellent series of articles on advertising agency accounting is now out of print, but may be seen in the library of the AICPA and in some of the libraries of the larger accounting firms.

Fields, Norman. A PRACTICAL GUIDE TO PROFIT MANAGEMENT FOR ADVERTISING AGENCIES. New York: Moore Publishing Co., 1958. v.p. facs. loose-leaf. (o.p.)

Part 1 describes agency compensation methods. Part 2 treats cost accounting theories as applied to agencies. Part 3 presents an advertising agency cost accounting system. Part 4 consists of a number of forms and detailed instructions to assist smaller agencies in setting up a cost accounting system.

Rubel, Ira W. ADVERTISING AGENCY FINANCIAL MANAGEMENT AND ACCOUNTING. New York: Funk & Wagnalls, 1940. 342p. forms. (o.p.)

Part II covers in detail the procedures to be followed in advertising agency accounting.

AIR CARRIERS

For regulations of the Civil Aeronautics Board, see the publications listed under the Board in Section 3, Governmental Regulation. Since the CAB has complete jurisdiction over the accounting used by the airlines, there is very little accounting literature on the subject.

International Air Transport Association. REVENUE ACCOUNTING MANUAL. Montreal: 1964- . loose-leaf.

Consists of interline revenue accounting rules (Part A), Traffic Conference Resolutions relating to revenue accounting matters (Part B) and miscellaneous industry agreements, listings and specifications (Part C).

Kennedy, Ralph D. and McMullen, Stewart Y. "Statements of Air Carriers." In their FINANCIAL STATEMENTS: FORM ANALYSIS AND INTERPRETATION, 5th ed. Homewood, Illinois: Richard D. Irwin, 1968. pp.552-66.

A brief description of air carrier accounting. Gives explanations of items to be found on an airline's balance sheet and shows how to analyze the financial and operating data.

Rules Service Company. CIVIL AERONAUTICS BOARD ECONOMIC AND PROCEDURAL REGULATIONS. Washington, D.C.: 1959- . loose-leaf.

Updated monthly, this service contains CAB uniform systems of accounts, procedural regulations and policy statements.

U.S. Civil Aeronautics Board. ACCOUNTING AND REPORTING INTERPRETATION LETTERS. Washington, D.C.: 1957- . pap.

Issued very occasionally, these releases offer interpretations of the CAB Economic Regulations.

U.S. Civil Aeronautics Board. UNIFORM SYSTEM OF ACCOUNTS AND REPORTS FOR CERTIFICATED ROUTE AIR CARRIERS. Washington, D.C.: U.S. Government Printing Office, June 1, 1961. loose-leaf. pap.

Constantly revised, the revisions are available on subscription basis.

AIRPORTS

Cunningham, Joseph M. AIRPORT ACCOUNTS, rev. ed. Chicago: Municipal Finance Officers Association of the United States and Canada, 1962. 29p. pap.

Presents a classification of accounts which is primarily intended for municipalities and therefore conforms to the principles of municipal accounting. But since the classification is basically that of an enterprise fund, it can easily be adapted to the private operation of an airport.

Dannenbrink, T.D. "Airports." In Williams, Robert I. and Doris, Lillian, ENCYCLOPEDIA OF ACCOUNTING SYSTEMS, Vol. I. Englewood Cliffs, New Jersey: Prentice-Hall, 1956. chap. 2.

Includes a chart of accounts with explanations of accounts peculiar to the operation of an airport.

Philadelphia. City. Department of Commerce. Division of Aviation. MANUAL OF ACCOUNTING PROCEDURES, PHILADELPHIA INTERNATIONAL AIRPORT, NORTH PHILADELPHIA AIRPORT (Specialized Departmental Accounting Procedure, No. 22003). Philadelphia: Office of the Director of Finance, January 1, 1958. v.p. figures, forms. pap.

Available in the library of the American Institute of CPA's if not from the publisher, this is a detailed classification of accounts based upon the Civil Aeronautics Administration's recommended uniform classification of accounts, but adapted to the particular needs of the Philadelphia operation.

AUTOMOBILE DEALERS

Lino, Daniel J. FINANCIAL AND OPERATIONAL ANALYSIS OF THE AUTOMOBILE DEALERSHIP. Miami, Florida: Automotive Finance Association, 1963. 148p.

A simple but complete explanation of the automobile dealer's financial and operating statements.

BANKS

For regulations of the Board of Governors of the Federal Reserve System, see Section 3, Governmental Regulation, Federal Reserve System.

American Bankers Association. Country Bank Operations Committee. ACCRUAL ACCOUNTING FOR BANKS. New York: 1967. 46p. charts, tables. pap.

Offers suggested methods of accruing income and expense items most generally found in the financial accounts of banks.

American Bankers Association. Technical Information Service. BANK AUDIT BIBLIOGRAPHY, 1949-1964. New York: 1965. 10p. pap.

A list of "selected reference material which provides suitable information concerning bank audits and internal check and control in banks." The first section, covering the years from 1949 through 1958, was prepared by the AICPA Committee on Bank Auditing and was published in THE JOURNAL OF ACCOUNTANCY, Vol. 7, No. 2, February 1959.

American Institute of Certified Public Accountants. Committee on Bank Accounting and Auditing. AUDITS OF BANKS (an AICPA Industry Audit Guide). New York: 1968. 171p. forms. pap. supplement, 1969.

A comprehensive report which describes the independent auditor's role in the banking industry, the accounting and financial reporting practices peculiar to that industry, and the special factors to be considered in the audit of a bank.

American Institute of Certified Public Accountants. BANK ACCOUNTING PRACTICES AND THEIR RELATIONSHIP TO GENERALLY ACCEPTED ACCOUNTING PRINCIPLES. Unpublished committee paper, New York, 1962. 17p. processed.

An unpublished, but widely distributed position paper prepared by the Committee for discussion purposes with members of the banking industry and others.

Austin, Walter G., Jr. FINANCIAL ACCOUNTING AND REPORTING BY COMMERCIAL BANKS IN THE UNITED STATES. Unpublished Ph.D. thesis, University of Texas, 1964. Ann Arbor, Michigan: University Microfilms, 1964. 316p. biblio., tables. processed. pap.

An interesting study based on the accounting and reporting practices of 600 commercial banks. The author proposes detailed financial statements for banks and suggests applicable financial accounting and reporting practices. Appendices contain questionnaires sent to the 600 banks, to state regulatory agencies and to leading public accountants together with discussions of the response received.

Bank Administration Institute. ACCRUAL ACCOUNTING. Park Ridge, Illinois: 1959. 122p. figures.

Presents the advantages of accrual accounting over cash basis accounting for banks.

Bank Administration Institute. AUDIT PROGRAM FOR THE SMALLER BANK. Park Ridge, Illinois: 1950. 115p. forms. pap.

Excellent guide to the maintenance of good accounting and auditing controls in the smaller bank. Chapters VI-IX serve as a combined chart and manual of accounts, with concise explanations of the character of each account.

Bank Administration Institute. AUDIT QUESTIONNAIRE CHECK LIST, by Harry E. Mertz. Park Ridge, Illinois: 1954. 22p. pap.

A check list of internal audits and controls.

Bank Administration Institute. THE NABAC MANUAL OF BANK ACCOUNTING, AUDITING AND OPERATION, 3rd ed. Park Ridge, Illinois: 1963. 290p. chart of accounts, forms.

Authoritative manual on bank accounting to be used as either a policy manual or a reference guide.

Bank Administration Institute. Accounting Commission. ACCOUNTING BULLETINS, Nos. 1- . Park Ridge, Illinois: 1964- .

A series of bulletins expressing the formal opinions of an institute committee on the application of principles of accounting and statement presentations to banks. No. 1, SECURITIES ACCOUNTING; No. 2, CAPITAL AND EARNINGS ACCOUNTING; No. 3, LOAN LOSS AND RELATED RESERVE ACCOUNTING.

Bank Administration Institute. Accounting and Smaller Bank Commissions. REALISTIC ACCOUNTING AND REPORTING IN THE SMALLER BANK. Park Ridge, Illinois: 1968. 72p. forms, tables.

Describes a method which can be used by a small bank to install and maintain an accrual accounting system. Numerous illustrations.

Bank Administration Institute. Audit Commission. AUDITING BANK EDP SYSTEMS. Park Ridge, Illinois: 1968. 123p. biblio., charts, forms. pap.

Directed toward the bank auditor with no experience of EDP. Chapters lead from a discussion of the basic concepts of the internal audit function and the fundamentals of EDP to internal control and auditing in an EDP environment and a section on auditing the data processing department. Appendix A describes a number of computer audit programs.

Baughn, William H. and Walker, Charles E., eds. THE BANKERS' HANDBOOK. Homewood, Illinois: Dow Jones-Irwin 1966. charts, graphs, tables. 1231p.

Covers all aspects of banking. The following chapters relate to bank accounting and auditing:
Chap. 15: Accounting Systems in Banking
Chap. 16: Cost Analysis and Cost Control
Chap. 17: Internal Audit and Fraud Control
Chap. 18: External Audits for Banks

Board of Governors of the Federal Reserve System. INSTRUCTIONS FOR THE PREPARATION OF REPORTS OF CONDITION BY STATE MEMBER BANKS OF THE FEDERAL RESERVE SYSTEM. Washington, D.C.: June 1969. 54p. pap.

Board of Governors of the Federal Reserve System. INSTRUCTIONS FOR THE PREPARATION OF REPORTS OF INCOME AND DIVIDENDS BY STATE MEMBER BANKS OF THE FEDERAL RESERVE SYSTEM. Washington, D.C.: December 1961. 25p. pap.

Board of Governors of the Federal Reserve System. REGULATION F: SECURITIES OF MEMBER BANKS. Washington, D.C.: 1964. 27p. pap.

Issued pursuant to the Board's new responsibilities of enforcing member bank securities disclosure regulations. Includes forms F-1 through F-12 and F-20.

Corns, Marshall C. HOW TO AUDIT A BANK, 2nd rev. ed. Boston: Bankers Publishing Company, 1966. 460p. forms.

A simplified presentation of bank auditing.

Garcia, F.L. HOW TO ANALYZE A BANK STATEMENT, 4th ed. Boston: Bankers Publishing Co., 1966. 126p. biblio., tables.

Discusses presentation and analysis of bank financial data. Notes changes in bank reporting effected by the Securities Act Amendments of 1964. Numerous statistical tables.

New Jersey Bankers Association and New Jersey Society of Certified Public Accountants. SUGGESTED SCOPE OF BANK AUDITS BY INDEPENDENT PUBLIC ACCOUNTANTS. Riverton, New Jersey: 1956. 14p. pap.

A listing of the general points to be covered in an audit by examiners or accountants.

New York Clearing House Association Committee on Accounting Procedures. BANK COST ACCOUNTING PRINCIPLES AND PROCEDURES. New York: 1961. 65p. tables. pap.

Covers the determination of: the profitability of branches, departments, divisions; the profitability of specific types of services; unit costs of specific activities, such as paying of checks; the analysis of depositors' accounts.

Peat, Marwick, Mitchell & Co. ELECTRONICS AND BANKS. New York: 1956. 37p. pap.

Primary emphasis on application of electronics to depositor accounting. accounting.

Rankin, R.G. SAFEGUARDING THE BANK'S ASSETS. New York: New York State Bankers Association, 1953. 71p. pap.
Covers basic records and controls, directors' examinations and internal audits.

U.S. Treasury. Office of the Comptroller of the Currency. COMPTROLLER'S MANUAL FOR NATIONAL BANKS: LAWS, REGULATIONS, RULINGS. Washington, D.C.: 1963-. loose-leaf.
Updated as required by changes in banking laws and regulations. Available on subscription basis.

U.S. Treasury. Office of the Comptroller of the Currency. COMPTROLLER's MANUAL FOR REPRESENTATIVES IN TRUSTS: REGULATIONS, INSTRUCTIONS, OPINIONS. Washington, D.C.: 1963-. forms. loose-leaf.

A general guide in the examination of National Bank trust departments. Available on subscription basis.

U.S. Treasury. Office of the Comptroller of the Currency. COMPTROLLER'S POLICY GUIDELINES FOR NATIONAL BANK DIRECTORS. Washington, D.C.: September 1964. forms. loose-leaf.
Designed to assist the director, this manual is concerned solely with matters of policy, not with detailed procedures. Available on subscription basis.

U.S. Treasury. Office of the Comptroller of the Currency. DUTIES AND LIABILITIES OF DIRECTORS OF NATIONAL BANKS (Form 1417). Washington, D.C.: September 1965. 30p. pap.
Part VI contains instructions and suggestions concerning periodic examinations of banks "by directors or by any committee appointed by the directors or by accountants for such committee... ."

U.S. Treasury. Office of the Comptroller of the Currency. EXAMINATION OF AUTOMATION IN NATIONAL BANKS. Washington, D.C.: 1962, reprinted 1968. 59p. glossary, biblio. pap.
A manual designed to assist the National Bank Examiner in ascertaining that adequate audit controls have been established over automation. Covers machines and their functions, audit controls and techniques, examination procedures, etc.

U.S. Treasury. Office of the Comptroller of the Currency. INSTRUCTIONS, PROCEDURES, FORMS FOR NATIONAL BANK EXAMINERS. Washington, D.C.: September 1964-. 104p. forms. loose-leaf.
Intended to aid in uniform training of examing personnel. Available on subscription basis.

BEVERAGES

American Bottlers of Carbonated Beverages. ABCB STANDARD ACCOUNTING SYSTEM MANUAL, rev. ed. Washington, D.C.: National Soft Drink Association, 1950. 118p. forms. pap.
Opens with a chart of accounts; other sections include installation and operation of an accounting system, closing and cost statements, profit planning.

Brewers' Association of America. UNIFORM CLASSIFICATION OF ACCOUNTS FOR THE BREWING INDUSTRY, prepared by H.C. Goettsche & Co. Chicago: 1960. 95p. charts. pap.

Offers an accounting system which can be adapted to breweries of various sizes.

Goettsche, H.C. BREWERY ACCOUNTING, COMPLETE SYSTEM AND FORMS, 2nd ed. Crawfordsville, Indiana: Donnelley, 1939. 279p. forms. (o.p.)
Includes detailed classification and explanation of accounts.

Maxwell, George A. WINERY ACCOUNTING AND COST CONTROL. New York: Prentice-Hall, 1949. 143p. charts, forms. (o.p.)
Gives an accounting and cost control system to fit a hypothetical winery producing table wines, dessert wines, vermouth, high-proof and beverage brandy. Classification of accounts is also included.

Wiss, Aaron. FINANCIAL MANAGEMENT FOR BEER WHOLESALERS. Chicago: National Beer Wholesalers' Association of America, Inc., 1963. 105p. pap.
Recommends basic principles of financial management. Includes a suggested chart of accounts for a beer distributor.

BROKERAGE

See also Public Offerings

For additional publications and regulations issued by the Securities and Exchange Commission see Section 3, Governmental Regulation, Securities and Exchange Commission.

American Institute of Certified Public Accountants. AUDITS OF BROKERS OR DEALERS IN SECURITIES. New York: 1956. 71p. pap.
Excellent guide to the special problems encountered in the audit of brokerage firms. Describes accounting records usually kept by brokers and covers in detail the scope of examination and form of reports required.

Association of Stock Exchange Firms. BACKGROUND & OPERATIONS OF THE SECURITIES INDUSTRY, prepared by Bolt Beranek and Newman, Inc. New York: New York Institute of Finance, 1965. 222p. pap.
A programmed text directed toward those with no knowledge of the securities industry. Part 1 gives basic information concerning different types of securities, stock exchanges, etc. Part 2 studies in detail the actual operations of a brokerage firm.

Association of Stock Exchange Firms. Accounting Division. CHART OF ACCOUNTS, rev. ed. New York: 1968. v.p. pap.
A functional chart of accounts presented in card form.

Association of Stock Exchange Firms. MANUAL OF FORMS AND RECORDS FOR PROCESSING AND RECORDING TRANSACTIONS. New York: 1958. 48p. forms. pap. (o.p.)
Includes forms for the order, billing, credit, cashier's dividend, security record and accounting divisions.

Commerce Clearing House, Inc. NATIONAL ASSOCIATION OF SECURITIES DEALERS, INC. MANUAL. Chicago: 1967- . loose-leaf.

Familiarly known as the NASD MANUAL, this constantly updated service contains rules and regulations covering financial transactions and reports of brokers and dealers. Also includes general regulations, fair practice rules, policy interpretations, etc. A convenient paperbound reprint of the essential sections of the MANUAL, omitting NASD membership information, is also available.

Commerce Clearing House, Inc. NEW YORK STOCK EXCHANGE CONSTITUTION AND RULES (reprinted from the NEW YORK STOCK EXCHANGE GUIDE, Vol. 2). Chicago: 1967. v.p. pap.

A convenient reprint of one volume of a three-volume publication, this contains the full text of the Exchange's Constitution, general and miscellaneous rules, definitions of terms, etc. Rules 416, 417 and 418 deal with financial statements and reports. Rule 325 deals with the computation of capital requirements.

Eiteman, Wilford J., *et al.* THE STOCK MARKET, 4th ed. New York: McGraw-Hill Book Co., 1966. 576p. charts, forms, tables.

Covers the general functions of a stock market with detailed description of the organization and operation of the New York Stock Exchange. Final section discusses investor activity in the market, explaining the analysis of financial statements, stock value theories, etc.

Grossfield, Abraham. "Stockbroker - New York Stock Exchange Member Firm Audit." In Prentice-Hall, Inc., ENCYCLOPEDIA OF AUDITING TECHNIQUES, chap. 34.

Outlines the work done as it is scheduled day by day. brief glossary.

Hazard, John W. and Christie, Milton. THE INVESTMENT BUSINESS, A CONDENSATION OF THE SEC REPORT. New York: Harper & Row, 1964. 448p.

Contains no original research, but is strictly a condensation of the lengthy SEC special study of the securities markets. Appendix II consists of a table giving correlation by chapter between this book and the SEC study.

Krell, David. ADVANCED BROKERAGE ACCOUNTING. New York: Pace College, 1969. 228p. paper.

Prepared for use in classes at Pace College, this provides descriptions of schedules and forms used in brokerage accounting.

Leffler, George L. THE STOCK MARKET, 3rd ed., rev. by Loring C. Farwell. New York: Ronald Press, 1963. 666p. forms, illus., tables.

A non-technical description of the operations and functions of the stock market and the securities business.

Pace, Homer St. Clair and Koestler, Edward J. BROKERAGE ACCOUNTING, rev. ed. New York: Pace & Pace, 1950. 188p. exhibits, forms. mimeo. (o.p.)

Sections 1 and 2 cover the principles and procedures of stock and commodity brokerage. Section 3 deals with financial statements and reports.

Robbins, Sidney. THE SECURITIES MARKETS, OPERATIONS AND ISSUES. New York: Free Press of Glencoe, London: Collier-Macmillan Ltd., 1966. 319p. biblio.

Written by the chief economist of the 1963 Special Study of Securities Markets by the Securities and Exchange Commission, this book describes both legal and economic aspects of the securities markets, providing "an integrated approach" to their problems.

Thomson, John S. HANDBOOK FOR THE SECURITIES CASHIER, 3rd rev. ed. Los Angeles: Jerry Saltzer, 1959. 98p. facs.

Handbook which describes in detail the transactions which take place in the cashier's cage.

Thornton, F.W. STOCK BROKERAGE AND INVESTMENT HOUSE ACCOUNTING, WITH NOTES ON AUDITING PROCEDURE. New York: Harper & Bros., 1930. 196p. forms. (o.p.)

Part 1 deals with stock brokerage accounts; Part 2 with accounts of investment security dealers. Although now out of print, this book is still useful in providing descriptions of brokerage house transactions and the books used to record them.

U.S. Securities and Exchange Commission. FORM X-17A-5, rev. November 30, 1967. 10p. pap.

The form to be filed with the SEC by security brokers and dealers. Part I - Financial questionnaire; Part II - Supplementary information. Minimum audit requirements are also included.

U.S. Securities and Exchange Commission. GENERAL RULES AND REGULATIONS UNDER THE SECURITIES EXCHANGE ACT OF 1934, as in effect April 1, 1970. Washington, D.C.: Government Printing Office, 1968. 144p. pap.

This release is revised and updated constantly. Of particular interest to accountants with brokerage clients are the following rules: 15c3-1, net capital requirements for brokers and dealers.

17a-3, records to be made by certain exchange members, brokers and dealers.

17a-5, reports to be made by certain exchange members, brokers and dealers.

U.S. Securities and Exchange Commission. NET CAPITAL REQUIREMENTS FOR BROKERS AND DEALERS - INTERPRETATION AND GUIDE (Accounting Series Release, No. 107). Washington, D.C.: January 18, 1967. 29p. pap.

Intended to help brokers and dealers in complying with the SEC's "net capital" Rule 15c3-1. Part 1 explains the operation of Rule 15c3-1. Part 2 gives a hypothetical example of computation of capital pursuant to Rule 15c3-1, including a detailed trial balance sheet with explanation and a work sheet.

U.S. Securities and Exchange Commission. REPORT OF SPECIAL STUDY OF SECURITIES MARKETS OF THE SECURITIES AND EXCHANGE COMMISSION (88th Congress, 1st session, House document No. 95), 5 volumes. Washington, D.C.: U.S. Government Printing Office, 1963. charts, forms, tables. pap.

A monumental study in which the SEC, as directed by the Congress in 1961, reviewed the adequacy of investor protection in the securities markets. The study contains 176 recommendations for changes in the administration of various aspects of these markets. Proposals are included for raising the standards of the stock exchanges, the NASD (handling the over-the-counter market), investment advisers, and mutual funds among others. The SEC has, since the issuance of this Special Study, been taking up each of these suggestions in turn.

U.S. Securities and Exchange Commission. SECURITIES EXCHANGE ACT OF 1934, as amended to July 29, 1968. Washington, D.C.: U.S. Government Printing Office, 1968. 39p. pap.

Section 15 - Over-the-Counter Markets. Section 17 - Accounts and Records, Reports, Examinations of Exchanges, Members and Others.

Weiss, Ezra. REGISTRATION AND REGULATION OF BROKERS AND DEALERS. Washington, D.C.: Bureau of National Affairs, 1965. 391p.

An excellent handbook on the securities industry and the laws by which it is governed.

CEMETERIES

Mucklow, Walter. CEMETERY ACCOUNTS. New York: American Institute Publishing Co., 1935. 208p. exhibits, forms. (o.p.)

The only available text on this subject, this presents a comprehensive analysis of all financial activities of cemeteries.

CHURCHES

Crowe, J.M. and Moore, Merrill D. CHURCH FINANCE RECORD SYSTEM MANUAL. Nashville, Tennessee: Broadman Press, 1959. 48p. forms, tables. pap.

Describes a financial record system applicable to churches with congregational government. Definition of accounting terms, a chart of accounts for the general fund are included.

Gross, Malvern J., Jr. THE LAYMAN'S GUIDE TO PREPARING FINANCIAL

STATEMENTS FOR CHURCHES. New York: American Institute of Certified Public Accountants, 1966. 16p. pap.

A concise explanation of the major characteristics of church accounting. Several examples of good financial reports are included.

Holck, Manfred, Jr. ACCOUNTING METHODS FOR THE SMALL CHURCH. Minneapolis, Minnesota: Augsberg Publishing House, 1961. 108p. biblio., forms, tables.

Based on materials presented as a thesis for a Master's degree at Austin Presbyterian Seminary, Austin, Texas.

Walker, Arthur L. CHURCH ACCOUNTING METHODS (Church Business Management Series). Englewood Cliffs, New Jersey: Prentice-Hall, 1964. 171p. chart of accounts, biblio., charts, graphs. (Available from Interdenominational Book and Bible Company, Inc., 627 Broadway, New York, New York 10012.)

Offers a simple, basic approach to accounting adaptable to all churches.

CLUBS

Barbour, Henry Ogden. PRIVATE CLUB ADMINISTRATION. Washington, D.C.: Club Managers Association of America, 1968. 643p. charts, forms, tables.

Although this book covers all aspects of club management, accounting for clubs is discussed in several sections. Chapter VII, "Club Financing: Principles and Practices," by Fred W. Eckert is of particular interest.

Club Managers Association of America. UNIFORM SYSTEM OF ACCOUNTS FOR CLUBS, 2nd rev. ed. Washington, D.C.: 1967. 152p. forms.

Prepared by the accounting firms of Laventhol Krekstein Horwath & Horwath and Harris, Kerr, Forster & Company. Outlines one balance sheet presentation for city and country clubs, but separate statements of income and expense. Also includes provision for a summary of gross receipts from all sources.

Harris, Kerr, Forster & Company. CLUBS IN TOWN AND COUNTRY. New York: 1953- . charts, tables. pap.

Annual statistical review of the operations of 50 town and 50 country clubs. Statistical data presented in terms of averages, in geographical divisions and size classifications. Includes 10-year trend tables of income and expense for both types of clubs.

CONSTRUCTION

For regulations of the Federal Housing Authority concerning multifamily housing projects, see Section 3, Governmental Regulations, Department of Housing and Urban Development.

American Institute of Certified Public Accountants. AUDITS OF CONSTRUCTION CONTRACTORS. New York: 1965. 102p. tables. pap.

Combines two earlier pamphlets, GENERALLY ACCEPTED ACCOUNTING PRINCIPLES FOR CONTRACTORS and AUDITING IN THE CONSTRUCTION INDUSTRY in their entirety. Also includes specimen financial statements for construction contractors.

American Institute of Certified Public Accountants. LONG-TERM CONSTRUCTION-TYPE CONTRACTS (Accounting Research Bulletin No. 45). New York: October 1955. 3p. pap.

After describing both the percentage-of-completion and completed-contract accounting methods, the committee states its preference for the former method when estimates of cost and length of time to completion are fairly dependable. Otherwise, the completed-contract method is considered preferable.

Associated General Contractors of America. SUGGESTED GUIDE FOR FIELD COST ACCOUNTING FOR BUILDING CONTRACTORS. Washington, D.C.: 1961. 45p. forms. pap.

Intended as a guide for building contractors to use in establishing their own cost accounting systems. Presents a sample job for which the included forms are developed.

Bentley, Howard B. BUILDING CONSTRUCTION INFORMATION SOURCES (Management Information Guide, No. 2). Detroit, Michigan: Gale Research Co., 1964. 181p.

A detailed, annotated guide to construction literature. Includes dictionaries, encyclopedias, landbooks, government publications, periodicals, directories, indexes, etc.

Bureau of National Affairs, Inc. TAX ACCOUNTING PROBLEMS OF CONTRACTORS (Tax Management Portfolio, No. 75-2nd). Washington, D.C.: 1966. v.p. pap.

Discusses permissible accounting methods and techniques for using them in the operation of a contracting business.

Coombs, W.E. CONSTRUCTION ACCOUNTING AND FINANCIAL MANAGEMENT. New York: McGraw-Hill Book Co., 1958. 481p. forms.

A well-organized book directed toward the individual contractor, this gives a comprehensive review of accounting procedures in the construction industry.

National Association of Home Builders. Business Management Committee. THE ACCOUNTING SYSTEM FOR ALL BUILDERS. Washington, D.C.: August 1965. 32p. charts, tables. pap.

Presents an accounting system designed to be adapted to building operations of any size. Appendices give both short-form and long-form charts of accounts.

The Surety Association of America. CONSTRUCTION CONTRACTORS, THEIR SURETIES, BANKS, FINANCIAL STATEMENTS AND ACCOUNTING METHODS, A BIBLIOGRAPHY. New York: 1964. 38p. pap.

Good listing of articles, addresses, papers and the few available books on the accounting problems of the construction contractor.

Walker, Frank R. PRACTICAL ACCOUNTING AND COST KEEPING FOR CONTRACTORS, 6th ed., rev. Chicago: Frank R. Walker Co., 1968. 251p. forms.

A detailed manual of record-keeping for contractors.

Wolkstein, Harry W. ACCOUNTING METHODS AND CONTROLS FOR THE CONSTRUCTION INDUSTRY. Englewood Cliffs, New Jersey: Prentice-Hall, 1967. 316p. charts, facs., tables.

Points out the numerous ways in which the accountant can offer valuable assistance to the contractor, and, in so doing, presents a general description of accounting for the construction industry.

ELECTRICAL MANUFACTURING

American Institute of Certified Public Accountants. A MEDIUM-SIZED "SMALL LOAN" COMPANY; AN ELECTRONIC EQUIPMENT MANUFACTURER (Case Study in Auditing Procedure, No. 12). New York: 1958. 61p. pap.

The second part of this pamphlet describes the actual procedures followed by a practitioner in an audit of a multiplant company in the electronics manufacturing industry.

National Association of Electrical Distributors. SUGGESTED ACCOUNTING SYSTEM FOR ELECTRICAL SPECIALTY APPLIANCE DISTRIBUTORS (Information Bulletin, No. 739). New York: June 11, 1950. 21p. pap.

Available to members only, but can be read at library of National Association of Accountants.

National Electrical Manufacturers Association. UNIFORM ACCOUNTING MANUAL FOR THE ELECTRICAL MANUFACTURING INDUSTRY, 7th ed. New York: 1950, amended to 1960. v.p. forms, tables. loose-leaf.

Covers account classifications and definitions, accounting for investment in plant and equipment, accounting for costs, analysis of cost variances, financial operating statements and ratios.

ENTERTAINMENT

Carnegie Commission on Educational Television. PUBLIC TELEVISION: A PROGRAM FOR ACTION. New York: Harper & Row, 1967. 266p. graphs, tables.

The report of the Commission on a study of noncommercial television of general public interest rather than that of an instructional nature. The 12 recommendations are designed to strengthen and enlarge both such television systems in the United States.

Institute of Broadcasting Financial Management, Inc. ACCOUNTING MANUAL FOR BROADCASTERS. New York: 1963. tables. loose-leaf.

Covers normal transactions of broadcasting stations.

National Association of Broadcasters. ACCOUNTING MANUAL FOR RADIO STATIONS, rev. ed. Washington, D.C.: 1961. 24p. chart of accounts, forms. pap.

Contains a suggested chart of accounts, a short section on machine accounting, a typical billing system with forms and a brief description of accounting theory and practice designed for those without formal training in accounting.

National Association of Broadcasters. ACCOUNTING MANUAL FOR TELEVISION STATIONS, rev. ed. Washington, D.C.: 1959. 24p. forms. pap.

Designed to guide broadcasters in establishing basic accounting procedures for a TV station. A chart of accounts with definitions is given.

National Association of Educational Broadcasters. Educational Television Stations Division. THE FINANCING OF EDUCATIONAL TELEVISION STATIONS. Washington, D.C.: 1965. 189p. charts. pap.

A study on long-range financing of educational television which reviews present techniques and offers recommendations for the future.

New York. State. Attorney General. THEATRICAL ACCOUNTING (General Business Law, article 26-A, Chapter III, part 51). New York: New York State Department of Law, July 22, 1964. 16p. mimeo. pap.

Rules specify that reports are to be prepared by independent public accountants. Also, theatrical financial books "are to be organized in such a way as to fully record and clearly reflect all financial transactions."

New York. State. General Business Law. THEATRICAL SYNDICATION FINANCING (Article 26-A, as enacted by chapter 728 of the Laws of 1964). Albany, New York: 1964. 8p. pap.

The law giving statutory authority to the enforcement of theatrical accounting regulations by the office of the Attorney General.

Ogden, Warde B. THE TELEVISION BUSINESS; ACCOUNTING PROBLEMS OF A GROWTH INDUSTRY. New York: Ronald Press, 1961. 197p. glossary, charts, graphs.

A study of the business, accounting and financial practices involved in the production, distribution and broadcasting of television programs. Accounting for television film series is thoroughly covered.

Shemel, Sidney and Krasilovsky, M. William. THIS BUSINESS OF MUSIC, ed. by Paul Ackerman. New York: Billboard Publishing Co., 1964. 452p. forms, tables.

Although not specifically on accounting for the music business, this is of interest to accountants with clients in the field since it gives a sound presentation of the multitudinous aspects of the industry about which so little has been written. Chapter 13 is on taxation.

The authors wrote a second book, MORE ABOUT THIS BUSINESS OF MUSIC, published by Billboard Publishing Company in 1967, which covers material not included in their earlier work.

U.S. Federal Communications Commission. AM-FM BROADCAST FINANCIAL DATA. Washington, D.C.: 1935- . pap.

Annual listing of broadcast revenues, expenses and income before tax, based on reports submitted by all networks and stations.

Figures presented by size of area, by state and by cities besides the comparative national statistics.

U.S. Federal Communications Commission. TV BROADCAST FINANCIAL DATA. Washington, D.C.: 1948- . pap.

Annual compilation based on reports submitted by all networks and affiliated and other stations. Includes individual TV market data by cities.

ESTATES AND TRUSTS

See also advanced accounting volumes listed under Accounting and Auditing Textbooks.

Biskind, Elliott L. and Scanlon, John F. BOARDMAN'S ESTATE MANAGEMENT AND ACCOUNTING. New York: Clark Boardman, 1965- . v.p. forms, tables.

A successor volume to the out-of-print Dodge and Sullivan's ESTATE ADMINISTRATION AND ACCOUNTING, this book is a useful reference in matters connected with New York Surrogate Court procedures. Does not include discussion of accounting principles and practices for estates and trusts, nor the distinctions between principal and income which were covered fully in the earlier volume.

Denhardt, J.G., Jr. COMPLETE GUIDE TO ESTATE ACCOUNTING AND TAXES. Englewood Cliffs, New Jersey: Prentice-Hall, 1964. 214p. forms, tables.

Basically for the layman rather than the professional accountant, this is useful because there is so little literature on the subject.

Dodge, Chester J. and Sullivan, John F. ESTATE ADMINISTRATION AND ACCOUNTING (Lawyers and accountants edition). New York: Boardman, 1940, with 1940-50 supplement. 872p. forms, tables. (o.p.)

Excellent presentation not only of estate administration, but of the accounting principles and practices for estates and trusts.

Prentice-Hall, Inc. "Estates and Trusts - Corporate Fiduciary." "Estates and Trusts - Individual Fiduciary." In ENCYCLOPEDIA OF ACCOUNTING FORMS AND REPORTS. New York: 1964. Volume 3, pp.141-173.

Illustrations and descriptions of forms to be used in both corporate and individual fiduciary estate transactions.

Stephenson, Gilbert Thomas. ESTATES AND TRUSTS, 4th ed. New York: Appleton-Century-Crofts, 1965. 463p. biblio.

Although containing little information specifically on estate accounting, this is the best of the textbooks on estates and trusts. "Collateral reading" lists at end of each chapter.

Tanguy, Lewis L. and Gaffney, Thomas J. "Fiduciary Accounting - Estates and Trusts." In Prentice-Hall, Inc. ACCOUNTANT'S ENCYCLOPEDIA. New York: 1962. pp.1017-70.

Opens with the basic terminology and procedures in fiduciary accounting. Explains the role of the public accountant with particular emphasis on types of engagements and working arrangements. Discusses special accounting and tax problems. The final section describes the accounting system.

Wixon, Rufus, ed. "Fiduciary Accounting." In his ACCOUNTANTS' HANDBOOK. New York: Ronald Press, 1956. sec. 26.

Covers legal background and accounting procedure for private trusts, charitable trusts and foundations, decedents' estates. The final two sections deal with bankruptcy procedures.

EXPORT — IMPORT

Goldner, Jack. FOREIGN TRADE ACCOUNTING AND MANAGEMENT HANDBOOK. Chicago: Commerce Clearing House, 1967. 542p. biblio., forms, tables.

Explains exporting and importing procedures and overseas operations and describes the related accounting methods and controls for companies engaged in foreign trade. Detailed case studies of ten different types of companies in the export and import business and companies with foreign subsidiaries.

Shaterian, William S. EXPORT - IMPORT BANKING, THE DOCUMENTS AND FINANCIAL OPERATIONS OF FOREIGN TRADE, 2nd ed. New York: Ronald Press, 1956. 518p. forms.

Still the authoritative work on the forms and procedures involved in export-import banking. Sections on the foreign departments of banks, documents of foreign trade and financial operations of foreign trade.

FARMS

American Institute of Certified Public Accountants. A MEDIUM-SIZED DAIRY (Case Study in Auditing Procedure, No. 14). New York: 1962. 35p. pap.

Case study of an actual examination of a dairy, submitted by a member of the Institute's Committee on Auditing Procedure.

Hopkins, John A. and Heady, Earl O. FARM RECORDS AND ACCOUNTING, 5th ed. Ames, Iowa: Iowa State University Press, 1962. 391p. tables.

Sections on bookkeeping records, valuation and depreciation of farm inventory, farm financial accounts, analysis of farm records, income taxes, enterprise accounts and farm budgeting and planning.

Joint Committee on Standardization of Farm Management Accounting. ACCOUNTING AND PLANNING FOR FARM MANAGEMENT. Brisbane, Queensland, Australia: Queensland Department of Primary Industries, 1966. 160p. biblio., tables.

An excellent detailed presentation of a practical, uniform system of farm management accounting. Covers the preparation and interpretation of accounting information and use of accounting data for planning and control.

Mallyon, C.A. THE PRINCIPLES AND PRACTICE OF FARM MANAGEMENT ACCOUNTING. Sydney: The Law Book Co. of Australasia Pty. Ltd., 1961. 363p. selected biblio., tables.

Reviews all aspects of farm accounting. Sections on installation and operation of the accounting system, presentation and analysis of accounts, budgeting and project accounting.

New Zealand Society of Accountants. Farm Research Committee. FARM

ACCOUNTING IN NEW ZEALAND. Wellington, New Zealand: 1965; supplement, 1966. 166p. glossary of farm terms, tables. pap.
A recommended form of accounts for livestock farming which can be easily adjusted with minor changes in individual circumstances.

Oppenheimer, Harold L. COWBOY ARITHMETIC: CATTLE AS AN INVESTMENT, 2nd ed. Danville, Illinois: Interstate, 1964. 226p. biblio., facs., photos., tables.
Although concentrating primarily on investment tax aspects of cattle breeding, this book gives useful background information on historical and economic aspects of the livestock industry.

Oppenheimer, Harold L. COWBOY ECONOMICS: RURAL LAND AS AN INVESTMENT. Danville, Illinois: Interstate, 1966. 285p. charts, maps, photos, tables.
Analyzes ranching and cattle breeding from the economic, management and tax viewpoints. Good background information. Historical and operational reference guide bibliography included.

FIDUCIARY

See Estates and Trusts

FINANCE COMPANIES

American Institute of Certified Public Accountants. A MEDIUM-SIZED "SMALL LOAN" COMPANY (Case Studies in Auditing Procedure, No. 12). New York: 1958. pp.11-38. pap.
A case study on an actual examination of a small loan company, submitted by a member of the Institute's Committee on Auditing Procedure.

American Institute of Certified Public Accountants. A SMALL LOAN (CONSUMER FINANCE) COMPANY (Case Studies in Auditing Procedure, No. 13). New York: 1962. pp.33-57. pap.
A case study submitted by a member of the Institute's Committee on Auditing Procedure describing an actual audit of a small loan company.

American Institute of Certified Public Accountants. A SMALLER COMMERCIAL FINANCE COMPANY (Case Studies in Auditing Procedure, No. 10). New York: 1956. 43p. pap. (o.p.)
Case study submitted by a member of the Institute's Committee on Auditing Procedure covering an actual examination of a commercial finance company.

Canadian Institute of Chartered Accountants. FINANCE COMPANIES - THEIR ACCOUNTING, FINANCIAL STATEMENT PRESENTATION, AND AUDITING (Research Study, No. 9), by St. Elmo V. Smith. Toronto: October 1967. 71p. pap.
A study of the finance company industry in Canada and all aspects of its accounting requirements.

FOOD

American Institute of Certified Public Accountants. A CORN PROCESSING COMPANY (Case Studies in Auditing Procedure, No. 5). New York: 1947.

64p. pap. (o.p.)

Case study submitted by a member of the Institute's Committee on Auditing Procedure covering an actual examination of a corn processing company.

American Institute of Certified Public Accountants. A GRAIN COMPANY (Case Studies in Auditing Procedure, No. 7). New York: 1949. 50p. pap. (o.p.)

Case study submitted by a member of the Institute's Committee on Auditing Procedure covering an actual examination of a grain company.

Grain and Feed Dealers National Association. Financial Information Committee. MANAGEMENT ACCOUNTING MANUAL. Washington, D.C.: 1968. v.p. chart of accounts, forms.

Offers a computerized uniform accounting system for the grain, feed and farm supply industry. Developed by the Association's Financial Information Committee under the direction of Peat, Marwick, Mitchell & Co. in cooperation with The National Cash Register Company. The system may also be prepared manually.

LeMoine, Joseph F. IMPROVING ACCOUNTING PROCEDURES IN FOOD BROKER FIRMS. Newark, Delaware: Food Distribution Section, University of Delaware, 1964. 58p. chart of accounts. pap.

Prepared under a Small Business Administration Management Research grant to the University of Delaware. Reports on existing accounting practices among food brokers and recommends a uniform system of accounts for the industry.

National Association of Frozen Food Packers. A COST ACCOUNTING MANUAL FOR FROZEN FOOD PACKERS, rev. ed. Washington: 1958. 76p. exhibits, forms. pap.

Presents the basic cost accounting system most generally used in the frozen food packing industry with the intent of encouraging a uniform method of cost accounting within the industry.

U.S. Department of Agriculture. Agricultural Marketing Service. IMPROVED METHODS AMONG WHOLESALE FOOD DISTRIBUTORS: FOR INVENTORY CONTROL, SALES ACCOUNTING, AND SHIPMENT OF MERCHANDISE (Marketing Research Report No. 271). Washington, D.C.: U.S. Government Printing Office, 1958. 75p. charts, diagrs., illus., tables. pap.

Report based on research by Fraser and Torbet. Reviews both manual and tabulating machine methods, finding that an annual business volume of approximately six million is necessary before automatic equipment pays its way.

U.S. Department of Agriculture. Economic Research Service. Marketing Economics Division. A GUIDE TO UNIFORM COST AND FINANCIAL ACCOUNTING FOR POULTRY PROCESSORS. Washington, D.C.: U.S. Government Printing Office, June 1961. 144p. charts, tables. pap.

Presents three types of cost systems of varying complexity. Chart of accounts and account codes are included.

U.S. Farmer Cooperative Service (Department of Agriculture). GUIDE TO UNIFORM ACCOUNTING FOR LOCKER AND FREEZER PROVISIONERS (Agriculture Handbook, No. 163). Washington, D.C.: U.S. Government Printing

Office, August 1959. 53p. forms. pap.
Explains the uniform accounting system and offers guides for using it.

U.S. Farmer Cooperative Service (Department of Agriculture). MANAGEMENT ACCOUNTING FOR FROZEN FOOD LOCKER AND RELATED PLANTS, by Robert L. Dickens. Washington, D.C.: U.S. Government Printing Office, 1961. 117p. forms. pap.
Objective of this study was to develop accounting procedures and techniques that would provide cost information needed for small business management.

FOUNDRIES

See also Iron and Steel

Belt, Robert E. FOUNDRY COST ACCOUNTING, PRACTICE AND PROCEDURE, 2nd rev. ed. Cleveland, Ohio: Penton Publishing Co., 1926. 267p. forms. (o.p.)
Includes procedures for a gray iron, malleable iron, and steel foundry.

British Steel Founders' Association. STEEL FOUNDRY COSTING. London: Gee & Co. (Publishers) Ltd., 1965. 110p. tables.
Prepared by a subcommittee of the Accountants Committee of the Association. Offers a basic cost system to be used as a model by all British steel foundries.

Court, H.P. and Harrison, W.E. THE ELEMENTS OF FOUNDRY COSTING. London: The Council of Ironfoundry Associations, 1956. 91p. figures. pap.
Gives a sound cost system for the foundry industry.

Gray and Ductile Iron Founders' Society, Inc. ADVANCED COST ACCOUNTING METHODS FOR GRAY IRON FOUNDRIES (Cost Manual No. 2). Cleveland, Ohio: 1954. 119p. pap.
With Cost Manual No. 1 (1949) included as a supplement, this manual was intended to induce foundries to advance from the level of cost practice illustrated in the earlier manual to the advanced methods shown here. Suggested cost methods for several departments are given in some detail: the melting, molding, core, cleaning and shipping departments.

Malleable Founders' Society. Committee on Cost Accounting. MANUAL OF PRINCIPLES AND PROCEDURES OF COST ACCOUNTING FOR THE MALLEABLE IRON INDUSTRY. Cleveland, Ohio: 1949. 37p. pap.
Provides for segregation and accumulation of costs by productive departments, service departments and general cost divisions. A definition of terms listing is given.

Non-ferrous Founders' Society, Inc. MANUAL OF BASIC COST PRINCIPLES WITH CHART OF ACCOUNTS AND COST DICTIONARY FOR NON-FERROUS FOUNDRIES, 3rd ed. Cleveland, Ohio: 1954. 56p. pap.
Provides both a simplified and an expanded cost system. Chart of accounts and cost dictionary are included in this manual.

Steel Founders' Society of America. Management Accounting Program Committee. MANAGEMENT CONTROLS, Bulletins No. 1-20. Cleveland, Ohio:

1959-61. pap. (o.p.)
An excellent series of bulletins prepared by Price Waterhouse & Co. for the Steel Founders' Society which deal with accounting and control problems of steel foundries in a concrete way. Subject index was issued in May 1961.

GOVERNMENT AND MUNICIPAL

See also Hospitals and Schools and Colleges

American Association of State Highway Officials. MANUAL OF UNIFORM ACCOUNTING PROCEDURES. Washington, D.C.: 1958-1960. 202p. forms.
Sections on chart of accounts, highway control, internal auditing, administration and engineering, construction accounting, maintenance accounting, equipment accounting, budgets, purchasing and stores. Chapter 1 gives definitions of terms used in all aspects of highway construction and maintenance including accounting terminology.

Burkhead, Jesse. GOVERNMENT BUDGETING. New York: John H. Wiley & Sons, 1956. 510p. charts, forms, tables.
Discusses historical background of governmental budgeting. Describes the classification of budget data, the various phases of federal budgeting such as agency budgeting, and specialized budget problems. Bibliographies at the end of each chapter.

Harris, Walter O. MUNICIPAL PUBLIC WORKS COST ACCOUNTING MANUAL. Chicago: Public Administration Service, 1955. 107p. chart of accounts, forms. pap.
Intended as a basic cost accounting manual for the installation and maintenance of cost accounts for public works and water utility operations.

Kerrigan, Harry D. FUND ACCOUNTING. New York: McGraw-Hill, 1969. 533p. Terminology of government accounting, pp.478-512. charts, tables.
Covers fund accounting concepts and techniques for the municipal and the non-profit organization.

Kohler, Eric and Wright, Howard W. ACCOUNTING IN THE FEDERAL GOVERNMENT. Englewood Cliffs, New Jersey: Prentice-Hall, 1956. 291p. biblio.
First chapters deal with aspects of local government accounting, the remainder with federal agency accounting. Chapters on the General Accounting Office, Bureau of the Budget, Treasury Department and General Services Administration. Also covers accounting for costs, management and transaction controls, internal auditing, revolving funds, construction accounting and federal purchasing.

Mikesell, R.M. and Hay, Leon E. GOVERNMENTAL ACCOUNTING, 4th ed. Homewood, Illinois: Richard D. Irwin, 1969. 772p. charts, graphs.
Describes the accounting procedures used in all the generally recognized funds employed in governmental accounting. Governmental accounting terminology, pp.694-737.

National Committee on Governmental Accounting. GOVERNMENTAL

ACCOUNTING, AUDITING AND FINANCIAL REPORTING. Chicago: Municipal Finance Officers Association of the United States and Canada, 1968. 248p. forms, tables.

This authoritative work on governmental accounting combines and revises two earlier publications, MUNICIPAL ACCOUNTING AND AUDITING and A STANDARD CLASSIFICATION OF MUNICIPAL ACCOUNTS. Describes principles and procedures of accounting, budgeting, auditing and financial reporting for all governmental units other than national governments and their agencies. Classifications of balance sheet, revenue and expenditure accounts which are explained in detail can be adapted to all types and sizes of governmental units. Terminology and classification of accounts are given.

National Committee on Governmental Accounting. SIMPLIFIED MUNICIPAL ACCOUNTING: A MANUAL FOR SMALLER GOVERNMENTAL UNITS. Chicago: 1950. 162p. forms. (o.p.)

Practical working manual.

Normanton, E.L. THE ACCOUNTABILITY AND AUDIT OF GOVERNMENTS. Manchester, England: The University Press; New York: Praeger, 1966. 472p.

Describes the development, in law and practice of the state audit in Great Britain and other Western countries as well as the broader subject of public accountability.

Tenner, Irving and Lynn, Edward S. MUNICIPAL AND GOVERNMENTAL ACCOUNTING, 4th ed. (Prentice-Hall Accounting Series). Englewood Cliffs, New Jersey: Prentice-Hall, 1960. 592p. Governmental accounting terminology, biblio.

Includes material on performance budgeting.

GOVERNMENT CONTRACTS

See Also Section 3, Governmental Regulation, for the following government agencies, other than the Department of Defense, also responsible for procurement regulations: Atomic Energy Commission, Defense Supply Agency (listed under Department of Defense), National Aeronautics and Space Administration and the Renegotiation Board.

Commerce Clearing House. GOVERNMENT CONTRACTS GUIDE. Chicago: 1967- . pap.

A convenient handbook on government contract problems. Based on CCH service GOVERNMENT CONTRACTS REPORTS, footnotes key the references to specific paragraphs in the much more comprehensive service. Checklist of contract clauses to be used in different types of contracts included in each edition. Good subject index.

Cuneo, Gilbert A. GOVERNMENT CONTRACTS HANDBOOK. Washington, D.C.: Machinery and Allied Products Institute and Council for Technological Advancement, 1962. 384p. forms.

A "practical working handbook" for the businessman involved in government contract work. Bibliographies at the end of each chapter.

Electronic Industries Association. DEFENSE CONTRACT TERMINATION GUIDE. Washington, D.C.: 1964. 114p. pap.

A handy guide for the use of industry in following the basic procedures set forth in Sections VIII and XV of the Armed Services Procurement Regulations. Not to be used as an official set of rules. Includes a convenient "Termination Flow Chart."

Gunzer, C. Richard. RENEGOTIATION PRACTICE AND PROCEDURE. New Fairfield, Connecticut: 1962- . v.p. biblio., forms, tables. loose-leaf.
Covers methods of gathering, presenting and pleading facts in renegotiation.

Machinery and Allied Products Institute and Council for Technological Advancement. THE GOVERNMENT CONTRACTOR AND THE GENERAL ACCOUNTING OFFICE. Washington, D.C.: 1966. 225p.
An excellent report which discusses historical development of the General Accounting Office, its general functions and its role in government procurement. Concentrates on the GAO's contract audit function.

Paul, Jack. UNITED STATES GOVERNMENT CONTRACTS & SUBCONTRACTS. Philadelphia: Joint Committee on Continuing Legal Education of the American Law Institute and the American Bar Association, 1964. 769p.
Written primarily for the lawyer, this is a good presentation of the principles and procedures of federal procurement. Highlights problems with which an attorney should be ready to cope.

Sweeney, Henry W. "Accounting for Government Contracts." In Prentice-Hall, Inc., ACCOUNTANT'S ENCYCLOPEDIA, Vol. 3. New York: 1962. chap. 35.
Describes different types of contracts and procedures for obtaining them, government definition of allowable and unallowable costs, and termination and price renegotiation of government contracts.

Trueger, Paul M. ACCOUNTING GUIDE FOR DEFENSE CONTRACTS, 5th ed. Chicago: Commerce Clearing House, 1966. 798p. forms.
A comprehensive and detailed guide on government procurement policies and practices with particular emphasis on the accounting methods required in dealing with defense contracts.

U.S. Department of Defense. ARMED SERVICES PROCUREMENT REGULATIONS. Washington, D.C.: U.S. Government Printing Office, 1969-. loose-leaf.
The essential source of information on government procurement regulations. Its section on "Contract Cost Principles" contains general cost principles and procedures for the determination and allowance of costs in connection with the negotiation and administration of cost-reimbursement type contracts. Available on subscription basis.

U.S. Department of Defense. ARMED SERVICES PROCUREMENT REGULATION MANUAL FOR CONTRACT PRICING. Washington, D.C.: U.S. Government Printing Office, February 1969-. loose-leaf. paper.
Contains detailed discussion and examples in order to illustrate application of pricing policy to pricing problems. Based on policies expressed in the Armed Services Procurement Regulations, but does not contain material which is directive in nature.

U.S. Department of Defense and National Aeronautics and Space Administration. INCENTIVE CONTRACTING GUIDE, prepared by the Office of Assistant Secretary of Defense (Installations and Logistics). Washington, D.C.: U.S. Government Printing Office, 1969. 254p. charts. pap.

Gives the policy, principles and practice governing the application of incentives of various kinds (cost, schedule, etc.) to a number of procurement situations.

U.S. General Accounting Office. AUDITS OF GOVERNMENT CONTRACTS. Washington, D.C.: U.S. Government Printing Office, 1966. 31p. pap.

A brief presentation of information on the authority, purposes, objectives and related auditing and reporting practices of the GAO in carrying out its responsibilities to those government contractors whose contracts are subject to GAO audit.

HOSPITALS

American Hospital Association. ACCOUNTING MANUAL FOR LONG-TERM CARE INSTITUTIONS. Chicago: 1968. 129p. chart of accounts, forms.

Emphasizes the use of accounting and financial management in these institutions. Sections on a specialized chart of accounts, cash, inventories, payroll, cost finding, budgeting, and financial and statistical reports.

American Hospital Association. BOOKKEEPING PROCEDURES AND BUSINESS PRACTICES FOR SMALL HOSPITALS. Chicago: 1956. 170p. forms, illus. pap.

A guide for small hospitals in the establishment of financial management programs.

American Hospital Association. BUDGETING PROCEDURES FOR HOSPITALS. Chicago: 1961. 78p. forms, illus. pap.

An effective budget program for hospitals.

American Hospital Association. CHART OF ACCOUNTS FOR HOSPITALS. Chicago: 1966. 143p. charts. pap.

Intended to serve as the basis for all accounting manuals published by the American Hospital Association. The other manuals simply develop the recommended classification of accounts into systems and procedures for further use by hospitals.

American Hospital Association. COST FINDING AND RATE SETTING FOR HOSPITALS. Chicago: 1968. 111p. charts, forms, tables. pap.

A major revision and expansion of the 1957 COST FINDING FOR HOSPITALS. Describes methods of compiling, analyzing and interpreting cost data as an aid in establishing and maintaining financial information to be used in hospital management decisions.

American Hospital Association. HOSPITAL LITERATURE INDEX. Published quarterly with annual and five-year cumulations.

Classified listing of books, pamphlets and articles on hospital administration and management, including accounting. Approximately 95% of technical articles in HOSPITAL ACCOUNTING magazine are listed. Available on subscription basis.

American Hospital Association. INTERNAL CONTROL AND INTERNAL AUDITING FOR HOSPITALS. Chicago: 1969. 66p. chart. pap.

A general guide to establishing a system of internal control in a hospital.

American Hospital Association. UNIFORM HOSPITAL DEFINITIONS. Chicago: 1960. 54p. pap.

Gives recommendations for standard hospital definitions specifically designed in relation to uniform accounting procedures. Originally published as Chapter 1 in 1960 UNIFORM CHART OF ACCOUNTS AND DEFINITIONS FOR HOSPITALS, since superseded by 1966 CHART OF ACCOUNTS FOR HOSPITALS.

American Institute of Certified Public Accountants. A HOSPITAL (Case Studies in Auditing Procedure, No. 11). New York: 1956. 45p. chart, exhibits. pap.

Presents an actual audit of a hospital, submitted by a member of the Institute's Committee on Auditing Procedure.

American Institute of Certified Public Accountants. MEDICARE AUDIT GUIDE (Industry Audit Guide). New York: 1969. 52p. pap.

Provides guidance to the independent auditor examining and reporting on statements of reimbursable costs under the Medicare program.

Canadian Hospital Association. THE CANADIAN HOSPITAL ACCOUNTING MANUAL: ACCOUNTING AND STATISTICAL PRINCIPLES AND PROCEDURES FOR CANADIAN HOSPITALS, 2nd ed. Toronto: [1959] 211p. chart of accounts, charts, graphs, tables. pap.

Canadian Institute of Chartered Accountants. Committee on Accounting and Auditing Research. THE HOSPITAL AUDIT (Research Study, No. 7). 58p. biblio. pap.

Covers the special features of hospital accounting and internal control as well as the responsibilities of the auditor and of hospital boards and administrators.

Commerce Clearing House, Inc. COMPLETE GUIDE TO MEDICARE, as of January 2, 1968. 432p. pap.

Handbook which includes the full texts of pertinent laws, final regulations, and detailed explanations of official material.

Harris, Kerr, Forster & Company. ACCOUNTING MANUAL FOR NURSING HOMES. New York: 1967. 21p. charts, tables. pap.

Intended to give practical guidance to nursing homes in the management and recording of financial transactions.

Hay, Leon E. BUDGETING AND COST ANALYSIS FOR HOSPITAL MANAGEMENT, 2nd ed. Bloomington, Indiana: Pressler Publications, 1963. 311p. charts, graphs.

Shows how to apply the principles of budgeting and cost analysis to the financial problems of hospitals. Numerous tables in both the "Budgeting" and the "Cost Analysis" sections.

Lybrand, Ross Bros. & Montgomery. ACCOUNTING AND ECONOMIC ASPECTS OF THE MEDICARE PROGRAM TO HEALTH CARE INSTITUTIONS (Lybrand Newsletter Special Report). New York: February 1966. 27p. pap.

Directed toward the hospital administrator, this pamphlet not only explains the determination of reasonable costs in some detail, but also gives background information about the Medicare program and outlines procedures for billing and admission of patients. Includes a brief checklist and bibliography. A supplement dated July 1966 is entitled COST DETERMINATION AND REIMBURSEMENT REQUIREMENTS OF THE MEDICARE PROGRAM.

Martin, T. Leroy. HOSPITAL ACCOUNTING, PRINCIPLES AND PRACTICE, 3rd ed. Chicago: Physicians' Record Company, 1958. 296p. tables.

A good detailed presentation of hospital accounting which was originally developed for a graduate hospital accounting course. A fundamental knowledge of accounting is required of the reader.

Seawell, L. Vann. HOSPITAL ACCOUNTING AND FINANCIAL MANAGEMENT. Berwyn, Illinois: Physicians' Record Company, 1964. 528p. charts, forms, tables.

A sequel to the 1960 text by the same author, PRINCIPLES OF HOSPITAL ACCOUNTING. Emphasis is placed on the utilization of information found in accounting reports for effective hospital management, planning and control. Uniform classification of accounts, pp.78-87.

Seawell, L. Vann. PRINCIPLES OF HOSPITAL ACCOUNTING. Berwyn, Illinois: Physicians' Record Company, 1960. 384p.

Gives the fundamental principles and procedures of hospital accounting. Directed toward the non-accountant.

Taylor, Philip J. and Nelson, Benjamin O. MANAGEMENT ACCOUNTING FOR HOSPITALS. Philadelphia: W.B. Saunders Company, 1964. 449p. chart of accounts, biblio., charts, tables.

Giving complete coverage of hospital accounting reports, this book reflects the collective experience of the partners and staff of Lybrand, Ross Bros. & Montgomery.

U.S. Department of Health, Education, and Welfare. Social Security Administration. AUDIT PROGRAM FOR HOSPITALS UNDER THE HEALTH INSURANCE FOR THE AGED ACT - TITLE XVIII (HIM-16). Washington, D.C.: 1968. 16p. pap.

Offers detailed instructions for audit program for hospitals operating under Medicare. Includes suggested forms of certification. A similar publication dealing with extended care facilities (nursing homes) is the AUDIT PROGRAM FOR EXTENDED CARE FACILITIES UNDER THE HEALTH INSURANCE FOR AGED ACT, TITLE XVIII (HIM-18), also published in 1968.

U.S. Department of Health, Education, and Welfare. HOSPITAL MANUAL (HIM-10), rev. ed. Washington, D.C.: U.S. Government Printing Office, April 1967. 122p. forms. pap.

A procedural manual designed for use by hospitals which will be billing for services furnished under Medicare.

U.S. Department of Health, Education, and Welfare. PRINCIPLES OF REIMBURSEMENT FOR PROVIDER COSTS (HIM-5). Washington, D.C.: U.S. Government Printing Office, May 1966. 30p. pap.

Gives Medicare accounting regulations for allowable and unallowable costs. Discusses methods by which costs of services to Medicare beneficiaries are determined.

U.S. Department of Health, Education, and Welfare. PROVIDER REIMBURSEMENT MANUAL (HIM-15). Washington, D.C.: U.S. Government Printing Office, 1967. 19p. pap.

A manual to be used by intermediaries in computing reasonable costs of services furnished under Medicare. Each chapter is being published as completed. Chapter 1, entitled DEPRECIATION (HIM 15), 15 p., July 1967.

U.S. Department of Health, Education, and Welfare. Social Security Administration Library. MEDICARE, A BIBLIOGRAPHY OF SELECTED REFERENCES, 1966/1967. Washington, D.C.: U.S. Government Printing Office, 1968. 88p. pap.

Classified, annotated bibliography of significant books, pamphlets and articles on the subject acquired by the Social Security Administration Library during Medicare's first year. Lists of the most valuable periodicals and indexing and abstracting services are included.

HOTELS AND MOTELS

American Hotel and Motel Association. UNIFORM SYSTEM OF ACCOUNTS AND EXPENSE DICTIONARY FOR MOTELS, MOTOR HOTELS, SMALL HOTELS. New York: 1962. 128p. forms.

Section I contains illustrative balance sheet for a motel, motor hotel or small hotel. Section II gives illustrative operating statements for properties with very little restaurant activity (includes motels with concession-basis restaurants). Section III contains illustrative operating statements for properties with extensive restaurant operations.

American Motor Hotel Association. UNIFORM CLASSIFICATION OF ACCOUNTS FOR MOTELS AND MOTOR HOTELS. Temple, Texas: Tourist Court Journal, rev. printing, 1965. 84p. chart of accounts.

Non-technical manual intended for motel owners and managers.

Harris, Kerr, Forster & Company. TRENDS IN THE HOTEL-MOTEL BUSINESS. New York: 1935- . charts, tables. pap.

Financial analyses of the hotel industry, arranged by transient, residential and resort hotels and by motels and motor hotels.

Horwath, Ernest B., et al. HOTEL ACCOUNTING, 3rd ed. New York: Ronald Press, 1963. 519p. chart, forms, tables.

Gives background of the hotel industry and hotel operation before going into an exhaustive study of accounting and control methods in the field. Simplified system of accounts for small hotels is included.

Hotel Association of New York City, Inc. UNIFORM SYSTEM OF ACCOUNTS FOR HOTELS, 6th rev. ed. New York: 1961. 102p.

Adopted by the American Hotel Association of United States and Canada.

Laventhol Krekstein Horwath & Horwath. LODGING INDUSTRY. New York: 1931- . charts, tables. pap.

Operating ratios of 100 hotels located in a number of different cities. Issued annually.

Merriam, Kemper W. A SIMPLIFIED SYSTEM OF ACCOUNTING FOR THE SMALL MOTEL (Special Studies, No. 9). Tucson, Arizona: Bureau of Business Research, University of Arizona, 1954. 37p. forms. pap.

Presents a bookkeeping system for the tourist motel operator.

Tourist Court Journal. ANNUAL MOTEL FINANCIAL REPORT. Temple, Texas: Tourist Court Journal Company, Inc., 1938- .

Published annually in the July issue of the TOURIST COURT JOURNAL, this study gives 30-year records and 11-year comparative statistics of expenses and profits from room sales. Also presents operations averages by geographic area and by motel size.

INSURANCE

Also of importance to accountants in this field are the rules, regulations and laws promulgated by state authorities.

American Institute of Certified Public Accountants. AUDITS OF FIRE AND CASUALTY INSURANCE COMPANIES. New York: 1966. 84p. glossary. pap.

Describes the nature of the fire and casualty insurance business, the methods of accounting and recordkeeping and the prescribed financial reporting principles and practices. Includes suggested audit procedures as guidelines.

Beardsley, Charles M. LIFE COMPANY ANNUAL STATEMENT HANDBOOK. Columbus, Ohio: Charles M. Beardsley and Associates, Inc., 1962. v.p. tables.

Designed as a workbook to assist those seeking specific guides to the preparation of annual statements for U.S. life insurance companies.

Beardsley, Charles M. NEW ITEMS IN THE ... ANNUAL STATEMENT FOR LIFE INSURANCE COMPANIES. Columbus, Ohio: Charles M. Beardsley & Associates, Inc., 1966- . forms, tables. pap.

Annual work designed to help the insurance financial officer in preparing his annual statement blanks. Numerous Illustrations. Latest instructions for completing life, accident and health statement blanks compiled by the National Association of Insurance Commissioners is included as an appendix.

Huebner, S.S. and Black, Kenneth, Jr. LIFE INSURANCE, 6th ed. New York: Appleton-Century-Crofts, 1964. 831p. charts, forms, formulas, tables.

One of the best texts on the life insurance field. Chapters 42 and 43 are entitled "Interpreting Life Insurance Company Financial Statements: I and II," and cover the accounting aspects in some detail.

Institute of Life Insurance. LIFE INSURANCE FACT BOOK. New York: 1946- . charts, tables. pap.

Excellent annual compilation of insurance statistics, annual statement tabulations, etc. Includes mortality tables and a glossary of insurance terms.

Insurance Accounting and Statistical Association. INSURANCE ACCOUNTING,

FIRE AND CASUALTY, 2nd ed., ed. by W. Rogers Hammond. Philadelphia: Chilton, 1965. 358p. exhibits.

An excellent guide to basic accounting principles as applied to the specialized field of fire and casualty insurance.

Kerrmann, F. M. LIFE INSURANCE RECORDKEEPING AND ACCOUNTING. New York: Life Office Management Association, 1960. 224p. chart of accounts, forms. pap.

Describes the fundamentals and the methods of the recordkeeping processes used in the life insurance industry.

Life Office Management Association. PRINCIPLES OF LIFE INSURANCE, 2 vols. Homewood, Illinois: Richard D. Irwin, 1964. tables.

Volume 1 outlines basic principles of life insurance, legal aspects, taxation, etc. Volume 2 deals with organizational concepts and functions required to run a life insurance company. Chapter 13 (Vol. 2) is on financial statements.

Lybrand, Ross Bros. & Montgomery. COMMENTS ON INSURANCE COMPANY ACCOUNTING PRACTICES. New York: 1964. 26p. pap.

A discussion of specific areas in which insurance company accounting practices differ from generally accepted accounting principles. Part 1 is on accounting for life insurance companies; Part 2 covers fire and casualty companies.

Maclean, Joseph B. LIFE INSURANCE, 9th ed. New York: McGraw-Hill Book Co., 1962. 631p.

Provides excellent coverage of the entire life insurance field. Chapter 16 deals with financial statements.

Michelbacher, G.F. MULTIPLE-LINE INSURANCE. New York: McGraw-Hill Book Co., 1957. 674p. biblio., forms, tables.

Chapters 8, "Audits of Exposure," and 19, "The Financial Statement," are of particular interest to accountants in the insurance field.

National Association of Insurance Commissioners. Committee on Valuation of Securities. VALUATION OF SECURITIES AS OF DECEMBER 31 ... New York: 1945- . loose-leaf.

Annual publication giving notations as to amortizability of each bond and market values of stocks to be used in the companies' annual statements.

New York. State. Insurance Department. EXAMINATION OF INSURANCE COMPANIES, 7 vols. New York: 1953-55. (o.p.)

A series of lectures delivered before the examiners of the New York State Department of Insurance. Volume 7 is an Index volume.

Peat, Marwick, Mitchell & Co. FEDERAL TAXATION OF LIFE INSURANCE COMPANIES. [Chicago]: February 1968. 80p. pap.

Gives background material on, and a summary of, the Life Insurance Company Income Tax Act of 1959. Main portion discusses tax planning for acquisitions and mergers, purchase or sale of a block of insurance contracts, utilization of operations losses, foreign tax credits and consolidated returns. Section on Internal Revenue Service problems and procedures.

Raymond, Robert H. FINANCIAL STATEMENTS OF LIFE INSURANCE COMPANIES. Unpublished Ph.D. thesis, Michigan State University, 1964. 333p. tables. pap. (Available from University Microfilms.)

Points up the difference between insurance company financial statements and those of commercial and industrial firms, particularly if the insurance company's financial information is limited to that included in the life insurance Convention Blank required by state insurance departments.

Special Libraries Association. Insurance Division. INSURANCE LITERATURE. Ten times a year.

Annotated listings of publications and articles on insurance, which are arranged by type of insurance covered.

This division also compiles a classified INSURANCE PERIODICALS INDEX, which is published monthly in BEST'S REVIEW: LIFE/HEALTH, and BEST'S REVIEW: PROPERTY/LIABILITY, both published by A.M. Best. Annual cumulations are available from the Insurance Division, Special Libraries Association.

Special Libraries Association. Insurance Division. INSURANCE LITERATURE.
Van House, Charles L. and Hammond, W. Rogers. ACCOUNTING FOR LIFE INSURANCE COMPANIES. Homewood, Ill.: Richard D. Irwin, 1969. 524p. forms, glossary.

Published for the Life Office Management Association, this textbook describes the various accounting processes used in connection with the different insurance functions: agents' commissions, policy benefits, claim settlements, etc.

IRON AND STEEL

See also Foundries

American Institute of Certified Public Accountants. A STEEL FABRICATING COMPANY (Case Studies in Auditing Procedure, No. 8). New York: 1950. pp.9-22. pap. (o.p.)

An actual examination of a steel fabricating company, submitted by a member of the Institute's Committee on Auditing Procedure.

American Institute of Steel Construction, Inc. A.I.S.C. COST MANUAL, A MANUAL OF STANDARD PRACTICE FOR STRUCTURAL STEEL COST ACCOUNTING, 2nd ed. New York: 1942. 98p.

Outlines a simple but complete cost system under four divisions: cost outline, cost recording, job costs, and estimating and pricing.

American Iron and Steel Institute. ANNUAL STATISTICAL REPORT. New York: 1856- . tables.

Contains statistics, many of them covering 10-year periods, on iron and steel production, shipments, employment, etc. Some of the statistics in this report are reproduced in chart form in the Institute's annual pamphlet publication, CHARTING STEEL'S PROGRESS.

Iron Age. THE IRON AGE STEEL INDUSTRY FINANCIAL ANALYSIS. Philadelphia: Chilton, 1958- . tables. pap.

Thirty-nine U.S. steel companies are covered in this annual financial analysis which is published each year in the April issue of IRON AGE magazine.

Kuhn, Loeb & Co. ANNUAL FINANCIAL RÉSUMÉ OF NINE MAJOR STEEL COMPANIES, 1950/1959- . New York: 1960- . tables. pap.

Financial information on the nine largest U.S. steel companies, compiled from company annual reports and 10-K reports filed with the SEC. Numerous comparative ratio tables as well as individual company data. Glossary of financial terms included.

Steel. ANNUAL FINANCIAL ANALYSIS OF THE STEEL INDUSTRY. Cleveland, Ohio: Penton, 1925- . charts, tables. pap.

Appearing each year in an early April issue of STEEL magazine, this analysis gives financial information on 34 individual U.S. steel companies.

LABOR UNIONS

For regulations of the Office of Labor Management and Welfare-Pension Reports see publications listed under that agency in Section 3, Governmental Regulation.

California Society of Certified Public Accountants. San Francisco Chapter. Committee on Labor Unions and Welfare Funds. REPORTING REQUIREMENTS FOR EMPLOYEE BENEFIT PLANS AND LABOR UNIONS. San Francisco, California: May 15, 1964. 57p. selected biblio. pap.

Intended as a reference guide for the complex reports to be filed for these funds.

Fischer, Harry C. ACCOUNTING AND OFFICE MANUAL FOR LABOR UNIONS. Washington, D.C.: Bureau of National Affairs, 1961. 223p. forms. mimeo.

A detailed presentation of the financial reporting of a labor union.

Kozmetsky, George. FINANCIAL REPORTS OF LABOR UNIONS. Boston: Division of Research, Graduate School of Business Administration, Harvard University, 1950. 292p. exhibits. (o.p.)

A comprehensive study of the financial reporting of the international labor unions. In addition to an examination of current reporting practice, the author includes background information, criteria for improvement of reports and a study of the relationship between financial reports and union administration.

LAW FIRMS

A number of state bar associations have issued pamphlets on various aspects of financial management of law firms which may be obtained upon written request.

American Bar Association. Committee on Economics of Law Practice. ADMINISTRATION AND FINANCIAL MANAGEMENT IN A LAW FIRM, by Clark Sloat and Richard D. Fitzgerald (Economics of Law Practice Series, pamphlet No. 10). New York: Mathew Bender, 1965. 95p. forms. pap.

Serves as a guide to principles and procedures of managing the administrative and financial affairs of a professional law practice.

American Bar Association. THE LAWYER'S HANDBOOK. St. Paul, Minnesota: West Publishing Co., 1962. 587p.

Contains chapters on bookkeeping for the law office, accounting systems, pegboard systems and financial and statistical reports for law firms. Accounting systems bibliography included.

Biegler, John C. and Basson, Milton B. FINANCIAL AND STATISTICAL REPORTS IN ADMINISTERING A LAW FIRM. New York: Price Waterhouse & Co., 1961. 30p. pap.

Includes seven basic statements and schedules needed for effective financial management of a law firm.

Burroughs Corporation. Todd Division. ACCOUNTING FOR SMALL PROFESSIONAL OFFICES. THE ATTORNEY'S OFFICE, by Robert L. White (The Accountants' Service Bulletin, No. 251). Rochester, New York: January-February, 1963. 5p. forms. pap.

Concentrates on recordkeeping aspects of accounting for a law office.

Burroughs Corporation. Todd Division. AN ACCOUNTING SYSTEM FOR ATTORNEYS, by Arthur A. Hartman (The Accountants' Service Bulletin, No. 241). Rochester, New York: May 1961. 4p. forms. pap.

Describes a system established in a law firm of four partners, three associates, six secretaries and one receptionist-bookkeeper.

Prentice-Hall, Inc. A LAWYER'S PRACTICE MANUAL. Englewood Cliffs, New Jersey: 1964. 269p.

Based on a survey of the economics of law practice by the Missouri Bar Association. Includes a brief chapter on how to keep financial records.

LUMBER

Mountain States Lumber Dealers Association. FINANCIAL MANAGEMENT AND STANDARDIZED ACCOUNTING PROCEDURES FOR RETAIL LUMBER DEALERS. Salt Lake City, Utah: 1963. v.p. loose-leaf.

Prepared by the Management Services Division of Ernst & Ernst. Section 1 deals with accounting procedures, Section 2 with management controls. Chart of accounts included in Section 1.

Mucklow, Walter and Associates. LUMBER ACCOUNTS. New York: American Institute Publishing Co., 1936. 472p. forms. (o.p.)

Describes physical operations and processes in the lumber industry in addition to suggested accounting systems. Although out of print, this is still a valuable book.

Noltemeyer, Vincent E. ACCOUNTING AND COST CONTROLS IN THE HARDWOOD CONVERSION INDUSTRY, rev. ed. Nashville, Tennessee: Hardwood Dimension Manufacturers Association, 1965. 49p. forms, tables. pap.

Seeks to explain accounting and cost control principles rather than basic bookkeeping techniques. Detailed classification of accounts given.

MACHINERY

American Institute of Certified Public Accountants. AN ELECTRONIC EQUIPMENT MANUFACTURER (Case Studies in Auditing Procedure, No. 12). New York: 1958. pp. 39-61. pap.

A case study submitted by a member of the Institute's Committee on Auditing Procedure covering an actual examination of an electronic equipment manufacturer.

American Institute of Certified Public Accountants. A LOADING AND HAULING EQUIPMENT MANUFACTURER (Case Studies in Auditing Procedure, No. 1). New York: 1947. 32p. pap.

A case study submitted by a member of the Institute's committee covering an actual examination of a loading and hauling equipment manufacturer.

American Institute of Certified Public Accountants. THE MACHINE MANUFACTURING COMPANY (Case Studies in Internal Control, No. 2). New York: 1950. 38p. pap.

Describes a case in which an accountant evaluates the internal control situation and applies his findings in an actual audit.

Machinery and Allied Products Institute. MAPI ACCOUNTING MANUAL, PREPARED FOR THE MACHINERY AND ALLIED PRODUCTS, INDUSTRIAL EQUIPMENT AND CAPITAL GOODS PRODUCING INDUSTRIES. Chicago: 1952. v.p. biblio.

Intended as a guide to suitable accounting methods to be used in the capital goods industries.

National Screw Machine Products Association. BASIC PRINCIPLES OF COST CONTROL FOR THE SCREW MACHINE PRODUCTS INDUSTRY, 2nd ed. Cleveland, Ohio: 1951. 32p. pap.

Offers a cost accounting system recommended for the entire industry. ESTIMATING MANUAL, 1958; CHART OF ACCOUNTS, 1961.

MEAT PACKING

American Meat Institute. Accounting Committee. ACCOUNTING FOR MEAT PACKING. Chicago: AMI Center for Continuing Education, 1963. 223p. charts, tables.

A non-technical presentation of accounting systems for the meat packing industry intended for use in the Institute's home study accounting course. It is, however, comprehensive enough to be useful to the trained accountant unfamiliar with the industry. Chart of accounts given.

National Independent Meat Packers Association. ACCOUNTING MANUAL FOR MEAT PACKERS. Washington, D.C.: 1956. 111p. loose-leaf.

A cost accounting manual which, instead of dealing with pricing, is concerned with the development of an accounting system which will clearly show the small meat packer his departmental and product costs.

Price Waterhouse & Co. FINANCIAL PLANNING AND CONTROL IN THE MEAT INDUSTRY. Chicago: AMI Center for Continuing Education, 1967. 281p. biblio., charts, forms.

Prepared in cooperation with the Accounting Committee of the American Meat Institute. Shows how modern financial management techniques could be applied in the meat industry to increase effectiveness of operation and planning and to maximize profits.

Western States Meat Packers Association, Inc. COST CONTROL MANUAL. San Francisco, California: 1958. 225p. forms. loose-leaf.

Not a bookkeeping text. Developed as a system of controls to be used by management in the meatpacking industry in evaluating performance and setting product costs at a profitable level.

MINES

Ameican Bureau of Metal Statistics. YEARBOOK. New York: 1920-. tables.
Annual publication containing various statistical records of nonferrous metals on a world-wide basis. Miscellaneous tables include annual average prices back to 1913.

American Metal Market. METAL STATISTICS. New York: 1908-. tables.
Annual publication containing statistics and prices on all metals. Most tables give comparative figures for five or more previous years. Includes production statistics.

American Metal Market. MINES REGISTER, 1968-1969, 28th ed. New York: 1968. 598p. tables
A comprehensive listing of active and inactive mining companies in North, South and Central America, the West Indies, the Philippines and other metal-producing countries. Also contains 10-year comparative statistics on copper, zinc, lead, nickel, gold and silver.

Canadian Institute of Chartered Accountants. FINANCIAL REPORTING FOR NON-PRODUCING MINING COMPANIES (Research Study, No. 8). Toronto: 1967. 39p. pap.
The report of a C.I.C.A. Study Group who, after reviewing financial statements of non-producing mining companies, propose certain standards of disclosure to be followed by such companies.

Field, Robert E. FINANCIAL REPORTING IN THE EXTRACTIVE INDUSTRIES (Accounting Research Study No. 11). New York: American Institute of Certified Public Accountants, 1969. 198p. glossary, selected bibliography, tables. pap.
In this study which covers financial reporting for the extractive industries of petroleum and natural gas, coal, metals and nonmetallic minerals, natural resources are treated as similar to inventory rather than to plant and equipment. Extractive operations are described in detail as well as the accounting principles and practices applicable to these operations.

Hoover, Theodore Jesse. THE ECONOMICS OF MINING (NON-FEROUS METALS), 3rd ed. Stanford, California: Stanford University Press, 1948. 561p. tables. (o.p.)
Intended as a textbook for mining schools, but also useful to the practicing mining engineer. The three sections cover mine valuation, organization and management. Bibliographies at the end of each chapter.

Little, A.J. and MacDonald, W.L. MINING ACCOUNTING IN CANADA, AN OUTLINE OF ACCOUNTING AND INCOME TAX PROBLEMS PECULIAR TO THE INDUSTRY. Toronto: Canadian Institute of Chartered Accountants, 1960. 69p.
Intended as a guide to current accounting practices in the mining industry, not a theoretical discussion of these practices. Covers accounting for mining rights and for exploration companies, depletion allowances, producing mines and mines in the development state, etc. Two chapters on income tax exemptions and problems peculiar to the mining industry.

Merriam, Kemper Williams. COST ACCOUNTING FOR THE MINING, MILLING, AND SMELTING OF COPPER ORES. Unpublished Ph.D. thesis, University of Texas, 1957. [University Microfilms, 1965] 311p. chart of accounts, biblio., charts. xerox.

Part 1 gives detailed description of copper mining, milling and smelting processes. Part 2 discusses cost accounting principles for these processes, illustrated by analysis of operating cost summaries as prepared regularly for each process or department of a copper plant

Montana. Bureau of Mines and Geology. HANDBOOK FOR SMALL MINING ENTERPRISES IN MONTANA (Bulletin 39). Butte, Montana: May 1964. 228p. diagrs., forms, tables. pap.

Prepared by the Montana Bureau of Mines and Geology under a Small Business Administration grant, this manual for the small mine owner explains, in detail, how he can operate his mine more efficiently. Chapter 8, "Mine Accounting," by D.J. Emblem includes a section on reports to management. Chapter 9, "Minerals Benefication Accounting," by G.G. Griswold, Jr. covers metallurgical accounting, cost accounting and economics. Bibliographies at end of some chapters.

Parks, Roland D. EXAMINATION AND VALUATION OF MINERAL PROPERTY, 4th ed. Reading, Massachusetts: Addison-Wesley, 1957. 525p. biblio., charts, photos., tables.

Section 1, "Mine Examination" covers planning of field work, geological investigation, sampling procedures and calculations, the estimation of ore and other assets, and economic considerations. Sections 2, 3 and 4 deal in detail with valuation of mineral properties including oil. Section 5 consists of valuation tables.

Peele, Robert, ed. MINING ENGINEERS HANDBOOK, 3rd ed., 2 vols. New York: John H. Wiley & Sons, 1941. v.p. charts, illus., tables.

A comprehensive handbook. Section 20 is on "Mine Organization and Accounts." Bibliographies at the end of each section.

Peloubet, Maurice E. "Accounting for the Extractive Industries." In ECONOMICS OF THE MINERAL INDUSTRIES, 2nd ed., ed. by E.H. Robie. New York: American Institute of Mining, Metallurgical and Petroleum Engineers, Inc., 1964. chap. 9, part 1.

Covers requirements of accounting systems for the extractive industries, depletion and depreciation, operating costs, income reporting, SEC and tax requirements. Includes a number of examples of statement presentation and a detailed, classified bibliography.

U.S. Bureau of Mines (Department of the Interior). COST ACCOUNTING AND CONTROL AT CALUMET DIVISION, CALUMET & HECLA, INC., CALUMET, MICHIGAN (Information Circular 8044), by B.C. Peterson, et al. Washington, D.C.: U.S. Government Printing Office, 1962. 37p. illus. pap.

Good example of the successful use of cost accounting.

U.S. Bureau of Mines (Department of the Interior). LIST OF BUREAU OF MINES PUBLICATIONS AND ARTICLES, January 1, 1960 to December 31, 1964, by Rita D. Sylvester. Washington, D.C.: U.S. Government Printing Office, 1965. 301p. pap.

Comprehensive listing of Bureau reports and articles by Bureau authors published outside the Bureau. Supplements the 50-year LIST OF PUBLICATIONS ISSUED BY THE BUREAU OF MINES,

July 1, 1910 to January 1, 1960 and the 50-year LIST OF ARTICLES BY BUREAU AUTHORS PUBLISHED OUTSIDE THE BUREAU, July 1, 1910 to January 1, 1960, both still available from the U.S. Government Printing Office. Complete subject and author indexes.

U.S. Bureau of Mines (Department of the Interior). MINERALS YEARBOOK, 4 vols. Washington, D.C.: U.S. Government Printing Office, 1932- .
Annual statistical volume of the Bureau, presently published in four volumes. Vol. 1, Metals and Minerals; Vol. 2, Mineral Fuels; Vol. 3, Area Reports: Domestic; Vol. 4, Area Reports: International.

Willcox, Frank. MINE ACCOUNTING AND FINANCIAL ADMINISTRATION. New York: Pitman, 1949. 497p. forms. (o.p.)
Although out-of-print, this is still considered an excellent text. Explains briefly different aspects of mining operations and then goes on to show how they are handled in the accounting records. Appendices on Canadian mining industry and taxation.

MOTOR TRANSPORTATION

American Transit Association. CLASSIFICATION OF ACCOUNTS FOR BUS OPERATING COMPANIES WITH ANNUAL OPERATING REVENUES LESS THAN $100,000. New York: 1926. 24p. pap.
Condensed classification for use by the smaller bus companies.

American Transit Association. CLASSIFICATION OF ACCOUNTS FOR BUS OPERATING COMPANIES WITH ANNUAL OPERATING REVENUES MORE THAN $100,000. New York: 1925. 72p. pap.
Standard classification including not only operating revenues and expenses but also income, property and general balance sheets.

American Trucking Associations, Inc. A.T.A. ACCOUNTING SERVICE, 2 vols. Washington, D.C.: 1948- . loose-leaf.
Sec. A: ICC Uniform System of Accounts.
Sec. A-1: Chart of Accounts.
Sec. B: ICC Motor Carrier Accounting Interpretations.
Sec. C: Index of account numbers for over 5,800 motor carrier operations.
Sec. D: I.C.C. Statistical Requirements and Definitions. Guides on how to obtain statistical information required in ICC annual report.
Sec. E: Suggested forms and accounting controls for cash receipts, accounts payable, etc.
Sec. F: ICC regulations governing destruction of records.
Sec. G: Outlines records necessary for tax purposes.

American Trucking Associations, Inc. National Accounting and Finance Council. LENDING LIBRARY CATALOG. Washington, D.C.: 1968. 67p. pap.
An annotated listing of the materials in the Council's financial lending library which can be borrowed by its members. Supplements issued periodically.

Price Waterhouse & Co. HOUSEHOLD GOODS MOVING AND STORAGE

INDUSTRY ACCOUNTING AND PROCEDURES MANUAL. Chicago: National Moving and Storage Technical Association. 1967. v.p. loose-leaf.

Underwritten by the National Moving and Storage Technical Foundation, this manual provides a comprehensive management information system for the industry. Section I contains the general accounting manual; Section II describes operating and related accounting and reporting procedures; Section III consists of an accounting manual for ICC reporting.

U.S. Department of Commerce. Office of Transportation Research. COST ACCOUNTING SYSTEM FOR GROUND MODES OF TRANSPORTATION CARRIERS, 3 vols. in 5 parts. Springfield, Virginia: Clearinghouse, 1966.

Vol. 1: Railroad manual (PB 173 201-1) and (PB 173 201-2)
Vol. 2: Motors manual (PB 173 202-1) and (PB 173 202-2)
Vol. 3: Barge manual (PB 173 203)

In 1964, the firms of Lybrand, Ross Bros. & Montgomery and United Research, Inc. were awarded a joint contract by the Office of Transportation Research to develop concepts for improved accounting systems for rail, motor and waterway carriers. The contractors disagreed fundamentally on "the nature and capability of accountancy and its proper role in cost-determination." Since the final report was felt by the United Research staff to "express to an undue extent" the concepts of Lybrand, Ross Bros. & Montgomery, a small follow-on contract was awarded to United Research to present an explanation of their opinions.

Therefore, each of these volumes contains two reports applicable to the particular mode of transportation. The first section, by Lybrand, Ross Bros. & Montgomery offers general accounting principles and concepts and an accounting manual for each mode; the second section, by United Research, provides a chart of accounts and a manual of work measurement procedures for each mode. Each volume contains a glossary prepared by Lybrand, Ross Bros. & Montgomery and a work measurement bibliography by United Research on the particular mode of transportation covered in that volume.

U.S. Interstate Commerce Commission. UNIFORM SYSTEM OF ACCOUNTS FOR CLASS I AND CLASS II COMMON AND CONTRACT MOTOR CARRIERS OF PROPERTY, PRESCRIBED BY THE I.C.C. IN ACCORDANCE WITH PART II OF THE INTERSTATE COMMERCE ACT...as rev. to January 1, 1969. Washington, D.C.: U.S. Government Printing Office, 1969. 74p. pap.

Revisions are available on a free standing order basis from the ICC.

MOTION PICTURE

See Entertainment

MUSIC

See Entertainment

NON - PROFIT ORGANIZATION

American Institute of Certified Public Accountants. AUDITS OF VOLUNTARY HEALTH AND WELFARE ORGANIZATIONS (AICPA Industry Audit Guide). New York: 1967. 72p. pap.

Designed to help the independent auditor in his examination of voluntary health and welfare organizations, this booklet does not offer generally accepted accounting principles for this type of audit. Instead, it discusses the accounting practices currently being followed by such organizations and appropriate reporting of these practices.

Canadian Welfare Council. CANADIAN STANDARDS OF ACCOUNTING AND FINANCIAL REPORTING FOR VOLUNTARY ORGANIZATIONS. Ottawa, Canada: 1967. 20p. pap.

Prepared by a committee representing the Canadian Welfare Council, The Canadian Institute of Chartered Accountants, Community Funds and Councils of Canada, and the National Agency Review Committee. The committee endorses the standards recommended in the U.S. publication, STANDARDS OF ACCOUNTING AND FINANCIAL REPORTING FOR VOLUNTARY AND WELFARE AGENCIES issued by the National Health Council in 1965. This pamphlet consists of four pages outlining recommended accounting standards for Canadian voluntary organizations, supplemented by examples of financial statements for large and small agencies.

The committee did not deal with details of accounting and techniques since this was amply covered in the U.S. publication.

Englander, Louis. ACCOUNTING PRINCIPLES AND PROCEDURES OF PHILANTHROPIC INSTITUTIONS. New York: The New York Community Trust, 1957. 46p. pap.

A report based on an investigation of a representative cross-section of philanthropic institutions from which the author concludes that enough similarities exist to justify the formulation of a statement of generally accepted accounting principles for philanthropic institutions.

Henke, Emerson O. ACCOUNTING FOR NONPROFIT ORGANIZATIONS. Belmont, California: Wadsworth, 1966. 159p. pap.

Prepared as a textbook for accounting students on the graduate level. Questions and problems at end of each chapter.

National Health Council and the National Social Welfare Assembly. STANDARDS OF ACCOUNTING AND FINANCIAL REPORTING FOR VOLUNTARY HEALTH AND WELFARE ORGANIZATIONS. New York: National Health Council, 1965. 130p.

The primary objective of this study, the first comprehensive work of its kind, was to devise standards for uniform financial reporting by voluntary health and welfare associations (excluding hospitals) that would disclose clearly to contributors all significant facts concerning an organization's financial management.

Van Fenstermaker, Joseph. CASH MANAGEMENT: MANAGING THE CASH FLOWS, BANK BALANCES, AND SHORT-TERM INVESTMENTS OF NON-PROFIT INSTITUTIONS. Kent, Ohio: Kent State University Press, 1966. 80p. biblio., tables. loose-leaf.

A non technical book designed to help the financial officer in the administration of his cash management system.

PAPER

American Paper Institute. A PAPER INDUSTRY REPORT ON ACCOUNTING PRINCIPLES AND PRACTICES FOLLOWED FOR FINANCIAL REPORTING PURPOSES. New York: 1967. 31p. tables. pap.

A survey of the accounting practices followed by 101 firms in the paper industry, compiled by Arthur Andersen & Co. for the American Paper Institute.

Book Paper Manufacturers Association. PRINCIPLES OF COST ACCOUNTING FOR THE BOOK PAPER INDUSTRY, prepared by Scovell, Wellington & Company. [New York]: March 1948. 78p. charts. pap. (Available from American Paper Institute.)

Offers a cost accounting plan designed to show present and estimated future product costs and to provide a means of controlling the cost of milling operations.

National Paper Trade Association, Inc. PAPER DISTRIBUTION: A GUIDE TO MANAGEMENT CONTROL. New York: 1964. 29p. chart of accounts, glossary. pap.

Offers recommended accounting procedures which should provide paper merchants with improved financial control and increased profits.

PETROLEUM

American Association of Oilwell Drilling Contractors. Accounting Committee. ACCOUNTING MANUAL FOR THE OILWELL DRILLING INDUSTRY, 3rd ed. Dallas, Texas: 1957. 225p. glossary, oil field abbreviations. tables.

A technical guide for the accountant in the drilling industry.

American Petroleum Institute. Division of Finance and Accounting: REPORT OF CERTAIN PETROLEUM INDUSTRY ACCOUNTING PRACTICES. New York: 1965. 84p. glossary, tables. pap.

The first authoritative study of its kind, this deals with accounting methods now being used by 34 representative petroleum companies.

A RESURVEY AS OF DECEMBER 1966 was published in 1967 by the American Petroleum Institute to determine to what extent companies might have changed accounting practices since the 1965 survey. (30p. pap.)

Andersen, Arthur & Co. ACCOUNTING FOR OIL AND GAS EXPLORATION COSTS. [Chicago]: 1963. 37p. tables. pap.

Presents the argument that full-cost accounting (the capitalization of all costs incurred in finding oil reserves and the amortization of these costs over the reserves found on a company-wide unit of production basis) should be adopted by the oil and gas industry.

Breeding, Clark W. and Burton, A. Gordon. INCOME TAXATION OF OIL AND GAS PRODUCTION, 2nd ed. Englewood Cliffs, New Jersey: Prentice-Hall, 1961. v.p. tables. loose-leaf.

Excellent presentation of oil and gas income taxation principles and practices.

Chase Manhattan Bank. Energy Division. ANNUAL FINANCIAL ANALYSIS OF A GROUP OF PETROLEUM COMPANIES. New York: 1945- . charts, photos., tables. pap.

Based on information obtained from annual reports to stockholders and to SEC and from data developed from other sources. This annual pamphlet covers approximately 30 companies, the number of companies varying throughout the years, primarily as a result of mergers, but this does not significantly affect comparative data. Chapters on income statement, source and use of funds, and balance sheet information. Fifteen statistical tables include prior year's figures. Available without charge from the Energy Division, Chase Manhattan Bank.

Coutts, W.B. ACCOUNTING PROBLEMS IN THE OIL AND GAS INDUSTRY. Toronto: Canadian Institute of Chartered Accountants, 1963. 52p. biblio. pap.

Studies accounting practices in use in the petroleum industry with regard to drilling and exploration costs, carrying charges on undeveloped properties, depletion and amortization and recognition of "fair value" of oil and gas reserves. Offers recommendations to be followed in order to provide greater uniformity in financial statements.

Field, Robert E. FINANCIAL REPORTING IN THE EXTRACTIVE INDUSTRIES (Accounting Research Study No. 11). New York: American Institute of Certified Public Accountants, 1969. 198p. glossary, selected bibliography, tables. pap.

In this study which covers financial reporting for the extractive industries of petroleum and natural gas, coal, metals and nonmetallic minerals, natural resources are treated as similar to inventory rather than to plant and equipment. Extractive operations are described in detail as well as the accounting principles and practices applicable to these operations.

Irving, Robert H., Jr. and Draper, Verden R. ACCOUNTING PRACTICES IN THE PETROLEUM INDUSTRY. New York: Ronald Press, 1958. 247p. glosary, graphs.

Explains and illustrates the accounting methods used in every phase of the oil industry.

Miller, Kenneth G. OIL AND GAS FEDERAL INCOME TAXATION, Chicago: Commerce Clearing House, 1966- . Three supplements a year. pap.

"...prime purpose...to correlate the four areas of law, regulation, rulings and court decisions." The author also includes descriptions of accepted practices in certain "areas of uncertainty" which have not been covered by published pronouncements.

Petroleum Accountants Society of Oklahoma. MATERIAL CLASSIFICATION MANUAL. Tulsa, Oklahoma: Ross-Martin Company, 1960. 51p. tables. pap.

Alphabetical list of material and equipment used in producing, manufacturing and pipe line exploration and research operations of the petroleum industry. Classified between controllable and non-controllable items for accounting treatment.

Porter, Stanley P. PETROLEUM ACCOUNTING PRACTICES. New York: McGraw-Hill Book Co., 1965. 557p. figures.

Comprehensive review of current accounting practices in the United States petroleum industry.

Smith, C. Aubrey and Brock, Horace R. ACCOUNTING FOR OIL AND GAS PRODUCERS. Englewood Cliffs, New Jersey: Prentice-Hall, 1959. 536p. facs.

Includes background information on geological activities, drilling operations, etc., in the petroleum industry, as well as the presentation of accounting principles, practices and procedures.

Southwestern Legal Foundation. OIL AND GAS ACCOUNTING. Proceedings of the...Institute on Oil and Gas Accounting, September 1965- . Albany, New York: Mathew Bender, 1966- .

Collections of papers from annual Institutes which are presented under the auspices of the International Oil and Gas Educational Center, Dallas, Texas. Subjects range over all aspects of petroleum accounting.

Taher, Abdulhady Hassan. INCOME DETERMINATION IN THE INTERNATIONAL PETROLEUM INDUSTRY. London: Pergamon Press Ltd.; New York: Pergamon Press, Inc., 1966. 243p. biblio., charts, tables.

This dissertation, submitted as partial requirement for a Ph.D. degree, presents a novel approach to the problem of measuring net income and rate of return of the international petroleum trading and processing organizations.

U.S. Federal Power Commission. DEPRECIATION PRACTICES OF NATURAL GAS COMPANIES, CLASS A AND B. Washington, D.C.: U.S. Government Printing Office, 1961. 8p. tables. pap.

Presents information on natural gas companies operating in interstate commerce over which ICC has jurisdiction. Straight-line depreciation method used by all companies in the study.

Waller, Robert E. OIL ACCOUNTING, PRINCIPLES OF OIL EXPLORATION AND PRODUCTION ACCOUNTING IN CANADA. Toronto: University of Toronto Press (for Canadian Institute of Chartered Accountants), 1956. 99p. code of accounts, glossary of terms, exhibit.

The emphasis is on establishing some standardization in petroleum accounting techniques which are most appropriate to Canadian conditions.

PLASTICS

Society of the Plastics Industry, Inc. ACCOUNTING MANUAL FOR THE PLASTICS INDUSTRY. New York: 1946. 180p. classification of accounts, forms.

Covers financial statements; classification of ledger accounts; sales analyses; accounting for manufacturing costs, labor, general expenses; depreciation rates; cost formulas; suggested forms and procedures.

PRINTING AND PUBLISHING

American Institute of Certified Public Accountants. A NEWSPAPER PUBLISHER (Case Studies in Auditing Procedure, No. 2). New York: 1947. 34p. pap. (o.p.)

Case submitted by a member of the Institute's Committee on Auditing Procedure covering an actual examination of a newspaper publisher.

American Institute of Certified Public Accountants. A WHOLESALE DISTRIBUTOR OF NEWSPAPERS AND MAGAZINES (Case Studies in Auditing Procedure, No. 9). New York: 1951. 46p. pap. (o.p.)

Case study submitted by a member of the Institute's Committee on Auditing Procedure covering an actual examination of a wholesale distributor of newspapers and magazines.

American Photo-Engravers Association. MANUAL OF THE STANDARD COST AND ACCOUNTING SYSTEMS OF THE AMERICAN PHOTO-ENGRAVERS ASSOCIATION. Chicago: 1946. 104p. forms.

Provides standard cost systems for both shops employing more than five men and shops employing five or less.

Business Forms Institute. ACCOUNTING AND COST CONTROL MANUAL, prepared by Stevenson, Jordan & Harrison, Inc. Greenwich, Connecticut: 1962. v.p. pap. (o.p.)

Intended to provide a uniform method of accounting for the industry, this manual can be adapted to the small, medium or large company. Chart of accounts included as an appendix.

Institute of Newspaper Controllers and Finance Officers. INTERNAL CONTROL AND AUDIT FOR NEWSPAPERS. Harmon-on-Hudson, New York: 1965. 179p. biblio., charts, forms.

Designed to provide systems of internal control and audit techniques for both large and small newspapers. Appendix gives check lists for all key areas requiring strict internal control.

Institute of Newspaper Controllers and Finance Officers. PROFIT PLANNING FOR NEWSPAPERS. Fair Haven, New Jersey: 1966. 50p. biblio., charts, forms, tables. pap.

Discusses long-range and yearly profit planning for newspaper enterprises, with emphasis on the budgeting process.

Institute of Newspaper Controllers and Finance Officers. REPORTING TO NEWSPAPER MANAGEMENT. Fair Haven, New Jersey: 1968. 55p. biblio., charts, forms. pap.

Emphasizes the concepts and principles of management reporting rather than the techniques of financial reporting. Examples of key newspaper reports are given.

Institute of Newspaper Controllers and Finance Officers. STANDARD CHART OF ACCOUNTS FOR NEWSPAPERS, rev. New York: 1961. 38p. pap.

Groups expense accounts by function and employs both four-digit and five-digit forms so that it can be useful to both large and small newspapers.

International Typographic Composition Association. COST ACCOUNTING MANUAL. Washington, D.C.: 1962. 84p. forms. pap.

A cost accounting system specifically adapted to the needs of the typographic composition plant. Provides an accounting system, a budgeted hourly rate system and a cost system. Available to members only, but can be seen at the National Association of Accountants' library.

Magazine Publishers Association, Inc. MANUAL OF UNIFORM ACCOUNTING FOR MAGAZINE PUBLISHERS. New York: 1960. v.p. forms. loose-leaf.

Sections on classification of accounts, definitions of accounts, multi-publication houses and sample forms.

National Association of Photo-Lithographers. A STUDY OF A SIMPLIFIED METHOD FOR BUILDING BUDGETED HOURLY COST RATES IN A LITHOGRAPHIC PLANT, rev. New York: 1962. 88p. pap.

Offers a suggested procedure for establishing hourly cost rates in lithographic plant cost centers.

PUBLIC UTILITIES

See also Asset Accounting

For regulations of the Federal Communications Commission, Federal Power Commission and the Rural Electrification System, see publications listed under these agencies in Section 3, Governmental Regulation.

Public utilities are regulated by state as well as by federal commissions both as to rates and accounting. The intrastate activities of certain types of utilities, e.g. gas distribution companies, are subject only to state regulation. Decisions of both federal and state commissions are listed in PUBLIC UTILITIES REPORTS, CONTAINING DECISIONS OF THE REGULATORY COMMISSIONS AND OF STATE AND FEDERAL COURTS (1st-3rd series. Annual digest; bi-weekly advance sheets. Washington, D.C.: Public Utilities Reports, Inc., 1915- .) This publisher has also issued two cumulative digests: P.U.R. DIGEST, 1915-1932, and P.U.R. DIGEST, 2nd SERIES, 1933-1962 with supplements to date.

An interesting bibliography on public utility accounting which includes a number of out of print items not listed here can be found in Management Information Guide No. 7, PUBLIC UTILITIES INFORMATION SOURCES, by Florine E. Hunt, chapter 3. (Detroit: Gale Research Co., 1965).

American Gas Association, Accounting Section, and Edison Electric Institute, Accounting Division. ACCOUNTING COMPENDIUM REPORT. New York: 1934- . pap.

Abstracts of accounting papers in proceedings volume of the annual National Conference of Electric and Gas Utility Accountants and other AGA and EEI publications, arranged in classified form. The 1934 volume covers the years 1919 through 1933.

American Gas Association and Edison Electric Institute. Joint Subcommittee on Financial Reporting. FINANCIAL REPORTING PRACTICES AND TRENDS AS DISCLOSED BY AN ANALYSIS OF THE ANNUAL REPORTS TO STOCKHOLDERS OF 56 GAS AND ELECTRIC UTILITIES FOR THE YEARS ... New York: 1949- . tables. pap.

These annual studies, each of which includes data for the previous three years have covered the same companies since 1949. The 56 companies reviewed include 13 electric, 22 gas and 21 combination electric and gas companies. A list of these companies is included.

American Institute of Certified Public Accountants. A PUBLIC UTILITY (Case Studies in Auditing Procedure, No. 4). New York: 1947. 32p. pap. (o.p.)

Case study submitted by a member of the Institute's Committee on Auditing Procedure covering an actual examination of a public utility.

BOOKS

American Water Works Association. WATER RATES MANUAL (AWWA MI Rates Manual). New York: 1960. 61p. tables. pap.

A reprinting of a 1954 report of the AWWA Committee on Water Rates and a collection of "certain portions of classical papers on the subject of water rates." Includes an outline for allocation of plant and expenses.

Foster, J. Rhoades and Rodey, Bernard S., Jr. PUBLIC UTILITY ACCOUNTING. New York: Prentice-Hall, 1951. 690p. charts, forms, tables. (o.p.)

The best work on all phases of public utility accounting. Special coverage of uniform system of accounts, depreciation accounting, and reports to regulatory authorities.

Harvey, John L. "Audit of a Public Utility." In Prentice-Hall, ENCYCLOPEDIA OF AUDITING TECHNIQUES, Vol. 2. Englewood Cliffs, New Jersey: 1966. chap. 30.

Presents a detailed case history of an actual audit.

Hendriksen, Eldon S. PRICE-LEVEL ADJUSTMENTS OF FINANCIAL STATEMENTS - AN EVALUATION AND CASE STUDY OF TWO PUBLIC UTILITY FIRMS. Pullman, Washington: Washington State University Press, 1961. 133p. tables.

Suggests use of present value in accounting statements to be determined by a price index. Several price indexes are applied to statements of Washington Water Power Company and Portland General Electric Company as examples.

Livingstone, John Leslie. THE EFFECTS OF ALTERNATIVE ACCOUNTING METHODS ON REGULATORY RATE OF RETURN DECISIONS IN THE ELECTRIC UTILITY INDUSTRY. Unpublished Ph.D. thesis, Stanford University, 1966. Ann Arbor, Michigan: University Microfilms, 1966. 244p. biblio., charts, tables. pap.

A comprehensive study of two critical issues involving alternate accounting methods used in the determination of permitted rates of return for electric utility companies. Detailed analyses relating to (1) the methods of valuing the rate base and questions about historical costs, current costs and changes in the general price level, and (2) the accounting for tax reductions when accelerated depreciation is used for tax purposes but not for financial reporting. Chapters VII and VIII provide a mathematical formulation as a "normative model" which is applied to the industry in order to evaluate the regulatory use of alternative tax accounting methods.

Municipal Finance Officers Association and the American Water Works Association. MANUAL OF WATER WORKS ACCOUNTING. Chicago: Municipal Finance Officers Association, 1938. 505p. biblio., list of terms, tables. (o.p.)

Currently being revised, this work is still of value since it is the only one in its field. Classification of accounts, classes A and B, and C and D utilities.

Nash, Luther R. ANATOMY OF DEPRECIATION: A DISCUSSION OF UTILITY ACCOUNTING METHODS FROM TIME TO TIME IN EFFECT OR PROPOSED BY REGULATORY OR UTILITY REPRESENTATIVES, WITH PARTICULAR REFERENCE TO RECENT CONTROVERSIES. Washington, D.C.: Public Utilities Reports, Inc., 1947. 224p. chart, photos., tables.

Gives early accounting history and the development of government regulation in utility accounting. Presents arguments for straight-line, retirement accounting and reserve-size methods.

Nash, Luther R. THE ECONOMICS OF PUBLIC UTILITIES, 2nd ed. New York: McGraw-Hill Book Co., 1931. 526p. (o.p.)

A comprehensive study of the utility industry. Chapter 5 covers accounting methods.

National Association of Regulatory Utility Commissioners and the Federal Communications Commission. Cooperative Committee on Communications Problems. SEPARATIONS MANUAL. Washington, D.C.: NARUC, April 1963. 96p. pap.

Develops a system of procedure for allocating telephone property costs, revenues, expenses, taxes and reserves between State and Interstate jurisdictions. Addenda are added regularly.

National Association of Regulatory Utility Commissioners. BULLETIN SERVICE. Washington, D.C.: Available on annual subscription basis.

The official organ of NARUC. Published one or more times a week, the BULLETIN lists events affecting regulation of all utilities and includes digests of important regulatory commission and court decisions.

National Association of Regulatory Utility Commissioners. UNIFORM SYSTEM OF ACCOUNTS FOR ELECTRIC UTILITIES, 1958.

Class A & B - Accounts for utilities having annual electric operating revenues of $1,000,000 or more.
Class C - Accounts for utilities having annual electric operating revenues of $150,000. 125p.
Class D - Accounts for utilities having annual electric operating revenues of less than $150,000. 59p.

National Association of Regulatory Utility Commissioners. UNIFORM SYSTEM OF ACCOUNTS FOR GAS UTILITIES. 1958.

Class A & B - Accounts for utilities having annual gas operating revenues of $1,000,000 or more.
Class C - Accounts for utilities having annual gas operating revenues of $150,000 or more but less than $1,000,000.
Class D - Accounts for utilities having annual gas operating revenues of less than $150,000.

National Association of Regulatory Utility Commissioners. UNIFORM SYSTEM OF ACCOUNTS FOR WATER UTILITIES, 1957.

Class A & B - Accounts for utilities having annual water operating revenues of $250,000 or more. 128p.
Class C - Accounts for utilities having annual water operating revenues of $50,000 or more but less than $250,000. 100p.
Class D - Accounts for utilities having annual water operating revenues of less than $50,000. 64p.

National Association of Regulatory Utility Commissioners. Committee on Accounts and Statistics. INTERPRETATIONS OF UNIFORM SYSTEM OF ACCOUNTS FOR ELECTRIC, GAS AND WATER UTILITIES. Washington, D.C.: 1967, supplements to date. v.p. loose-leaf.

A summary of interpretations to the uniform systems of accounts adopted by NARUC in 1957 and 1958. Additional interpretations are added as a need for clarification on certain points becomes apparent.

National Association of Regulatory Utility Commissioners. Committee on Depreciation. REPORTS. Washington, D.C.: 1939- .

The most important of these annual reports is the single volume containing the 1943 and 1944 reports. The 1943 report was the result of a four-year study of depreciation methods and included the committee's recommendations. The 1944 report contains objections to these recommendations raised within the utility industry and modifications of certain sections of the earlier report. Together, these reports give a clear picture of depreciation methods used by most utilities.

National Association of Regulatory Utility Commissioners. Committee on Engineering. Subcommittee on Depreciation. PUBLIC UTILITY DEPRECIATION PRACTICES. Washington, D.C.: 1968. 447p. biblio., charts, tables.

Gives practical operating practices and methods for determining the depreciation of public utility property for regulatory purposes. Numerous supporting charts and graphs.

National Conference of Electric and Gas Utility Accountants. PROCEEDINGS. New York: American Gas Association and Edison Electric Institute, 1937- .

This annual conference covers all aspects of public utility accounting, internal auditing, tax accounting, etc. A good source of current thinking on important questions.

Phillips, C.F., Jr. "Accounting and Financial Control." In his THE ECONOMICS OF REGULATION: THEORY AND PRACTICE IN THE TRANSPORTATION AND PUBLIC UTILITY INDUSTRIES. Homewood, Illinois: Richard D. Irwin, 1965. pp.144-76.

Illustrates development of regulated uniform systems of accounts.

Stone & Webster Service Corporation. ACCOUNTING AND RATEMAKING TREATMENT OF INCOME TAX EFFECTS OF ACCELERATED/LIBERALIZED DEPRECIATION, INVESTMENT TAX CREDIT/GUIDELINE DEPRECIATION. New York: August 1964. v.p. pap.

Periodically updated. Holders of volumes are notified of new editions. A "Master Summary" sheet indicates preferences of certain federal and state regulatory agencies for one of the four accounting methods indicated in the title.

U.S. Federal Power Commission. ELECTRIC UTILITY DEPRECIATION PRACTICES, 1961. CLASSES A AND B PRIVATELY OWNED COMPANIES. Washington, D.C.: U.S. Government Printing Office, 1964. 10p. tables. pap.

Tables show comparative figures for the various types of depreciation accounting used by 222 companies in their 1961 annual reports.

U.S. Federal Power Commission. FEDERAL AND STATE COMMISSION JURISDICTION AND REGULATION OF ELECTRIC, GAS, AND TELEPHONE UTILITIES, 1967, prepared in cooperation with National Association of Regulatory Utility Commissioners and the Federal Communications Commission. Washington,

D.C.: U.S. Government Printing Office, 1968. tables. pap.
Section F, "Accounting, Auditing, and Annual Reports" and Section G, "Financial and Corporate Regulation" are of particular interest.

U.S. Federal Power Commission. GLOSSARY OF IMPORTANT POWER AND RATE TERMS, ABREVIATIONS, AND UNITS OF MEASUREMENT. Washington, D.C.: U.S. Government Printing Office, 1965. 43p. biblio. pap.
Prepared under the direction of the Inter-Agency Committee on Water Resources, this handy little booklet provides an excellent alphabetic Index to its list of definitions.

RADIO

See Entertainment

RAILROADS

Association of American Railroads. Accounting Division. RAILWAY ACCOUNTING RULES, effective September 1, 1967. Washington, D.C.: 1967. 400p. forms.
Contains mandatory and recommended accounting rules, forms and rules of order of the Accounting Division of the Association of American Railroads.

Bunnell, Edward H. RAILROAD ACCOUNTING AND STATISTICS. Chicago: Watson, 1955. 287p. charts, forms, illus. (o.p.)
Gives historical background of railway accounting as well as the current accounting practices of the industry.

Locklin, D. Philip. ECONOMICS OF TRANSPORTATION, 6th ed. Homewood, Illinois: Richard D. Irwin, 1966. 894p. charts, forms, maps.
Discusses the whole field of transportation with extended coverage of the railroads. Chapter 24 is on "Railroad Accounts and Accounting Regulation." Selected references at end of each chapter.

U.S. Department of Commerce. Office of Transportation Research. COST ACCOUNTING SYSTEM FOR GROUND MODES OF TRANSPORTATION CARRIERS, 3 vols. in 5 parts. Springfield, Virginia: Clearinghouse, 1966.
Vol. 1: Railroad manual (PB 173 201-1) and (PB 173 201-2)
Vol. 2: Motors manual (PB 173 202-1) and (PB 173 202-2)
Vol. 3: Barge manual (PB 173 203)

In 1964, the firms of Lybrand, Ross Bros. & Montgomery and United Research, Inc. were awarded a joint contract by the Office of Transportation Research to develop concepts for improved accounting systems for rail, motor and waterway carriers. The contractors disagreed fundamentally on "the nature and capability of accountancy and its proper role in cost-determination." Since the final report was felt by the United Research staff to "express to an undue extent" the concepts of Lybrand, Ross Bros. & Montgomery, a small follow-on contract was awarded to United Research to present an explanation of their opinions.

Therefore, each of these volumes contains two reports applicable to the particular mode of transportation. The first section, by

Lybrand, Ross Bros. & Montgomery offers general accounting principles and concepts and an accounting manual for each mode; the second section, by United Research, provides a chart of accounts and a manual of work measurement procedures for each mode. Each volume contains a glossary prepared by Lybrand, Ross Bros. & Montgomery and a work measurement bibliography by United Research on the particular mode of transportation covered in that volume.

U.S. Interstate Commerce Commission. Bureau of Accounts. INTERPRETATIONS OF THE UNIFORM SYSTEM OF ACCOUNTS FOR RAILROAD COMPANIES, ACCOUNTING SERIES CIRCULAR NO. 130, effective September 1, 1962. Washington, D.C.: U.S. Government Printing Office, 1962. 61p. pap.

Informal interpretations to be followed in absence of specific prescribed accounting regulations or other authoritative decisions of the I.C.C. Available free on standing order from the ICC.

U.S. Interstate Commerce Commission. Bureau of Accounts. UNIFORM SYSTEM OF ACCOUNTS FOR RAILROAD COMPANIES, PRESCRIBED BY THE I.C.C. IN ACCORDANCE WITH SECTION 20 OF THE INTERSTATE COMMERCE ACT...as amended to January 1, 1968. Washington, D.C.: U.S. Government Printing Office, 1968. 113p. pap.

This is kept up to date by supplements available free on standing order from the ICC, entitled "Accounting Series Circulars."

REAL ESTATE

Australian Society of Accountants. New South Wales Division, Accounting for Long-Term Projects Committee. ACCOUNTING FOR LONG-TERM LAND DEVELOPMENT PROJECTS (A Research Study Report, SOCIETY BULLETIN, No. 1, November 1967). Melbourne, Australia: 1967. 32p. pap.

Not an official statement of the Society, this committee report describes the organization, management, financing, commercial assessment, and financial accounting for long-term land development projects.

Babb, Janice B. and Dordick, Beverly F. REAL ESTATE INFORMATION SOURCES (Management Information Guide, No. 1). Detroit, Michigan: Gale Research Co., 1963. 317p.

A comprehensive listing of literature on the utility or investment use of real estate.

Bernstein, Benjamin and Reed, Alvin S. A GUIDE TO RECORD-KEEPING FOR SYNDICATED REAL ESTATE TRANSACTIONS (The Accountants' Service Bulletin, No. 246). Rochester, New York: Burroughs Company, Todd Division, March-April, 1962. 7p. chart of accounts, forms, illus. pap.

Deals with the establishment of records for real estate which is primarily for sale.

Downs, James C. Jr. "Records and Accounting." In his PRINCIPLES OF REAL ESTATE MANAGEMENT, 8th ed. Chicago: Institute of Real Estate Management, 1964. pp.339-413.

Very basic summary of recordkeeping and accounting for property management. Includes a brief bibliography.

The Institute of Real Estate Management of the National Association of Real

Estate Boards. A COST ACCOUNTING SYSTEM FOR THE REAL ESTATE OFFICE (Fundamentals and Standards Bulletin, No. 105). Chicago: July 1958. 14p. charts, schedules. pap.

Practical presentation of cost allocation methods. Includes several types of management department cost analyses charts and a typical organization chart.

National Association of Building Owners and Managers. UNIFORM ACCOUNTING FOR OFFICE BUILDINGS (Service Bulletin, No. 24). Chicago: Sept. 30, 1956. 7p. pap.

The standard accounting system for office buildings, incorporating a new chart of accounts.

New York State Society of Certified Public Accountants. Real Estate Accounting Committee. BIBLIOGRAPHY OF REAL ESTATE ACCOUNTING AND TAXATION LITERATURE. New York: June 30, 1959. 42p. pap.

Good bibliography, composed chiefly of magazine articles.

RESTAURANTS

American Institute of Certified Public Accountants. A SMALL RESTAURANT (Case Studies in Auditing Procedure, No. 8). New York: 1950. pp.25-37. pap. (o.p.)

A case study submitted by a member of the Institute's Committee on Auditing Procedure covering an actual examination of a small restaurant.

Dukas, Peter and Lundberg, Donald E. HOW TO OPERATE A RESTAURANT. New York: Ahrens Publishing Co., 1960. 286p. forms, photos.

Includes chapters on "The Profit and Loss Statement," "Let Your Profit and Loss Statement Work for You" and "The Dynamics of Accounting." List of training films, pp.270-3.

Laventhol Krekstein Horwath & Horwath. ANNUAL STUDY OF RESTAURANT OPERATIONS. New York: 1959- .

Published annually in the firm publication, THE LKHH ACCOUNTANT, this study includes a comparative summary of ratios for profit and loss statement figures with the previous year.

National Restaurant Association. A FINANCIAL ANALYSIS OF THE RESTAURANT INDUSTRY: CORPORATIONS, PARTNERSHIPS, AND INDIVIDUALLY OWNED OPERATIONS. Chicago: 1963. 108p. biblio., tables. pap.

A detailed study of six financial ratios and their value to the restaurant operator. Ratios covered are: current ratio, net sales to net working capital, net profit to total net worth, net profit to total assets, net sales to fixed assets and net profit to net sales.

National Restaurant Association. UNIFORM SYSTEM OF ACCOUNTS FOR RESTAURANTS, 4th rev. ed., prepared by Laventhol Krekstein Horwath & Horwath. Chicago: 1968. 150p. forms, tables.

Includes sample statements and forms. Appendices deal with food and beverage cost control. An earlier publication, RECORD KEEPING FOR THE SMALL RESTAURANT, has been incorporated in this edition.

U.S. Small Business Administration. STARTING AND MANAGING A SMALL RESTAURANT (Starting and Managing Series), by Paul Fairbrook. Washington,

D.C.: U.S. Government Printing Office, 1964. 124p. biblio., forms. pap.
Chapter on profits through accounting.

RETAIL TRADE

American Institute of Certified Public Accountants. A DEPARTMENT STORE (Case Studies in Auditing Procedure, No. 3). New York: 1947. 57p. pap. (o.p.)
A case study submitted by a member of the Institute's Committee on Auditing Procedure covering an actual examination of a department store.

Bell, Hermon F. and Moscarello, Louis C. RETAIL MERCHANDISE ACCOUNTING, 3rd ed. New York: Ronald Press, 1961. 487p. forms, tables.
The best of the texts on retail accounting. Includes several chapters on the LIFO method with special reference to retailers. New edition in preparation.

Brown, Milton P. and May, Eleanor G. OPERATING RESULTS OF MULTI-UNIT DEPARTMENT STORES (Bureau of Business Research Bulletin, No. 159). Boston: Graduate School of Business Administration, Harvard University, 1961. v.p. tables. pap.
A detailed study of operating figures: margins, expenses and profits of multi-unit department stores. Brief text (8 pages) on the problems of branch store accounting.

Canadian Institute of Chartered Accountants. SMALL RETAIL STORE ACCOUNTING. Toronto: January, 1959. 42p. pap. (o.p.)
A compilation of six articles on various aspects of control, budgeting and accounting procedures previously published in THE CANADIAN CHARTERED ACCOUNTANT and one chapter on income tax especially written for this pamphlet. Designed to help the small retailer in the successful financial operation of his business.

Chute, A. Hamilton. A SELECTED AND ANNOTATED BIBLIOGRAPHY OF RETAILING, rev. (Bibliography Series, No. 5). Austin, Texas: Bureau of Business Research, University of Texas, 1964. 118p. pap.
Comprehensive bibliography of retail publications. Classified by broad subject areas. Includes a listing of selected magazine articles.

Cornell University. OPERATING RESULTS OF FOOD CHAINS. Ithaca, New York: 1954- . tables. pap.
Annual study, financed by the National Association of Food Chains which surveys the margins, expenses and profits of over 50 food chains. Includes selected financial ratio tables covering the current and previous five years.

Davidson, William R. and Doody, Alton F. "Retail Accounting and Expense Management." In their RETAILING MANAGEMENT, 3rd ed. New York: Ronald Press, 1966, part VIII, pp.749-864.
Contains chapters on accounting statements and the cost method of accounting, retail method of accounting, expense analysis and expense management. Includes ten cases and problems.

Duncan, Delbert J. and Phillips, Charles F. RETAILING, PRINCIPLES AND METHODS, 7th ed. Homewood, Illinois: Richard D. Irwin, 1967. 826p. charts, forms, photos., tables.

An excellent retailing text. Section 7 on "Retail Control" includes chapters on the cost method of accounting control, the retail inventory method and merchandise management accounting and expense control. Supplementary readings at the end of each chapter.

Fairchild Publications, Inc. FAIRCHILD'S FINANCIAL MANUAL OF RETAIL STORES. New York: 1937- . pap. Annual.

Gives a comparative review of sales and profits for the larger chains and financial data for the industry as well as the alphabetic manual listing of retail stores.

Helfert, Erich A., et al. CONTROLLERSHIP IN DEPARTMENT STORES. Boston: Division of Research, Graduate School of Business Administration, Harvard University, 1965. 154p. tables.

Indicates that department store controllers must shift from being simply financial accountants to a wider role as planner and advisor to management.

McNair, Malcolm P. and Hersum, Anita C. RETAIL INVENTORY METHOD AND LIFO. New York: McGraw-Hill Book Co., 1952. 466p. biblio., tables. (o.p.)

Excellent presentation of the two methods of inventory valuation: the "retail method," a means of arriving at cost from a physical inventory taken at current retail prices, and Lifo, the "last-in-first-out" method. The author outlines his reasons why he feels Lifo has a future in the retail business although it is not widely used at present.

National Association of Food Chains. STANDARD MANUAL OF ACCOUNTS FOR THE FOOD CHAIN INDUSTRY, rev. ed., developed by the Controllers Conference of the Association. Washington, D.C.: February 1968. 80p. pap.

A guide to the reporting and control of operating expenses and the recording of sales in the food chain industry. Describes accounting procedures for food manufacturing and processing operations.

National Association of Retail Grocers of the United States. FINANCIAL AND OPERATING STANDARDS FOR SUPERMARKETS, by Eric C. Oesterle and W. David Downey. Chicago: 1965. 162p. charts, tables. pap.

Based on a sample of 418 supermarkets, classified by sales volume and by specific operating characteristics within these groupings. Brief descriptions of obvious patterns precede the actual standards outlined for the various types of operations. Includes a system for evaluating the performance of a supermarket. Definition of accounting terms included.

National Association of Retail Grocers of the United States in cooperation with Frazer and Torbet. UNIFORM ACCOUNTING MANUAL FOR SUPERETTE AND SUPERMARKET OPERATORS. Milwaukee, Wisconsin: [1963]. 134p. forms. pap.

Presents the manual method of record keeping to be used as a guide to retail operations. Based on "C.T.P." concept pioneered by NARGUS which refers to the "difference between each department's gross profits and direct departmental controllable expenses."

National Retail Merchants Association. Controllers Congress. MERCHANDISING AND OPERATING RESULTS OF DEPARTMENT AND SPECIALITY STORES. New York: 1935-. pap. 1969 ed. in 4 vols.

This annual study presents data on department, specialty and branch stores arranged by size. Includes a number of total store ratios on sales, profits, expenses, etc.

National Retail Merchants Association. Controllers Congress. INTERNAL AUDITING FOR RETAIL STORES. New York: 1957. 64p. pap. (o.p.)

Prepared by the Milwaukee Retail Controllers' Association for the Controllers' Congress, this brief manual seeks to aid stores in setting up an effective internal audit program or in checking the effectiveness of a system currently in effect.

National Retail Merchants Association. Controllers Congress. OPERATING RESULTS OF DEPARTMENT AND SPECIALTY STORES. New York: 1963- . pap.

From 1920 to 1963 these studies were issued by the Harvard University Graduate School of Business Administration under the direction of Malcolm P. McNair, the outstanding authority in the retail field. The NRMA studies institute different bases for most of the tables, so care should be taken in any historical comparison of the figures in these studies. In addition to a brief review of retail trade activity during the year, these volumes contain tabulations on total store incóme, expense and profit financial data based on classifications incorporated in the association's RETAIL ACCOUNTING MANUAL. Financial ratios are also included.

National Retail Merchants Association. Controllers Congress. RETAIL ACCOUNTING MANUAL. New York: 1962. v.p. charts, tables. loose-leaf.

Based on the expense center approach, this manual presents accounting systems for both single and multi-unit stores which can be adapted by smaller stores.

Oklahoma. University. Bureau of Business Research. ACCOUNTING AND FINANCIAL DATA FOR RETAIL STORES: PRIMARY PURPOSES AND USES, by Homer A. Brown and Alva A. Cummings. Norman, Okla: March 1964. 78p. tables.

Presents a summary of findings on a survey of recordkeeping practices of a number of small retailers with recommendations for improvement. Describes an adequate accounting system and outlines the uses of accounting information. Final chapter covers specialized statements and schedules: cash flow, source and application of funds, budgets and schedule of insurance coverage.

Powers, James T. EXECUTIVE COMPENSATION IN RETAILING...in cooperation with Sam Flanel. New York: National Retail Merchants Association, Controllers' Congress, 1966. v.p. tables. loose-leaf.

A survey of executive compensation practices in department and specialty stores. Analyzes compensation in retailing and compares retail compensation with that of other industries. The bulk of the survey is made up of tables giving the dollar salary, bonus and total compensation figures for the 18 top executive positions in the 125 firms participating in the survey, grouped by size of store as indicated by sales volume. Appendices give representative bonus, retirement, profit sharing and stock option plans.

Super Market Institute. INDEX OF SUPER MARKET ARTICLES. Chicago: 1966. pap.

Annual listing of articles and reports about super market operations. Classified under numerous categories, this annotated bibliography also provides a detailed cross-reference index.

U.S. Small Business Administration. FINANCIAL RECORDKEEPING FOR SMALL STORES (Small Business Management Series, No. 32), by Robert C. Ragan. Washington, D.C.: U.S. Government Printing Office, 1966. 138p. charts, forms. pap.

Describes a basic recordkeeping system which the small-store owner can handle without professional assistance.

Urban Land Institute. Community Builders Council. STANDARD MANUAL OF EXPENSE ACCOUNTS FOR SHOPPING CENTERS. Washington, D.C.: 1961. 25p. pap.

Concentrates on the expense accounting area.

Wingate, John W. and Schaller, Elmer O. TECHNIQUES OF RETAIL MERCHANDISING, 2nd ed. Englewood Cliffs, New Jersey: Prentice-Hall, 1956. 592p. selected biblio., charts, facs., tables.

Part One, on "Profits," and Part Four, on "Planning and Control," are of most interest to accountants.

SAVINGS AND LOAN ASSOCIATIONS

For regulations of the Federal Home Loan Bank Board, see the publications listed under that agency in Section 3, Governmental Accounting.

American Institute of Certified Public Accountants. AUDITS OF SAVINGS AND LOAN ASSOCIATIONS. New York: 1962. 78p. pap.

Excellent guide for audits of these associations. Appendices give supervisory regulations and a chart of accounts.

Conway, Lawrence V. SAVINGS AND LOAN ACCOUNTING, 2nd ed. Chicago: American Savings and Loan Institute Press, 1965. 477p. glossary, facs., forms.

Prepared as a text for a course given by the American Savings and Loan Institute, this book presents a general outline of accounting concepts as well as the specific accounting principles relating to savings and loan association accounting procedures.

United States Savings and Loan League. STANDARD ACCOUNTING MANUAL FOR SAVINGS AND LOAN ASSOCIATIONS. Chicago: 1956. 99p. forms, tables. pap.

A classification of accounts comprises pp. 1-37. Following chapters cover accounting for various types of loans, interest rates, taxes and insurance, savings account bonus, and earnings distribution.

SCHOOLS AND COLLEGES

In addition to the following items, a number of state departments of education have prepared accounting guides to be used by the schools within their state system.

American Council on Education. COLLEGE AND UNIVERSITY BUSINESS ADMINISTRATION, rev. ed. Washington, D.C.: 1968. 327p. biblio.

The authoritative work on accounting for colleges and universities. Part 1 covers the principles of administration. Part 2, entitled "Principles of Accounting and Reporting" contains the material of greatest interest to accountants. Chapters on budgetary accounting, financial reports, balance sheet, fund accounting, internal control and audits. Appendix A: Chart of accounts; Appendix B: Illustrative forms; Appendix C: Terminology; Appendix D: Depreciation and revewal and replacement of plant assets.

American Council on Education. PLANNING FOR EFFECTIVE RESOURCE ALLOCATION IN UNIVERSITIES, prepared by Harry Williams of the Institute for Defense Analyses. Washington, D.C.: 1966. 88p. biblio., charts. pap.

Outlines a system of program budgeting for use in universities.

American Institute of Certified Public Accountants. PUBLIC SCHOOL COSTS. New York: 1963. 28p. pap.

Designed to provide basic guidelines which can help school board members and taxpayers make rational decisions on public school financial policies.

Mitchell, Herbert S. MANUAL FOR SCHOOL ACCOUNTING. Danville, Illinois: Interstate, 1961. 101p. charts. pap.

Presents a basic accounting system for school districts. Two later manuals by this author outline budget and management accounting systems for schools: SCHOOL ACCOUNTING FOR FINANCIAL MANAGEMENT (Interstate, 1964) and SCHOOL BUDGET POLICIES FOR FINANCIAL CONTROL (Interstate, 1962).

National Association of College and University Business Officers. ANNOTATED TABULATIONS OF COLLEGE AND UNIVERSITY ACCOUNTING PRACTICES. Washington, D.C.: American Council on Education, 1964. 64p. pap.

These tabulations show that the majority of these institutions and their auditors followed standards recommended in Volume 1 of COLLEGE AND UNIVERSITY BUSINESS ADMINISTRATION published by the Council in 1962, since superseded by the 1968 one-volume revised edition.

National Association of Independent Schools. ACCOUNTING FOR INDEPENDENT SCHOOLS. Boston: June 1969. 112p. biblio., chart of accounts, glossary, forms, pap.

Prepared by Peat, Marwick, Mitchell & Co., this manual is intended to develop uniform accounting practices and procedures for independent schools, to provide guidelines for uniform terminology and account classifications, and to generally assist the schools in the preparation of financial statements.

New York. State. Audit and Control Department, Municipal Affairs Division. UNIFORM SYSTEM OF ACCOUNTS FOR SCHOOL DISTRICTS, DOUBLE-ENTRY BASIS. Albany, New York: 1965. v.p. forms. loose-leaf.

Designed for use by all school districts employing eight or more teachers.

Ryan, Leo V. AN ACCOUNTING MANUAL FOR CATHOLIC ELEMENTARY AND SECONDARY SCHOOLS. Washington, D.C.: National Catholic Educational Association, 1963. 115p. forms. pap.

Adapted from the U.S. Office of Education's 1957 FINANCIAL ACCOUNTING FOR LOCAL AND STATE SCHOOL SYSTEMS. The Catholic school system, in evolving from a series of autonomous units into "an integrated network of schools requiring common financial supervision" is in urgent need of a uniform system of accounting. This manual is offered as a basis for such a system.

Swanson, John, et al. FINANCIAL ANALYSIS OF CURRENT OPERATIONS OF COLLEGES AND UNIVERSITIES. Ann Arbor, Michigan: Institute of Public Administration, University of Michigan, 1966. 459p. glossary, biblio., charts, graphs, tables. pap. (o.p.)

A study based on personal interviews and material received from 110 U.S. colleges and universities, 16 governing boards and coordinating agencies, five budget directors and three regional associations. Discusses procedures for financial analysis which are supplementary to the institution's basic financial accounting. The particular factors analyzed in detail are instruction, research, services to the public, services to the academic community and general support.

U.S. Department of Health, Education and Welfare. Office of Education. FINANCIAL ACCOUNTING FOR LOCAL AND STATE SCHOOL SYSTEMS, STANDARD RECEIPT AND EXPENDITURE ACCOUNTS (Handbook II, Bulletin 1957, No. 4). Washington, D.C.: U.S. Government Printing Office, 1957. 255p. Classification of accounts, glossary. pap.

The basic guide to accounting for state and local school systems in the United States. Chapters on the classification and definitions of receipt, expenditure and clearing accounts; analyzing expenditures; recording receipts and expenditures; financial accounting terminology.

U.S. Department of Health, Education and Welfare. Office of Education. GUIDE TO COLLEGE AND UNIVERSITY BUSINESS MANAGEMENT, by Paul K. Nance, et al. Washington, D.C.: U.S. Government Printing Office, 1965. 175p. charts, photos. pap.

Designed for business managers of small to medium sized institutions, this pamphlet covers among other aspects the financial functions of college business management. Bibliographies at the end of each chapter.

U.S. Department of Health, Education and Welfare. Office of Education. PRINCIPLES OF PUBLIC SCHOOL ACCOUNTING (Handbook II-B). Washington, D.C.: U.S. Government Printing Office, 1967. 280p. glossary, forms. pap.

A comprehensive handbook on school accounting records and systems. Early chapters cover basic information on financial accounting which may be skipped by the more knowledgeable.

SHIPPING

For additional regulations of the Interstate Commerce Commission and the Maritime Administration, see publications listed under those agencies in Section 3, Governmental Regulation.

Cheng, Philip C. STEAMSHIP ACCOUNTING. Cambridge, Maryland: Cornell Maritime Press, 1969. 192p. charts of accounts, forms, tables.

The only book on accounting for the steamship industry. The author emphasizes the application of accounting principles and theory to the shipping business.

Ferguson, Allen R., _et al_. THE ECONOMIC VALUE OF THE UNITED STATES MERCHANT MARINE. Evanston, Illinois: Transportation Center, Northwestern University, 1961. 567p. biblio., tables.

Excellent overall economic review of the subject. Part II, "Costs of the Program," is of particular interest to accountants.

Poole, Arthur B. "Accounting Policy and Practice." In McDowell, Carl E. and Gibbs, Helen M., OCEAN TRANSPORTATION. New York: McGraw-Hill Book Co., 1954. pp.288-306. (o.p.)

Practical approach to steamship accounting by a financial vice-president of a large shipping company. Sections on accounts related to operating statements, accounts related to balance sheet, accounting methods and procedures, cost accounting and contrasts between steamship and other industry accounting.

U.S. Department of Commerce. Office of Transportation Research. COST ACCOUNTING SYSTEM FOR GROUND MODES OF TRANSPORTATION CARRIERS, 3 vols. in 5 parts. Springfield, Virginia: Clearinghouse, 1966.

Vol. 1: Railroad manuals (PB 173 201-1) and (PB 173 201-2)
Vol. 2: Motors manuals (PB 173 202-1) and (PB 173 202-2)
Vol. 3: Barge manual (PB 173 203)

In 1964, the firms of Lybrand, Ross Bros. & Montgomery and United Research, Inc. were awarded a joint contract by the Office of Transportation Research to develop concepts for improved accounting systems for rail, motor and waterway carriers. The contractors disagreed fundamentally on "the nature and capability of accountancy and its proper role in cost-determination." Since the final report was felt by the United Research staff to "express to an undue extent" the concepts of Lybrand, Ross Bros. & Montgomery, a small follow-on contract was awarded to United Research to present an explanation of their opinions.

Therefore, each of those volumes contains two reports applicable to the particular mode of transportation. The first section, by Lybrand, Ross Bros. & Montgomery offers general accounting principles and concepts and an accounting manual for each mode; the second section, by United Research, provides a chart of accounts and a manual of work measurement procedures for each mode. Each volume contains a glossary prepared by Lybrand, Ross Bros. & Montgomery and a work measurement bibliography by United Research on the particular mode of transportation covered in that volume.

U.S. Interstate Commerce Commission. UNIFORM SYSTEM OF ACCOUNTS FOR MARITIME CARRIERS PRESCRIBED BY THE INTERSTATE COMMERCE COMMISSION FOR MARITIME CARRIERS, effective January 1, 1951. Washington, D.C.: 1950, with subsequent orders. pap.

U.S. Maritime Administration (Department of Commerce). MANUAL OF PROCEDURES. ACCOUNTING INSTRUCTIONS, Nos. 1- . Washington, D.C.: 1955- .

Issued periodically as inserts to the Office of Finance MANUAL OF PROCEDURES, these are rules and regulations relating to subsidized shipping. Available on standing order.

U.S. National Archives and Records Service. CODE OF FEDERAL REGULATIONS. TITLE 46: SHIPPING, Part 200 to end. Washington, D.C.: U.S. Government Printing Office, 1970, with cumulative supplements.

Basic volume includes all rules and regulations effective as of January 1, 1970. Supplements contain changes and additions as published in the FEDERAL REGISTER subsequent to this date. Of particular interest to accountants is Chapter II which contains the policy, practice and procedure as well as the regulations of the Federal Maritime Board and the Maritime Administration.

The contents of this CODE OF FEDERAL REGULATIONS as well as the FEDERAL REGISTER are considered by law prima facie evidence of the text of the original document.

Winter, William D. MARINE INSURANCE, ITS PRINCIPLES AND PRACTICE, 3rd ed. New York: McGraw-Hill Book Co., 1952. 571p. biblio., forms, tables.

A comprehensive text on all aspects of marine insurance which is of interest to accountants dealing with the shipping industry.

TELEVISION

See Entertainment

TEXTILES

American Apparel Manufacturers Association, Inc. COST ACCOUNTING MANUAL FOR THE APPAREL INDUSTRY. Nashville, Tennessee: Southern Garment Manufacturers Association, 1955. [American Apparel Manufacturers Association] 18p. pap.

A cost accounting manual designed to explain the methods to be used in determining the cost of a specific garment or lot number.

The American Cotton Manufacturers Institute, Inc. COTTON TEXTILE COSTS, 2nd ed. Charlotte, North Carolina: 1950. 101p. charts, forms. (o.p.)

A study of modern cost accounting methods and their application to the cotton textile manufacturing industry.

American Institute of Certified Public Accountants. THE TEXTILE COMPANY (Case Studies in Internal Control, No. 1). New York: 1950. 60p. pap.

Based on an actual case in which internal control procedures were reviewed. A lengthy internal control questionnaire checklist is given which includes handwritten comments by auditor at end of each section concerning adequacy of the system.

Kopycinski, Joseph V. TEXTILE INDUSTRY INFORMATION SOURCES (Management Information Guide, No. 4). Detroit, Michigan: Gale Research Co., 1964. 194p.

A detailed guide to the literature of the textile industry. Includes a section listing the larger collections of textile literature.

New York State Society of Certified Public Accountants. Committee on Textile Accounting. BIBLIOGRAPHY, TEXTILE ACCOUNTING. New York: September 30, 1966. 6p. mimeo.

Consists mainly of magazine articles.

Shinn, W.E. ELEMENTS OF TEXTILE COSTING, 2nd ed. Metuchen, New Jersey: Textile Book Service, 1965. 105p. graphs. pap. mimeo.

This book is primarily concerned with the cost of textile goods at the mill in finished form ready for the market, so does not include selling, advertising promotion or marketing costs.

Silk and Rayon Printers and Dyers Association of America, Inc. UNIFORM COST METHODS. New York: 1949. 51p. forms.

Suggests a simple, practical method for smaller companies and a more detailed method for the larger firms.

THEATRE

See Entertainment

WAREHOUSES AND WAREHOUSE RECEIPTS

American Bankers Association. A BANKER'S GUIDE TO WAREHOUSE RECEIPT FINANCING. New York: 1966. 48p. pap.

Offered as a handy guide to bankers to help them in reviewing procedures on loans secured by warehouse receipts.

American Institute of Certified Public Accountants. PUBLIC WAREHOUSES - CONTROLS AND AUDITING PROCEDURES FOR GOODS HELD (Statements on Auditing Procedure, No. 37). New York: September 1966. 16p. pap.

Covers internal control of the warehouseman and the auditing procedures of the independent auditor with regard to goods held in the warehouse.

American Warehousemen's Association. PUBLIC MERCHANDISE WAREHOUSING, AN OPERATIONS MANUAL. PART VII: COST ACCOUNTING FOR THE WAREHOUSEMAN. Chicago: 1962. 16p. pap.

A basic accounting manual which can be used to pinpoint costs by warehousemen with only a slight knowledge of bookkeeping.

Andersen, Arthur & Co. WAREHOUSES AND WAREHOUSE RECEIPTS. [Chicago]: July 1964. 61p. pap.

Gives background information and the main factors which an auditor should consider in examining financial statements of a warehouse company, a depositor of goods in a warehouse or a lender holding warehouse receipts as collateral for a loan. Uniform Warehouse Receipts Act is also included.

Jacoby, Neil H. and Saulnier, Raymond J. FINANCING INVENTORY ON FIELD WAREHOUSE RECEIPTS. New York: National Bureau of Economic Research, 1944. 107p. charts, tables.

Although not of recent date, this study is still useful since it is longer and more detailed than other more current publications on warehouse receipts.

National Association of Refrigerated Warehouses, Inc. WAREHOUSE RECEIPTS

AND THE UNIFORM COMMERCIAL CODE, by John W. MacDonald. Washington, D.C.: 1966. 23p. pap.

An excellent pamphlet which covers in detail the most important aspects of the Uniform Commercial Code concerned with the issuing, handling and use of warehouse receipts as collateral. Pages 15 through 23 contain excerpts from the Code appropriate to warehouse receipts. Available without charge from the NAWW; a staff-prepared digest of the study is also available.

The New York Clearing House Association. WAREHOUSE RECEIPT FINANCING. [New York]: July 1965. 19p. exhibits. pap.

Makes recommendations for tighter controls, listing ten specific steps to be adopted. Includes a suggested questionnaire to be filled out by the warehouseman.

WINERY

See Beverages

STATISTICAL AND MATHEMATICAL METHODS

See also Operations Research

American Institute of Certified Public Accountants. AN AUDITOR'S APPROACH TO STATISTICAL SAMPLING, No. 1- . New York: 1967- . pap.

A series of programmed self-study texts on statistical sampling techniques in auditing, prepared by Teaching Systems Corporation. No. 1: AN INTRODUCTION TO STATISTICAL CONCEPTS AND ESTIMATION OF DOLLAR VALUES, covers basic statistical concepts and illustrates the practical application of unrestricted random sampling.

No. 2: SAMPLING FOR ATTRIBUTES, deals with sampling for specific characteristics, such as "the frequency of occurrence of a certain event."

No. 3: STRATIFIED RANDOM SAMPLING, describes in detail the techniques of stratified random sampling and the reasons for using such a plan.

Arkin, Herbert. HANDBOOK OF SAMPLING FOR AUDITING AND ACCOUNTING. New York: McGraw-Hill Book Co., 1963. v.p. tables. loose-leaf.

Presents basic concepts involved in statistical methods in language easily understood by average accountant.

Arkin, Herbert and Colton, Raymond R. STATISTICAL METHODS, 5th. ed. (College Outline Series, No. 27.) New York: Barnes & Noble, 1970. 360p. tables. pap.

A small handbook which describes concisely the various statistical techniques and theories. Bibliographies at the end of each chapter.

Bierman, Harold, et al. QUANTITATIVE ANALYSIS FOR BUSINESS DECISIONS, 3rd. ed. Homewood, Illinois: Richard D. Irwin, 1969. 654p. charts, tables.

Reviews new statistical and mathematical techniques now being applied to business decision-making. Brief bibliographies at end of some chapters.

Brown, R. Gene and Vance, Lawrence L. SAMPLING TABLES FOR ESTIMATING ERROR RATES OR OTHER PROPORTIONS. Berkeley, California: University of California, 1961. 219p. tables. (o.p.)
Offers tables prepared primarily for the use of accountants and auditors in the application of sampling techniques.

Cissell, Robert and Helen. MATHEMATICS OF FINANCE, 3rd ed. Boston: Houghton Mifflin, 1969. 346p. charts, diagrs., forms, tables.
A textbook which is also directed towards helping the financial analyst in making his decisions. Includes chapters on bonds and stocks.

Cochran, William G. SAMPLING TECHNIQUES, 2nd ed. New York: John H. Wiley & Sons, 1963. 421p. tables.
For advanced students, this textbook describes sampling theory as developed in sample surveys and presents illustrations of the various sampling methods. Bibliographies at the end of each chapter.

Croxton, Frederick E., et al. PRACTICAL BUSINESS STATISTICS, 4th ed. Englewood Cliffs, New Jersey: Prentice-Hall, 1969. 464p. charts, illus., tables.
A textbook covering all aspects of statistical methods including statistical sampling.

Curtis, Arthur B. and Cooper, William J. MATHEMATICS OF ACCOUNTING, 4th ed., revised by William James McCallion. Englewood Cliffs, New Jersey: Prentice-Hall, 1961. 576p. tables.
Part 1 covers commercial arithmetic and simple interest with applications. Part 2 covers commercial algebra and compound interest with applications.

Cyert, R.M. and Davidson, H. Justin. STATISTICAL SAMPLING FOR ACCOUNTING INFORMATION. Englewood Cliffs, New Jersey: Prentice-Hall, 1962. 224p. selected biblio., charts, tables.
Shows how to use statistical sampling methods in solving accounting problems without the necessity of higher mathematical training.

Dean, Burton V., et al. MATHEMATICS FOR MODERN MANAGEMENT. New York: John H. Wiley & Sons, 1963. 456p. charts, graphs.
Textbook which emphasizes the application of operations research techniques to business decision making. Part V briefly covers interest, annuities, investments and actuarial tables.

Financial Publishing Company. MONTHLY PAYMENT DIRECT REDUCTION LOAN AMORTIZATION TABLES, 11th ed. Boston: 1967. v.p. tables.
Shows equal monthly payments required to amortize a $1,000 loan, including the amount of interest and principal in each payment and the balance outstanding at any time during the life of the loan. A volume giving quarterly, semiannual or annual payments is available from the same publisher.

Gushee, Charles H., ed. FINANCIAL COMPOUND INTEREST AND ANNUITY TABLES, 4th ed. Boston: Financial Publishing Co., 1966. 884p. tables.

Contains the six standard tables for compound interest work for a wider range of rates and a greater number of periods than other sources. Tables covered are: amount of 1; amount of 1 per period; sinking fund or periodic payment, amounting to 1; present worth of 1; present worth of 1 per period; periodic payment worth 1 today.

Hill, Henry P., et al. SAMPLING IN AUDITING, A SIMPLIFIED GUIDE AND STATISTICAL TABLES. New York: Ronald Press, 1962. 57p. biblio., tables.

Shows how to apply statistical sampling techniques to auditing problems.

Hummel, Paul M. and Seebeck, Charles L. MATHEMATICS OF FINANCE, 2nd ed. New York: McGraw-Hill Book Co., 1956. 384p. tables.

A clearly written textbook presentation of the mathematics of investment and finance. Describes interest rates, annuities, perpetuities, depreciation methods, etc. Kent's Compound Interest and Annuity Tables are given.

Institute of Internal Auditors. SAMPLING MANUAL FOR AUDITORS, rev. ed. New York: 1967. v.p. glossary, biblio., tables. pap.

An illustrated guide to statistical sampling techniques and procedures directed toward the auditor. Originally issued by the General Auditing Department of Lockheed Aircraft Corporation for its own use, the great interest generated by this manual led to its being offered to the Institute by Lockheed for reproduction and distribution.

Kendall, M.G. and Smith, B. Babington. TABLES OF RANDOM SAMPLING NUMBERS, 2nd series (Tracts for Computers, No. XXIV). London: Cambridge University Press, 1939, reprinted 1961. 70p. tables. pap.

A series of 100,000 random digits in a handy little paperback.

Lipkin, Lawrence, et al. ACCOUNTANTS HANDBOOK OF FORMULAS AND TABLES. Englewood Cliffs, New Jersey: Prentice-Hall, 1963. 340p. tables.

Presentation of the formulas useful in making accounting decisions are followed by examples demonstrating their use.

Miller, Robert B. STATISTICAL CONCEPTS AND APPLICATIONS: A NON-MATHEMATICAL EXPLANATION. Chicago: Science Research Associates, 1968. 192p. glossary, selected biblio., charts. pap.

Directed toward "the educated layman" who is neither a mathematician nor a statistician, this book explains concepts in and applications of various statistical techniques.

Moroney, M.J. FACTS FROM FIGURES, 3rd rev. ed. Baltimore, Maryland: Penguin, 1956. 472p. biblio., charts, tables. pap.

Prepared for non-mathematicians, this well-written little book explains clearly and graphically the various statistical techniques used in business and research.

O'Hara, John B. and Clelland, Richard C. EFFECTIVE USE OF STATISTICS IN ACCOUNTING AND BUSINESS, ILLUSTRATIVE CASES. New York: Holt, Rinehart and Winston, 1964. 231p. charts, graphs, tables.

Presents applications of simple statistical methods to financial management problems.

Rand Corporation. A MILLION RANDOM DIGITS WITH 100,000 NORMAL DEVIATES. Glencoe, Illinois: Free Press of Glencoe, 1955. 225p. tables.
Presents the largest published digit table for use in random sampling.

Schmid, Calvin F. HANDBOOK OF GRAPHIC PRESENTATION. New York: Ronald Press, 1954. 324p. charts, forms, graphs, illus., maps, tables.
Good working manual for those who have to present statistical information in graphic form.

Slonim, Morris James. SAMPLING IN A NUTSHELL. New York: Simon and Schuster, 1966. 158p. charts, tables. pap.
A handy elementary guide to sampling written in an easy style.

Treffetzs, Kenneth L. and Hills, E. Justin. MATHEMATICS OF BUSINESS, ACCOUNTING AND FINANCE. New York: Harper, 1956. 605p. tables.
Reviews fundamental arithmetical operations and algebraic principles as well as simple and compound interest and discount, installment credit, annuities and life insurance.

Vance, Lawrence L. and Neter, John. STATISTICAL SAMPLING FOR AUDITORS AND ACCOUNTANTS. New York: John H. Wiley & Sons, 1956. 310p. charts, tables. (o.p.)
An excellent basic handbook for the uninitiated in statistical sampling.

Walsh Killian Lebens, Inc. YATES MUNICIPAL BOND EVALUATOR DIRECTORY. New York: 1966. tables. pap.
Comprehensive listing of municipal bonds which has greatly simplified the process of appraising the value of these bonds. References in the DIRECTORY are made to certain pages in the weekly supplement, MUNICIPAL BOND EVALUATOR, on which maturities are listed along the left side of each page and coupons are listed across the top. The intersection of the coupon column and the maturity row give the yield and dollar value of the bonds.

SYSTEMS

We include in this section only material on accounting and control systems and a few general works on systems and procedures. Comprehensive coverage of all aspects of systems and procedures is provided by Management Information Guide No. 12 in this series, SYSTEMS AND PROCEDURES, INCLUDING OFFICE MANAGEMENT, by Chester Morrill, Jr., published in 1967 by Gale Research Company.

Anthony, Robert N. PLANNING AND CONTROL SYSTEMS: A FRAMEWORK FOR ANALYSIS. Boston: Division of Research, Graduate School of Business Administration, Harvard University, 1965. 192p. biblio.
In place of the usual planning and control framework for designing a system the author suggests a framework based on the divisions of strategic planning, management control and operational control.

Association for Systems Management. BUSINESS SYSTEMS, 3rd ed. Cleveland: 1969. charts, forms, tables.
"How-to-do" systems manual containing descriptions of various ac-

counting and office procedures systems, each contributed by different members of the Association. Bibliographies at end of each chapter.

Baily, Henry Heaton. SPECIALIZED ACCOUNTING SYSTEMS, INCLUDING CONSTRUCTION AND INSTALLATION, 2nd ed. New York: John H. Wiley & Sons, 1951. 590p. charts, forms. (o.p.)
Gives background and accounting system information for several business fields on which there is not too much written material available: grain and stock brokerage, railroads, banks, fire and life insurance.

Carrithers, Wallace M. and Weinwurm, E.H. BUSINESS INFORMATION AND ACCOUNTING SYSTEMS. Columbus, Ohio: Chas. E. Merrill, 1967. 748p. charts, forms, photos, tables.
Includes accounting systems within the framework of information systems. The first half of the book covers basic concepts and organization of information systems and data processing.

Gillespie, Cecil. ACCOUNTING SYSTEMS, PROCEDURES AND METHODS, 2nd ed. Englewood Cliffs, New Jersey: Prentice-Hall, 1961. 641p. charts, diagrs., forms.
Shows how to review the business, establish the system, and prepare the manual or report.

Heckert, J. Brooks and Kerrigan, H.D. ACCOUNTING SYSTEMS, DESIGN AND INSTALLATION, 3rd ed. New York: Ronald Press, 1967. 673p. charts, forms, illus., photos.
Concentrates on the accounting system as a means of collecting and reporting information. Numerous visual aids help to explain the descriptions of basic business procedures.

Lasser Institute, J.K., ed. HANDBOOK OF ACCOUNTING METHODS, 3rd ed. New York: Van Nostrand, 1964. 970p. forms.
Short first section covers basic accounting system practice. Second section is composed of 97 chapters on specific accounting problems of various industries, businesses, etc., each written by a different contributor.

Lazzaro, Victor, ed. SYSTEMS AND PROCEDURES, A HANDBOOK FOR BUSINESS AND INDUSTRY, 2nd ed. Englewood Cliffs, New Jersey: Prentice-Hall, 1968. 544p. charts, forms, tables.
The more important of the systems and procedures techniques are covered by various authorities: work measurement, EDP, PERT, forms control, management information systems, etc.

Moore, Francis E. and Stettler, Howard F. ACCOUNTING SYSTEMS FOR MANAGEMENT CONTROL. Homewood, Illinois: Richard D. Irwin, 1963. 712p. charts, forms, illus.
Emphasizes the management viewpoint. Sections on management considerations in accounting systems, elements of the accounting system, systems for the operating functions of business, design and installation of accounting systems.

National Society of Public Accountants. PORTFOLIO OF ACCOUNTING

SYSTEMS FOR SMALL AND MEDIUM-SIZED BUSINESSES, 2 vols., ed. by Marjorie D. James. Englewood Cliffs, New Jersey: Prentice-Hall, 1968. charts, forms.

Covers accounting procedures and controls for 69 types of businesses, each one described by an expert in that field.

Nelson, Oscar S. and Woods, Richard S. ACCOUNTING SYSTEMS AND DATA PROCESSING. Cincinnati: South-Western Publishing Co., 1961. 655p. charts, illus., tables.

Advocates a unified treatment of accounting systems and data processing. Text is in three parts: organization and use of accounting information, nature of systems design, and automated data processing systems.

Pendery, John A. and Keeling, B. Lewis. PAYROLL RECORDS AND ACCOUNTING, SOCIAL SECURITY AND INCOME TAX WITHHOLDING. Cincinnati: South-Western Publishing Co., 1969. 254p. forms, photos., tables. pap.

Updated annually, this textbook gives a simplified explanation of basic payroll systems and accounting methods. Chapters 8 and 9 are on payroll accounting systems and payroll accounting.

Prentice-Hall, Inc. Editorial Staff. "Accounting Systems and Procedures." In ACCOUNTANT'S ENCYCLOPEDIA. New York: 1962, Vol. II, part 5.

Five articles covering objectives and techniques of systems installation, forms design and control, internal report preparation, integrated data processing and electronic data processing.

Printice-Hall, Inc. Editorial Staff. ENCYCLOPEDIC DICTIONARY OF SYSTEMS AND PROCEDURES. Englewood Cliffs, New Jersey: Prentice-Hall, 1966. 679p.

A dictionary of systems operations, methods and procedures written in non-technical language.

Prentice-Hall, Inc. Editorial Staff. HANDBOOK OF SUCCESSFUL OPERATING SYSTEMS AND PROCEDURES, WITH FORMS. Englewood Cliffs, New Jersey: Prentice-Hall, 1964. 779p. charts, forms.

Forms and reports used in accounting systems: manual, mechanical and electronic.

Randall, Clarence B. and Burgly, Sally Weimar. SYSTEMS AND PROCEDURES FOR BUSINESS DATA PROCESSING , 2nd ed. Cincinnati: South-Western Publishing Co., 1968. 624p. charts, diagrs., forms, illus.

A textbook covering systems fundamentals, machine indoctrination, essential operations, specialized techniques in integrated data processing, data processing applications for accounting systems.

Whiteside, Conon D. ACCOUNTING SYSTEMS FOR THE SMALL AND MEDIUM-SIZED BUSINESS. Englewood Cliffs, New Jersey: Prentice-Hall, 1961. 264p. forms.

A detailed presentation of accounting systems for wholesale, retail and service trades as well as for the small or medium-sized manufacturing plant. Numerous graphic illustrations are included.

Williams, Robert I. and Doris, Lillian. ENCYCLOPEDIA OF ACCOUNTING SYSTEMS, 5 vols. Englewood Cliffs, New Jersey: Prentice-Hall, 1956. forms.

Describes and illustrates accounting systems for a variety of industries, businesses and professions.

TAX ACCOUNTING

See also Section 4, Tax Practice

American Institute of Certified Public Accountants. ACCOUNTING FOR INCOME TAXES (Opinions of the Accounting Principles Board, No. 11). New York: December 1967. 33p. pap.

Authoritative statement on the treatment of interperiod allocation of income taxes.

American Institute of Certified Public Accountants. ACCOUNTING FOR INCOME TAXES: AN INTERPRETATION OF APB OPINION NO. 11, by Donald J. Bevis and Raymond E. Perry. New York: 1969. 70p. tables. pap.

Offers guidelines for practical application of APB Opinion No. 11. Includes complete text of the Opinion.

Andersen, Arthur & Co. ACCOUNTING FOR INCOME TAXES. [Chicago]: 1961. 81p. pap.

"...states views of our Firm with respect to the direction of future development of accounting for income taxes and relates our conclusions to sound accounting principles."

Bardes, Philip, et al., eds. MONTGOMERY'S FEDERAL TAXES, 39th ed. New York: Ronald Press, 1964. v.p.

Tax accounting methods are covered in chapters 7 and 8: "Tax Basis of Property" and "Accounting Periods and Methods."

Black, Homer A. INTERPERIOD ALLOCATION OF CORPORATE INCOME TAXES (Accounting Research Study, No. 9). New York: American Institute of Certified Public Accountants, 1966. 133p. pap.

Reviews three alternative concepts of interperiod income tax allocation, relating them to accounting practice: the liability method, the deferred method and the net of tax method.

Haskins & Sells. INVESTMENT CREDIT AND DEPRECIATION GUIDELINES; ACCOUNTING METHODS AND IMPACT ON NET INCOME AND FUNDS FROM OPERATIONS. [New York]: May 1963. 24p. pap.

Summarizes the accounting methods used in the 1962 annual reports of 465 listed companies with respect to the investment credit and depreciation guidelines tax provisions.

Keller, Thomas F. ACCOUNTING FOR CORPORATE INCOME TAXES (Michigan Business Studies, Vol. XV, No. 2). Ann Arbor: Bureau of Business Research, University of Michigan, 1961. 161p.

A monograph which concentrates on the treatment of the annual income tax charge in annual financial statements. The author is in favor of inter-period tax allocation.

Lasser, J.K., ed. HANDBOOK OF TAX ACCOUNTING METHODS. New York: Van Nostrand, 1951. 1108p. biblio., illus. (o.p.)

Gives principles and general methods of tax accounting. Covers the specific tax problems of 91 businesses and industries.

Moyer, C.A. and Mautz, R.K. "Influence of Federal Income Taxation on Financial Reporting." In their INTERMEDIATE ACCOUNTING, A FUNCTIONAL APPROACH. New York: John H. Wiley & Sons, 1962. chap. 16.
Outlines the differences between statements of income and surplus to be used for accounting purposes and those to be used for tax purposes.

Price Waterhouse & Co. IS GENERALLY ACCEPTED ACCOUNTING FOR INCOME TAXES POSSIBLY MISLEADING INVESTORS? A STATEMENT OF POSITION ON INCOME TAX ALLOCATION. New York: 1967. 27p. tables. pap.
Price Waterhouse & Co. differs with the position expressed in the AICPA Accounting Research Study No. 9 concerning deferred tax allocation accounting, feeling that such deferred income taxes are not likely ever to be paid and thus should not always be offset against income in financial statements. Includes a study of the accounting practices of 100 companies as to the treatment of accelerated depreciation and installment sales.

VALUATION

American Society of Appraisers. APPRAISAL AND VALUATION MANUAL. New York: 1956- . charts, tables.
A biennial publication which contains field-tested experiences of specialists in various areas of appraisal and valuation practice. Cumulative index in current volume covers all previous volumes.

Bonbright, James C. THE VALUATION OF PROPERTY, 2 vols. Charlottesville, Virginia: The Michie Company, 1965. 1,271p.
Originally published in 1937, this is a classic on the nature and measurement of value.

Harvard University. Graduate School of Business Administration. Accounting Round Table. THE MEASUREMENT OF PROPERTY, PLANT AND EQUIPMENT IN FINANCIAL STATEMENTS. Boston: 1964. 86p. ports. pap.
Summary of proceedings of an accounting round-table composed of participants from insurance companies, banks, the public accounting profession and the academic community.

Helfert, Erich A. VALUATION: CONCEPTS AND PRACTICE. Belmont, California: Wadsworth, 1966. 127p. biblio., charts, tables. pap.
After discussing various concepts of value in the first chapter, the author goes on to discuss valuation of recorded assets and liabilities, cash flows, corporate enterprises and corporation securities.

McMichael, Stanley L. MC MICHAEL'S APPRAISING MANUAL, 4th ed. Englewood Cliffs, New Jersey: Prentice-Hall, 1951. 749p. appraising biblio., charts, diagrs., tables.
Covers all aspects of the real estate appraisal field.

Marston, Winfrey, et al. ENGINEERING VALUATION AND DEPRECIATION, 2nd ed. New York: McGraw-Hill Book Co., 1953. [Iowa State University Press] 524p. charts, graphs.
Discusses the procedures involved in the appraisal of industrial property.

National Association of Insurance Commissioners. Committee on Valuation of Securities. VALUATION OF SECURITIES AS OF DECEMBER 31... New York: 1945- .

Annual publication which gives "notations as to amortizability of each bond to be used in the companies' annual statements... ."

WRITING AND REPORTS

Brown, Leland. EFFECTIVE BUSINESS REPORT WRITING, 2nd ed. Englewood Cliffs, New Jersey: Prentice-Hall, 1963. 432p. biblio., facs., forms.

Comprehensive presentation of the principles of business report writing. Numerous illustrations.

Comer, David B. and Spillman, Ralph R. MODERN TECHNICAL AND INDUSTRIAL REPORTS. New York: Putnam, 1962. 445p. biblio., charts, graphs.

Concentrates on report writing. Advises how to organize and present material forcefully.

Crouch, W. George and Zetler, Robert L. A GUIDE TO TECHNICAL WRITING, 3rd ed. New York: Ronald Press, 1964. 453p.

Discusses various types of business communication: letters, reports, articles, speeches. Selected bibliography and general reading list included.

deMare, George. COMMUNICATING FOR LEADERSHIP - A GUIDE FOR BUSINESS EXECUTIVES. New York: Ronald Press, 1968. 283p.

Well-written book which gives practical advice on written and oral communications between the businessman and the people with whom he deals.

Graves, Harold F. and Hoffman, Lyne S.S. REPORT WRITING, 4th ed. Englewood Cliffs, New Jersey: Prentice-Hall, 1965. 296p. charts, forms, photos.

Practical textbook on report writing. Special handbook section includes details of "mechanics" such as punctuation, usage, spelling, etc. Bibliography of abstracts and index.

Hunter, Laura Grace. THE LANGUAGE OF AUDIT REPORTS. Washington, D.C.: U.S. Government Printing Office, 1957. 93p. pap.

Excellent pamphlet giving advice on how to make audit reports "clear, concise and correct." Most of the illustrations come from audit reports.

Lesikar, R.V. REPORT WRITING FOR BUSINESS, 3rd ed. Homewood, Illinoise: Richard D. Irwin, 1969. 440p. forms, illus., tables.

Covers a number of business problems on which reports must be prepared. Bibliography of basic business sources is included.

Lewis, Ronello B. ACCOUNTING REPORTS FOR MANAGEMENT. Englewood Cliffs, New Jersey: Prentice-Hall, 1957. 197p. forms, tables.

Shows how to present effective and easily understandable accounting reports to the non-financial executive. Numerous forms illustrate the author's ideas.

Palen, Jennie M. REPORT WRITING FOR ACCOUNTANTS. Englewood Cliffs, New Jersey: Prentice-Hall, 1955. 616p. charts, forms.

Chapters 1-19 and 28 describe in detail the types of reports for which the independent auditor is responsible. Chapters 20-22 cover the comment section in audit reports and chapters 23-25 discuss techniques of writing these comments. Remaining chapters on "The Right Word," "Presentations" and "Review, Typing and Delivery."

Prentice-Hall, Inc. ENCYCLOPEDIA OF ACCOUNTING FORMS AND REPORTS, 3 vols. Englewood Cliffs, New Jersey: 1964. forms.

Vol. 1: Forms and reports used in accounting practice. Vol. 2: Forms and reports used in accounting systems (later reprinted as separate volume, HANDBOOK OF SUCCESSFUL OPERATING SYSTEMS AND PROCEDURES WITH FORMS). Vol. 3: Forms and reports used in specific industries.

Sklare, Arnold B. CREATIVE REPORT WRITING. New York: McGraw-Hill Book Co., 1964. 444p. biblio., charts, forms.

Reviews all types of modern business reports and explains how to set them up imaginatively and effectively.

Winfrey, Robley. TECHNICAL AND BUSINESS REPORT PREPARATION, 3rd ed. Ames, Iowa: Iowa State University Press, 1962. 350p. charts, diagrs., forms, illus., tables.

Offers techniques by which technically sound, clearly written reports can be presented in an attractive format. Collateral reading references included.

Section 9

PERIODICALS

Section 9

PERIODICALS

Periodicals play an important role in the expression of current accounting thought. Viewpoints concerning accounting theory and practice are developed in the accounting journals long before they are recorded in book form, if, in fact, they are ever so formalized.

Since the periodical literature is a prime source of information for the accountant, the accounting indexes described in Section 6, Bibliographies and Indexes, should be an essential part of his library. The most important of these is the ACCOUNTANTS' INDEX, published every two years by the American Institute of Certified Public Accountants. The other basic accounting index is ACCOUNTING ARTICLES, updated monthly, published by Commerce Clearing House, Inc.

The most comprehensive of the standard periodical directories are the AYER DIRECTORY OF NEWSPAPERS AND PERIODICALS (annually, N.W. Ayer & Son, Inc.), THE STANDARD PERIODICAL DIRECTORY (2nd ed., 1967, Oxbridge Publishing Company) and ULRICH'S INTERNATIONAL PERIODICALS DIRECTORY (Vols. I and II, 12th ed., 1968, annual supplements, R.R. Bowker Company). These directories all include sections in which the periodical titles are classified by subject matter.

In the following listing we have included only periodicals in the English language, with the exception of the official journals of certain foreign accounting institutes. All these official journals cover all aspects of accounting of interest to the members of their institutes. We have divided the entries into Journals, U.S. State Society Journals and Bulletins, and Related Business Periodicals.

ACCOUNTING JOURNALS

ABACUS. Sydney University Press, Press Building, University of Sydney, Sydney, New South Wales 2006, Australia. Semiannual.
Edited by R.J. Chambers. A scholarly publication, with contributors from all countries.

ACCOUNTANCY. Institute of Chartered Accountants in England and Wales, 26-34 Old Street, London E.C.1, England. Monthly.
Long established official journal of the Institute.

DE ACCOUNTANT. Nederlands Institute van Accountants, Herengracht 491, Amsterdam C. Netherlands. Monthly.

Official journal of the Netherlands Institute.

THE ACCOUNTANT. Gee & Co. Ltd., 151 Strand, London W.C.2, England. Weekly.

The most authoritative of the journals not published by an accounting institute. Covers all aspects of accountancy.

THE ACCOUNTANTS' DIGEST. Editor, L.L. Briggs, 13 Bay View Street, Burlington, Vermont 05401. Quarterly.

Digests of selected articles from accounting journals of the English-speaking world.

ACCOUNTANTS' JOURNAL. New Zealand Society of Accountants, Box 10046, Wellington, New Zealand. Monthly.

Official journal of the New Zealand Society.

THE ACCOUNTANTS' JOURNAL. Philippine Institute of Certified Public Accountants, San Luis Terraces Building, T.M. Kalaw, Ermita, Manila, Philippines. Quarterly.

Official journal of the Philippine Institute.

THE ACCOUNTANT'S MAGAZINE. Institute of Chartered Accountants of Scotland. Accountants' Publishing Co., Ltd., 27 Queen Street, Edinburgh 2, Scotland. Monthly.

Official journal of the Scottish Institute.

ACCOUNTANTS' WEEKLY REPORT. Prentice-Hall, Inc., Englewood Cliffs, New Jersey 07632. Weekly.

Contains brief digests of current tax decisions and rulings.

ACCOUNTING. Brooklyn College Accounting Alumni Association, Brooklyn College, Brooklyn, New York 21010. Irregular.

Articles on accounting and related matters by practicing accountants, lawyers, etc., in addition to those by Brooklyn College accounting professors.

THE ACCOUNTING FORUM. Accounting Students, Bernard M. Baruch School of Business and Public Administration, The City College, 17 Lexington Avenue, New York, New York 10010. Semiannual.

Includes articles on accounting topics by accountants in public practice in addition to those by City College accounting instructors and students. Includes CPA examination questions and answers.

THE ACCOUNTING PRACTITIONERS REPORT. Hanover Lamont Corporation, 89 Beach Street, Boston, Massachusetts 02111. Monthly.

A newsletter containing accounting, tax and legal developments of interest to accountants.

ACCOUNTING RESEARCH ASSOCIATION NEWSLETTER. Accounting Research Association, American Institute of Certified Public Accountants, 666 Fifth Avenue, New York, New York 10019. Irregular.

Offers current news about research activities of importance to the accounting profession.

THE ACCOUNTING REVIEW. American Accounting Association, Curtis-Reed Plaza, Menasha, Wisconsin. Quarterly.

Principal contributors are accounting professors.

Excellent, detailed book reviews. Since 1967, the January issue has included a section on "Research in Accounting," which lists accounting theses by subject.

THE ACCOUNTING SEMINAR. Long Island University Accounting Society, Accounting Department, Long Island University, Zeckendorf Campus, Brooklyn, New York 11201. Annual.

Articles by Long Island University accounting professors and students as well as contributions by accountants engaged in public practice.

THE ARTHUR ANDERSEN CHRONICLE. Arthur Andersen & Co., 69 W. Washington Street, Chicago, Illinois 60602. Quarterly.

Published by Arthur Andersen & Co. for staff members, but available to others upon request.

ASSOCIATION OF WATER TRANSPORTATION ACCOUNTING OFFICERS BULLETIN. Association of Water Transportation Accounting Officers, P.O. Box 53, Bowling Green Station, New York, New York 10004. Irregular.

Contains minutes of Association luncheon meetings and reprints or digests of talks delivered at those meetings.

THE AUDITOR. Faculty of Auditors, 36 Ebury Street, Victoria, London S.W.1, England. Quarterly.

The official journal of the Faculty of Auditors. Contains articles and news on accounting, legal and tax matters of interest to the auditing profession.

AUSTRALIAN ACCOUNTANT. (Australian Society of Accountants; Australasian Institute of Cost Accountants) Accountants Publishing Company, Ltd., 49 Exhibition Street, Melbourne, Australia. Monthly.

Official journal of the Australian Society.

BUDGETING. Planning Executives Institute, 16 Park Place, Oxford, Ohio 45056. Bimonthly.

Emphasis on budgeting and control.

CANADIAN CHARTERED ACCOUNTANT. Canadian Institute of Chartered Accountants, 250 Bloor Street, E., Toronto 5, Ontario, Canada. Monthly.

Official journal of Canadian Institute. Includes regular section in the French language.

CERTIFIED ACCOUNTANTS JOURNAL. Association of Certified and Corporate Accountants, Ltd., 22 Bedford Square, London W.C.1, England. Monthly.

Official journal of the Association. Emphasis on management accounting.

THE CERTIFIED GENERAL ACCOUNTANT. Certified General Accountants' Associations of Canada, 25 Adelaide Street, E., Toronto 1, Ontario, Canada. 5/year.

Emphasis on management accounting. Includes articles in the French language.

CHARTERED ACCOUNTANT. Institute of Chartered Accountants of India, Box 268. Indraprastha Marg, New Delhi 1, India. Monthly.

Official journal of the Indian Institute.

CHARTERED ACCOUNTANT IN AUSTRALIA. Institute of Chartered Accountants in Australia, Box 3921, G.P.O., Sydney 2001, Australia. Monthly.

Official journal of the Australian Institute.

COOPERATIVE ACCOUNTANT. National Society of Accountants for Cooperatives, Box 4765, Duke Station, Durham, North Carolina 27706. Quarterly.
Official journal of the National Society. Articles on accounting management for agricultural cooperatives.

COST AND MANAGEMENT. Society of Industrial and Cost Accountants of Canada, Box 176, 154 Main Street E., Hamilton, Ontario, Canada. Monthly.
Official journal of the Society. Emphasis on management accounting and cost analysis and control. Articles in French and English.

THE C.P.A. American Institute of Certified Public Accountants, 666 Fifth Avenue, New York, New York 10019. Monthly.
Reports on association activities and current professional developments. Contains the earliest public printing of the numbered opinions of the AICPA Ethics Committee.

DIE WIRTSCHAFTSPRUFUNG. Verlagsbuchhandlund des Instituts der Wirtschaftsprufer, 4 Dusseldorf, Postfach 10226, Germany. Irregular.
Official journal of the German Institute of Certified Accountants.

E. & E. Ernst & Ernst. 1300 Union Commerce Building, Cleveland, Ohio 44115. Quarterly.
Journal published by Ernst & Ernst for firm personnel, but available to others upon request.

FEDERAL ACCOUNTANT. Federal Government Accountants Association, 1523 L Street, N.W., Washington, D.C. 20005. Quarterly.
Covers general accounting and auditing topics, but emphasis is given to developments in the federal government of interest to businessmen and accountants.

FINANCIAL EXECUTIVE. Financial Executives Institute, 50 W. 44th Street, New York, New York 10036. Monthly.
Offers material on financial management of interest to corporate controllers and treasurers.

FINANZAS Y CONTABILIDAD. Editorial Finanzas, S. De R. L., Av Hidalgo No. 5, Piso 9, Mexico 1, D.F. Monthly.
Contains articles on accounting and finance in Spanish.

FRANCE COMPTABLE. Compagnie Professionnelle des Chefs de Comptabilite et des Comptables Brevetes Par l'Etat, SPICA, 30 rue Concorcet, Paris 9e, France. Quarterly.
The official journal of this particular French accounting society.

GAO REVIEW. Superintendent of Documents, U.S. Government Printing Office, Washington, D.C. 20402. Quarterly.
Published for the accounting and auditing staffs of the U.S. General Accounting Office, but available to others on subscription basis.

H & S REPORTS. Haskins & Sells, 2 Broadway, New York, New York 10004. Quarterly.
Journal published by Haskins & Sells for firm personnel, but available to others upon request.

HOSPITAL FINANCIAL MANAGEMENT. Hospital Financial Management Association, 840 North Lake Shore Drive, Chicago, Illinois 60611. 10/year.

Journal of the Association. Contains articles on hospital accounting, management, administration and control.

INDUSTRIAL ACCOUNTANT QUARTERLY. Pakistan Institute of Industrial Accountants, P.I.I.A. Building, Soldier Bazaar, Karachi-3, Pakistan. Quarterly.

Emphasis on management accounting

THE INTERNAL AUDITOR. Institute of Internal Auditors, 170 Broadway, New York, New York 10038. Bimonthly.

Emphasis on internal auditing and control.

THE INTERNATIONAL ACCOUNTANT. Association of International Accountants, Temple Chambers, Temple Avenue, London E.C.4, England. Quarterly.

Official journal of the Association. Directed toward professional, commercial and management accountants "throughout the world," but emphasis is mainly on material of interest to professional accountants in the British Commonwealth countries.

THE INTERNATIONAL JOURNAL OF ACCOUNTING, EDUCATION AND RESEARCH. Center for International Education and Research in Accounting, 320 Commerce West, University of Illinois, Urbana, Illinois 61801. Semiannual.

Includes material on international accounting and subjects of international accounting interest.

THE INTERPRETER. Insurance Accounting and Statistical Association, International Office P.O. Box 139, Kansas City, Missouri 64141. Monthly.

Covers insurance accounting and statistics.

IRISH ACCOUNTANT AND SECRETARY. Morris and Co., 1-2 Rutland Place, Cavendish Row, Dublin 1, Ireland. Bimonthly.

Articles on accounting practices, procedures and systems.

THE JOURNAL OF ACCOUNTANCY. American Institute of Certified Public Accountants, 666 Fifth Avenue, New York, New York 10019. Monthly.

Official journal of the AICPA. Articles on accounting, tax and professional development activities of interest to accountants and financial executives. Subscriptions can include the semiannual CPA examination supplements.

JOURNAL OF ACCOUNTING RESEARCH. Institute of Professional Accounting. Graduate School of Business, University of Chicago, Chicago, Illinois 60637, and London School of Economics and Political Science, University of London, at Baltimore, Maryland 21202. Semiannual.

Emphasis is on accounting theory rather than on the more practical aspects of accountancy. Annual supplement on empirical research in accounting.

JOURNAL UEC. Union Europeenne des Experts Comptables, Economiques et Financiers, 139, rue du Faubourg Saint-Honore, Paris 8^e, France. Quarterly.

Official journal of the UEC. Contains articles on international accounting matters published in French, German and English. Includes pronouncements of the UEC.

THE LKHH ACCOUNTANT (formerly THE HORWATH ACCOUNTANT). Laventhol Krekstein Horwath & Horwath, 866 Third Avenue, New York, New York 10022. Quarterly.

Special emphasis on accounting for hotels, motels, clubs, hospitals, restaurants and institutions. Includes annual studies on club and restaurant operations. Published for employees of Laventhol Krekstein

Horwath & Horwath, but available to others upon request.

LYBRAND JOURNAL. Lybrand, Ross Bros. & Montgomery, 60 Broad Street, New York, New York 10004. Quarterly.
Published for staff and clients of Lybrand, Ross Bros. & Montgomery, but available to others upon request.

THE MAGAZINE OF BANK ADMINISTRATION (formerly AUDITGRAM). Bank Administration Institute, 303 South Northwest Highway, P.O. Box 500, Park Ridge, Illinois 60068. Monthly.
Emphasis on bank operations, internal audit and control.

MANAGEMENT ACCOUNTING (formerly COST ACCOUNTANT). Institute of Cost and Works Accountants, 63 Portland Place, London, W.1, England. Monthly.
The official journal of the Institute. Articles on current developments in cost and management accounting in various industries.

MANAGEMENT ACCOUNTING (formerly NAA BULLETIN). National Association of Accountants, 505 Park Avenue, New York, New York 10022. Monthly.
Technical articles in areas related to management accounting such as cost accounting and control, budgeting, planning and forecasting. Available only to members of NAA.

MANAGEMENT SERVICES. American Institute of Certified Public Accountants, 666 Fifth Avenue, New York, New York 10019. Bimonthly.
Covers both financial and non-financial aspects of business management, planning and control systems.

NATIONAL PUBLIC ACCOUNTANT. National Society of Public Accountants, 1717 Pennsylvania Avenue, N.W., Washington, D.C. 20006. Monthly.
Official journal of the Society. Offers articles on practical aspects of accounting with emphasis on accounting for taxes.

NEWSPAPER CONTROLLER. Institute of Newspaper Controllers and Finance Officers, Inc., P.O. Box 68, Fair Haven, New Jersey 07701. Monthly.
Brief articles on various aspects of financial management in the newspaper publishing industry.

THE PARKISTAN ACCOUNTANT. Institute of Chartered Accountants of Pakistan, El-Markaz, Bunder Road, Karachi, 3, Pakistan. Quarterly.
Official journal of the Institute.

THE PRACTICAL ACCOUNTANT. The Institute for Continuing Professional Development, Inc., 40 West 57th Street, New York, New York 10019. Bimonthly.
Emphasis on accounting for taxes.

PRICE WATERHOUSE REVIEW. Price Waterhouse & Co., 60 Broad Street, New York, New York 10004. Quarterly.
Published for the staff of Price Waterhouse & Co., but available to others upon request.

RETAIL CONTROL. Controllers Congress, National Retail Merchants Association, 100 West 31st Street, New York, New York 10001. Monthly, September - June.
Covers internal auditing and control in the retail industry.

REVISION OG REGNSKABSVAESEN. Foreningen af Statsautoriserede Revisorer, Kronprinssegade 8, 1306 Copenhagen K., Denmark. Monthly.
Official journal of the Danish Institute. Contains an occasional article in the English language.

ROEH HACHESHBON. The Institute of Certified Public Accountants in Israel, P.O. Box 29281, 1, Montefiore Street, Tel Aviv, Israel. Monthly.
The official journal of the Institute. Although published in Hebrew, brief digests of the articles are given in English in the Table of Contents.

SDL NEWSLETTER. S.D. Leidesdorf & Co., 125 Park Avenue, New York, New York 10017. Quarterly.
Published by S.D. Leidesdorf & Co. for their staff, but available to others upon request.

THE SOUTH AFRICAN CHARTERED ACCOUNTANT. The National Council of Chartered Accountants, Harland House, Loveday Street, P.O. Box 964, Johannesburg, South Africa. Monthly.
Official journal of the Joint Council of the Societies of Chartered Accountants of South Africa. Text in Afrikaans and English.

SPHERE. Alexander Grant & Company, 380 Madison Avenue, New York, New York 10017. Quarterly.
Published by Alexander Grant & Company for members of its staff, but available to others upon request.

TEMPO. Touche, Ross, Bailey & Smart, P.O. Box 441, Wall Street Station, New York, New York 10005. Quarterly.
Published by Touche, Ross, Bailey & Smart for their staff, but available to others upon request.

THE TRANSCRIPT. Harris, Kerr, Forster & Company, 420 Lexington Avenue, New York, New York 10017. Monthly.
Articles on restaurant, club and institutional accounting. Published for Harris, Kerr, Forster & Company staff, but available to others upon request.

U.S. ARMY AUDIT AGENCY BULLETIN. Superintendent of Documents, U.S. Government Printing Office, Washington, D.C. 20402. Quarterly.
Emphasis is on accounting and auditing in the federal government, but also includes general articles on accounting, auditing, management, professional development, etc.

THE WOMAN CPA. American Woman's Society of Certified Public Accountants and the American Society of Women Accountants, 327 South La Salle Street, Chicago, Illinois 60604. Bimonthly.
Official publication of the two societies of women accountants which offers articles on all aspects of accountancy.

WORLD. Peat, Marwick, Mitchell & Co., 70 Pine Street, New York, New York 10005. Quarterly.
Published for the staff of Peat, Marwick, Mitchell & Co., but available to others upon request.

THE ARTHUR YOUNG JOURNAL. Arthur Young & Co., 277 Park Avenue, New York, New York 10017. Quarterly.

Published for the staff of Arthur Young & Co., but available to others upon request.

U.S. STATE SOCIETIES JOURNALS AND BULLETINS (EXCLUDING NEWSLETTERS)

(Arizona) THE QUARTERLY. Arizona Society of Certified Public Accountants, 3130 North Third Avenue, Phoenix, Arizona 85013. Quarterly.

THE CALIFORNIA CPA QUARTERLY. California Society of Certified Public Accountants, 1000 Welch Road, Palo Alto, California 94304. Quarterly.

COLORADO CPA REPORT. Colorado Society of Certified Public Accountants, 1200 Lincoln Street, Denver, Colorado 80203. Quarterly.

THE CONNECTICUT C.P.A. Connecticut Society of Certified Public Accountants, 179 Allyn Street, Hartford, Connecticut 06103. Quarterly.

(District of Columbia) THE CERTIFICATE. District of Columbia Institute of Certified Public Accountants, 1200 18th Street, Washington, D.C. 20036. 9/year.

THE FLORIDA CERTIFIED PUBLIC ACCOUNTANT. Florida Institute of Certified Public Accountants, Box 14287, Gainesville, Florida 32601. Semiannual.

THE GEORGIA C.P.A. Georgia Society of Certified Public Accountant, Inc., 1504 William-Oliver Building, Atlanta, Georgia 30303. Quarterly.

ILLINOIS CERTIFIED PUBLIC ACCOUNTANT. Illinois Society of Certified Public Accountants, 208 South LaSalle Street, Chicago, Illinois 60604. Quarterly.

THE KENTUCKY ACCOUNTANT. Kentucky Society of Certified Public Accountants, 310 West Liberty Street, Louisville, Kentucky 40202. Monthly.

THE LOUISIANA CERTIFIED PUBLIC ACCOUNTANT. Society of Louisiana Certified Public Accountants, 822 Perdido Street, New Orleans, Louisiana 70112. Quarterly.

THE MARYLAND CPA QUARTERLY. Maryland Association of Certified Public Accountants, Keyser Building, Baltimore, Maryland 21202. Quarterly.

MASSACHUSETTS CPA REVIEW. Massachusetts Society of Certified Public Accountants, Inc., One Center Plaza, Boston, Massachusetts 02108. Bimonthly.

THE MICHIGAN CERTIFIED PUBLIC ACCOUNTANT. Michigan Association of Certified Public Accountants, 1311 E. Jefferson Avenue, Detroit, Michigan 48207. Bimonthly.

(Minnesota) THE FOOTNOTE. Minnesota Society of Certified Public Accountants, 1102 Wesley Temple Building, Minneapolis, Minnesota 55403. Monthly.

THE MISSISSIPPI CERTIFIED PUBLIC ACCOUNTANT. Mississippi Society of Certified Public Accountants, P.O. Box 808, Jackson, Mississippi 39205. Annual.

(Missouri) THE ASSET. Missouri Society of Certified Public Accountants, 1925 Railway Exchange Building, St. Louis, Missouri 63101. 10/year.

MONTANA CPA. The Montana Society of Certified Public Accountants, 801 East Beckwith, Missoula, Montana 59801. Irregular.

THE NEBRASKA C.P.A. MAGAZINE. Nebraska Society of Certified Public Accountants, 811 Mulder Drive, Lincoln, Nebraska 68510. Semiannual.

THE NEW JERSEY CPA. New Jersey Society of Certified Public Accountants, 550 Broad Street, Newark, New Jersey 07102. Quarterly.

THE NEW YORK CERTIFIED PUBLIC ACCOUNTANT. New York State Society of Certified Public Accountants, 355 Lexington Avenue, New York, New York 10017. Monthly.

Excellent journal carrying articles of interest to all public and private accountants, financial officers, analysts, etc. Regular departments on accounting and auditing, CPA practice, administration, estate planning, management services and federal, state and local taxation.

THE OHIO CPA. Ohio Society of Certified Public Accountants, 79 East State Street, Columbus, Ohio 43215. Quarterly.

THE OKLAHOMA C.P.A. Oklahoma Society for Certified Public Accountants, 506 Sequoyah Building, Oklahoma City, Oklahoma 73105. Quarterly.

THE PENNSYLVANIA CPA SPOKESMAN. Pennsylvania Institute of Certified Public Accountants, Lewis Tower Building, Philadelphia, Pennsylvania 19102. 5/year.

THE TENNESSEE CPA. Tennessee Society of Certified Public Accountants, 161 Eighth Avenue, North, Nashville, Tennessee 37203. Monthly.

TEXAS CPA - THE TEXAS CERTIFIED PUBLIC ACCOUNTANT. Texas Society of Certified Public Accountants, 200 Corrigan Tower, Dallas, Texas 75201. Quarterly.

VIRGINIA ACCOUNTANT. Virginia Society of Certified Public Accountants, 809 Mutual Building, Richmond, Virginia 23219. Quarterly.

THE WEST VIRGINIA CPA. West Virginia Society of Certified Public Accountants, P.O. Box 1142, Charleston, West Virginia 25324. Quarterly.

WISCONSIN C.P.A. Wisconsin Society of Certified Public Accountants, 176 West Wisconsin Avenue, Milwaukee, Wisconsin 53203. Quarterly.

RELATED BUSINESS PERIODICALS

THE APPRAISAL JOURNAL. American Institute of Real Estate Appraisers of the National Association of Real Estate Boards, 36 South Wabash Avenue, Chicago, Illinois 60603. Quarterly.

In its coverage of all aspects of real estate valuation, this magazine often includes industry cost statistics which are useful to the accountant.

BARRON'S. Dow Jones & Company, Inc., 200 Burnett Road, Chicopee, Massachusetts 01021. Weekly.

National business and finance weekly. Also contains weekly stock prices and other statistical information.

BUSINESS HORIZONS. Graduate School of Business, Indiana University, Bloomington, Indiana 47401. Bimonthly.

Covers all aspects of business trends and procedures. Section entitled "Research Clearinghouse" lists current research projects of interest to businessmen and includes an accounting and control category.

BUSINESS INTERNATIONAL. Business International Corporation, 757 Third Avenue, New York, New York 10017. Weekly.

Brief summaries of news of current interest to managers of international corporations.

BUSINESS WEEK. McGraw-Hill Book Co., Inc., 330 West 42nd Street, New York, New York 10036. Weekly.

Excellent magazine offering news on all phases of business: production, labor, finance, marketing, research, exports, economics, transportation, labor relations and new products. Includes articles on individual companies.

CALIFORNIA MANAGEMENT REVIEW. University of California Press, Berkeley, California 94720. Quarterly.

Published for the Graduate Schools of Business Administration of California, Berkeley and Los Angeles. Attempts to "serve as a bridge between creative thought about management and executive action." Covers all aspects of management theory and practice.

CHANGING TIMES. The Kiplinger Washington Editors, Inc., Editors Park, Maryland 20782. Monthly.

Discusses subjects of general interest in a lively style. Numerous "how to" articles covering wide variety of topics of interest to small businessmen and homeowners.

COLUMBIA LAW REVIEW. Columbia Law School, Columbia University, 435 West 116th Street, New York, New York 10027. Monthly.

Journal published by Columbia Law School students covering wide range of legal matters.

THE COMMERCIAL AND FINANCIAL CHRONICLE. William B. Dana, 25 Park Place, New York, New York 10007. Semiweekly.

Monday issue contains security prices, corporation news, bank clearings, etc. Thursday issue contains general business news, business advertising, reprints of corporate executives' speeches, etc.

The BANK AND QUOTATION RECORD, a monthly companion publication of the CHRONICLE contains stock prices for securities listed on all U.S. stock exchanges and includes a large number of prices for over-the-counter securities.

THE CONFERENCE BOARD RECORD. National Industrial Conference Board, Inc., 845 Third Avenue, New York, New York 10022. Monthly.

Includes articles by business executives as well as by NICB researchers and analysts on economic and financial subjects. Available only to NICB associates.

DAILY REPORT FOR EXECUTIVES. The Bureau of National Affairs, Inc., 1231 25th Street, N.W., Washington, D.C. 20037. Daily.

Excellent digest of daily legislative, tax, financial and economic developments of importance to business executives.

DUN'S REVIEW. Dun & Bradstreet Publications Corporation, P.O. Box 3088,

Grand Central Station, New York, New York 10017. Monthly.
Covers general business and investment topics. Includes numerous articles on individual companies.

FINANCIAL ANALYSTS JOURNAL. Financial Analysts Federation, 477 Madison Avenue, New York, New York 10022. Bimonthly.
Covers investment management and security analysis. Classified, cumulative index, volumes 1-22, 1945-1966.

FINANCIAL WORLD. Guenther Publishing Corporation, 17 Battery Place, New York, New York 10004. Weekly.
Covers business and financial investment news. Includes articles on individual companies. Late October issue each year contains "Annual Report Awards" for corporation reports to stockholders based on clarity of presentation of financial material and attractiveness of layout.

FORBES. Forbes, Inc., 60 Fifth Avenue, New York, New York 10011. Semimonthly.
Covers business and investment news. Includes articles on individual companies. January 1st issue contains the "Annual Report on American Industry" in which Forbes ranks the top 500 publicly held U.S. corporations by growth and profitability. Reviews of each major industry including its largest companies are included. Also issues an annual directory of companies ranked by assets, revenues, market values and net profits.

FORTUNE. Time, Inc., 540 N. Michigan Avenue, Chicago, Illinois 60611. Monthly.
Dedicated to the professional management man. Articles of general and cultural interest as well as those relating to business management, finance, marketing, production, etc. Includes articles covering individual corporations, industries and professions. Publishes, annually, a listing popularly known as "Fortune's 500," ranking the 500 largest U.S. industrial corporations by sales.

HARVARD BUSINESS REVIEW. Graduate School of Business Administration, Harvard University, Boston, Massachusetts. Bimonthly.
One of the best of the business journals, this covers all aspects of corporate finance and administration.

HARVARD LAW REVIEW. Harvard Law Review Association, Gannett House, Cambridge, Massachusetts 02138. 8/year, November - June.
Issued by the students of Harvard Law School. This journal covers entire range of legal topics.

THE JOURNAL OF BUSINESS. University of Chicago Press, 5750 Ellis Avenue, Chicago, Illinois 60637. Quarterly.
Edited by the faculty of the Graduate School of Business, University of Chicago. Offers analytical approach to business operations and problems. January issue contains a classified list of accepted doctoral dissertations with a section on accounting.

THE JOURNAL OF COMMERCIAL BANK LENDING (formerly ROBERT MORRIS ASSOCIATES BULLETIN). Robert Morris Associates, Philadelphia National Bank Building, Philadelphia, Pennsylvania 19107. Monthly.

Articles on bank credit and financial policies. Includes a number of articles on bank financial reporting, since this association works closely with the AICPA on improving the standards of bank reporting.

THE JOURNAL OF FINANCE. American Finance Association, Executive Secretary and Treasurer, Robert A. Kavesh, Graduate School of Business, New York University, 100 Trinity Place, New York, New York 10006, 5/year.

Emphasis is on finance and economics. Includes a regular section on abstracts of doctoral dissertations.

JOURNAL OF SYSTEMS MANAGEMENT (formerly SYSTEMS AND PROCEDURES JOURNAL). Systems and Procedures Association, 24587 Bagley Road, Cleveland, Ohio 44138. Bimonthly.

Articles on business and industrial management systems and procedures.

THE JOURNAL OF TAXATION. Journal of Taxation, Inc., 125 East 56th Street, New York, New York 10022. Monthly.

A journal of current news and comment for professional tax men.

KIPLINGER TAX LETTER. The Kiplinger Washington Editors, 1729 H Street, N.W. Washington, D.C. 20006. Biweekly.

News concerning political and legal developments on tax matters of importance to businessmen.

KIPLINGER WASHINGTON LETTER. The Kiplinger Washington Editors, 1729 H Street, N.W. Washington, D.C. 20006. Weekly.

Brief news items and opinions concerning business and political trends and events of importance to the corporate executive.

J.K. LASSER TAX REPORT. Business Reports, Inc., 1 West Avenue, Larchmont, New York 10538. Semimonthly.

Brief summaries of current tax activities.

MANAGEMENT REVIEW. American Management Association, Inc., 135 West 50th Street, New York, New York 10020. Monthly.

Composed of reprints and digests of articles in current business periodicals.

MERGERS AND ACQUISITIONS, THE JOURNAL OF CORPORATE VENTURE. Mergers & Acquisitions, Inc., 1725 K Street N.W., Washington, D.C. 20006. Bimonthly.

Articles on financial and management aspects of business combinations. News of current merger activities. Listing of recent corporate acquisitions.

MICHIGAN BUSINESS REVIEW. Graduate School of Business Administration, The University of Michigan, Ann Arbor, Michigan 48104. Bimonthly.

Emphasis on business and applied economics.

NATIONAL TAX JOURNAL. National Tax Association, 100 East Broad Street, Columbus, Ohio 43215. Quarterly.

Official journal of the Association. Articles on federal, state and local government tax matters.

THE OFFICE. Office Publications Company, 73 Southfield Avenue, Stamford,

Connecticut 06904. Monthly.

Articles on office management and systems with emphasis on new equipment and automation. Includes articles on financial management and control.

OPERATIONS RESEARCH. Operations Research Society of America, 428 Preston Street, Baltimore, Maryland 21202. Bimonthly.

Official journal of the Society. Excellent presentations of current operational problems solved by operations research techniques.

PUBLIC UTILITIES FORTNIGHTLY. Public Utilities Reports, Inc., 332 Pennsylvania Building, 425 13th Street, N.W., Washington, D.C. 20004. Biweekly.

Covers federal and state regulations and court decisions on public utility matters. Includes articles on accounting for public utilities.

SURVEY OF CURRENT BUSINESS. Office of Business Economics, U.S. Department of Commerce. Published by the Superintendent of Documents, U.S. Government Printing Office, Washington, D.C. 20402. Monthly.

Covers current business trends and outlook. Lengthy statistical section brings up-to-date the figures in the annual STATISTICAL ABSTRACT, also issued by the Department of Commerce. Weekly statistical supplement is sent to all subscribers, not available on separate subscription.

TAX BAROMETER. Washington Publications, Inc., 444 Madison Avenue, New York, New York 10022. Weekly.

Newsletter covering federal income, estate and gift taxation.

THE TAX EXECUTIVE. Tax Executives Institute, Inc., 1111 E Street, N.W., Washington, D.C. 20004. Quarterly.

Covers tax problems and developments, including articles on accounting for taxes.

TAX LAW REVIEW. New York University School of Law, 40 Washington Square South, New York, New York 10003. Bimonthly.

Articles on all aspects of tax law and legislation.

TAX POLICY. Tax Institute of America, 457 Nassau Street, Princeton, New Jersey 08540. Bimonthly.

Reprints of speeches and articles on taxation and related subjects.

TAXATION. Taxation Publishing Co., Ltd., 98 Park Street, London W1, England. Weekly.

Covers the legal aspects, the practice and administration of taxation.

TAXATION FOR ACCOUNTANTS. Taxation for Accountants, 125 East 56th Street, New York, New York 10022. Bimonthly.

A tax magazine for the accountant in general practice.

TAXES, THE TAX MAGAZINE. Commerce Clearing House, Inc., 4025 West Peterson Avenue, Chicago, Illinois 60646. Monthly.

Articles on current tax subjects including tax legislation, interpretations of tax laws, etc.

TAXES ON PARADE. Commerce Clearing House, Inc., 4025 West Peterson Avenue, Chicago, Illinois 60646. Weekly.

Brief digest of current tax news including Tax Court regular and memo decisions.

U.S. TAX WEEK. Mathew Bender & Co., Inc., 235 East 45th Street, New York, New York 10017. Weekly.

Digests of court decisions, revenue rulings and related tax releases arranged by subject. Includes category on "Accounting Methods and Periods."

THE YALE LAW JOURNAL. Yale Law Journal Company, 127 Wall Street, New Haven, Connecticut. Monthly, November-January, March-July inclusive.

Published by The Yale Law School. Covers wide range of legal matters.

Section 10

SERVICES

Section 10

SERVICES

In addition to the numerous tax and regulatory services listed here, we have included several corporate information and general services we feel would be useful to the accountant. However, this is definitely a restricted listing of services. A comprehensive annotated listing of financial services is given in the DIRECTORY OF BUSINESS AND FINANCIAL SERVICES, edited by Mary A. McNierney and published by the Special Libraries Association in 1963.

Although we have listed only a selected few of their services, complete lists of their publications are available from all the publishers included in this section.

American Management Association, 135 West 50th Street, New York, New York 10020.

EXECUTIVE COMPENSATION SERVICE. Annual. Domestic Compensation Service consists of 11 volumes, covering top management, middle management, administrative and technical, sales personnel, supervisory management, current and deferred compensation, stock purchase plans, salary administration and control, benefits and employment contracts, corporate directorships, current compensation references (bibliography). INTERNATIONAL COMPENSATION SERVICE consists of 11 volumes covering compensation in the United Kingdom, West Germany, Mexico, Brazil, Belgium, Netherlands, Switzerland, France, Argentina and Venezuela. Volume 1 in this series is a comprehensive report on U.S. Expatriate Compensation.

Appeal Printing Company, Inc., 130 Cedar Street, New York, New York 10006.

APPEAL SECURITIES ACT HANDBOOK. Supplemented as required. A compilation of the Federal securities acts.

Auerbach Corporation and Auerbach Info, Inc., 121 North Broad Street, Philadelphia, Pennsylvania 19107.

AUERBACH STANDARD EDP REPORTS, 8 vols. Supplemented as required. Reports on all major U.S. computer systems. Condensed version of this service is available in the one volume AUERBACH COMPUTER NOTEBOOK FOR ACCOUNTANTS, subscriptions to which are available through the American Institute of CPAs at greatly reduced rates for members.

AUERBACH DATA COMMUNICATIONS REPORTS, 2 vols. Supplemented as required. Covers digital data communications equipment and techniques.

AUERBACH DATA HANDLING REPORTS, 2 vols. Supplemented as required. A guide to the selection and application of support equipment and supplies used in conjunction with computer systems.

Mathew Bender & Company, Inc., 1275 Broadway, Albany, New York 12201.
BUSINESS ORGANIZATIONS, 16 vols. Supplements as required.

CURRENT LEGAL FORMS WITH TAX ANALYSIS, by Jacob Rabkin and Mark H. Johnson, 13 vols. Supplemented as required.

ESTATE AND INCOME TAX TECHNIQUES, by the J.K. Lasser Tax Institute, 5 vols. Supplemented as required.

FEDERAL INCOME, GIFT AND ESTATE TAXATION, by Jacob Rabkin and Mark H. Johnson, 9 vols. Monthly supplements.

FOREIGN TAX AND TRADE BRIEFS, by Walter H. Diamond. Monthly supplements.

LABOR RELATIONS REPORTER, over 100 bound and loose-leaf volumes. Semiweekly supplements.

TAX TECHNIQUES FOR FOUNDATIONS AND OTHER EXEMPT ORGANIZATIONS, by Stanley Weithorn, 2 vols. Monthly supplements.

A. M. Best Company, Park Avenue, Morristown, New Jersey 07960.
BEST'S FLITCRAFT COMPEND. Annual. Tabular statistics and general information on life insurance companies.

BEST'S INSURANCE REPORTS. Annual. LIFE-HEALTH, 1 vol.; PROPERTY-LIABILITY, 1 vol.

The Blue List Publishing Company, Inc., 345 Hudson Street, New York, New York 10014.
THE BLUE LIST OF CURRENT MUNICIPAL OFFERINGS. Daily.

Bureau of National Affairs, 1231 24th Street, N.W., Washington, D.C. 20037.
TAX MANAGEMENT. Biweekly supplements. Consists of separate Portfolios on important tax topics which are revised as required. A new Portfolio is issued every two weeks.

Callaghan & Co., 6141 North Cicero Avenue, Chicago, Illinois 60646.
MERTENS-LAW OF FEDERAL INCOME TAXATION, 34 vols. Monthly supplements.

Clark Boardman Company, Ltd., 435 Hudson Street, New York, New York 10014.
BOARDMAN'S ESTATE MANAGEMENT AND ACCOUNTING: LAW - FORM - TEXT. Annual.

Commerce Clearing House, Inc., 4025 West Peterson Avenue, Chicago, Illinois 60646.
ACCOUNTANCY LAW REPORTS, 2 vols. Monthly supplements.

ACCOUNTING ARTICLES. Monthly supplements.

ATOMIC ENERGY LAW REPORTS, 4 vols. Weekly supplements.

BALANCE OF PAYMENTS REPORTS. Weekly supplements.

BLUE SKY LAW REPORTS, 3 vols. Monthly supplements. State blue sky law regulations and statutes. All legal investment laws and some insurance control laws.

CAPITAL CHANGES REPORTS, 5 vols. Weekly supplements. Analyzes changes in capital structure of corporations due to reorganizations, mergers, rights, etc.

CODE AND REGULATIONS, 3 vols. Monthly supplements. Texts of Internal Revenue Code and income, estate and gift tax regulations.

COMMON MARKET REPORTS, 2 vols. Biweekly supplements.

CONGRESSIONAL INDEX. Weekly supplements. Self-contained weekly report of all congressional activity.

CONGRESSIONAL LEGISLATIVE REPORTING, 2 vols. Weekly supplements. Provides bills on any selected subject from introduction through enactment. Includes CONGRESSIONAL INDEX.

CONSUMER CREDIT GUIDE, 2 vols. Biweekly supplements.

CONTRACT APPEALS DECISIONS. Monthly supplements. Includes two-volume, bound, annual edition of BOARD OF CONTRACT APPEALS DECISIONS.

CORPORATION LAW GUIDE, 2 vols. Weekly supplements.

FEDERAL BANKING LAW REPORTS, 4 vols. Weekly supplements.

FEDERAL ESTATE & GIFT TAX REPORTS, 2 vols. Weekly supplements.

FEDERAL EXCISE TAX REPORTS. Weekly supplements.

FEDERAL INCOME TAX REGULATIONS, 2 vols. Monthly supplements.

FEDERAL SECURITIES LAW REPORTS, 5 vols. Weekly supplements.

FEDERAL AND STATE CARRIERS REPORTS, 5 vols. Biweekly supplements.

FEDERAL TAX ARTICLES, 2 vols. Monthly supplements.

FEDERAL TAX GUIDE REPORTS, 4 vols. Weekly supplements. Volume 1, Control Edition, available separately.

GOVERNMENT CONTRACTS REPORTS, 8 vols. Weekly supplements.

INHERITANCE, ESTATE & GIFT TAX REPORTS. Weekly supplements. Federal and all states, 7 vols.; federal and home state, 5 vols.; home state only, 2 vols.

LABOR LAW GUIDE, 2 vols. Weekly supplements.

LABOR LAW REPORTS, 12 vols. Weekly supplements. EMPLOYMENT PRACTICES and WAGE AND HOURS sections available separately.

MEDICARE AND MEDICAID GUIDE. Biweekly supplements.

MUTUAL FUNDS REPORTS. Biweekly supplements.

PAYROLL TAX GUIDE, 2 vols. Biweekly supplements.

PENSION PLAN GUIDE, 4 vols. Biweekly supplements.

SEC ACCOUNTING RULES. Supplemented as required. Contains accounting regulations and releases of the Securities and Exchange Commission.

SECURED TRANSACTIONS GUIDE, 4 vols. Biweekly supplements.

STANDARD FEDERAL TAX REPORTS (INCOME, EXCISE, ESTATE & GIFT TAXES), 14 vols. Weekly supplements.

STATE TAX GUIDE. Biweekly supplements. Information about taxes of all states, arranged by states and by taxes.

STATE TAX REPORTS. Monthly supplements. Specialized volumes for each state, District of Columbia and Puerto Rico.

TAX COURT REPORTS, 3 vols. Weekly supplements. Available with all prior TC Memorandum Decisions.

TAX LIBRARY. Consists of the following five units: Standard Federal Income Tax; Tax Court Reports; Local State Tax Report; United States Tax Cases (USTC); and Tax Court Memo Decisions (TCM).

TAX TREATIES. Monthly supplements. Covers treaties concluded between United States and foreign countries.

TRADE REGULATION REPORTS, 5 vols. Weekly supplements. Available with all prior Trade Cases.

UNEMPLOYMENT INSURANCE REPORTS (SOCIAL SECURITY). Weekly supplements. Federal and all states, 13 vols.; federal and home state, 3 vols.; federal only, 3 vols.

U.S. TAX CASES, 51 vols. Semiannual volumes.

UTILITIES LAW REPORTS, 3 vols. Weekly supplements.

Copley International Corporation, 330 Madison Avenue, New York, New York 10017.

THE GALLATIN INTERNATIONAL BUSINESS SERVICE, 7 vols. BUSINESS INTELLIGENCE service consists of volumes on Africa, the Americas, Asia-Oceania and Europe. INTERNATIONAL BUSINESS AIDS, SPECIAL REPORTS and STATISTICAL INDICATORS are single volumes. A fortnightly GALLATIN LETTER discusses current international developments.

Dun & Bradstreet, Inc., 99 Church Street, New York, New York 10008.

INTERNATIONAL MARKET GUIDES. Semiannual revisions. Continental Europe, 3 vols.; Latin America, 2 vols. Dun & Bradstreet also publishes a number of reference books and market guides on individual foreign countries.

MIDDLE MARKET DIRECTORY. Annual, with two supplements a year. Covers the 27,000 businesses in the U.S. with a net worth between $500,000 and $1,000,000.

MILLION DOLLAR DIRECTORY. Annual, with two supplements a year. Covers the 31,000 U.S. corporations with a net worth of $1,000,000 a year or more.

REFERENCE BOOK OF CORPORATE MANAGEMENTS. Annual. Provides biographical information on principal officers and directors of 1,500 of the largest U.S. corporations.

REFERENCE BOOK OF MANUFACTURERS, 2 vols. Annual. Available to subscribers to the Dun & Bradstreet Reporting Service. Covers approximately 328,000 U.S. manufacturers.

REFERENCE BOOKS, 4 vols. Bimonthly revisions. Gives credit ratings for approximately 2,500,000 United States and Canadian companies. Included in Dun & Bradstreet Reporting Service.

REPORTING SERVICE. Credit rating service on U.S. and Canadian corporations available on individual contract basis.
Dun & Bradstreet also provides INTERNATIONAL CREDIT REPORTS on foreign companies located in countries other than the U.S. and Canada.

Financial Information, Inc., 114 Liberty Street, New York, New York 10006.
FINANCIAL STOCK GUIDE SERVICE. Monthly. Gives information on stocks of industrial companies and banks.

Financial Publishing Company, 82 Brookline Avenue, Boston, Massachusetts 02115.
INVESTORS BOND VALUES TABLES. Yields and values of bonds paying interest semiannually.

MONTHLY PAYMENT DIRECT REDUCTION LOAN AMORTIZATION TABLES.

First National City Bank, 399 Park Avenue, New York, New York 10022.
FOREIGN INFORMATION SERVICE, 6 vols. Monthly supplements.

Institute for Business Planning, 2 West 13th Street, New York, New York 10011.
COMPLETE ESTATE AND LIFE PLANNING, 3 vols. Monthly supplements. Includes one volume each on estate and life insurance planning and one volume of estate planning forms. Newsletters, "LIFE INSURANCE IDEAS" and "ESTATE PLANNING IDEAS," issued semimonthly.

CORPORATE PLANNING. Monthly supplements. "CORPORATE PLANNING IDEAS" newsletter issued semimonthly.

FORMS OF BUSINESS AGREEMENTS AND RESOLUTIONS. Monthly supplements.

MUTUAL FUND INVESTMENT PLANNING. Monthly supplements.

"MUTUAL FUND INVESTMENT IDEAS" newsletter issued semimonthly.

PAY PLANNING, 3 vols. Monthly supplements. Includes a volume of pay planning forms. "PAY PLANNING IDEAS" newsletter issued semimonthly.

REAL ESTATE INVESTMENT PLANNING, 3 vols. Monthly supplements. "REAL ESTATE INVESTMENT IDEAS" newsletter issued semimonthly.

TAX PLANNING, 2 vols. Monthly supplements. Semimonthly publication, TAX PLANNING IDEAS covers current news of tax matters.

Lofit Publications, Inc., Saugerties, New York 12477.

MERTENS' LAW OF FEDERAL GIFT AND ESTATE TAXATION, 8 vols. Monthly supplements. Consists of six bound volumes, one loose-leaf volume of supplements and one loose-leaf volume of current information concerning restatements of the law.

Moody's Investors Service, Inc., 99 Church Street, New York, New York 10007.

DIVIDEND SERVICE. Semiweekly, with weekly and monthly cumulative issues. Annual edition.

MOODY'S BANK AND FINANCE MANUAL. Semiweekly supplements.

MOODY'S BOND RECORD. Monthly.

MOODY'S INDUSTRIAL MANUAL. Semiweekly supplements.

MOODY'S MUNICIPAL AND GOVERNMENT MANUALS. Semiweekly supplements.

MOODY'S PUBLIC UTILITY MANUAL. Semiweekly supplements.

MOODY'S TRANSPORTATION MANUAL. Semiweekly supplements.

The National Quotation Bureau, Inc., 116 Nassau Street, New York, New York 10038.

NATIONAL DAILY QUOTATION SERVICE. Daily, with monthly and semiannual cumulations.

NATIONAL MONTHLY BOND SUMMARY. Monthly, with semiannual cumulations. Summarization of bond market quotations, cumulated for the past six months.

NATIONAL MONTHLY STOCK SUMMARY. Monthly, with semiannual cumulations. Summarization of stock market quotations, cumulated for the past six months.

Pandick Press, 345 Hudson Street, New York, New York 10013.

PANDICK PRESS, INC. SERVICE. Supplemented as required. Covers regulations on the preparation of registration statements under Securities Act of 1933, applications and statements under Trust Indenture Act of 1939 and materials for certain matters under Section 13 and 14 of the S.E.C. Act of 1934.

R.L. Polk & Company, Polk Directory Building 431 Howard Street, Detroit, Michigan 48231.

POLK'S BANK DIRECTORY. Semiannual. Covers U.S. and foreign banks.

Prentice-Hall, Inc., Englewood Cliffs, New Jersey 07632.

AMERICAN FEDERAL TAX REPORTS, 74 vols. Semiannual. Verbatim reprints of every federal tax decision reported from 1796 to date.

CAPITAL ADJUSTMENTS, 4 vols. Weekly supplements. Gives current tax status of corporations, changes in capital structure.

COMMUNICATIONS. Monthly supplements. Compilation of methods and forms used by employers in communicating with employees.

CORPORATION GUIDE. Biweekly supplements. A one volume digest of material in CORPORATION SERVICE.

CORPORATION SERVICE, 6 vols. Biweekly supplements. Covers corporate law. Available for all states, any one state or group of states.

CUMULATIVE CHANGES, 2 vols. Irregular supplements. Gives exact wording of each amended section of the 1954 Code and Regulations as of any given date.

EXCISE TAXES. Biweekly supplements.

FEDERAL BANK, 4 vols. Monthly supplements. Consists of two volumes, CONTROL OF BANKING and FEDERAL AIDS TO FINANCING with two additional volumes of loose-leaf supplements.

FEDERAL TAX CITATOR, 5 vols. Monthly supplements. Gives judicial history of each federal tax case issues and rulings, listing all other cases and rulings where it is cited.

FEDERAL TAX GUIDE, 3 vols. Weekly supplements.

FEDERAL TAX LIBRARY. Consists of sets of the following Prentice-Hall services: American Federal Tax Reports; Citator; Cumulative Changes; Federal Tax Service; Tax Court Service; and Current Tax Court Service.

FEDERAL TAX SERVICE, 8 vols. Weekly supplements. Additional available volumes on EXCISE TAXES and ESTATE & GIFT.

INHERITANCE TAXES, 3 vols. Biweekly supplements.

LABOR RELATIONS GUIDE, 2 vols. Weekly supplements.

OIL AND GAS TAXES, 2 vols. Monthly supplements. One volume is INCOME TAXATION OF OIL AND GAS, by Clark W. Breeding and A. Gordon Burton. The other loose-leaf volume contains current information.

PAYROLL GUIDE. Supplemented every three weeks.

PENSION AND PROFIT SHARING, 2 vols. Biweekly supplements. Available with PENSION AND PROFIT SHARING FORMS volume.

PENSION AND PROFIT SHARING FORMS. Monthly supplements.

PERSONNEL POLICIES AND PRACTICES. Biweekly supplements.

SALES TAX, 7 vol. Weekly supplements. Covers all states and cities which impose sales, use, receipts and similar taxes.

SECURITIES REGULATIONS, 2 vols. Semimonthly supplements. Covers all laws administered by the SEC. SECURITIES REGULATION GUIDE is a one-volume digest of the more important of these laws.

SOCIAL SECURITY - UNEMPLOYMENT COMPENSATION, 2 vols. Monthly supplements. Full text of federal social security (including Medicare) and unemployment tax laws.

STATE AND LOCAL TAXES. Weekly supplements. Available for any and all states. ALL STATES UNIT covers in chart, table and calendar form which taxes are imposed by which state.

STATE TAX GUIDE. Weekly supplements. One-volume guide to tax rules in each state and District of Columbia.

TAX COURT, 3 vols. Weekly supplements. Contains every Tax Court (and BTA) reported and memorandum decisions. Bound volumes of memorandum decisions available from 1928 to date.

TAX IDEAS - TRANSACTION GUIDE, 2 vols. Biweekly supplements. Outlines tax effects of transactions.

TAX TREATIES. Monthly supplements. Official text of all U.S. treaties with foreign countries.

WAGE-HOUR GUIDE. Weekly supplements.

WILLS AND TRUSTS FORMS. Monthly supplements.

WILLS, ESTATES AND TRUSTS, 4 vols. Monthly supplements.

Public Utilities Reports, Inc., Pennsylvania Building, Washington, D.C. 20004.

FEDERAL UTILITY REGULATION ANNOTATED (FPC). Biweekly supplements. Covers current commission and court decisions on administration of the Natural Gas Act and the Federal Power Act by the Federal Power Commission.

FEDERAL UTILITY REGULATION ANNOTATED (SEC). Monthly supplements. Current commission and court decisions on administration of the Public Utility Holding Company Act of 1935 by the Securities and Exchange Commission.

PUR ADVANCE SHEETS. Biweekly. Full texts of the opinions on all important decisions of state and federal regulatory commissions and court cases on appeal including Supreme Court.

PUR EXECUTIVE INFORMATION SERVICE. Weekly letter on federal and state developments affecting public utilities.

Rand McNally & Company, P.O. Box 7600, Chicago, Illinois 60680.

RAND McNALLY INTERNATIONAL BANKERS DIRECTORY. Semiannual.

S.M. Rubel and Associates, 53 West Jackson Boulevard, Chicago, Illinois 60604.
SBIC EVALUATION SERVICE. Monthly supplements. Financial analysis and news reports of small business investment companies.

Rules Service Company, 1001 15th Street, N.W. Washington, D.C. 20005.
CIVIL AERONAUTICS BOARD ECONOMIC AND PROCEDURAL REGULATIONS. Monthly supplements.

Standard & Poor's Corporation, 345 Hudson Street, New York, New York 10014.
BOND GUIDE. Monthly supplements.

CALLED BOND RECORD. Semiweekly supplements, with cumulative weekly and quarterly issues.

CORPORATION RECORDS, 6 vols., and Daily News Service volume. Bimonthly supplements. Arranged alphabetically. Covers all major U.S. and foreign corporations and their securities. Available on subscription with or without Daily News Service volume.

DIVIDEND RECORD. Daily, with cumulative supplements weekly, monthly and annually. Quarterly cumulative sections also available on subscription.

INDUSTRY SURVEYS, 2 vols. Annual basic surveys on 44 leading industries with several current surveys issued during each year.

POOR'S REGISTER OF CORPORATIONS. DIRECTORS AND EXECUTIVES. Annual, with three cumulative supplements a year. Covers the United States and Canada. Separate sections, each arranged alphabetically, one listing corporations and their officers and directors, the other listing individuals and their business affiliations.

REGISTERED BOND INTEREST RECORD. Weekly cumulative supplements. Alphabetical listing of payments, record and payment dates.

REVIEW OF SECURITIES REGULATION. Bimonthly supplements.

STATUS OF BONDS. Five supplements a year. Directory of coupon-paying agents.

STOCK GUIDE. Monthly. Covers approximately 4,750 common and preferred stocks, listed and OTC.

TRADE AND SECURITIES, STATISTICS. Monthly supplements.

Standard Statistics Company, Inc., 345 Hudson Street, New York, New York 10014.
ISL DAILY STOCK PRICE INDEX - AMERICAN STOCK EXCHANGE. Quarterly issues. Produced by the Investment Statistics Laboratory on computer from magnetic tape. Available on punched cards and tape as well as in bound hardcover copies.

ISL DAILY STOCK PRICE INDEX - NEW YORK STOCK EXCHANGE. Quarterly issues. Also available on punched cards and magnetic tape.

Standard Rate & Data Service, Inc., 5201 Old Orchard Rd., Skokie, Illinois 60076.

STANDARD RATE AND DATA SERVICE, 18 sections. Monthly editions give up-to-date advertising rates in U.S., Canadian and certain foreign media such as newspapers, magazines, television, radio, etc.

Tax Research Institute of America, Inc., 589 Fifth Avenue, New York, New York 10017.

TAX COORDINATOR, 6 vols. Biweekly supplements.

Arthur Wiesenberger Services, Division of Nuveen Corp., 61 Broadway, New York, New York 10006.

INVESTMENT COMPANIES. Annual, with quarterly supplements. Information on all the larger open and closed end companies in the United States and Canada.

Walsh Killian Lebens, Inc., 511 Locust Street, St. Louis, Missouri 63101.

YATES MUNICIPAL BOND EVALUATOR DIRECTORY. Weekly supplements. Comprehensive listing of municipal bonds useful in appraising their values. References in DIRECTORY are made to certain pages in the weekly supplement, MUNICIPAL BOND EVALUATOR, in which maturities and coupons are listed in such a way that the yield and dollar value of the bonds are easily obtained.

Section 11

BASIC ACCOUNTING LIBRARY

Section 11

BASIC ACCOUNTING LIBRARY

BIBLIOGRAPHIES AND INDEXES

ACCOUNTANTS' INDEX. New York: American Institute of Certified Public Accountants. Biennial.

ACCOUNTING ARTICLES. Chicago: Commerce Clearing House, Inc. Monthly.

BUSINESS PERIODICALS INDEX. New York: H.W. Wilson Company. Monthly, with periodic cumulations including annual bound volume.

FUNK & SCOTT INDEX OF CORPORATIONS AND INDUSTRIES. Cleveland, Ohio: Funk & Scott Publishing Company. Weekly, with monthly, semiannual and annual cumulations.

SELECTED LIST OF BOOKS SUGGESTED FOR AN ACCOUNTANT'S LIBRARY. New York: American Institute of Certified Public Accountants, Library. Irregular.

YOUR REFERENCE LIBRARY. New York: National Association of Accountants, Technical Service Department. Annual.

HANDBOOKS

ACCOUNTANTS' HANDBOOK, by Rufus Wixon. New York: Ronald Press, 1956. v.p.

ACCOUNTANTS' COST HANDBOOK, 2nd ed., ed. by Robert I. Dickey. New York: Ronald Press, 1960. v.p. (5th ed. to be published in 1970).

ACCOUNTING PRACTICE MANAGEMENT HANDBOOK. New York: American Institute of Certified Public Accountants, 1962. 952p.

DICTIONARY FOR ACCOUNTANTS, 4th ed., by Eric Kohler. Englewood Cliffs, New Jersey: Prentice-Hall, 1970. 464p.

ENCYCLOPEDIA OF ACCOUNTING SYSTEMS, 5 vols., by Robert I. Williams and Lillian Doris. Englewood Cliffs, New Jersey: Prentice-Hall, 1956.

ENCYCLOPEDIA OF AUDITING TECHNIQUES, 2 vols., ed. by Jennie M. Palen. Englewood Cliffs, New Jersey: Prentice-Hall, 1966.

ENCYCLOPEDIA OF COST ACCOUNTING SYSTEMS, 3 vols. Englewood Cliffs, New Jersey: Prentice-Hall, 1965.

FINANCIAL HANDBOOK, 4th ed., rev. printing, by Jules I. Bogen. New York: Ronald Press, 1968. v.p.

HANDBOOK OF ACCOUNTING METHODS, 3rd ed., ed. by J.K. Lasser Institute. New York: Van Nostrand, 1964. 976p.

HANDBOOK OF AUDITING METHODS, ed. by J.K. Lasser. New York: Van Nostrand, 1953. 769p.

INDUSTRIAL ACCOUNTANT'S HANDBOOK, ed. by Wyman P. Fiske and John A. Beckett. Englewood Cliffs, New Jersey: Prentice-Hall, 1954.

OPERATIONAL AUDITING HANDBOOK, by Bradford Cadmus. New York: Institute of Internal Auditors, 1964. 474p.

PERIODICALS

ACCOUNTING JOURNALS

ACCOUNTANCY. Monthly.

THE ACCOUNTANT. Weekly.

THE ACCOUNTANTS DIGEST. Quarterly.

ACCOUNTING RESEARCH ASSOCIATION NEWSLETTER. Irregular.

THE ACCOUNTING REVIEW. Quarterly.

CANADIAN CHARTERED ACCOUNTANT. Monthly.

THE C.P.A. Monthly.

FINANCIAL EXECUTIVE. Monthly.

THE INTERNAL AUDITOR. Bimonthly.

THE JOURNAL OF ACCOUNTANCY. Monthly.

JOURNAL OF ACCOUNTING RESEARCH. Semiannual.

JOURNAL UEC. Quarterly.

MANAGEMENT ACCOUNTING (formerly NAA BULLETIN). Monthly.

MANAGEMENT SERVICES. Bimonthly.

RELATED BUSINESS PERIODICALS

BANK AND QUOTATION RECORD. Weekly.

BARRON'S. Weekly.

BUSINESS WEEK. Weekly.

THE COMMERCIAL AND FINANCIAL CHRONICLE. Semiweekly.

FINANCIAL ANALYSTS JOURNAL. Bimonthly.

FINANCIAL WORLD. Weekly.

FORBES. Semimonthly.

FORTUNE. Monthly.

HARVARD BUSINESS REVIEW. Bimonthly.

THE JOURNAL OF TAXATION. Monthly.

MERGERS AND ACQUISITIONS, THE JOURNAL OF CORPORATE. VENTURE

OPERATIONS RESEARCH. Bimonthly.

PUBLIC UTILITIES FORTNIGHTLY. Biweekly.

SURVEY OF CURRENT BUSINESS. Monthly.

TAX LAW JOURNAL. Bimonthly.

TAXATION FOR ACCOUNTANTS. Bimonthly.

TAXES, THE TAX MAGAZINE. Monthly.

VENTURE. Bimonthly.

BOOKS

The following selections are arranged in the same classifications as the far more comprehensive listing in Section 8, Books. The detailed annotations have been omitted here, but can be easily located in Section 8.

ACCOUNTANCY PROFESSION

Carey, John L. THE CPA PLANS FOR THE FUTURE. New York: American Institute of Certified Public Accountants, 1965. 541p.

ACCOUNTANTS' EDUCATION

Roy, Robert H. and MacNeil, James H. HORIZONS FOR A PROFESSION: THE COMMON BODY OF KNOWLEDGE FOR CERTIFIED PUBLIC ACCOUNTANTS. New York: American Institute of Certified Public Accountants, 1967. 354p. charts, illus., tables.

ACCOUNTING AND AUDITING TEXTBOOK

Finney, H.A. and Miller, Herbert E. PRINCIPLES OF ACCOUNTING, ADVANCED. 5th ed. Englewood Cliffs, New Jersey: Prentice-Hall, 1960. 847p. forms.

Finney, H.A. and Miller, Herbert E. PRINCIPLES OF ACCOUNTING, INTERMEDIATE. 6th ed. Englewood Cliffs, New Jersey: Prentice-Hall, 1965. forms.

Finney, H.A. and Miller, Herbert E. PRINCIPLES OF ACCOUNTING, INTRODUCTORY. 6th ed. Englewood Cliffs, New Jersey: Prentice-Hall, 1963. 704p. forms.

Montgomery, Robert H. MONTGOMERY'S AUDITING, by Norman J. Lenhart and Philip L. Defliese, 8th ed. New York: Ronald Press, 1957. 766p.

Simons, Harry and Karrenbrock, Wilbert E. ADVANCED ACCOUNTING, COMPREHENSIVE VOLUME, 4th ed. Cincinnati: South-Western Publishing Co., 1968. 1056p. tables.

Simons, Harry and Karrenbrock, Wilbert E. INTERMEDIATE ACCOUNTING COMPREHENSIVE VOLUME, 4th ed. Cincinnati: South-Western Publishing Co., 1964. 980p. forms.

ACCOUNTING PRINCIPLES AND PROCEDURES

American Institute of Certified Public Accountants. ACCOUNTING RESEARCH STUDIES, No. 1- . New York: 1961- .

American Institute of Certified Public Accountants. APB ACCOUNTING PRINCIPLES, 2 vols. Chicago: Commerce Clearing House, 1968- .

American Institute of Certified Public Accountants. OPINIONS OF THE ACCOUNTING PRINCIPLES BOARD, No. 1- . New York: 1962- .

Paton, William A. and Littleton, A.C. AN INTRODUCTION TO CORPORATE ACCOUNTING STANDARDS (American Accounting Association Monograph, No. 3). Madison, Wisconsin: American Accounting Association, reprinted 1962. 178p. pap.

ACCOUNTING THEORY

American Accounting Association. A STATEMENT OF BASIC ACCOUNTING THEORY. Evanston, Illinois: 1966. 106p. pap.

Littleton, A.C. THE STRUCTURE OF ACCOUNTING THEORY (American Accounting Association Monograph, No. 5). Menasha, Wisconsin: American Accounting Association, 1953. 242p. pap.

Littleton, A.C. and Zimmerman, V.K. ACCOUNTING THEORY: CONTINUITY AND CHANGE. Englewood Cliffs, New Jersey: Prentice-Hall, 1962. 282p.

Moonitz, Maurice and Littleton, A.C., eds. SIGNIFICANT ACCOUNTING ESSAYS. Englewood Cliffs, New Jersey: Prentice-Hall, 1965. 529p.

AUDITING

American Institute of Certified Public Accountants. CASE STUDIES IN AUDITING PROCEDURE, No. 1- . New York: 1947- . pap.

American Institute of Certified Public Accountants. INDUSTRY AUDIT GUIDES. New York: 1956- .

American Institute of Certified Public Accountants. SPECIAL REPORTS: APPLICATION OF STATEMENT ON AUDITING PROCEDURE NO. 28. New York: 1960. 96p. pap.

American Institute of Certified Public Accountants. STATEMENTS ON AUDITING PROCEDURE, No. 1- . New York: 1939- . pap.

Cooper, Vivian R.V. MANUAL OF AUDITING, 2nd ed. London: Gee & Co. (Publishers) Ltd., 1969. 704p.

Lasser, J.K., ed. HANDBOOK OF AUDITING METHODS. See HANDBOOKS, this section.

Montgomery, Robert H. MONTGOMERY'S AUDITING, by Norman J. Lenhart and Philip L. Defliese, 8th ed. New York: Ronald Press, 1957. 766p.

National Conference of Bankers and Certified Public Accountants. THE AUDITOR'S REPORT, ITS MEANING AND SIGNIFICANCE. New York: American Institute of Certified Public Accountants, 1967. 30p. illus. pap.

Prentice-Hall, Inc. ENCYCLOPEDIA OF AUDITING TECHNIQUES. See HANDBOOKS, this section.

AUDITING AND THE COMPUTER

Corcoran, A. Wayne and Istvan, Donald F. THE AUDIT AND THE PUNCHED CARD, AN INTRODUCTION (Bureau of Business Research Monograph No. 101).

Columbus, Ohio: Bureau of Business Research, Ohio State University, 1961. 90p. facs. pap.

Davis, Gordon B. AUDITING AND EDP. New York: American Institute of Certified Public Accountants, 1968. 353p. charts, forms, tables.

Porter, W. Thomas, Jr. AUDITING ELECTRONIC SYSTEMS. Belmont, California: Wadsworth, 1966. 125p. figures.

BUDGETING

Deardon, John. COST AND BUDGET ANALYSIS. Englewood Cliffs, New Jersey: Prentice-Hall, 1962. 219p. charts, illus.

Heckert, J. Brooks and Willson, James D. BUSINESS BUDGETING AND CONTROL, 3rd ed. New York: Ronald Press, 1967. 596p. charts, forms, tables.

Heiser, Herman C. BUDGETING - PRINCIPLES AND PRACTICE. New York: Ronald Press, 1959. 415p. figures, graphs.

Rautenstrauch, Walter and Villers Raymond. BUDGETARY CONTROL, 2nd ed. New York: Funk & Wagnalls, 1968. 368p. charts, forms, tables.

Welsch, Glenn A. BUDGETING: PROFIT-PLANNING AND CONTROL, 2nd ed. Englewood Cliffs, New Jersey: Prentice-Hall, 1964. 600p.

CPA EXAMINATIONS

American Institute of Certified Public Accountants. CPA EXAMINATIONS. New York: 1921- .

American Institute of Certified Public Accountants. INFORMATION FOR CPA CANDIDATES. New York: 1970. 50p. pap.

Behling, Robert P. CPA REQUIREMENTS, 2nd ed. Whitewater, Wisconsin: Wisconsin State University (Whitewater), 1968. 230p.

Horngren, Charles T. and Leer, J. Arthur. CPA PROBLEMS AND APPROACHES TO SOLUTIONS, 3rd ed., 2 vols. Englewood Cliffs, New Jersey: Prentice-Hall, 1969.

Miller, Herbert E., ed. C.P.A. REVIEW MANUAL, 3rd ed. Englewood Cliffs, New Jersey: Prentice-Hall, 1966. 640p. charts, tables.

U.S. Army Audit Agency, in cooperation with the American Institute of Certified Public Accountants. PROVISIONS IN CPA LAWS & REGULATIONS, rev. July 1, 1968. Washington, D.C.: U.S. Government Printing Office. 81p. tables. pap.

CONSOLIDATED STATEMENTS

Childs, William H. CONSOLIDATED FINANCIAL STATEMENTS, PRINCIPLES AND PROCEDURE. Ithaca, New York: Cornell University Press, 1949. 368p.

Robson, Sir Thomas B. HOLDING COMPANIES AND THEIR SUBSIDIARIES, CONSOLIDATED AND OTHER GROUP ACCOUNTS, PRINCIPLES AND PROCEDURE, 4th ed. London: Gee & Co., 1969. 148p.

CONTROLLERSHIP

Anderson, David R. and Schnidt, Leo A. PRACTICAL CONTROLLERSHIP, rev. ed. Homewood, Illinois: Richard D. Irwin, 1961. 777p.

Heckert, J. Brooks and Willson, James D. CONTROLLERSHIP, 2nd ed. New York: Ronald Press, 1963. 816p. charts, forms, tables.

Prentice-Hall Editorial Staff. CORPORATE TREASURER'S AND CONTROLLER'S ENCYCLOPEDIA, 4 vols. Englewood Cliffs, New Jersey: Prentice-Hall, 1969.

CORPORATIONS — FINANCIAL MANAGEMENT

Bogen, Jules I. FINANCIAL HANDBOOK. See HANDBOOKS, this section.

Dewing, Arthur S. THE FINANCIAL POLICY OF CORPORATIONS, 5th ed., 2 vols. New York: Ronald Press, 1953.

Gerstenberg, Charles W. FINANCIAL ORGANIZATION AND MANAGEMENT OF BUSINESS, 4th rev. ed. Englewood Cliffs, New Jersey: Prentice-Hall, 1959. 640p. charts, tables.

Gilbert, Lewis D. and Gilbert, John J. ANNUAL REPORT OF STOCKHOLDER ACTIVITIES AT CORPORATION MEETINGS. New York: 1939- . pap.

Guthman, Harry G. and Dougall, Herbert E. CORPORATE FINANCIAL POLICY, 4th ed. Englewood Cliffs, New Jersey: Prentice-Hall, 1962. 795p.

CORPORATIONS — INDUSTRIAL MANAGEMENT

Greisman, Bernard, ed. J.K. LASSER'S BUSINESS MANAGEMENT HANDBOOK, 3rd ed., rev. and expanded. New York: McGraw-Hill Book Co., 1968. 784p. charts.

Maynard, Harold B., ed. HANDBOOK OF BUSINESS ADMINISTRATION. New York: McGraw-Hill Book Co., 1967. v.p. charts, tables.

Maynard, Harold B. INDUSTRIAL ENGINEERING HANDBOOK, 2nd ed. New York: McGraw-Hill Book Co., 1963. v.p. charts, forms, illus., tables.

Newman, William H. and Logan, James P. BUSINESS POLICIES AND CENTRAL MANAGEMENT, 5th ed. Cincinnati: South-Western Publishing Co., 1965. 960p. charts, tables.

Toan, Arthur B., Jr. USING INFORMATION TO MANAGE. New York: Ronald Press, 1968. 161p. charts, tables.

Wylie, Harry L., ed. OFFICE MANAGEMENT HANDBOOK, 2nd ed. New York: Ronald Press, 1958. v.p. diagrs., forms, tables.

COST ACCOUNTING

Dickey, Robert I., ed. ACCOUNTANTS' COST HANDBOOK. See HANDBOOKS, this section.

Fiske, Wyman P. and Beckett, John A., eds. INDUSTRIAL ACCOUNTANT'S HANDBOOK. See HANDBOOKS, this section.

Gillespie, Cecil. COST ACCOUNTING AND CONTROL. Englewood Cliffs, New Jersey: Prentice-Hall, 1957. 839p. charts, exhibits, forms.

Gillespie, Cecil. STANDARD AND DIRECT COSTING, 3rd ed. Englewood Cliffs, New Jersey: Prentice-Hall, 1962. 337p. charts, forms, tables.

Horngren, Charles T. COST ACCOUNTING, A MANAGERIAL EXPHASIS,

2nd ed. Englewood Cliffs, New Jersey: Prentice-Hall, 1967. 896p. charts.

Matz, Adolph, et al. COST ACCOUNTING, 4th ed. Cincinnati: South-Western Publishing Co., 1967. 973p. charts, tables.

National Association of Accountants. NAA RESEARCH REPORTS. New York: 1969 . pap.

Neuner, John J.W. COST ACCOUNTING: PRINCIPLES AND PRACTICE, 7th ed. Homewood, Illinois: Richard D. Irwin, 1967. 859p. charts, forms, tables.

Prentice-Hall Editorial Staff. ENCYCLOPEDIA OF COST ACCOUNTING SYSTEMS. See HANDBOOKS, this section.

Shillinglaw, Gordon. COST ACCOUNTING: ANALYSIS AND CONTROL, rev. ed. Homewood, Illinois: Richard D. Irwin, 1967. 931p. charts, tables.

CREDIT AND COLLECTION

Cole, Robert H. CONSUMER AND COMMERCIAL CREDIT MANAGEMENT, 3rd ed. Homewood, Illinois: Richard D. Irwin, 1968. 631p. forms, tables.

Credit Research Foundation. CREDIT MANAGEMENT HANDBOOK, 2nd ed. Homewood, Illinois: Richard D. Irwin, 1965. 812p. figures, tables.

Shultz, William J. and Reinhardt, Hedwig. CREDIT AND COLLECTION MANAGEMENT, 3rd ed. Englewood Cliffs, New Jersey: Prentice-Hall, 1962. 655p. forms, illus., tables.

EDP AND THE ACCOUNTANT

Adamson, Lee J., et al. ACCOUNTANTS' DATA PROCESSING SERVICES, MODERN METHODS IN SERVING SMALL CLIENTS. New York: Ronald Press, 1964. 202p. charts, forms, illus.

Gregory, Robert H. and VanHorn, Richard L. AUTOMATIC DATA-PROCESSING SYSTEMS, PRINCIPLES AND PROCEDURES, 2nd ed. Belmont, California: Wadsworth, 1963. 827p. charts, tables.

McRae, Thomas W. THE IMPACT OF COMPUTERS ON ACCOUNTING. New York: John H. Wiley & Sons, 1964. 304p. charts, forms, tables.

Price Waterhouse & Co. MANAGEMENT CONTROL OF ELECTRONIC DATA PROCESSING. White Plains, New York: International Business Machines, 1965. 39p. pap.

System Development Corporation. COMPUTER RESEARCH STUDIES, Nos. 1-6. New York: American Institute of Certified Public Accountants, 1966-68. pap.

EXECUTIVE COMPENSATION

American Management Association. EXECUTIVE COMPENSATION SERVICE. See SERVICES, this section.

Casey, William J. PAY PLANS. See SERVICES, this section, under Institute for Business Planning.

National Industrial Conference Board. TOP EXECUTIVE COMPENSATION, by Harland Fox. (Studies in Personnel Policy, No. 213.) New York: 1969. 82p. charts, tables. pap.

Washington, George T., et al. COMPENSATING THE CORPORATE EXECUTIVE, 3rd ed., 2 vols. New York: Ronald Press, 1962.

FINANCIAL RATIOS

Accounting Corporation of America. BAROMETER OF SMALL BUSINESS. San Diego, California: 1948- . pap.

Dun & Bradstreet, Inc. KEY BUSINESS RATIOS. New York: 1931- . pap.

Morris, Robert, Associates. SOURCES OF COMPOSITE FINANCIAL DATA, A BIBLIOGRAPHY. Philadelphia: 1967. 24p. pap.

Morris, Robert, Associates. STATEMENT STUDIES. Philadelphia: 1923- . pap.

News Front. 15,000 LEADING U.S. CORPORATIONS. New York: 1966. 226p. charts, graphs, tables. pap.

Standard & Poor's Corporation. STANDARD AND POOR'S INDUSTRY SURVEYS. See SERVICES, this section.

FINANCIAL STATEMENTS AND ANALYSIS

American Institute of Certified Public Accountants. ACCOUNTING TRENDS AND TECHNIQUES. New York: 1948- .

Foulke, Roy A. PRACTICAL FINANCIAL STATEMENT ANALYSIS, 6th ed. New York: McGraw-Hill Book Co., 1968. 736p. tables.

Kennedy, Ralph Dale and McMullen, Steward Yarwood. FINANCIAL STATEMENTS: FORM, ANALYSIS, AND INTERPRETATION, 5th ed. Homewood, Illinois: Richard D. Irwin, 1968. 744p. illus., tables.

Mautz, R.K. FINANCIAL REPORTING BY DIVERSIFIED COMPANIES. New York: Financial Executives Research Foundation, 1968. 398p. charts, tables.

National Association of Accountants. EXTERNAL REPORTING FOR SEGMENTS OF A BUSINESS, by Morton Backer and Walter B. McFarland. New York: 1968. 112p. charts, forms, tables. pap.

Rappaport, Alfred, et al. PUBLIC REPORTING BY CONGLOMERATES. Englewood Cliffs, New Jersey: Prentice-Hall, 1968. 172p. forms.

FRAUD AND DEFALCATIONS

Cardwell, Harvey. THE PRINCIPLES OF AUDIT SURVEILLANCE. Princeton: Van Nostrand, 1960. 475p. forms.

Jaspan, Norman and Black, Hillel. THE THIEF IN THE WHITE COLLAR. Philadelphia: Lippincott, 1960. 254p.

Pratt, Lester A. BANK FRAUDS: THEIR DETECTION AND PREVENTION, 2nd ed. New York: Ronald Press, 1965. 284p. figures.

INTERNAL AUDITING AND CONTROL

American Institute of Certified Public Accountants. CASE STUDIES IN INTERNAL CONTROL, Nos. 1- . New York: 1950- . pap.

American Institute of Certified Public Accountants. INTERNAL CONTROL. New York: 1949. 24p. pap.

Brink, Victor Z. INTERNAL AUDITING, rev. by James A. Cashin, 2nd ed. New York: Ronald Press, 1958. 478p. chart.

Cadmus, Bradford and Child, Arthur, J.E. INTERNAL CONTROL AGAINST FRAUD AND WASTE. Englewood Cliffs, New Jersey: Prentice-Hall, 1953. 330p. (Available from the Institute of Internal Auditors.)

Walker, W.A. and Davies, W.R. INDUSTRIAL INTERNAL AUDITING. New York: McGraw-Hill Book Co., 1951. [University Microfilms] 329p. forms.

INTERNATIONAL ACCOUNTING

American Institute of Certified Public Accountants. PROFESSIONAL ACCOUNTING IN 25 COUNTRIES. New York: 1964. v.p. exhibits.

Hepworth, Samuel R. REPORTING FOREIGN OPERATIONS (Michigan Business Studies, Vol. 12, No. 5.) Ann Arbor, Michigan: Bureau of Business Research, University of Michigan, 1956. 211p. tables.

Mueller, Gerhard G. A BIBLIOGRAPHY OF INTERNATIONAL ACCOUNTING, rev. ed. Seattle, Washington: University of Washington, 1968. 66p. processed. pap. (Copies available from author.)

Mueller, Gerhard G. INTERNATIONAL ACCOUNTING. New York: Macmillan, 1967. 269p.

INVENTORY

American Institute of Certified Public Accountants. CASE STUDIES IN THE OBSERVATION OF INVENTORY. New York: 1959. 62p. pap.

American Institute of Certified Public Accountants. PRACTICAL TECHNIQUES AND POLICIES FOR INVENTORY CONTROL (Management Services Technical Study, No. 6). New York: 1968. 79p. charts. pap.

Hoffman, Raymond A. INVENTORIES, A GUIDE TO THEIR CONTROL, COSTING, AND EFFECT UPON INCOME AND TAXES. New York: Ronald Press, 1962. 382p. tables. Currently being revised.

LAW

Bergh, Louis O. and Conyngton, Thomas. BUSINESS LAW, 6th ed. New York: Ronald Press, 1964. 1006p. forms.

Black, Henry C. BLACK'S LAW DICTIONARY WITH GUIDE TO PRONUNCIATION, 4th ed. St. Paul, Minnesota: West Publishing Co., 1957. 1882p.

Dickerson, R.W.V. ACCOUNTANTS AND THE LAW OF NEGLIGENCE. Toronto: Canadian Institute of Chartered Accountants, 1966. 663p.

Dohr, James L., et al. ACCOUNTING AND THE LAW, CASES AND MATERIALS, 3rd ed. Brooklyn: Foundation Press, 1964. 713p.

Lavine, A. Lincoln. MODERN BUSINESS LAW, 2nd ed. Englewood Cliffs, New Jersey: Prentice-Hall, 1963. 860p.

LEASING

Cohen, Albert H. LONG TERM LEASES: PROBLEMS OF TAXATION, FINANCE AND ACCOUNTING (Michigan Business Studies, Vol. 11, No. 5). Ann Arbor, Michigan: Bureau of Business Research, School of Business Administration, University of Michigan, 1954. 149p. tables. pap.

Metz, Donald H. LEASING: STANDARDS AND PROCEDURES. Kaukauna, Wisconsin: Thomas Publications, Ltd., 1968. v.p. forms, photos, tables. loose-leaf.

National Industrial Conference Board. LEASING IN INDUSTRY (Business Policy Study, No. 127), by Henry G. Hamel. New York: 1968. 117p. tables. pap.

MANAGEMENT ACCOUNTING

Anthony, Robert N. MANAGEMENT ACCOUNTING TEXT AND CASES, 4th ed. Homewood, Illinois: Richard D. Irwin, 1970. 490p. charts, forms, tables.

Gordon, Myron J. and Shillinglaw, Gordon. ACCOUNTING: A MANAGEMENT APPROACH, 4th ed. Homewood, Illinois: Richard D. Irwin, 1969. 855p.

Horngren, Charles T. ACCOUNTING FOR MANAGEMENT CONTROL: AN INTRODUCTION, 2nd ed. Englewood Cliffs, New Jersey: Prentice-Hall, 1970. 606p. graphs, tables.

Keller, I. Wayne and Ferrara, William L. MANAGEMENT ACCOUNTING FOR PROFIT CONTROL, 2nd ed. New York: McGraw-Hill Book Co., 1966. 744p. charts, forms, tables.

Kohler, Eric L. ACCOUNTING FOR MANAGEMENT. Englewood Cliffs, New Jersey: Prentice-Hall, 1965. 275p. tables.

McFarland, Walter B. CONCEPTS FOR MANAGEMENT ACCOUNTING. New York: National Association of Accountants, 1966. 176p. illus.

Peloubet, Maurice E. THE FINANCIAL EXECUTIVE AND THE NEW ACCOUNTING. New York: Ronald Press, 1967. 237p.

MANAGEMENT AUDIT

Cadmus, Bradford. OPERATIONAL AUDITING HANDBOOK. See HANDBOOKS, this section.

Martindell, Jackson. THE APPRAISAL OF MANAGEMENT, FOR EXECUTIVES AND INVESTORS, rev. ed. New York: Harper & Row, 1965. 253p. charts, tables.

Peloubet, Sidney W. and Heaton, Herbert. INTEGRATED AUDITING. New York: Ronald Press, 1958. 282p. forms.

MANAGEMENT OF AN ACCOUNTING PRACTICE

American Institute of Certified Public Accountants. ACCOUNTING PRACTICE MANAGEMENT HANDBOOK. See HANDBOOKS, this section.

American Institute of Certified Public Accountants. MANAGEMENT OF AN ACCOUNTING PRACTICE, Bulletins 14- . (Bulletins 1-13, issued originally as "Economics of an Accounting Practice" series have been incorporated in the ACCOUNTING PRACTICE MANAGEMENT HANDBOOK.) New York: 1961-

Prentice-Hall, Inc. COMPLETE GUIDE TO A PROFITABLE ACCOUNTING PRACTICE. Englewood Cliffs, New Jersey: 1965. 797p. charts, forms.

MERGERS AND ACQUISTIONS

Choka, Allen D. BUYING, SELLING AND MERGING BUSINESSES. Philadelphia: American Law Institute, Joint Committee on Continuing Legal Education, 1965. 204p. pap.

Financial Executives Research Foundation. MERGERS AND ACQUISITIONS: PLANNING AND ACTION, by Clarence I. Drayton, et al, under the direction of G. Richard Young. New York: 1963. 237p. tables.

Fox, Byron E. and Eleanor M. CORPORATE ACQUISITIONS AND MERGERS. New York: Mathew Bender, 1968. 800p. tables. loose-leaf.

Hennessy, J.H., Jr. ACQUIRING AND MERGING BUSINESSES. Englewood Cliffs, New Jersey: Prentice-Hall, 1966. 286p.

McCarthy, George D. ACQUISITIONS AND MERGERS. New York: Ronald Press, 1963. 353p. tables.

National Industrial Conference Board. MERGERS AND MARKETS, 6th ed. by Betty Bock (Studies in Business Economics, No. 100). New York: 1968. 223p. pap.

Practising Law Institute. MERGING, BUYING AND SELLING BUSINESSES. New York: 1966. 222p. pap.

Short, Robert A. BUSINESS MERGERS, HOW AND WHEN TO TRANSACT THEM. Englewood Cliffs, New Jersey: Prentice-Hall, 1967. 223p. photo.

U.S. Department of Justice. MERGER GUIDELINES. Washington, D.C.: May 30, 1968. 27p. pap. mimeo.

OPERATIONS RESEARCH

Ackoff, Russell L. and Sasieni, Maurice W. FUNDAMENTALS OF OPERATIONS RESEARCH. New York: John H. Wiley & Sons, 1968. 467p. charts, formulas.

Ackoff, Russell L. and Rivett, Patrick. A MANAGER'S GUIDE TO OPERATIONS RESEARCH. New York: John H. Wiley & Sons, 1963. 117p.

Churchman, C. West, et al. INTRODUCTION TO OPERATIONS RESEARCH. New York: John H. Wiley & Sons, 1957. 645p. charts, diagrs., tables.

Miller, David W. and Starr, Martin K. EXECUTIVE DECISIONS AND OPERATIONS RESEARCH. Englewood Cliffs, New Jersey: Prentice-Hall, 1960. 456p. charts, tables.

Operations Research Society of America. INTERNATIONAL ABSTRACTS IN OPERATIONS RESEARCH. Baltimore, Maryland: bimonthly.

Operations Research Society of America. PROGRESS IN OPERATIONS RESEARCH, 3 vols. Volume 1 (PUBLICATIONS IN OPERATIONS RESEARCH NO. 5) ed. by Russell L. Ackoff. Volume 2 (PUBLICATIONS IN OPERATIONS RESEARCH NO. 9) ed. by David B. Hertz and Roger T. Eddison. Volume 3 (PUBLICATIONS IN OPERATIONS RESEARCH NO. 16) ed. by Julius S. Aronofsky. New York: John H. Wiley & Sons, 1961, 1964, 1969.

Saaty, Thomas L. MATHEMATICAL METHODS OF OPERATIONS RESEARCH. New York: McGraw-Hill Book Co., 1959. 433p. formulas, tables.

PENSIONS AND PROFIT SHARING

American Institute of Certified Public Accountants. ACCOUNTING FOR THE COST OF PENSION PLANS: TEXT AND EXPLANATORY COMMENTS ON APB OPINION NO. 8. New York: 1968. 109p. charts, tables. pap.

Bankers Trust Company. 1970 STUDY OF INDUSTRIAL RETIREMENT PLANS. New York: 1970. 313p. tables. pap.

Biegel, Herman C., et al. PENSIONS AND PROFIT SHARING, 3rd ed. Washington, D.C.: Bureau of National Affairs, Inc., 1964. 283p. forms, tables.

Council of Profit Sharing Industries. PROFIT SHARING MANUAL, 3rd ed., ed. by Joseph B. Meier. Chicago: 1957. 436p. forms, photos.

McGill, Dan M. FUNDAMENTALS OF PRIVATE PENSIONS, 2nd ed. Homewood, Illinois: Richard D. Irwin, 1964. 441p. tables.

Melone, Joseph J. and Allen, Everett T., Jr. PENSION PLANNING: PENSIONS, PROFIT SHARING, AND OTHER DEFERRED COMPENSATION PLANS. Homewood, Illinois: Dow Jones-Irwin, Inc., 1966. 416p. charts, tables.

Rothman, David C. ESTABLISHING & ADMINISTERING PENSION & PROFIT SHARING PLANS AND TRUST FUNDS (Taxation Practice Handbook 20). Philadelphia: Joint Committee on Continuing Legal Education of the American Law Institute and the American Bar Association, 1967. 259p. pap.

PRICE LEVEL CHANGES

Jones, Ralph Coughenour. EFFECTS OF PRICE LEVEL CHANGES ON BUSINESS INCOME, CAPITAL AND TAXES. [Columbus, Ohio]: American Accounting Association, 1956. 207. charts, tables. pap.

Jones, Ralph Coughenour. PRICE LEVEL CHANGES AND FINANCIAL STATEMENTS - CASE STUDIES FOR FOUR COMPANIES. [Columbus, Ohio]: American Accounting Association, 1955. 189p. charts, tables. pap.

Mason, Perry. PRICE LEVEL CHANGES AND FINANCIAL STATEMENTS, BASIC CONCEPTS AND METHODS. Columbus, Ohio: American Accounting Association, 1956. 28p. tables. pap.

Sweeney, Henry W. STABILIZED ACCOUNTING. New York: Holt, Rinehart & Winston, 1964. 274p. tables.

PROFESSIONAL ETHICS

American Institute of Certified Public Accountants. CODE OF PROFESSIONAL ETHICS...AND INTERPRETIVE OPINIONS, as amended December 31, 1969. New York: 1970. 31p. pap.

Carey, John L. and Doherty, William O. ETHICAL STANDARDS OF THE ACCOUNTING PROFESSION. New York: American Institute of Certified Public Accountants, 1966. 330p.

PUBLIC OFFERINGS

American Stock Exchange. AMERICAN STOCK EXCHANGE GUIDE. Chicago: Commerce Clearing House, April 1968- . loose-leaf.

Investment Dealers Digest. CORPORATE FINANCING, 1950-1966, 3 vols. New York: 1962-1967.

Investment Dealers Digest. CORPORATE FINANCING DIRECTORY. New York: 1942- . pap.

Loss, Louis. SECURITIES REGULATION, 2nd ed., 3 vols. Boston: Little, Brown, 1961.

New York Stock Exchange. COMPANY MANUAL. New York: 1954- . loose-leaf.

Rappaport, Louis H. SEC ACCOUNTING PRACTICE AND PROCEDURE, 2nd ed., rev. printing. New York: Ronald Press, 1966. v.p.

Robinson, Gerald J. GOING PUBLIC, SUCCESSFUL SECURITIES UNDERWRITING. New York: Clark, Boardman, 1961. 353p.

U.S. Securities and Exchange Commission. ACCOUNTING SERIES RELEASES. Washington, D.C.: 1937- .

Winter, Elmer L. A COMPLETE GUIDE TO MAKING A PUBLIC STOCK OFFERING. Englewood Cliffs, New Jersey: Prentice-Hall, 1962. 269p.

RECORDS RETENTION

Mitchell, William E. RECORDS RETENTION, rev. ed. Evansville, Indiana: Ellsworth Publishing Co., 1967. 72p. tables. pap.

New Jersey Society of Certified Public Accountants. A FAST GUIDE TO RECORD RETENTION, by Morris B. Kadin, ed. by Theodore Cohn. Newark, New Jersey: August 1967. 33p. pap.

Office of the Federal Register (National Archives and Records Service, General Services Administration). GUIDE TO RECORD RETENTION REQUIREMENTS. Washington, D.C.: U.S. Government Printing Office v.p. pap.

Record Controls, Inc. RETENTION AND PRESERVATION OF RECORDS WITH DESTRUCTION SCHEDULES, 7th ed. Chicago: 1967. 62p. forms, tables. pap.

SMALL BUSINESS

Gibson, James L. and Haynes, W. Warren. ACCOUNTING IN SMALL BUSINESS DECISIONS. Lexington, Kentucky: University of Kentucky Press, 1963. 133p.

Institute of Continuing Legal Education. SMALL BUSINESS FINANCING LIBRARY, 3 vols., ed. by Jay V. Grimm, Robert L. Knauss and Bernard Goodwin. Ann Arbor, Michigan: 1966. v.p. forms, tables.

U.S. Small Business Administration. COST ACCOUNTING FOR SMALL MANUFACTURERS, by R. Lee Brummet. Washington, D.C.: 1953. 99p. charts, facs., tables. pap.

U.S. Small Business Administration. PUBLIC ACCOUNTING SERVICES FOR SMALL MANUFACTURERS, by Robert E. Witschey (Small Business Management Series, No. 5). Washington, D.C.: 1954. 21p. pap.

Zeff, Stephen A. USES OF ACCOUNTING FOR SMALL BUSINESS (Michigan Business Report, No. 39). Ann Arbor, Michigan: Bureau of Business Research, University of Michigan, 1962. 79p. pap.

Specialized Accounting

In this section we include only titles in the Government and Municipal, Government Contracts, and Non-profit Organizations categories. For books on accounting for specific industries, see Specialized Accounting in Section 8, Books.

Government and Municipal

Kohler, Eric and Wright, Howard W. ACCOUNTING IN THE FEDERAL GOVERNMENT. Englewood Cliffs, New Jersey: Prentice-Hall, 1956. 291p.

Mikesell, R.M. and Hay, Leon E. GOVERNMENTAL ACCOUNTING, 4th ed. Homewood, Illinois: Richard D. Irwin, 1969. 772p. charts, graphs.

National Committee on Governmental Accounting. GOVERNMENTAL ACCOUNTING, AUDITING AND FINANCIAL REPORTING. Chicago: Municipal Finance Officers Association of the United States and Canada, 1968. 248p. forms, tables.

National Committee on Governmental Accounting. SIMPLIFIED MUNICIPAL ACCOUNTING: A MANUAL FOR SMALLER GOVERNMENTAL UNITS. Chicago: 1950. 162p. forms.

Tenner, Irving and Lynn, Edward S. MUNICIPAL AND GOVERNMENTAL ACCOUNTING, 4th ed. (Prentice-Hall Accounting Series.) Englewood Cliffs, New Jersey: Prentice-Hall, 1960. 592p.

Government Contracts

Commerce Clearing House. GOVERNMENT CONTRACTS REPORTS. See SERVICES, this section.

Machinery and Allied Products Institute and Council for Technological Advancement. THE GOVERNMENT CONTRACTOR AND THE GENERAL ACCOUNTING OFFICE. Washington, D.C.: 1966. 225p.

Trueger, Paul M. ACCOUNTING GUIDE FOR DEFENSE CONTRACTS, 5th ed. Chicago: Commerce Clearing House, 1966. 798p. forms.

U.S. Department of Defense. ARMED SERVICES PROCUREMENT REGULATIONS. Washington, D.C.: U.S. Government Printing Office, 1963- . loose-leaf.

U.S. Department of Defense. ARMED SERVICES PROCUREMENT REGULATION MANUAL FOR CONTRACT PRICING. Washington, D.C.: U.S. Government Printing Office, February 1969-. loose-leaf. pap.

U.S. Department of Defense and National Aeronautics and Space Administration. INCENTIVE CONTRACTING GUIDE, prepared by the Office of Assistant Secretary of Defense (Installations and Logistics). Washington, D.C.: U.S. Government Printing Office 1969. 254p. charts. pap.

U.S. General Accounting Office. AUDITS OF GOVERNMENT CONTRACTS. Washington, D.C.: U.S. Government Printing Office, 1966. 31p. pap.

Non-Profit Organizations

American Institute of Certified Public Accountants. AUDITS OF VOLUNTARY HEALTH AND WELFARE ORGANIZATIONS (AICPA Industry Audit Guide). New York: 1967. 72p. pap.

National Health Council and the National Social Welfare Assembly. STANDARDS OF ACCOUNTING AND FINANCIAL REPORTING FOR VOLUNTARY

HEALTH AND WELFARE ORGANIZATIONS. New York: National Health Council, 1965. 130p.

STATISTICAL AND MATHEMATICAL METHODS

American Institute of Certified Public Accountants. AN AUDITOR'S APPROACH TO STATISTICAL SAMPLING, No. 1- . New York: 1967- . pap.

Arkin, Herbert. HANDBOOK OF SAMPLING FOR AUDITING AND ACCOUNTING. New York: McGraw-Hill Book Co., 1963. v.p. tables. loose-leaf.

Arkin, Herbert and Colton, Raymond R. STATISTICAL METHODS, 5th ed., rev. (College Outline Series, No. 27.) New York: Barnes & Noble, 1969. 287p. tables. pap.

Croxton, Frederick E., et al. PRACTICAL BUSINESS STATISTICS, 4th ed. Englewood Cliffs, New Jersey: Prentice-Hall, 1969. 464p. charts, illus., tables.

Curtis, Arthur B. and Cooper, William J. MATHEMATICS OF ACCOUNTING, 4th ed., rev. by William James McCallion, Englewood Cliffs, New Jersey: Prentice-Hall, 1961. 576p. tables.

Cyert, R.M. and Davidson, H. Justin. STATISTICAL SAMPLING FOR ACCOUNTING INFORMATION. Englewood Cliffs, New Jersey: Prentice-Hall, 1962. 224p. charts, tables.

Gushee, Charles H., ed. FINANCIAL COMPOUND INTEREST AND ANNUITY TABLES, 4th ed. Boston: Financial Publishing Co., 1966. 884p. tables.

Hill, Henry P., et al. SAMPLING IN AUDITING, A SIMPLIFIED GUIDE AND STATISTICAL TABLES. New York: Ronald Press, 1962. 57p. tables.

Institute of Internal Auditors. SAMPLING MANUAL FOR AUDITORS, rev. ed. New York: 1967. v.p. tables. pap.

Kendall, M.G. and Smith, B. Babington. TABLES OF RANDOM SAMPLING NUMBERS, 2nd series (Tracts for Computers, No. XXIV). London: Cambridge University Press, 1939, reprinted 1961. 70p. tables. pap.

Lipkin, Lawrence, et al. ACCOUNTANTS HANDBOOK OF FORMULAS AND TABLES. Englewood Cliffs, New Jersey: Prentice-Hall, 1963. 340p. tables.

Moroney, M.J. FACTS FROM FIGURES, 3rd rev. ed. Baltimore, Maryland: Penguin, 1956. 472p. charts, tables. pap.

O'Hara, John B. and Clelland, Richard C. EFFECTIVE USE OF STATISTICS IN ACCOUNTING AND BUSINESS, ILLUSTRATIVE CASES. New York: Holt, Rinehart & Winston, 1964. 231p. charts, graphs, tables.

Rand Corporation. A MILLION RANDOM DIGITS WITH 100,000 NORMAL DEVIATES. Glencoe, Illinois: Free Press of Glencoe, 1955. 225p. tables.

Schmid, Calvin F. HANDBOOK OF GRAPHIC PRESENTATION. New York: Ronald Press, 1954. 324p. charts, forms, graphs, illus., maps, tables.

Treffetzs, Kenneth L. and Hills, E. Justin. MATHEMATICS OF BUSINESS, ACCOUNTING AND FINANCE. New York: Harper, 1956. 605p. tables.

SYSTEMS

Gillespie, Cecil. ACCOUNTING SYSTEMS, PROCEDURES AND METHODS, 2nd ed. Englewood Cliffs, New Jersey: Prentice-Hall, 1961. 641p. charts, diagrs., forms.

Heckert, J. Brooks and Kerrigan, H.D. ACCOUNTING SYSTEMS, DESIGN AND INSTALLATION, 3rd ed. New York: Ronald Press, 1967. 673p. charts, forms, illus., photos.

Lasser Institute, J.K., ed. HANDBOOK OF ACCOUNTING METHODS. See HANDBOOKS, this section.

National Society of Public Accountants. PORTFOLIO OF ACCOUNTING SYSTEMS FOR SMALL AND MEDIUM-SIZED BUSINESSES, 2 vols., ed. by Marjorie D. James. Englewood Cliffs, New Jersey: Prentice-Hall, 1968. charts, forms.

Whiteside, Conon D. ACCOUNTING SYSTEMS FOR THE SMALL AND MEDIUM-SIZED BUSINESS. Englewood Cliffs, New Jersey: Prentice-Hall, 1961. 264p. forms.

Williams, Robert I. and Doris, Lillian. ENCYCLOPEDIA OF ACCOUNTING SYSTEMS. See HANDBOOKS, this section.

TAX ACCOUNTING

American Institute of Certified Public Accountants. ACCOUNTING FOR INCOME TAXES: AN INTERPRETATION OF APB OPINION NO. 11, by Donald J. Bevis and Raymond E. Perry. New York: 1969. 70p. tables. pap.

Bardes, Philip, _et al._, eds. MONTGOMERY'S FEDERAL TAXES, 39th ed. New York: Ronald Press, 1964. v.p.

VALUATION

Bonbright, James C. THE VALUATION OF PROPERTY, 2 vols. Charlottesville, Virginia: The Michie Company, 1965. 1,271p.

Harvard University, Graduate School of Business Administration, Accounting Round Table. THE MEASUREMENT OF PROPERTY, PLANT AND EQUIPMENT IN FINANCIAL STATEMENTS. Boston: 1964. 86p. ports. pap.

McMichael, Stanley L. McMICHAEL'S APPRAISING MANUAL, 4th ed. Englewood Cliffs, New Jersey: Prentice-Hall, 1951. 749p. charts, diagrs., tables.

Marston, Winfrey, _et al._ ENGINEERING VALUATION AND DEPRECIATION, 2nd ed. New York: McGraw-Hill Book Co., 1953. [Iowa State University Press.] 524p. charts, graphs.

WRITING AND REPORTS

de Mare, George. COMMUNICATING FOR LEADERSHIP - A GUIDE FOR BUSINESS EXECUTIVES. New York: Ronald Press, 1968. 283p.

Hunter, Laura Grace. THE LANGUAGE OF AUDIT REPORTS. Washington, D.C.: U.S. Government Printing Office, 1957. 93p. pap.

Palen, Jennie M. REPORT WRITING FOR ACCOUNTANTS. Englewood Cliffs, New Jersey: Prentice-Hall, 1955. 616p. charts, forms.

SERVICES

Several of the services listed below cover the same material. For example, a smaller accounting library might want to take either Standard & Poor's CORPORATION RECORDS or Moody's MANUALS; a smaller tax department would use either the CCH STANDARD FEDERAL TAX REPORTS or the Prentice-Hall FEDERAL TAX SERVICE. We have listed these several services, all of which are excellent, in order to cover the field adequately. Brief descriptions in Section 10, Services, should be helpful in deciding which services to choose for a particular library.

American Management Association, 135 West 50th Street, New York, New York 10020. EXECUTIVE COMPENSATION SERVICE, 11 vols. Annual.

Appeal Printing Company, Inc., 130 Cedar Street, New York, New York 10006. APPEAL SECURITIES ACT HANDBOOK. Supplemented as required.

Auerbach Corporation and Auerbach Info, Inc., 121 North Broad Street, Philadelphia, Pennsylvania 19107. AUERBACH COMPUTER NOTEBOOK FOR ACCOUNTANTS.

Mathew Bender & Company, Inc., 1275 Broadway, Albany, New York 12200. FEDERAL INCOME, GIFT AND ESTATE TAXATION, by Jacob Rabkin and Mark H. Johnson, 9 vols. Monthly supplements.

A.M. Best Company, Park Avenue, Morristown, New Jersey 07960. BEST'S INSURANCE REPORTS: LIFE-HEALTH, 1 vol.; PROPERTY-LIABILITY, 1 vol.

The Blue List Publishing Company, Inc., 345 Hudson Street, New York, New York 10014. THE BLUE LIST OF CURRENT MUNICIPAL OFFERINGS. Daily.

Bureau of National Affairs, 1231 24th Street, N.W. Washington, D.C. 20037. TAX MANAGEMENT. Biweekly supplements.

Callaghan & Co., 6141 North Cicero Avenue, Chicago, Illinois 60646. MERTENS-LAW OF FEDERAL INCOME TAXATION, 34 vols. Monthly supplements.

Commerce Clearing House, Inc., 4025 West Peterson Avenue, Chicago, Illinois 60646.

ACCOUNTANCY LAW REPORTS, 2 vols. Monthly supplements.

BLUE SKY LAW REPORTS, 3 vols. Monthly supplements.

CAPITAL CHANGES REPORTS, 5 vols. Weekly supplements.

CONGRESSIONAL LEGISLATIVE REPORTING, 2 vols. Weekly supplements.

FEDERAL SECURITIES LAW REPORTS, 5 vols. Weekly supplements.

GOVERNMENT CONTRACTS REPORTS, 8 vols. Weekly supplements.

SEC ACCOUNTING RULES. Supplemented as required.

STANDARD FEDERAL TAX REPORTS (INCOME, EXCISE, ESTATE & GIFT TAXES), 14 vols. Weekly supplements.

U.S. TAX CASES, 51 vols. Semiannual volumes.

Dun & Bradstreet, Inc., 99 Church Street, New York, New York 10008. MIDDLE MARKET DIRECTORY. Annual, with two supplements a year. MILLION DOLLAR DIRECTORY. Annual, with two supplements a year.

Financial Information, Inc., 114 Liberty Street, New York, New York 10006. FINANCIAL STOCK GUIDE SERVICE. Monthly.

Institute for Business Planning, 2 West 13th Street, New York, New York 10011. PAY PLANNING, 3 vols. Monthly supplements. TAX PLANNING, 2 vols. Monthly supplements.

Lofit Publications, Inc., Saugerties, New York 12477. MERTENS' LAW OF FEDERAL GIFT AND ESTATE TAXATION, 8 vols. Monthly supplements.

Moody's Investors Service, Inc., 99 Church Street, New York, New York 10007.

DIVIDEND SERVICE. Semiweekly with weekly, monthly and annual cumulative issues.

MOODY'S BANK AND FINANCE MANUAL. Semiweekly supplements.

MOODY'S BOND RECORD. Monthly.

MOODY'S INDUSTRIAL MANUAL. Semiweekly supplements.

MOODY'S MUNICIPAL AND GOVERNMENT MANUALS. Semiweekly supplements.

MOODY'S PUBLIC UTILITY MANUALS. Semiweekly supplements.

MOODY'S TRANSPORTATION MANUAL. Semiweekly supplements.

The National Quotation Bureau, Inc., 116 Nassau Street, New York, New York 10038. NATIONAL MONTHLY BOND SUMMARY. Monthly, with semiannual cumulations. NATIONAL MONTHLY STOCK SUMMARY. Monthly, with semiannual cumulations.

Pandick Press, 345 Hudson Street, New York, New York 10013. PANDICK PRESS, INC. SERVICE. Supplemented as required.

Prentice-Hall, Inc., Englewood Cliffs, New Jersey 07632. AMERICAN FEDERAL TAX REPORTS, 74 vols., semiannual. CAPITAL ADJUSTMENTS, 4 vols., weekly supplements. CORPORATION GUIDE, biweekly supplements. FEDERAL TAX SERVICE, 8 vols., weekly supplements.

Public Utilities Reports, Inc., Pennsylvania Building, Washington, D.C. 20004. FEDERAL UTILITY REGULATION ANNOTATED (FPC), biweekly supplements. FEDERAL UTILITY REGULATION ANNOTATED (SEC), monthly supplements. PUR ADVANCE SHEETS, biweekly.

Rules Service Company, 1001 15th Street, N.W., Washington, D.C. 20005. CIVIL AERONAUTICS BOARD ECONOMIC AND PROCEDURAL REGULATIONS. Monthly supplements.

Standard & Poor's Corporation, 345 Hudson Street, New York, New York 10014.

BOND GUIDE. Monthly supplements.

CORPORATION RECORDS, 6 vols., and Daily News Service volume. Bimonthly supplements.

DIVIDEND RECORD. Daily, with weekly, monthly and annual cumulative supplements.

INDUSTRY SURVEYS, 2 vols. Supplemented every few months.

POOR'S REGISTER OF CORPORATIONS, DIRECTORS AND EXECUTIVES. Annual, with three cumulative supplements a year.

STOCK GUIDE. Monthly.

TRADE AND SECURITIES, STATISTICS. Monthly supplements.

Tax Research Institute of America, Inc., 589 Fifth Avenue, New York, New York 10017. TAX COORDINATOR, 6 vols. Biweekly supplements.

Standard Statistics Company, Inc., 345 Hudson Street, New York, New York 10014. ISL DAILY STOCK PRICE INDEX - AMERICAN STOCK EXCHANGE, quarterly issues. ISL DAILY STOCK PRICE INDEX - NEW YORK STOCK EXCHANGE, quarterly issues.

Arthur Wiesenberger Services, Division of Nuveen Corp., 61 Broadway, New York, New York 10006. INVESTMENT COMPANIES. Annual, with quarterly supplements.

Appendix A

STATE BOARDS OF ACCOUNTANCY

Appendix A

STATE BOARDS OF ACCOUNTANCY

ALABAMA STATE BOARD OF PUBLIC ACCOUNTANCY
William L. Flurry, CPA, Secretary-Treasurer
424 Bell Building
Montgomery, Alabama 36104

ALASKA STATE BOARD OF PUBLIC ACCOUNTANCY
Peter L. Kline, CPA, Secretary-Treasurer
206 National Bank of Alaska Building
Juneau, Alaska 99801

ARIZONA STATE BOARD OF ACCOUNTANCY
J. Carl Brooksby, CPA, Secretary
2450 Fourth Avenue
Yuma, Arizona 85364

ARKANSAS STATE BOARD OF ACCOUNTANCY
Glen F. Rogers, CPA, Secretary
803 Recta Building
Little Rock, Arkansas 72201

CALIFORNIA STATE BOARD OF ACCOUNTANCY
Harvey Shadle, Executive-Secretary
1021 O Street
Sacramento, California 95814

COLORADO STATE BOARD OF ACCOUNTANCY
Janet B. Noren, Executive-Secretary
110 State Services Building
Denver, Colorado 80203

CONNECTICUT STATE BOARD OF ACCOUNTANCY
Manuel Cole, CPA, Secretary
44 Gillette Street
Hartford, Connecticut 06105

DELEWARE STATE BOARD OF ACCOUNTANCY
William Markell, Administrative Secretary
Post Office Box 121
Newark, Delaware 19711

DISTRICT OF COLUMBIA BOARD OF ACCOUNTANCY
Robert Bernstein, CPA, Secretary
Department of Occupations and Professions
1200 Eighteenth Street, N.W.
Washington, D.C. 20036

FLORIDA STATE BOARD OF ACCOUNTANCY
Douglas H. Thompson, Executive Director
Box 14286
Gainesville, Florida 32601

GEORGIA STATE BOARD OF ACCOUNTANCY
Cecil L. Clifton, Joint Secretary
166 Pryor Street, S.W.
Atlanta, Georgia 30303

GUAM TERRITORIAL BOARD OF PUBLIC ACCOUNTANCY
Gerald B. Eppard, CPA, Chairman
% Peat, Marwick, Mitchell & Co.
Post Office Box P
Agana, Guam 96910

HAWAII BOARD OF ACCOUNTANCY
Robert E. Bekeart, Executive-Secretary
Department of Regulatory Agencies
Post Office 3469
Honolulu, Hawaii 96801

IDAHO STATE BOARD OF ACCOUNTANCY
Mrs. Connie A. Anderson, Executive-Secretary
Post Office Box 2896
Boise, Idaho 83701

ILLINOIS COMMITTEE ON ACCOUNTANCY
E. J. Smith, Clerk
707 South Sixth Street
Champaign, Illinois 61820

INDIANA STATE BOARD OF CERTIFIED ACCOUNTANTS
Charles W. Stout, Secretary
912 State Office Building
Indianapolis, Indiana 46204

IOWA BOARD OF ACCOUNTANCY
Thelma Crittenden, Executive-Secretary
627 Insurance Exchange Building
Des Moines, Iowa 50309

KANSAS BOARD OF ACCOUNTANCY
Sherwood W. Newton, CPA, Secretary
The University of Kansas
311 Summerfield Hall
Lawrence, Kansas 66044

KENTUCKY STATE BOARD OF ACCOUNTANCY
William J. Caldwell, Jr., Executive-Secretary
310 West Liberty
Louisville, Kentucky 40202

STATE BOARD OF CPAs OF LOUISIANA
Lydia F. Parek, Executive-Secretary
213 Louisiana State Office Building
325 Loyola Avenue
New Orleans, Louisiana 70125

MAINE BOARD OF ACCOUNTANCY
Lawrence E. Parker, Jr., CPA, Secretary
84 Harlow Street
Bangor, Maine 04401

MARYLAND STATE BOARD OF PUBLIC ACCOUNTANCY
William B. Tittsworth, CPA, Chairman
602 Keyser Building
Baltimore, Maryland 21202

MASSACHUSETTS BOARD OF PUBLIC ACCOUNTANCY
James P. Hannon, Executive-Secretary
State Office Building, Government Center
100 Cambridge Street
Boston, Massachusetts 02202

MICHIGAN BOARD OF ACCOUNTANCY
Robert E. Reames, CPA, Secretary
1033 South Washington Avenue
Lansing, Michigan 48926

MINNESOTA STATE BOARD OF ACCOUNTANCY
Clair G. Budke, Administrative Assistant
1102 Wesley Temple Building
Minneapolis, Minnesota 55403

MISSISSIPPI STATE BOARD OF PUBLIC ACCOUNTANCY
Evan Gallagher, CPA, Secretary
220 Barnett Building
Jackson, Mississippi 39201

MISSOURI STATE BOARD OF ACCOUNTANCY
Stuart E. White, Executive-Assistant
312 East Capitol Avenue
Post Office Box 613
Jefferson City, Missouri 65102

MONTANA STATE BOARD OF EXAMINERS IN ACCOUNTANCY
Henry O. Jordahl, Jr., CPA, Secretary
Post Office Box 817
Kalispell, Montana 59901

NEBRASKA STATE BOARD OF PUBLIC ACCOUNTANCY
Ray C. Johnson, Secretary
State Capitol Building
Room 2303
Lincoln, Nebraska 68509

NEVADA STATE BOARD OF ACCOUNTANCY
Miss Marguerite M. Callahan, Executive-Secretary
290 South Arlington Avenue
Reno, Nevada 89501

NEW HAMPSHIRE BOARD OF ACCOUNTANCY
Richard B. Morgan, Secretary
77 Water Street
Manchester, New Hampshire 03101

THE NEW JERSEY STATE BOARD OF CERTIFIED PUBLIC ACCOUNTANTS
Jerome M. Fien, CPA, Secretary
1100 Raymond Boulevard
Newark, New Jersey 07102

NEW MEXICO STATE BOARD OF PUBLIC ACCOUNTANCY
L. A. B. Parker, CPA, Executive-Secretary
6101 Marble, N.E.
Albuquerque, New Mexico 87110

NEW YORK STATE BOARD OF CERTIFIED PUBLIC ACCOUNTANT EXAMINERS
Robert G. Allyn, CPA, Executive-Secretary
800 North Pearl Street
Albany, New York 12204

NORTH CAROLINA STATE BOARD OF CPA EXAMINERS
Miss Katharine D. Guthrie, Executive Director
Post Office Box 1248
Chapel Hill, North Carolina 27514

NORTH DAKOTA STATE BOARD OF ACCOUNTANCY
R. D. Koppenhaver, CPA, Secretary
Box 8104, University Station
Grand Forks, North Dakota 58201

ACCOUNTANCY BOARD OF OHIO
Dan Joseph, Jr., Executive Director
21 West Broad Street
Columbus, Ohio 43215

OKLAHOMA STATE BOARD OF CERTIFIED PUBLIC ACCOUNTANCY
Mrs. Retha Duggan, Executive Assistant
506 Sequoyah Building
Oklahoma City, Oklahoma 73105

OREGON STATE BOARD OF ACCOUNTANCY
Mrs. Helen Garrett, Executive Secretary
158 Twelfth Street, N.E.
Salem, Oregon 97310

PENNSYLVANIA STATE BOARD OF EXAMINERS OF PUBLIC ACCOUNTANTS
Joseph W. Kettering, CPA, Secretary
1100 Lewis Tower Building
Philadelphia, Pennsylvania 19102

PUERTO RICO BOARD OF ACCOUNTANCY
Herminio Mendez Herrera, CPA, Secretary
Post Office Box 3271
San Juan, Puerto Rico 00904

RHODE ISLAND BOARD OF ACCOUNTANCY
Robert B. Scott, CPA, Secretary
2400 Industrial Bank Building
Providence, Rhode Island 02903

SOUTH CAROLINA BOARD OF CPA EXAMINERS
Robert A. Harden, CPA, Secretary-Treasurer
Post Office Box 627
Columbia, South Carolina 29202

SOUTH DAKOTA STATE BOARD OF ACCOUNTANCY
John E. Page, CPA, Executive Secretary
141 North Main Street
Sioux Falls, South Dakota 57102

TENNESSEE STATE BOARD OF ACCOUNTANCY
Clyde R. Watson, CPA, Secretary
Frost Building
161 Eighth Avenue North
Nashville, Tennessee 37203

TEXAS STATE BOARD OF PUBLIC ACCOUNTANCY
Miss Pauline Thomas, Administrative Director
Perry-Brooks Building
Austin, Texas 78701

UTAH COMMITTEE FOR PUBLIC ACCOUNTANCY
Floy W. McGinn, Director
Department of Registration
330 East Fourth South Street
Salt Lake City, Utah 84111

VERMONT STATE BOARD OF ACCOUNTANCY
Howard S. Rosen, CPA, Secretary
22 Wales Street
Rutland, Vermont 05701

VIRGINIA STATE BOARD OF ACCOUNTANCY
Turner N. Burton, Director
Post Office Box 1-X
Richmond, Virginia 23202

VIRGIN ISLANDS BOARD OF PUBLIC ACCOUNTANCY
Norman R. Cissel, CPA, President
Post Office Box 629
Christiansted, Saint Croix
Virgin Islands 00802

WASHINGTON STATE BOARD OF ACCOUNTANCY
Mrs. Peggy Holm, Secretary
1710 Smith Tower
Seattle, Washington 98104

WEST VIRGINIA BOARD OF ACCOUNTANCY
Arthur L. Baumgarner, CPA, Secretary
526 Kanawha Valley Building
Charleston, West Virginia 25322

WISCONSIN ACCOUNTING EXAMINING BOARD
Arthur E. Wegner, CPA, Secretary
110 North Henry Street
Madison, Wisconsin 53703

THE WYOMING STATE BOARD OF ACCOUNTANCY
LeRoy L. Lee, Executive Secretary
Post Office Box 1362
Laramie, Wyoming 82070

Appendix B

STATE SOCIETIES OF CPAs

Appendix B

STATE SOCIETIES OF CPAs

ALABAMA SOCIETY OF CPAs
David E. Young, Executive Secretary
Post Office Box 2765
Montgomery, Alabama 36105

ALASKA SOCIETY OF CPAs
William Dresser, CPA, Secretary-Treasurer
509 Northern Lights Boulevard
Anchorage, Alaska 99503

ARIZONA SOCIETY OF CPAs
Fred A. Cutler, Executive Director
3130 North Third Avenue, Suite 201
Phoenix, Arizona 85013

ARKANSAS SOCIETY OF CPAs
Miss Marque Schwarz, Administrative Assistant
803 Rector Building
Little Rock, Arkansas 72201

CALIFORNIA SOCIETY OF CPAs
Arthur M. Sargent, Executive Director
1000 Welch Road
Palo Alto, California 94304

COLORADO SOCIETY OF CPAs
Gordon H. Scheer, Executive Director
1200 Lincoln Street, Suite 530
Denver, Colorada 80203

CONNECTICUT SOCIETY OF CPAs
Jack Brooks, Executive Director
179 Allyn Street
Hartford, Connecticut 06103

D.C. INSTITUTE OF CPAs
Harvey R. Lampshire, Executive Director
1200 18th Street, N.W., Suite 915
Washington, D.C. 20036

DELAWARE SOCIETY OF CPAs
William A. Baldwin, CPA, Secretary-Treasurer
Frank Gunnip & Company
330 Delaware Trust Building
Wilmington, Delaware 19801

FLORIDA INSTITUTE OF CPAs
Clifford C. Beasley, Executive Director
Box 14287, University Station
Gainesville, Florida 32601

GEORGIA SOCIETY OF CPAs
James Martin, Jr., Executive Director
1504 William-Oliver Building
Atlanta, Georgia 30303

HAWAII SOCIETY OF CPAs
George Neale, Executive Director
P.O. Box 1754
Honolulu, Hawaii 96806

IDAHO SOCIETY OF CPAs
Mrs. Connie A. Anderson, Administrative Secretary
P.O. Box 2896
Boise, Idaho 83701

ILLINOIS SOCIETY OF CPAs
Miss Jeannette M. Cochrane, Executive Director
208 South LaSalle Street
Chicago, Illinois 60604

INDIANA ASSOCIATION OF CPAs
Jack E. Noble, Executive Director
439 Glendale Building
6100 North Keystone Avenue
Indianapolis, Indiana 46220

IOWA SOCIETY OF CPAs
Mr. K. L. Crittenden, Executive Secretary
627 Insurance Exchange Building
Des Moines, Iowa 50309

KANSAS SOCIETY OF CPAs
John Killian, Executive Director
517 Capitol Federal Savings Building
Topeka, Kansas 66603

KENTUCKY SOCIETY OF CPAs
William J. Caldwell, Jr., Executive Secretary
310 West Liberty Street, Room 415
Louisville, Kentucky 40202

SOCIETY OF LOUISIANA CPAs
Mrs. Mary Atkinson, Executive Secretary
822 Perdido Street, Suite 408
New Orleans, Louisiana 70112

MAINE SOCIETY OF PUBLIC ACCOUNTANTS
Owen C. Hall, CPA, Secretary
University of Maine
96 Falmouth Street
Portland, Maine 04103

MARYLAND ASSOCIATION OF CPAs
William B. McCloskey, CPA, Executive Director
1012 Keyser Building
Baltimore, Maryland 21202

MASSACHUSETTS SOCIETY OF CPAs
Miss Agnes L. Bixby, Executive Secretary
One Center Plaza
Boston, Massachusetts 02108

MICHIGAN ASSOCIATION OF CPAs
Gerald Phelan, Executive Director
1311 East Jefferson
Detroit, Michigan 48207

MINNESOTA SOCIETY OF CPAs
Mr. Clair G. Budke, Executive Director
1102 Wesley Temple Building
Minneapolis, Minnesota 55403

MISSISSIPPI SOCIETY OF CPAs
Mr. M. B. Swayze, Administrative Consultant
P.O. Box 808
Jackson, Mississippi 39205

MISSOURI SOCIETY OF CPAs
Donald E. Breimeier, Executive Director
1925 Railway Exchange Building
St. Louis, Missouri 63101

MONTANA SOCIETY OF CPAs
Fred Henningsen, CPA, Executive Secretary
801 East Beckwith
Missoula, Montana 59801

NEBRASKA SOCIETY OF CPAs
Arnold Magnuson, Executive Secretary
811 Mulder Drive
Lincoln, Nebraska 68510

NEVADA SOCIETY OF CPAs
Mrs. Marguerite Callahan, Executive Secretary
290 South Arlington Avenue
Reno, Nevada 89501

NEW HAMPSHIRE SOCIETY OF CPAs
Richard A. Charpentier, CPA, Secretary-Treasurer
875 Elm Street
Manchester, New Hampshire 03101

NEW JERSEY SOCIETY OF CPAs
Herbert J. Rohrbach, Jr., Executive Director
550 Broad Street, 11th Floor
Newark, New Jersey 07102

NEW MEXICO SOCIETY OF CPAs
Mrs. Wanda Yokley, Executive Secretary
120 Madeira, North East, Suite 102
Albuquerque, New Mexico 87108

NEW YORK STATE SOCIETY OF CPAs
Harold P. C. Howe, Executive Director
355 Lexington Avenue
New York, New York 10017

NORTH CAROLINA ASSOCIATION OF CPAs
Thomas C. Wagstaff, Executive Secretary
P.O. Box 1247
Chapel Hill, North Carolina 27514

NORTH DAKOTA SOCIETY OF CPAs
R. D. Koppenhaver, CPA, Secretary-Treasurer
Box 8104, University Station
Grand Forks, North Dakota 58201

OHIO SOCIETY OF CPAs
Victor A. Feldmiller, Executive Director
79 East State Street
Columbus, Ohio 43215

OKLAHOMA SOCIETY OF CPAs
Mrs. Retha Duggan, Executive Secretary
506 Sequoyah Building
Oklahoma City, Oklahoma 73105

OREGON SOCIETY OF CPAs
Robert W. Hensel, Executive Director
208 Oregon Bank Building
Portland, Oregon 97204

PENNSYLVANIA INSTITUTE OF CPAs
F. Willard Heintzelman, CPA, Executive Director
1100 Lewis Tower Building
Philadelphia, Pennsylvania 19102

INSTITUTO DE CONTADORES PUBLICOS AUTORIZADOS DE PUERTO RICO
Mrs. Isabel Miranda de Rivera, Executive Secretary
P.O. Box 9851
Santurce, Puerto Rico 00908

RHODE ISLAND SOCIETY OF CPAs
Stanley B. Thomas, Executive Secretary
87 Weybosset Street, Suite 528
Providence, Rhode Island 02903

SOUTH CAROLINA ASSOCIATION OF CPAs
Joseph E. Whitmire, CPA, Executive Secretary
P.O. Box 671
Columbia, South Carolina 29200

SOUTH DAKOTA SOCIETY OF CPAs
Holly A. Peterson, CPA, Secretary-Treasurer
University of South Dakota
Vermillion, South Dakota 57069

TENNESSEE SOCIETY OF CPAs
Nels T. Moody, Executive Director
Room 317, Frost Building
161 Eighth Avenue, North
Nashville, Tennessee 37203

TEXAS SOCIETY OF CPAs
William H. Quimby, Executive Director
200 Corrigan Tower
Dallas, Texas 75201

UTAH ASSOCIATION OF CPAs
Joseph F. Cowley, Jr., Executive Secretary
744 Northcrest Drive
Salt Lake City, Utah 84103

VERMONT SOCIETY OF CPAs
Thomas J. Tetreault, CPA, Secretary-Treasurer
2 Linden Street
Brattleboro, Vermont 05301

VIRGIN ISLANDS SOCIETY OF CPAs
Ezra A. Gomez, CPA, Secretary-Treasurer
Dronnigens Gade No. 15
Charlotte Amalie
St. Thomas, Virgin Islands 00801

VIRGINIA SOCIETY OF CPAs
Mrs. Patricia P. Koontz, Executive Secretary
809 Mutual Building
Richmond, Virginia 23219

WASHINGTON SOCIETY OF CPAs
Russell A. Davis, Executive Director
347 Logan Building
Seattle, Washington 98101

WEST VIRGINIA SOCIETY OF CPAs
Willard Phillips, Jr., Executive Director
P.O. Box 1142
Charleston, West Virginia 25324

WISCONSIN SOCIETY OF CPAs
Joseph Sperstad, Executive Secretary
176 West Wisconsin Avenue, Room 401
Milwaukee, Wisconsin 53203

WYOMING SOCIETY OF CPAs
LeRoy L. Lee, CPA, Executive Secretary
University Station, Box 3643
Laramie, Wyoming 82070

Appendix C

PUBLISHERS

Appendix C

PUBLISHERS

Addresses for periodicals are given in Section 9 and are not included here. The addresses of state societies of CPA's are given in another appendix and are therefore omitted from this one. With these exceptions, the following is a complete list of publishers and their addresses for publications cited in this book.

AMI Center for Continuing Education
59 East Van Buren Street
Chicago, Illinois 60605

Accountants International Study Group
Publications available from:
American Institute of CPAs
Canadian Institute of Chartered Accountants
Institute of Chartered Accountants in England and Wales
Institute of Chartered Accountants of Scotland
Institute of Chartered Accounts in Ireland

Accounting Corporation of America
1929 First Avenue
San Diego, California 92112

Accounting Studies Press
100 North LaSalle Street
Chicago, Illinois 60602

Addison-Wesley Publishing Company, Inc.
Reading, Massachusetts 01867

Ahrens Publishing Company, Inc.
116 West 14th Street
New York, New York 10011

Allyn & Bacon, Inc.
Orders and correspondence to:
Allyn & Bacon, Inc.
College Division
Rockleigh, New Jersey 07647

American Accounting Association
1507 Chicago Avenue
Evanston, Illinois 60201

American Apparel Manufacturers Association
2000 K Street, N.W.
Washington, D.C. 20006

American Association of Oilwell Drilling Contractors
505 North Ervay Street
Dallas, Texas 75201

American Association of State Highway Officials
917 National Press Building
Washington, D.C. 20004

American Bankers Association
90 Park Avenue
New York, New York 10016

American Bottlers of Carbonated Beverages
1128 16th Street, N.W.
Washington, D.C. 20026

American Bureau of Metal Statistics
50 Broadway
New York, New York 10004

American Council on Education
1785 Massachusetts Avenue, N.W.
Washington, D.C. 20036

American Gas Association
605 Third Avenue
New York, New York 10016

American Hospital Association
840 North Lake Shore Drive
Chicago, Illinois 60611

American Hotel and Motel Association
221 West 57th Street
New York, New York 10019

American Institute of Accountants
see: American Institute of Certified Public Accountants

American Institute of Certified Public Accountants
666 Fifth Avenue
New York, New 10019

American Institute of Mining, Metallurgical, and Petroleum Engineers, Inc.
345 East 47th Street
New York, New York 10017

American Institute of Steel Construction, Inc.
101 Park Avenue
New York, New York 10017

American Iron and Steel Institute
150 East 42nd Street
New York, New York 10017

American Law Institute
101 North 33 Street
Philadelphia, Pennsylvania 19104

American Management Association
135 West 50th Street
New York, New York 10020

American Metal Market Company
525 West 42nd Street
New York, New York 10036

American Motor Hotel Association
204 VFW Building
Kansas City, Missouri 64111

American Paper Institute
260 Madison Avenue
New York, New York 10016

American Petroleum Institute
1271 Avenue of the Americas
New York, New York 10020

American Research Council, Incorporated
Box 183
Rye, New York 10580

American Savings and Loan Institute Press
221 North LaSalle Street
Chicago, Illinois 60601

American Society of Appraisers
LaSalle Building
1028 Connecticut Avenue, N.W.
Washington, D.C. 20036

American Transit Association
355 Lexington Avenue
New York, New York 10017

American Trucking Associations, Inc.
1616 P Street, N.W.
Washington, D. C. 20036

American Warehousemen's Association
222 West Adams Street
Chicago, Illinois 60606

American Water Works Association
2 Park Avenue
New York, New York 10016

Andersen, Arthur and Co.
69 West Washington Street
Chicago, Illinois 60602

Appeal Printing Company
130 Cedar Street
New York, New York 10006

Appleton-Century-Cofts, Inc.
Division of Meredith Publication Corporation
440 Park Avenue South
New York, New York 10016

Arco Publishing Company, Inc.
219 Park Avenue South
New York, New York 10003

Associated General Contractors of America
1957 E Street, N. W.
Washington, D.C. 20006

Association of American Railroads
815 17th Street, N.W.
Washington, D.C. 20006

Association of Consulting Management Engineers, Inc.
347 Madison Avenue
New York, New York 10017

Association of National Advertisers, Inc.
155 East 44th Street
New York, New York 10017

Association of Reserve City Bankers
105 West Adams Street
Chicago, Illinois 60603

Association of Water Transportation Accounting Officers
P.O. Box 53, Bowling Green Station
New York, New York 10004

Auerbach Info, Inc.
121 North Broad Street
Philadelphia, Pennsylvania 19107

Augsburg Publishing House
426 South 5th Street
Minneapolis, Minnesota 55415

Australian Hire Purchase and Finance Conference
see: Institute of Chartered Accountants in Australia

Australian Society of Accountants
49 Exhibition Street
Melbourne, 3000, Australia

Automotive Finance Association
P.O. Box 1710
Miami, Florida 33101

Bank Administration Institute
303 South Northwest Highway
P.O. Box 500
Park Ridge, Illinois 60068

Bankers Publishing Company
89 Beach Street
Boston, Massachusetts 02111

Bankers Trust Company
280 Park Avenue
New York, New York 10017

Barnes and Noble, Inc.
105 Fifth Avenue
New York, New York 10003

Charles M. Beardsley & Associates, Inc.
71 East State Street
Columbus, Ohio 43215

Mathew Bender and Company, Inc.
235 East 45th Street
New York, New York 10017
Orders to:
1275 Broadway
Albany, New York 12201

Alfred M. Best Company, Inc.
Columbia Road and Park Avenue
Morristown, New Jersey 07960

R. R. Bowker Company
1180 Avenue of the Americas
New York, New York 10036

C. F. Braun and Company
1000 South Fremont Street
Alhambra, California 91801

Brewers Association of America
541 West Randolph Street
Chicago, Illinois 60606

Broadman Press
127 9th Avenue North
Nashville, Tennessee 37203

Brooklyn Public Library
Business Library and Science and Industry Division
Ingersoll Building
Grand Army Plaza
Brooklyn, New York 11238

Bureau of National Affairs
1231 25th Street, N.W.
Washington, D.C. 20037

Burroughs Corporation, Todd Division
University & Thomas Streets
Rochester, New York 14605

Business International Corporation
757 Third Avenue
New York, New York 10017

Business Reports, Inc.
2 East Avenue
Larchmont, New York 10538

Butterworth & Co. (Publishers), Ltd.
20 Loftus Street
Sydney, N.S.W., Australia

Callaghan and Company
6141 North Cicero Avenue
Chicago, Illinois 60646

Cambridge University Press
200 Euston Road
London N.W. 1, England

Canadian Hospital Association
25 Imperial Street
Toronto 7, Ontario, Canada

Canadian Institute of Chartered Accountants
250 Bloor Street E.
Toronto 5, Ontario, Canada

Canadian Welfare Council
55 Parkdale Avenue
Ottawa 3, Canada

Frank Cass & Company, Ltd.
67 Great Russell Street
London, W.C. 1, England

Center for International Education and Research in Accounting
see: University of Illinois, Center for International Education and Research in Accounting

Chapman & Hall, Ltd.
11 New Fetter Lane
London, E.C. 4, England

Chase Manhattan Bank
1 Chase Manhattan Plaza
New York, New York 10015

F. W. Cheshire, Pty., Ltd.
338 Little Collins Street
Melbourne, Australia

Chilton Book Company
401 Walnut Street
Philadelphia, Pennsylvania 19106

Clark Boardman Co., Ltd.
435 Hudson Street
New York, New York 10014

Clearinghouse for Federal, Scientific and Technical Information
5285 Port Royal Road
Springfield, Virginia 22151

Cleveland Public Library
Business and Technology Department
Cleveland, Ohio 44114

Club Managers Association of America
1030 15th Street, N.W.
Washington, D.C. 20005

Coda Publications
Box 1133
Studio City, California 91604

Collier-Macmillan Canada, Ltd.
70 Bond Street
Toronto, Canada

Collier-Macmillan, Ltd.
10 South Audley Street
London, W. 1, England

Columbia University Press
440 West 110th Street
New York, New York 10027

Commerce Clearinghouse
4025 West Peterson Avenue
Chicago, Illinois 60648

Computer Applications, Incorporated
555 Madison Avenue
New York, New York 10022

Conanan Educational Supply
2019 & 2059 Azcarraga
Manila, Philippines

Cornell Maritime Press, Inc.
Cambridge, Maryland 21613

Cornell University
205 Warren Hall
Ithaca, New York 14850

Cornell University Press
124 Roberts Place
Ithaca, New York 14850

Council of Ironfoundry Associations
14, Pall Mall
London, S.W. 1, England

Council of Profit Sharing Industries
29 North Wacker Drive
Chicago, Illinois 60606

Coward McCann, Inc.
200 Madison Avenue
New York, New York 10016

Crowell Collier and Macmillan
866 3rd Avenue
New York, New York 10022

Dartmouth College
Amos Tuck School of Business Administration
Hanover, New Hampshire 03755

Dartnell Corp.
4660 Ravenswood Avenue
Chicago, Illinois 60640

Data Processing Management Association
505 Busse Highway
Park Ridge, Illinois 60068

Document Index
Box 195
McLean, Virginia 22101

Dodd, Mead and Company
79 Madison Avenue
New York, New York 10016

Dow Jones - Irwin, Inc.
1818 Ridge Road
Homewood, Illinois 60430

Duke University
School of Law
Durham, North Carolina 27706

Dun and Bradstreet, Inc.
99 Church Street
New York, New York 10007

E. P. Dutton and Co., Inc.
201 Park Avenue South
New York, New York 10003

Economic Research Institute at the Stockholm School of Economics (abbreviation: EFI)
Sveavagen 65
113 50 Stockholm, Sweden

Edison Electric Institute
750 Third Avenue
New York, New York 10017

Educational Methods, Inc.
20 East Huron Street
Chicago, Illinois 60611

Electronic Industries Association
2001 Eye Street, N.W.
Washington, D.C. 20006

Ellsworth Publishing Co.
Box 3162, Parcel Post Annex
Evansville, Indiana 47700

Ernst & Ernst
1300 Union Commerce Building
Cleveland, Ohio 44115

Executive Reports Corporation, Division of Prentice-Hall, Inc.
Englewood Cliffs, New Jersey 07632

Fairchild Publications, Inc.
7 East 12th Street
New York, New York 10003

Federal Tax Press
P.O. Box 442
Branford, Connecticut 06405

Financial Analysts Federation
80 Federal Street
Boston, Massachusetts 02110

Financial Executives Institute
50 West 44th Street
New York, New York 10036

Financial Executives Research Foundation
50 West 44th Street
New York, New York 10036

Financial Publishing Company
82 Brookline Avenue
Boston, Massachusetts 02215

Foreningen af Statsautoriserede Revisorer
Kronprinsessegade 8
Copenhagen K, Denmark

Free Press of Glencoe
see: Macmillan Company

Funk & Scott Publishing Company
see: Predicasts, Inc.

Funk and Wagnalls
Division of Reader's Digest Books, Inc.
380 Madison Avenue
New York, New York 10017

Gale Research Company
Book Tower
Detroit, Michigan 48226

Gee & Co. (Publishers) Ltd.
151 Strand
London, W.C. 2, England

Gilbert, Lewis D. and John J.
1165 Park Avenue
New York, New York 10028

Government Printing Office
Superintendent of Documents
Washington, D.C. 20402

Grain and Feed Dealers National Association
401 Folger Building
Washington, D.C. 20005

Gray and Ductile Iron Founders' Society, Inc.
National City - East Sixth Building
Cleveland, Ohio 44114

Gunzer Publications
P.O. Box 204
New Fairfield, Connecticut 06810

HFL (Publishers) Ltd.
9 Bow Street, Covent Garden
London, W.C. 2, England

Harcourt, Brace and World, Inc.
757 Third Avenue
New York, New York 10017

Hardwood Dimension Manufacturers Association
3813 Hillsboro Road
Nashville, Tennessee 37212

Harper
see: Harper & Row

Harper and Row Publishers, Inc.
49 East 33rd Street
New York, New York 10016

Harris, Kerr, Forster and Co.
420 Lexington Avenue
New York, New York 10017

Harvard Business Review
Harvard Business School
Soldiers Field
Boston, Massachusetts 02163

Harvard University
Kittridge Hall
79 Garden Street
Cambridge, Massachusetts 02138

Harvard University
Graduate School of Business Administration
Soldiers Field
Boston, Massachusetts 02163

Haskins and Sells
2 Broadway
New York, New York 10004

D. C. Health & Company
285 Columbus Avenue
Boston, Massachusetts 02116

Her Majesty's Stationery Office
Box 569
London, S.E. 1, England
U.S. agent:
British Information Services
845 Third Avenue
New York, New York 10022

Holt, Rinehart and Winston, Inc.
Division of Columbia Broadcasting System
383 Madison Avenue
New York, New York 10017

Hotel Association of New York City, Inc.
141 West 51st Street
New York, New York 10019

Houghton Mifflin Company
2 Park Street
Boston, Massachusetts 02107

Hutchinson & Co. (Publishers) Ltd.
178-202 Great Portland Street
London, W. 1, England

Indiana University
School of Business
Bureau of Business Research
Bloomington, Indiana 47401

Institut der Wirtschaftsprufer in Deutschland e. V.
Cecilienallee 36
Postfach 10226
Dusseldorf, Germany

Institute for Business Planning Inc.
2 West 13th Street
New York, New York 10011

Institute of Broadcasting Financial Management
18 South Michigan Avenue
Chicago, Illinois 60603

Institute of Business Administration
University of Karachi
Karachi, India

Institute of Business and Economic Research
see: University of California

Institute of Chartered Accountants in Australia
Box 3921, General Post Office
Sydney, N.S.W., Australia

Institute of Chartered Accountants in England and Wales
Moorgate Place
London, E.C. 2, England

Institute of Chartered Accountants in Ireland
7 Fitzwilliam Place 2
Dublin, Ireland

Institute of Chartered Accountants of India
Indraprastha Marg
New Delhi 1, India

Institute of Chartered Accountants of Pakistan
El-Markaz, Bunder Road
Karachi 3, Pakistan

Institute of Chartered Accountants of Scotland
27 Queen Street
Edinburgh 2, Scotland

Institute of Continuing Legal Education
Hutchins Hall
Ann Arbor, Michigan 48102

Institute of Internal Auditors
60 Wall Street
New York, New York 10005

Institute of Life Insurance
277 Park Avenue
New York, New York 10017

Institute of Newspaper Controllers and Finance Officers
P.O. Box 68
Fair Haven, New Jersey 07701

Institute of Real Estate Management
155 East Superior Street
Chicago, Illinois 60611

Instituto Mexicano de Contadores Publicos
Madero 26 -2° Piso
Mexico 1, D.F., Mexico

International Air Transport Association
1060 University Street
Montreal 3, P. Q., Canada

International Business Machines Corporation
Technical Publications Department
112 East Post Road
White Plains, New York 10601
IBM publications can be obtained through IBM branch offices

International Consumer Credit Association
375 Jackson Avenue
Saint Louis, Missouri 63130

International Finance Corporation
1818 H Street, N.W.
Washington, D.C. 20433

International Monetary Fund
19th and H Streets, N.W.
Washington, D.C. 20431

International Textbook Company
Scranton, Pennsylvania 18515

International Typographic Composition Association
2233 Wisconsin Avenue, N.W.
Washington, D.C. 20007

Interstate Printers and Publishers, Inc.
19-27 North Jackson Street
Danville, Illinois 61832

Investment Dealers' Digest
150 Broadway
New York, New York 10038

Investment Index Company
Colonnade Building
University Circle
Cleveland, Ohio 44106

Iowa State University Press
Press Building
Ames, Iowa 50010

Richard D. Irwin, Inc.
1818 Ridge Road
Homewood, Illinois 60430

Japan Productivity Center
16-3-5 Ginza Chuoku
Tokyo, Japan

Joint Committee on Continuing Legal Education of the American Law Institute and the American Bar Association
Division of American Law Institute
101 North 33rd Street
Philadelphia, Pennsylvania 19104

Keith Business Library
Box 453
Ottawa, Canada

Kent State University Press
Kent, Ohio 44240

Kevmar Publications
Stratford, Connecticut 06497

Alfred A. Knopf, Inc.
501 Madison Avenue
New York, New York 10022

Kuhn, Loeb & Co.
40 Wall Street
New York, New York 10005

L. B. Associates
2215 Hudson Drive
Saint Louis, Missouri 63136

Laventhol Krekstein Horwath & Horwath
866 Third Avenue
New York, New York 10022

Law Book Company of Australia, Pty., Ltd.
127 Phillip Street
Sydney, Australia

Library Journal
see: R. R. Bowker Company

Life Office Management Association
757 Third Avenue
New York, New York 10017

J. B. Lippincott Company
East Washington Square
Philadelphia, Pennsylvania 19105

Little, Brown and Company
34 Beacon Street
Boston, Massachusetts 02106

Longmans, Green & Co., Ltd.
48 Grosvenor Street
London, W. 1, England

Lucas Brothers Publishers
909 Lowry Street
Columbia, Missouri 65201

Lybrand, Ross Brothers and Montgomery
60 Broad Street
New York, New York 10004

McGraw-Hill Book Company
330 West 42nd Street
New York, New York 10036

McGraw-Hill Company of Canada, Ltd.
253 Spadina Road
Toronto 4, Ontario, Canada

McGraw-Hill Publishing Company, Ltd.
34 Dover Street
London, W. 1, England

Machinery and Allied Products Institute
1200 18th Street, N.W.
Washington, D.C. 20036

Macmillan Company
Division of Crowell Collier and Macmillan
866 Third Avenue
New York, New York 10022

Macmillan Company of Canada
see: Collier-Macmillan Canada, Ltd.

Magazine Publishers Association, Inc.
575 Lexington Avenue
New York, New York 10022

Malleable Founders' Society
781 Union Commerce Building
Cleveland, Ohio 44115

Markham Publishing Company
3322 West Petersen Avenue
Chicago, Illinois 60645

Masterco Press
Box 382
Ann Arbor, Michigan 48106

Charles E. Merrill Publishing Company
Division of Bell and Howell Company
1300 Alum Creek Drive
Columbus, Ohio 43216

Michie Company
P.O. Box 57
Charlottesville, Virginia 22902

Michigan State University
Bureau of Business and Economic Research
East Lansing, Michigan 48823

Michigan State University Press
Box 550
East Lansing, Michigan 48823

Montana Bureau of Mines and Geology
Room 203-B, Main Hall
Montana School of Mines
Butte, Montana 57901

Morris, Robert, Associates
see: Robert Morris Associates

Mountain States Lumber Dealers Association
432 South Main Street
Salt Lake City, Utah 84101

Municipal Officers Association of the United States and Canada
1313 East 60th Street
Chicago, Illinois 60637

National Association of Accountants
505 Park Avenue
New York, New York 10022

National Association of Aluminum Distributors
1900 Arch Street
Philadelphia, Pennsylvania 19103

National Association of Building Owners and Managers
134 South LaSalle Street
Chicago, Illinois 60603

National Association of College and University Business Officers
1785 Massachusetts Avenue, N.W.
Washington, D.C. 20036

National Association of Cost Accountants
see: National Association of Accountants

National Association of Credit Management
44 East 23rd Street
New York, New York 10010

National Association of Educational Broadcasters
1346 Connecticut Avenue, N.W.
Washington, D.C. 20036

National Association of Food Chains
1725 Eye Street, N.W.
Washington, D.C. 20006

National Association of Frozen Food Packers
919 18th Street, N.W.
Washington, D.C. 20006

National Association of Home Builders
1625 L Street, N.W.
Washington, D.C. 20036

National Association of Independent Schools
4 Liberty Square
Boston, Massachusetts 02109

National Association of Insurance Commissioners, Committee on Valuation of Securities
60 Wall Street
New York, New York 10005

National Association of Photo-Lithographers
230 West 41st Street
New York, New York 10036

National Association of Railroad and Utilities Commissioners
see: National Association of Regulatory Utility Commissioners

National Association of Real Estate Boards
155 East Superior Street
Chicago, Illinois 60611

National Association of Refrigerated Warehouses
1210 Tower Building
Washington, D.C. 20005

National Association of Regulatory Utility Commissioners (NARUC)
3327 Interstate Commerce Building
Washington, D.C. 20044

National Association of Retail Grocers of the United States
360 North Michigan Avenue
Chicago, Illinois 60601

National Beer Wholesalers' Association of America, Inc.
6310 North Cicero Avenue
Chicago, Illinois 60646

National Bureau of Economic Research, Inc.
261 Madison Avenue
New York, New 10016

National Catholic Education Association
1785 Massachusetts Avenue, N.W.
Washington, D.C. 20006

National Committee on Government Accounting
1313 East 60th Street
Chicago, Illinois 60637

National Council of Chartered Accountants (S.A.)
Harland House, Loveday Street
P.O. Box 964
Johannesburg, South Africa

National Electrical Manufactures Association
155 East 44th Street
New York, New York 10017

National Health Council
1740 Broadway
New York, New York 10019

National Independent Meat Packers Association
1820 Massachusetts Avenue, N.W.
Washington, D.C. 20036

National Industrial Conference Board
845 Third Avenue
New York, New York 10022

National Paper Trade Association Inc.
220 East 42nd Street
New York, New York 10017

National Restaurant Association
1530 North Lake Shore Drive
Chicago, Illinois 60610

National Retail Merchants Association
100 West 31st Street
New York, New York 10001

National Screw Machine Products Association
2860 East 130th Street
Cleveland, Ohio 44120

National Soft Drink Association
1128 Sixteenth Street, N.W.
Washington, D.C. 20036

Thomas Nelson & Sons, Ltd.
91 Wellington Street W.
Toronto, Ontario, Canada

New Jersey Bankers Association
P.O. Box 573
Princeton, New Jersey 08540

New York Clearinghouse
100 Broad Street
New York, New York 10004

New York Community Trust
230 Park Avenue
New York, New York 10013

New York Institute of Finance
37 Wall Street
New York, New York 10005

New York State Bankers Association
405 Lexington Avenue
New York, New York 10017

New York State Department of Audit and Control
Division of Municipal Affairs
Albany, New York 12225

New York State Department of Commerce
112 State Street
Albany, New York 12207

New York State Department of Law
80 Centre Street
New York, New York 10013

New York State Society of Certified Public Accountants
355 Lexington Avenue
New York, New York 10017

New York Stock Exchange
11 Wall Street
New York, New York 10005

New York Times
229 West 43rd Street
New York, New York 10036

The New Yorker
25 West 43rd Street
New York, New York 10036

New Zealand Society of Accountants
Box 10046
Wellington, New Zealand

News Front
20 West 43rd Street
New York, New York 10036

Non-ferrous Founders' Society, Inc.
14600 Detroit Avenue
Cleveland, Ohio 44107

Northwestern University
Evanston, Illinois 60201

Ohio State University
1659 North High Street
Columbus, Ohio 43210

Operations Research Society of America
428 Preston Street
Baltimore, Maryland 21202

Oxbridge Publishing Company
420 Lexington Avenue
New York, New York 10017

Pace and Pace
5 Beekman Street
New York, New York 10038

Pandick Press, Inc.
345 Hudson Street
New York, New York 10014

Peat, Marwick, Mitchell & Co.
345 Park Avenue
New York, New York 10013

Penguin Books, Inc.
7110 Ambassador Road
Baltimore, Maryland 21207

Penton Publishing Company
1213 West 3rd Street
Cleveland, Ohio 44113

Pergamon Press, Inc.
44-01 21st Street
Long Island City, New York 11101

Pergamon Press, Ltd.
4 Fitzroy Square
London, W. 1, England

Philippine Institute of Certified Public Accountants
Social Communications Center Building
Magsaysay Boulevard & Santol Road
Manila, Philippines

Physicians' Record Company
3000 South Ridgeland Avenue
Berwyn, Illinois 60402

Pitman Publishing Corporation
20 East 46th Street
New York, New York 10017

Practising Law Institute
1133 Avenue of the Americas
New York, New York 10036

Praeger, Frederick A., Inc.
Division of Encyclopedia Britannica, Inc.
111 Fourth Avenue
New York, New York 10003

Predicasts, Inc.
10550 Park Lane
University Circle
Cleveland, Ohio 44106

Prentice-Hall, Inc.
Route 9W
Englewood Cliffs, New Jersey 07632

Presidents Publishing House, Inc.
230 Park Avenue
New York, New York 10017

Pressler Publications
Bloomington, Indiana 47401

Pride Waterhouse & Co.
60 Broad Street
New York, New York 10004

Princeton University Press
Princeton, New Jersey 08540

Profit Sharing Research Foundation
1718 Sherman Avenue
Evanston, Illinois 60201

Public Administration Service
1313 East 60th Street
Chicago, Illinois 60637

Public Affairs Information Service, Inc.
11 West 40th Street
New York, New York 10018

Public Library of Newark, New Jersey
Business Library
34 Commerce Street
Newark, New Jersey 07102

Public Utilities Reports, Inc.
332 Pennsylvania Building
Washington, D.C. 20004

G. P. Putnam's Sons
200 Madison Avenue
New York, New York 10016

Quadrangle Books, Inc.
180 North Wacker Drive
Chicago, Illinois 60606

Queens Printer and Controller of Stationery
Ottawa, Canada

Queensland Department of Primary Industries
William Street
Brisbane, Queensland, Australia

Record Controls, Inc.
209 South LaSalle Street
Chicago, Illinois 60604

Reinhold Publishing Corporation
Division of Chapman-Reinhold, Inc.
430 Park Avenue
New York, New York 10022

Robert Morris Associates
Philadelphia National Bank Building
Philadelphia, Pennsylvania 19107

Ronald Press Company
79 Madison Avenue
New York, New York 10010

Ross-Martin Company
P.O. Box 800
Tulsa, Oklahoma 74101

Rules Service Company
1001 15th Street, N.W.
Washington, D.C. 20005

Russell and Russell Publishers
Division of Atheneum Publishers
122 East 42nd Street
New York, New York 10017

Rutgers - The State University
New Brunswick, New Jersey 08903

Saltzer, Jerry
1145 South Holt Avenue
Los Angeles, California 90035

H. W. Satchwell & Co.
71 East State Street
Columbus, Ohio 43215

W. B. Saunders Company
West Washington Square
Philadelphia, Pennsylvania 19105

Science Research Associates
259 East Erie Street
Chicago, Illinois 60611

Silk and Rayon Printers and Dyers
Association of America, Inc.
7 Church Street
Paterson, New Jersey 07501

Simmons-Boardman Publishing
Corporation
Book Division
39 Church Street
New York, New York 10007

Simon and Schuster
630 Fifth Avenue
New York, New York 10020

Society of Industrial and Cost
Accountants of Canada
154 Main Street East
Hamiliton, Ontario, Canada

Society of the Plastics Industry
250 Park Avenue
New York, New York 10017

Sorg Printing Company
80 South Street
New York, New York 10038

South-Western Publishing Company
5101 Madison Road
Cincinnati, Ohio 45227

Special Libraries Association
235 Park Avenue South
New York, New York 10003

Standard and Poor's Corporation
345 Hudson Street
New York, New York 10014

Steel Service Center Institute
540 Terminal Tower
Cleveland, Ohio 44113

Stockholm Business Research
Institute
see: Economic Research Institute
at the Stockholm Economics

Stone & Webster Service Corporation
90 Broad Street
New York, New York 10004

Super Market Institute Incorporated
200 East Ontario Street
Chicago, Illinois 60611

Surety Association of America
110 William Street
New York, New York 10038

Sweet and Maxwell, Ltd.
11 New Fetter Lane
London, E.C. 4, England

Sweet and Maxwell (N.Z.), Ltd.
54 The Terrace
Wellington, New Zealand

Systems and Procedures Association
24587 Bagley Road
Cleveland, Ohio 44138

Tax Club Press
Arizona Land Title Building
199 North Store
Tucson, Arizona 85701

Tax Institute of America
457 Nassau Street
Princeton, New Jersey 08540

Technical Book Company
253 South Spring Street
Los Angeles, California 90012

Textile Book Service
52 Liberty Street
P.O. Box 656
Metuchen, New Jersey 08840

Thomas Publications, Ltd.
724 Desnoyer Street
Kaukauna, Wisconsin 54130

Thompson, Edward, Company
170 Old Country Road
Mineola, New York 11501

Tourist Court Journal
306 East Adams Avenue
Temple, Texas 76502

Tri-Ocean Books
62 Townsend Street
San Francisco, California 94107

Union Europeenne des Experts Comptables, Economiques et Financiers
139, rue du Faubourg Saint-Honore
Paris 8°, France

United Nations Publications
Sales Section
Room 1059
New York, New York 10017

U.S. Atomic Energy Commission
1717 H Street, N.W.
Washington, D.C. 20545

U.S. Bureau of the Budget
Executive Office Building
Washington, D.C. 20503

U.S. Civil Aeronautics Board
1825 Connecticut Avenue, N.W.
Washington, D.C. 20428

U.S. Comptroller of the Currency
15th Street and Pennsylvania Avenue, N.W.
Washington, D.C. 20220

U.S. Defense Supply Agency
Cameron Station
Alexandria, Virginia 22314

U.S. Department of Health, Education and Welfare
see: U.S. Social Security Administration

U.S. Department of Justice
Constitution Avenue and 10th Street, N.W.
Washington, D.C. 20530

United States Federal Communications Commission
Post Office Department Building
Washington, D.C. 20554

U.S. Federal Deposit Insurance Corporation
550 Seventeenth Street, N.W.
Washington, D.C. 20429

U.S. Federal Home Loan Bank Board
101 Indiana Avenue, N.W.
Washington, D.C. 20552

U.S. Federal Power Commission
General Accounting Office Building
441 G Street, N.W.
Washington, D.C. 20426

U.S. Federal Reserve System, Board of Governors of the Federal Reserve System
20th Street and Constitution Avenue, N.W.
Washington, D.C. 20551

U.S. Federal Trade Commission
Pennsylvania Avenue at Sixth Street, N.W.
Washington, D.C. 20580

U.S. General Accounting Office
441 G Street, N.W.
Washington, D.C. 20548

U.S. Internal Revenue Service
1111 Constitution Avenue, N.W.
Washington, D.C. 20224

U.S. Interstate Commerce Commission
12th Street and Constitution Avenue, N.W.
Washington, D.C. 20423

U.S. Maritime Administration
General Accounting Office Building
441 G Street, N.W.
Washington, D.C. 20235

U.S. Office of Economic Opportunity
1200 Nineteenth Street, N.W.
Washington, D.C. 20506

U.S. Office of Labor Management and Welfare-Pension Reports
14th Street and Constitution Avenue, N.W.
Washington, D.C. 20210

U.S. Securities and Exchange Commission
500 North Capital Street, N.W.
Washington, D.C. 20549

U.S. Small Business Administration
1441 L Street, N.W.
Washington, D.C. 20416

U.S. Social Security Administration
6401 Security Boulevard
Baltimore, Maryland 21235

U.S. Corporation Company
60 Wall Street
New York, New York 10005

U.S. Savings and Loan League
221 North LaSalle Street
Chicago, Illinois 60601

University Microfilms
300 North Zeeb Road
Ann Arbor, Michigan 48106

University of Alabama Press
Drawer 2877
University, Alabama 35486

University of Arizona
Tucson, Arizona 85700

University of California
Berkeley, California 94720

University of California Press
Berekeley, California 94720
also:
25 West 45th Street
New York, New York 10036

University of Chicago Press
5750 Ellis Avenue
Chicago, Illinois 60637

University of Florida
College of Business Administration,
Accounting Department
Gainesville, Florida 32601

University of Florida Press
15 Northwest 15th Street
Gainesville, Florida 32601

University of Illinois
Center for International Education
and Research in Accounting
College of Commerce and
Business Administration
Department of Accountancy
260 Commerce-West
Urbana, Illinois 61801

University of Illinois Press
Urbana, Illinois 61801

University of Kentucky Press
Lafferty Hall
University of Kentucky
Lexington, Kentucky 40506

University of Michigan
Graduate School of Business
Bureau of Business Research
Ann Arbor, Michigan 48104

University of Michigan
Institute of Public Administration
Bureau of Government
Ann Arbor, Michigan 48104

University of Oklahoma
Norman, Oklahoma 73069

University of Pennsylvania Press
3933 Walnut Street
Philadelphia, Pennsylvania 19104

University of Pittsburgh Press
3309 Cathedral of Learning
Pittsburgh, Pennsylvania 15213

University of Texas at Austin
Bureau of Business Research
Austin, Texas 78712

University of Texas at Austin
Graduate School of Business
Austin, Texas 78712

University of the State of New York
The State Education Department
Division of Professional Education
23 South Pearl Street
Albany, New York 10022

University of Toronto Press
Front Campus
University of Toronto
Toronto 5, Ontario, Canada
also:
1061 Kensington Avenue
Buffalo, New York 14215

University of Washington
Seattle, Washington 98105

University of Wichita
1845 Fairmount Street
Wichita, Kansas 67208

University Press
316-324 Oxford Road
Manchester, 13, England

Urban Land Institute
1200 18th Street, N.W.
Washington, D.C. 20036

Van Nostrand Company, Inc.
120 Alexander Street
Princeton, New Jersey 08540

Vantage Press Inc.
120 West 31st Street
New York, New York 10001

Wadsworth Publishing Company, Inc.
10 Davis Drive
Belmont, California 94002

Henry Z. Walck, Inc.
19 Union Square West
New York, New York 10003

Wall Street Journal
Dow Jones and Company, Inc.
30 Broad Street
New York, New York 10004

Frank R. Walker Company
5030 North Harlem Avenue
Chicago, Illinois 60656

Washington State University
College of Economics and Business
Bureau of Economics and Business Research
Pullman, Washington 99163

Washington State University Press
Pullman, Washington 99164

West Publishing Company
50 West Kellogg Boulevard
Saint Paul, Minnesota 55102

Western States Meat Packers Association Inc.
604 Mission Street
San Francisco, California 94105

John Wiley and Sons, Inc.
605 Third Avenue
New York, New York 10016

H. W. Wilson Company
950 University Avenue
Bronx, New York 10452

Wisconsin State University
Whitewater, Wisconsin 53190

World Publishing Company
2231 West 110th Street
Cleveland, Ohio 44102

Yates & Co.
819-21 Pine Street
Saint Louis, Missouri 63101

TITLE INDEX

AUTHOR—EDITOR INDEX

A

AUTHOR—EDITOR INDEX

B

E

F

G

M

N

T

U

V

AUTHOR—EDITOR INDEX

TITLE INDEX

A

TITLE INDEX

TITLE INDEX

C

D

G

H

I

J

K

L

M

O

P

S

T

U

V

W

SUBJECT INDEX

SUBJECT INDEX

A

B